Roots of Disorder

Roots of Disorder

Race and Criminal Justice in the American South, 1817–80

Christopher Waldrep

University of Illinois Press

Urbana and Chicago

20.95

© 1998 by the Board of Trustees of
the University of Illinois

Manufactured in the United States of America
1 2 3 4 5 C P 5 4 3 2 1
This book is printed on acid-free paper.

Library of Congress Cataloging-in-Publication Data
Waldrep, Christopher, 1951–
Roots of disorder : race and criminal justice in the American
South, 1817–80 / Christopher Waldrep.
p.   cm.
Includes bibliographical references and index.
ISBN 0-252-02425-7 (cloth : acid-free paper)
ISBN 0-252-06732-0 (pbk. : acid-free paper)
1. Criminal justice, Administration of—Mississippi—Warren
County—History. 2. Warren County (Miss.)—Race relations.
3. Discrimination in criminal justice administration—
Mississippi—Warren County—History. 4. Afro-Americans—
Legal status, laws, etc.—Mississippi—Warren County—
History. I. Title.
KFM7162.W35   1998
364.3'496073—ddc21   98-8929
CIP

To my mother,
Christine Waldrep,
and the memory of my father,
Reef Vuin Waldrep, Jr.

America! America!
God mend thine every flaw,
Confirm thy soul
In self-control
Thy liberty in law!

Contents

Methodological Note

This study of criminal justice is based on a database of crimes prosecuted in Warren County, Mississippi, from 1817 through the end of 1879. The sources for this database include the case files generated by Warren County's circuit court, criminal court, and county court. These papers are filed in the Natchez Trace Collection at the Center for American History, University of Texas, and the Old Court House Museum, Vicksburg, Mississippi. Typically, a case file includes a grand jury indictment, subpoenaes for witnesses, and a warrant for the defendant. But these papers can include a wealth of other information: transcripts of testimony, depositions, motions made by the district attorney and lawyers for the defense, jural instructions, and maps. These records are in good order at the Old Court House Museum. The files at the Center for American History at the University of Texas have not yet been processed and are not arranged in any particular order. I believe I located every extant Warren County case file in Texas by going through every box that could possibly contain such records. Cases appealed to a higher court furnished the most complete records. Some case files of appealed cases are in the Mississippi Department of Archives and History, RG 32, the High Court of Errors and Appeals Papers.

Circuit court clerks also maintained minute books, essentially diaries of actions taken by the court. These records are in the Circuit Court Clerk's Office, Vicksburg, Mississippi. An idiosyncratic system between 1838 and 1846 created overlapping minute books. Books O, P, and Q could not be located, creating a gap between 1846 and 1853. Fortunately, that period partly coincided with an especially good collection of case files in the Old Court House Museum. A complete set of case files, still in the original bundles created contemporaneously by the clerk, covered the November 1850 term through May 1854.

Before 1823, Mississippi's circuit courts were called superior courts. One superior court minute book covered from 1818 through 1822. A state docket book recorded criminal indictments from 1856 through 1869.

Mississippi's legislature created a criminal court to supplement the work of the circuit court in 1860. That court operated until 1869, when the legislature discontinued it. A minute book for the criminal court covered from 1867 through 1869. Case files from that court can be found at the Old Court House Museum and in the Natchez Trace Collection. County courts were created in 1865 and disbanded by the legislature in 1869. County court case files were found in both the Old Court House Museum and the Natchez Trace Collection. I located a county court docket book at the Old Court House Museum that allowed me to double-check the loose papers.

Defendants and victims had to be matched with census records to identify them by race (where not indicated in court records), literacy, and wealth. Not every person could be positively identified. Warren County had a mobile population that included many transients. In addition, some individuals had common names.

I categorized crimes as crimes against property, civil order, moral order, and person. Crimes against property included arson, malicious mischief, forgery, counterfeiting, false pretenses, embezzlement, and various types of larceny. Crimes against the civil order included perjury, escaping jail, maintaining a nuisance, dueling, disorderly conduct, exhibiting a deadly weapon, and vagrancy. Crimes against the moral order included adultery, fornication, violating Sabbath, incest, drunkenness, keeping a disorderly house, bigamy, gaming, and retailing liquor. Crimes against person included rape, various types of homicide, and assault.

Acknowledgments

Michael Les Benedict, Michael Fitzgerald, W. Fitzhugh Brundage, and Edward L. Ayers read earlier versions of this book, offering many helpful comments. Newton Key and Martin Hardeman shared their thoughts on ideas included herein, and Linda Kerber read a draft at a particularly critical stage and pulled me back from the precipice of error more than once. Vernon Burton and an anonymous reader for the University of Illinois Press read the manuscript and offered cogent, detailed, and crucial suggestions. Tom Appleton once again generously offered to read the final draft. Richard L. Wentworth, Emily Rogers, and Mary Giles at the University of Illinois Press guided the manuscript through the production process with professionalism and good humor. But whatever faults remain are mine.

Some of my first thoughts about this project germinated at the University of California at Irvine in 1991, when Michael Johnson hosted an excellent National Endowment for the Humanities summer seminar on freedom and slavery in the American South. Terry Finegan sent me his database of lynchings for Warren County, which helped a lot. Chris Morris aided me immeasurably by writing the social history of antebellum Warren County and Vicksburg. He further shared his computer database for the 1850 and 1860 censuses.

Jim Landis generously shared his research into the Zook murders. He showed me around Pennsylvania, and we spent an interesting day discussing murder in Mississippi. Without his work, I would never have known of that affair. Blanche Terry shared her enthusiasm for life. She also alerted me to the importance of the Irish in Vicksburg, John "Red Jack" McGuigan in particular.

Many librarians have provided essential services. The interlibrary loan staff at Eastern Illinois University's Booth Library must dread my approach with yet another bundle of request slips. Don Carleton opened the uncataloged portions of the Natchez Trace Collection at the University of Texas Center for American History. Gordon Cotton put me up week after week as I worked in Mississippi. Without his wonderful hospitality and amazing knowledge of Mississippi history, I would not have thought this book possible. In fact, I did not intend to write a book about Warren County until I met Gordon.

I could not have completed this work as efficiently as I did, and perhaps not at all, without grants from Eastern Illinois University's Council for Faculty Research, Eastern's College of Arts and Humanities, the National Endowment for the Humanities (FB-32231 and FE-27752-93), a Littleton-Griswold Research Grant from the American Historical Association, a Henry M. Phillips Research Grant in jurisprudence from the American Philosophical Society, a fellowship/grant-in-aid from the American Council of Learned Societies, and a grant from the American Bar Association's Commission on College and University Nonprofessional Legal Studies.

I first published the fruits of my research into Vicksburg grand juries in the *Chicago-Kent Law Review* in 1994. I kept Paul Finkelman's comments on that early article in mind as I wrote the book manuscript. Portions of chapter 5 originally appeared in the *Journal of American History* in March 1996. Thanks to the *Journal* for granting me permission to use that material here.

My parents awakened my interest in history, and my wife Pamela made it possible to pursue that interest. My daughters Janelle and Andrea made it fun to do so.

Roots of Disorder

Introduction

"Niggers . . . don't think the same way as humans. They all lie and steal and when they get drunk all they want is a white woman. You got to keep 'em down," one Georgia racist said in 1946.[1] Sometime in the dark past of white racism, a gruesome consensus emerged that black criminality could not be effectively punished by law. Only night-riding terrorists and lynchers could truly control black bestiality. Every white southerner understood what keeping African Americans "down" meant and what it did not mean. It did not mean going to law; it did not mean relying on a police state. It meant vigilante violence and lynching.

The chapters that follow trace the origins of that terrible paradigm to white southerners' legal culture. Many current understandings of law fit within a paradigm established early in the twentieth century by Roscoe Pound and other legal realists. Pound saw law as an instrument of politicians and people. In 1974 historian Eugene Genovese reworked Pound's instrumentalist theories into a subtle and perceptive argument that cleverly conceded considerable autonomy to law. No class could rule long, he wrote, "without some ability to present itself as the guardian of the interests and sentiments of those being ruled." Law enabled rulers to disguise the extent to which power rested on force. Allowing law partial autonomy, then, served the purpose of elites.[2] Writers like Genovese, committed to the primacy of class, imply that the public's attitude toward law has little force. If Genovese is correct, there is no point in studying the attitudes ordinary people harbor toward their legal institutions. With elites calling the shots, the beliefs of ordinary folk matter little. Many scholars have challenged this formulation, but it remains potent even today.[3]

It is, however, difficult to sustain such a proposition when studying folk violence. Some communities have suffered vigilante violence against the wishes of the majority, but more often vigilantes resemble a guerrilla army, operating with broad popular support. Like Mao's guerrilla fighters, they swim like fish in a friendly sea. For a hundred years after the Civil War the white South suppressed black southerners outside the law. Racism and economics motivated the perpetrators of this extralegal carnage, but whites' violence grew in a hothouse of more general hostility toward law and courts.

The choices ordinary people make between formal law and vigilante justice can be called their legal culture. This includes concepts and habits of justice as well as understandings of the role and potency of formal and informal rules, rights, and authority.[4] These attitudes build over a long period of time and come from many sources. In the antebellum South the operation of the law itself helped shape legal culture, as jurors and crime victims tried out their courts to see what worked and what did not. It is important to study the day-to-day operations of the courts because law itself plays a role in shaping the attitudes that encourage or discourage vigilantism. When legal tribunals seem corrupt or ineffective, people can take the punishment of crime out of court. Often when vigilantes ride, judges and lawyers approve, even if they do not actually ride with them. Southern lynchers had little confidence in the courts. "We want the crime *stoped.* Have you ever made an appeal to a negro audiance to stop it?" one lynching sympathizer asked the Tuskegee Institute. Another saw lynchings as the solution "to the delays of the law, the buying of juries, the corruptness of trial judges, the bribing of Governors."[5] Some of the chapters that follow will count the crimes ordinary people wanted enforced as a measure of how they wanted to use the law. During the antebellum era, shifts in legal discourse drove grand jurors, magistrates, and complainants to insist on increasingly tighter enforcement of laws designed to protect the interests of the whole community from individuals' greed.

But while legal discourse and practices helped shape popular attitudes about justice, so too did the nature of society. Feelings of community solidarity make law seem more or less necessary in a way that can incite or discourage the extralegal imposition of order.[6] Communities that imagine themselves as snug and unified feel a reduced need for law. Scandinavian fishermen, Bavarian villages, certain African tribes, and Israeli kibbutzniks all created tight webs of social relationships that discourage litigation. Traditional Japanese preferred conciliation and informal arbitration over lawsuits because resorting to legal authorities disturbed their harmonious communities. The strong communitarian impulse in early colonial Massachusetts similarly reduced recourse to law there. Church proceedings resolved conflicts without the formality of legal process. New Haven litigants, for example, settled their problems "in a private way," with friends acting as mediators. In such communities, arbitration and mediation occurred outside the law because community members felt a special social bond. Competitive, individualistic societies, on the other hand, fall prey to "excessive" litigiousness.[7]

For whites in Vicksburg and Warren County, the Civil War promoted solidarity. Nonetheless, the postbellum South could hardly be called cohesive; race may have been the lowest common denominator of white unity. This racism allowed whites to see themselves as a community, one threatened by blacks' crime. That sense of solidarity freed whites from the limits law and constitutionalism impose on punishing crime. To explain how this happened will require not so much study of legal discourse as an examination of the coming together white southerners experienced after the Civil War that made them less dependent on law. Readers will find more social history in that part of the book covering the Civil War and Reconstruction than in earlier chapters.

Writing about feelings of solidarity and community in the past can lead the unwary scholar into dangerous waters. Ferdinand Tonnies introduced nostalgic idealization into community studies in 1887 when he defined gemeinschaft (community) as a warm, personal, friendly, and old way of village life. To escape the sentimentalism that has long plagued community studies, scholars now sometimes define community merely as the concurrence of group and place, social interaction defined by geography and shaped by certain well-defined nodal points such as taverns, churches, or courthouses. That minimalist definition will serve, but with one important caveat. More than geography and social topography play a role in community formation. Members of community do, in fact, share secrets, understandings, ideology, and agreements as well as geography and nodal points. Competing communities can function within the same geographic space. To take just one example, South Carolina millworkers attracted to the demagogic lynching advocate Cole Blease formed a unified community, one they resolved to defend at any cost. That does not mean everyone in their geographic space joined their community. Shared ideology defines community; geography and social status merely sets its boundaries.[8]

People everywhere naturally form communities. But some places develop more intense community solidarity than others. Only communities with extraordinary gemeinschaft dare act collectively outside the law.[9] In a liberal universe of competing interests, legal rather than social ligaments bind the society together. The threat of a breakdown of cohesion can drive traditional communities into a tighter cohesion, making lynching more likely. When white communities felt besieged by outside forces, they naturally drew their wagons into a tighter, and sometimes more vicious, circle. Thinly populated white counties with a high rate of black population growth turned away from law more often than demographically stable regions. South Carolina millworkers fought for their community, even if middle-class professionals and merchants did not think they had one. Where a society agrees to structure its ordering mechanisms around courts and formal rules, vigilantism occurs less often.[10] As Jerold Auerbach put it, "Law begins where community ends."[11]

The place chosen for this particular study of law and community, Warren County, Mississippi, is no more typical of the South than Massachusetts is of the North. Like New England, Vicksburg represented its region in exaggerated form, "the most Southern place on earth." With a population 70 percent slave, Warren County slaveowners practiced a particularly intensive variety of plantation agriculture. Scene of a great Civil War battle, Vicksburg experienced war and occupation far more directly than most. Vicksburgers launched the white line movement, were perpetrators and victims of a bloody race riot in 1874, and saw at least nineteen lynchings in the New South era.[12] To trace the roots of southern racial violence, lynching-prone Warren County will serve as a good laboratory.

Even if Warren County is a good place to understand the South, one might still question the value of studying the South at all. Some see the entire South as a mere digression from the national narrative. And, at first glance, the South seems hopelessly lawless and backward in comparison to the industrializing North. Certainly nineteenth-century Warren County failed to give the same monopoly over the punishment of crime to government as did northern society.[13] It is tempting to view the balance between formal, state-sanctioned punishment and informal, extralegal discipline as a measure of progress toward modernity. Many adults today can remember shifts away from informal discipline. The state once permitted men to discipline their wives more freely than it does now. Police have felt more or less free at various times to administer an off-the-record beating to ethnic and racial minorities. Few schools now administer corporal punishment. Mothers and fathers still paddle children, but even that custom has come under attack.[14] By this measure of progress, Mississippi and the South seem hopelessly regressive by the North's more advanced standard, a sideshow to the main events in American history.

But Mississippi and Vicksburg may come closer to representing nineteenth-century America than most Americans realize. White Vicksburgers' racist-inspired doubts about the law jelled at a time when many whites all over America began to doubt that the Fourteenth Amendment had turned ex-slaves into true citizens. The story of Vicksburg begins with white exploitation of black labor through slavery, continues through white efforts to use the law to define blacks' place in society, and then proceeds to toleration of brutal vigilantism. This story is as fundamentally American as narratives of industrialization or urbanization. Northerners can look at the bloody violence in Vicksburg and deny that it represents America, but Vicksburgers' history of doubt about law reflected a skepticism common to all America, perhaps central to the national character.[15]

1

The Setting

Some say the Mississippi Delta begins in the lobby of Memphis's Peabody Hotel. More properly called the Yazoo-Mississippi Delta, it sweeps south from Memphis two hundred miles over vast plantations, ending in a line of walnut-covered bluffs above Natchez. Crime and violence in this place emerged from the landscape, the people who occupied it, and the passions unleashed by slavery. In any environment, what people call "crime" is peculiarly the product of society and culture. Community marks out the boundaries of appropriate behavior, demarking crime and deviance.[1] For most of the nineteenth century Warren County remained a frontier environment, a dangerously violent place where young men seized wealth in a slave society and then often moved on. The nature of the relationship between slaves and their owners helped shape the contours of violence in Warren County.

The first white pioneers came to what became Warren County long before the nineteenth century. The Choctaw living in the wooded bayous and ravines at the bottom of the Delta first saw Europeans when Hernando de Soto explored the lower Mississippi in the 1540s. At the end of the next century French missionaries scouted the region, building a mission and a fort at the mouth of the Yazoo River. The British came next, between 1768 and 1775, issuing land grants to pioneer settlers. After the American Revolution the Spanish displaced the British, establishing a fort at Walnut Hills. On paper the United States took control in 1795, but the Americans waited three years before moving into the Spanish fort, naming it Fort McHenry.[2]

At the end of the eighteenth century men and women from the old slave states of Virginia, the Carolinas, and Georgia came to southwest Mississippi. The settlers that went to what became Warren County settled along the Loosa Chitto, a tributary of the Mississippi now known as the Big Black, some sixty miles above Natchez. As they cut through cane and magnolia forests, these settlers may have thought they had left civilization behind. But from the beginning they maintained contacts, however tenuous, with the world. They raised corn, vegetables, and a few hogs. They hunted, trapped, and cut timber. In 1774 pioneers along the Mississippi petitioned Spanish authorities for a court to collect debts. The first settlers produced hogs, which they sold, probably for cash, on the New Orleans market. A later wave of immigrants raising cattle for market introduced slavery to the Loosa Chitto country. In 1795 John Barclay brought a cotton gin into the area, and local landowners rushed to have their own gins made by local mechanics.[3]

Well into the nineteenth century, pioneers continued to exchange well-established plantations with settled kin and community networks for a wilderness. The son of one pioneer remembered that his family moved through the influence of his mother. "My mother became dissatisfied," he wrote, meaning that she wanted to go west, "and through her influence my father became equally so."[4] Many more women dreaded separation from relatives and friends while young men sought manly independence and economic autonomy. The men wanted to test themselves on the frontier. As one put it, they yearned to "work alone, to take risks, to strive in a new land." The planters' sons who chose to journey west developed new patterns of behavior, more aggressive and self-absorbed. This reckless masculinity emphasized prodigious drinking, shooting, gambling, and whoring. As one young frontiersman told his brother, "You can live like a fighting cock with us."[5]

In 1809 the land around the bluffs above Natchez, between the Big Black and Mississippi rivers, became Warren County. A city—Vicksburg—grew on the Warren County side of the Mississippi, with commercial connections to New Orleans, New York, and London, although most migrants wanted to grow cotton, not a town. South Carolinian Elihu Hall Bay first laid out town lots, but legal wrangling converted his town site into someone else's cotton plantation. In 1814 Newit Vick, a Methodist minister, bought the land Bay had lost and planned a great city. But he died of yellow fever before he could do much about his dream. Vick's son decided to grow cotton instead of a town, but Vick's son-in-law sold lots and built a city.[6]

It is unlikely the "fighting cocks" who bought lots in Vicksburg formed a broad, homogeneous community. Vicksburg represented business opportunity and the indifferent market, not the kind of communal neighborhood rural folk recognized. To many the city that grew on the bluff overlooking the Mississippi River at Walnut Hills posed a threat to rural community life. Vick's new city attracted a diverse population. When Mississippi's legislature incorporated Vicksburg in 1825, about twenty Jewish families lived in the town. They migrated primarily from southern Germany, Bavaria, Badenia, and Alsace-Lorraine. Some journeyed from Prussia as well. The Sartorius brothers came, poor in material goods but bringing two Torah scrolls. Jewish Vicksburgers met in private homes but kept kosher. A second wave of Jewish settlers came after the mid-1840s, again mostly from Germany, but the new immigrants included many from Russia and Poland.[7] Irish Catholics also migrated to Vicksburg, and Father M. D. O'Reilly arrived in 1839 to establish a church. Both Jews and Catholics suffered from religious prejudice. About the Irish, one local grumbled that no one should "submit his neck to the yoke of priestly domination."[8]

Despite such prejudices, more and more Vicksburgers crowded into Father O'Reilly's mass and into Protestant churches as well. In the 1820s and 1830s Vicksburg grew with the cotton economy. As planters and their slaves carved plantations out of the wilderness, some began to recognize Vicksburg's value as a place to load their cotton bales onto steamboats bound for New Orleans. By 1835 Vicksburg had a population of 2,500. One traveler in 1836 thought the city looked prosperous, with "a great number of flat boats loaded with produce" at the city wharf. Another visitor thought the area "mad with speculation," a frontier booming with would-be planters hungry to commence cultivating the Delta. Men on the make crowded the streets, "gentlemen adventurers who think they have nothing more to do than come South and be the Lord of a Cotton Plantation and a hundred slaves." Such men made Vicksburg; the next year it became the county seat of Warren County.[9]

African Americans also came to Warren County and Vicksburg. The first slaves came in small groups, working land that later supported big plantation gangs. In 1810, 473 slaves resided in Warren County alongside 622 white pioneers. In 1824 three-quarters of the slaveowners held ten or fewer slaves, and no one owned more than fifty-four. The average slaveowner had six slaves, and half of the taxpayers owned at least one. Slaveowners hired their slaves out to neighbors, so many "nonslaveowners" had the use of neighborhood slaves.[10] As time passed, African Americans lived on larger plantations.[11] In 1820 census enumerators counted 1,287 slaves in Warren County and only a slightly larger number of free whites. By 1830 slaves outnumbered whites. Ten years later the 10,493 slaves living in Warren County outnumbered the whites two to one. Slaveowners constructed new quarters behind increasingly bigger big houses to accommodate larger gangs of slaves. In 1810 the average slaveowner held six slaves, and by 1860 that figure had reached thirteen. In 1830 the largest slaveowner in the county had ninety-five slaves. Thirty years later two men owned three times that number. That year the twenty-two largest slaveholders owned 2,739 slaves, or 20 percent of all the slaves in Warren County.[12]

* * *

Warren County slaves produced ever-larger cotton crops—more than thirty thousand bales by 1840, more than any other county in Mississippi but one. Huge profits could be made. In the 1850s Warren County farmers put thirty-two thousand new acres under the plow. The number of farms decreased, and fewer planters drove bigger slave gangs on expanded plantations. Cotton generated so much money that large planters devoted little time or space to growing food. They bought it for slaves rather than take precious acres away from cotton. Planters who lived in log cabins moved into mansions that sometimes rivaled those of the Natchez nabobs.[13]

Scanty evidence makes it difficult to know much about the nature of life for slaves on most Warren County plantations. Much is known, however, about the atypical plantations of Joseph and Jefferson Davis in Davis Bend, south of Vicksburg. A lawyer and delegate to the 1817 state constitutional convention, Joseph Davis's enthusiasm for the ideas of the English social reformer Robert Owen led him to give up a promising political career. In 1818 he bought eleven thousand acres in isolated Davis Bend with the intention of constructing a utopian community of slaves along the lines advocated by Owen. He housed his slaves in comfortable cottages with plaster walls and fireplaces and eschewed the authoritarianism characteristic of most southern planters. He established a court where slave juries heard complaints of misbehavior. No slave was punished on Davis's plantation except upon conviction by a jury of peers. Not even the overseers could whip a slave without going through Davis's court. Davis's eccentric ideas apparently cost him no money. By 1860 he owned 345 slaves; only eight other Mississippians owned more than three hundred. Although never as convinced by Owen's teachings as his elder brother, Jefferson Davis adopted Joseph's scheme, including the court with slave jurors.[14]

Davis's slave "utopia" was anything but typical in Warren County or anywhere else. Historians generally characterize master-slave relations as either paternalistic or more openly hostile. Whites invented paternalism to justify slavery: Slaves had a duty to labor for their owners, but whites had a reciprocal obligation to care for their slaves. Some slaveowners talked of the "love" they felt for "their people." Whites regularly claimed in public speeches and writings, and also privately, that God had placed the childlike Africans in their care. As slavery matured, owners took an increased interest in their slaves' spiritual lives. The white church welcomed blacks more warmly than any other white institution. Slaveowners resisted teaching their property to read but often gathered slaves around and read aloud from the scriptures. Many slaves understood the true nature of this arrangement and exploited it, negotiating for better conditions on paternalistic grounds.[15]

Viewed through another prism, slaveowners and their slaves engaged in a constant, bitter struggle. Although fewer slave revolts occurred in the American South than in other slaveholding regions of the world, American slaves practiced day-to-day resistance, breaking their tools, shirking, and "misunderstanding" instructions. They commonly staged work slowdowns and other campaigns of passive resistance.[16] But comprehending slaveowners as paternalists or slaves as engaged in a kind of guerrilla war against slavery assumes that the actors in the slavery drama calculated the consequences of all their acts. More likely, emotions and missed cues also played a role in day-to-day life on plantations.

Jared Reese Cook's Hard Times Plantation east of Vicksburg probably offers a more typical picture of life for slaves and whites than Joseph Davis's experiment. Jared's wife, Minerva, kept a detailed diary from 1855 through 1858. Minerva Cook worked closely with the house servants, almost as a partner with them in household production. She sewed alongside her seamstress and prepared the sausage that her butler sold in Vicksburg. But Minerva Cook had only a partial view of slavery. She had nothing to do with the field hands, observing once that no civilized person should ever have a word to say to "Negroes," who used horrible and vulgar language. Small children had to be shielded from them. She meant the field hands not her house slaves; she spent more time talking to them than to her cold and indifferent husband or her small children.[17]

If Minerva Cook had only a constricted view of slavery, her description of life in the big house is nonetheless revealing. Jessy, her butler and driver, appears on virtually every page. Hardly engaged in a guerrilla war against white people, he regularly went unescorted to town and neigh-

boring plantations. Cook headed a thriving household economy, produc-
ing chickens, eggs, butter, sausage, and similar saleable items. Jessy's job
was to market the output in Vicksburg. He worked the market, selling
sausage one day, butter the next, and bought flour and other necessities
for the plantation as well. Never punished, he seemed completely trustworthy. Jane the seamstress could outwork anyone. She would make thirty
shirts for adult men or the same number of dresses for adult women in a
single week, all properly backstitched, strong and neat. On a long summer day she could cut out a coat for her master in the morning and finish
it by twilight, handsome, pressed, and ready to wear the next day. Cook
was impressed and noted only a single flaw in her slave's character. Jane
did not want children and did everything possible to lose them when
pregnant. Cook reflected little on this peculiarity, apparently never considering that Jane might not want to bring children into the life she lived.[18]

Victorians understood human nature as a balance between passion and
civilizing influences. Civilization, political rules, and manners could hardly restrain the human capacity for irrational violence. Impatient with
logical systems as explanations for human behavior and deeply pessimistic
about human nature, southerners wrote about, thought about, and worried about passion. Ministers preached against the "Impetuosity and Bad
Effects of Passion" or the "madness of a quick and inflammable temper."
They feared that it ruled their lives and breathed within every human
breast, and, perhaps because of their apprehensions, it often did.[19] Minerva Cook worked only with the gentlest "servants," and her impressions
of slavery left out the field hands, often the most rebellious class of slaves.
Even so, she struggled to subdue her temper, her only fault as she saw it.
The slaves could be so trying and provoking, making it hard not to "fly
into a passion and treat them rougher than they ought to be treated."
Cook wrote that although her heart was filled with sympathy for her
slaves, her passion could not always be controlled.

The murders committed in Warren County record the human error
and emotional lapses—the passions—inherent in slavery as in all human
endeavors. Both whites and blacks murdered but in different ways. Plantation overseers sometimes killed their black laborers. Resistant slaves had
to calculate carefully their protest so as to avoid exciting overseers beyond
the bounds of reason. Slaves could break tools and perform their duties
slowly or not at all, but they had to be careful not to frustrate overseers
too much at the wrong moment.

White overseers may have been paternalistic, but managing even sub-
tly rebellious people can be wearing. On a Sunday afternoon in 1835, for

example, George, a teenager owned by Alexander McNeil, antagonized overseer Joseph Wade. Wade's former employers remembered him as a "good and tight overseer, but not cruel." He had to maintain his reputation as a strict disciplinarian to keep his job. Even finding future employment depended on getting a good recommendation. George may not have known just how far he could push a white man with a whip. One can imagine a teasing, rambunctious teenager pushing too far.

George may have consciously warred against white authority, or his war may have been the one waged by all teenagers when confronted with maladroit adult authority. For his part, Wade claimed that he had meant only to chastise George but lost his temper and beat the young slave nearly to death. Very agitated, the overseer ran to his employer. McNeil remembered later that Wade wailed that "if the Boy did die that he never would undertake business again & expressed a great deal of contrition &c." McNeil summoned a doctor and sent Wade back to his quarters. While the doctor examined the dying George, finding most of the flesh beaten from his back, Wade continued to wrestle with his conscience. At midnight he returned to his employer, offering to pay for the slave and vowing to leave the plantation immediately. He did, but authorities arrested him and tried him for murder.[20]

There were other instances of whites erupting with irrational anger when their authority had been challenged. In 1846 Arthur Jordan, an overseer, and two others beat to death a slave named Lewis. Lewis had resisted Jordan's instructions, and the overseer had called on Thomas Winter and James Scott, both white, to subdue him. In the ensuing fight Lewis tried to drown Scott, who, enraged by the slave's impudence, beat him to death with a shovel. As in the Wade case, the white men had been infuriated by a slave's unexpected resistance. Their anger boiled over, and they carried their "discipline" too far. Scott and Winter fled the county, and Jordan was tried for murder. The proceedings ended in a mistrial, after several delays authorities finally gave up on convicting him rather than go to trial again.[21]

Although these cases do not prove that there was constant warfare between whites and blacks, they do suggest that slavery created an emotional roller-coaster that sometimes drove participants to murder. The stress of day-to-day slave management drove some whites to murder regardless of abstract feelings of good will toward a supposedly inferior race. Joseph Wade's killing of George suggests how a misstep could lead to murder, even in a society committed to paternalism. And some African Americans did resist their owners in the most dramatic way, looking for an opportunity to strike at the enemy. We probably only know about their most inept or brazen murders. In 1857, for example, not long after Francis Jefferson Coleman wrote a will freeing his favorite slaves, a mysterious intruder slipped into the planter's bedroom and killed him with a hatchet. No one ever identified the killer.[22]

Slaves' frightening volatility persuaded rural Warren County's white minority that they had to band together, neighbor relying on neighbor. While Vicksburg became a place of competition and individualism, the countryside harbored many small communities, neighborhoods dominated by patriarchs and ruling families. More than in the North, whites in the South learned an ethic of self-reliance. When dealing with an uncooperative or violent slave one could hardly call on the sheriff. He was too far away; besides, slaves had to be convinced that their owners could control them. Slavery convinced Mississippians that they needed very little government generally. Slaves, and most other things, could be managed informally. Neighbor helping neighbor could not only keep the peace and control slaves but could also best build roads and levees.[23]

In Vicksburg the Delta collides with deep ravines and little walnut-covered hills. Warren County harbored competing social landscapes as well. Irish Catholics, German Jews, townsfolk, and planters all claimed Warren County as home. Outside Vicksburg, on the plantations, a less ethnically diverse elite ruled. Contradictions rent that world, too, as paternalism competed with the day-to-day realities of slavery. Whites espoused paternalistic values and preached against the "madness" of a quick temper. Slaves' resistance and the violence necessary to subjugate people unleased passions that could drive even the most committed paternalists to bloody violence—to murder.

2

Law and Mob Law

Antebellum Vicksburg established a national reputation for extralegal violence. The fiery abolitionist William Lloyd Garrison excoriated "Vicksburg Lynch law" on the pages of his journal, the *Liberator*.[1] A great Civil War battle eclipsed Vicksburg's antebellum fame for lynching, but modern historians still regard the city's prewar lynching and vigilantism as classic southern behavior. In the antebellum South, we are told, government hardly restrained violent moods, and passion trumped law.[2] The abolitionist and former slave Frederick Douglass captured an elemental truth when he described every plantation as "a little nation of its own. . . . The laws and institutions of the state . . . touch it nowhere."[3]

Although Douglass brilliantly expressed a fundamental reality of slavery, many truths made up the total experience. In Warren County, the mob and the lawyer rode through the same social and cultural landscape. Sometimes the lawyer was in the mob and sometimes the mob entered the courtroom, or at least stood at the door. This duality characterized not just Warren County but all of America. The tension between constitutionalism and extralegal violence is a central paradox of American society.[4] Through the entire antebellum period in Warren County informal ordering occurred outside court, both on and off plantations; the slaveowner and overseer, the crowd in the street, and the duelist all offered order without government.[5] Informal community justice coexisted with formal law, enforced in the courthouse. Yet at the same time, no one should argue that Warren County's governmental institutions were weak or too feeble to maintain order. When whites in Warren County claimed that only the riot, the duel, or the mob could effectively control crime, they made a choice not forced on them by an enfeebled court system. That duality of constitutionalism and its nemesis characterized Warren County.

* * *

Mississippians wove their commitment to constitutionalism and extralegal ordering into the structure of their legal system. For most whites, the journey through Mississippi's criminal justice system began before a justice of the peace. Justice of the peace courts embodied the dual nature of Warren County ordering, embodying both informal community justice and formal law. William Faulkner described a Mississippi justice of the peace in his fictional Yoknapatawpha County as the "chief man of the county . . . the largest landholder . . . the fountainhead if not of law at least of advice."[6] Faulkner exaggerated. Petty politicians, magistrates faced the prospect of defeat at the polls biennially. Some Warren County planters with larger holdings in land and slaves served as magistrates, but justices often owned little land and no slaves. The magistrates' wealth resembled that of the general population of male heads of households.[7]

The impression Warren Countians had of their magistrates may well have been even more modest than the reality. One of the richest, John Townsend, owned sixty-four slaves and $23,550 in real estate. But even Townsend did not conform to Faulkner's characterization of magistrates as the "chief man" of their counties. Neighbors said that despite his great wealth, "He seemed very poor when you looked at his house & his dress." Only two Warren County justices reported their occupation to census enumerators as "magistrate." Those two men, Simeon George and Lazarus Lindsey, served as justices for many years, long enough to regard themselves as professionals. It seems likely their neighbors considered them to be =ore fully magistrates than the planters, farmers, merchants, and carpenters who also did a term or two as justice of the peace. George owned $2,500 in real estate, well below the county mean for male heads of household ($6,609), and Lindsey had no real estate at all. Neither owned a slave. Probably few wealthy planters wanted a job that filled their days with other people's arguments over trivial sums of money and brought the victims of small crimes to their door in the night.[8]

Not just in Mississippi but all over America, justices of the peace were popular, accessible, efficient, and trustworthy—close to the life of the people and "set up to handle the small disputes of the average man." Holding court in the back of a store, under a tree, in their home, or anywhere else they chose, justices of the peace often seemed to enforce neighborhood conceptions of right and wrong as much as formal law.[9]

Faulkner's picture of JPs as fountainheads more of advice than law misses the extent to which magistrates dispensed formal law to their neighborhoods. One student of frontier magistrates found that almost a third had legal education and almost all had access to law books. Warren County justices occasionally made a career of law enforcement. Magistrate Alfred W. Brien eventually practiced law for fifty years and served in the legislature.[10] James Cornell served as city treasurer and clerk as well as justice of the peace before being admitted to the bar.[11] Magistrate Lawrence Sterne Houghton had no sympathy with abolitionists, insisting that Mississippi's slaves lived better lives than poor white men in the North. But Houghton remained unwavering in his commitment to the Union and to law. Despite his repudiation of secession, voters advanced him from justice of the peace to probate judge at the end of 1860.[12]

Mississippi law directed magistrates to try any breach of contract, suits for the recovery of personal property or for damages done by wandering livestock, or for injury to personal property where the damages did not exceed $50. Much of their business involved small debts. The statute required justices to keep a record of their proceedings so the loser could appeal to circuit court.[13] The justices also had jurisdiction over a miscellany of criminal offenses. JPs could jail vagrants for ten days and fine anyone caught selling liquor within two miles of a church, assaulting someone after winning or losing a bet, or "pull[ing] down any advertisement authorized by law."[14]

Slaves charged with offenses too serious to be punished informally by the slave patrol also went before justices of the peace. To guard against slaves' entry into the most formal forums of the criminal justice system, Mississippi's 1820 statute allowed any white person to complain before a justice of the peace when assaulted verbally by a slave or free person of color. The justice could not decide the case for himself but had to summon two slaveowners to sit with him. Acting as judges and jury, the trio could administer thirty-nine lashes and order the defendant pilloried.[15]

Justices of the peace had powers beyond misdemeanors; they were the first to hear complaints from victims of felonies. If the complaint sounded reasonable, the magistrate would order his constable to summon the person complained of and then listen to both sides. He could dismiss the case and release the accused on bail or he could order the defendant held in jail until the next grand jury. Since the grand jury met only twice a year that could involve months of incarceration.[16]

Along with law, community values and neighborhood politics played important roles in determining who went before justices of the peace. With no police force available, JPs had to rely on the reports of ordinary citizens. That meant that most criminal cases they heard involved assaults. Whites in the antebellum era expected their courts to settle quarrels, punishing assaults and other violent crimes. Few justice of the peace records survive, but their criminal dockets probably resembled those of circuit courts. Between 1817 and 1822, the period covered by Warren County's oldest surviving circuit court minute book, more than a third of the indictments grand jurors returned alleged crimes against person, and almost all of those involved cases of assault (forty). If indictments for fighting (twenty-two) are added to those for assault, those two crimes account for more than half of all the indictments returned in those years.[17]

Ordinary citizens determined which crimes went before justice of the peace courts; their values and priorities determined that authorities would prosecute more assault crimes than any other offense. Crime detection was a weak spot in the system because the government deployed no detectives or investigators to uncover crime. The sheriff never went looking for criminals except in response to a court order. The system depended on ordinary citizens to identify suspects and furnish evidence. Public opinion, therefore, played a decisive role in determining who went to court. The Stephen Lewis case illustrates how a heinous crime could mobilize public opinion against a murderer, even one who had killed a slave. In this case a murderer went to court only because his neighbors wanted him put on trial; they could easily have gone the other way.

Around noon on Wednesday, March 2, 1831, Lewis's neighbors could hear him curse his slave laborers, and for two hours they listened to the sharp crack of his whip, which prompted a "mighty begging" from one of his victims. Lewis, they knew, generally used the largest kind of overseers' whip. As they put it later with considerable understatement, neighbors John Slater, Absalom Fletcher, and James Hamilton decided that Lewis had "fallen out" with some of his slaves. The following Tuesday or Wednesday, Slater and Fletcher noticed a slave named Daniel was missing from Lewis's small slave force.[18]

Although juries did not like to convict in such cases, it was a crime to murder a slave in Mississippi.[19] In theory, law protected the lives of slaves. Lewis tested the theory. No statute or Supreme Court precedent could make Slater, Fletcher, and Hamilton turn their neighbor over to authorities. Had they decided to do nothing, no one would ever have known about their suspicions. With no professional police force to investigate crimes, it is unlikely Lewis would have come to the attention of authorities.

Lewis had alienated his neighbors by talking openly of murder. After asking Wylin Bohannon if he had ever seen a person with lockjaw, Lewis described Daniel as a "troublesome fellow and subject to fits" although submissive. Whoever had sold Daniel to Lewis had not told him about the slave's medical problems. Lewis felt cheated and growled that he "meant to put him out of the way or return him to his former owner." Lewis had no legal recourse against the man who sold him the defective human merchandise. Just across the river the buyers of unsound slaves could, under Louisiana's civil code, force sellers to make good on slaves who had hidden defects. Those buyers enjoyed an implied warranty. In Mississippi the rule was the opposite: caveat emptor, let the buyer beware.[20] Lewis had killed Daniel for economic calculations. He had bought a defective slave. He had not only lost the original purchase price but also bore the continuing costs of maintaining the property. It made economic sense to discard the merchandise, but when he expressed such sentiments he crossed a line established by his community. Bohannon recalled that he "declined holding any conversation with Lewis." Lewis may have threatened Daniel in front of other neighbors or Bohannon may have gossiped. However the word got around, Lewis's threats to kill Daniel probably predisposed his neighbors to turn him in.[21]

Neither Slater nor Fletcher liked Lewis, and that may also have motivated them to report their neighbor's brutality. Perhaps they felt genuine sympathy for the plight of a slave owned by a man in the habit of carrying the biggest whip available. But it seems more likely they, and the neighborhood generally, regarded Lewis as an outlaw, a dangerous man, violent beyond the bounds set by his community. In any case, Slater made his pivotal decision to complain to a justice of the peace on Saturday, March 12.[22]

The justice urged Slater to investigate further. The magistrate did not do this as a way of putting Slater off, for he visited Slater's house twice on Sunday to ask questions and issue instructions. Finally, on the following Tuesday, Fletcher reported that he had found Daniel's grave. Lewis had secretly buried his slave on the point of a ridge, no more than eighteen or twenty inches deep. Instead of using a coffin he laid some boards around the body. One foot protruded from the ground. The coroner issued a warrant and assembled a jury at the gravesite. They found Daniel and also discovered burnt places on his body where Lewis had applied fiery brands; the skin on Daniel's back had been beaten entirely off. Sickened authorities arrested Lewis.[23]

Ordinary citizens could also influence the criminal justice system through the grand jury. In the 1830s defendants like Stephen Lewis faced grand juries dominated by men owning fewer than five slaves. Authorities tried to make sure that citizens serving on grand juries understood the limitations law imposed on their inquiries. The circuit judge lectured jurors on their duties and the laws they could enforce. Then they retired to their room while the court worked through the civil docket. Victims and witnesses shuffled into their room. The district attorney stayed in the jury room and advised the jurors, but they decided whom to call. The jurors looked at the case of each defendant jailed by a justice of the peace. If they thought the evidence justified it the district attorney proposed a bill of indictment. That was usually a single sheet of paper detailing who assaulted whom and how and when they did it. If the jurors refused to indict, or, in the language of lawyers, if they "no billed" the proposed indictment, it went no further. Warren County's earliest records show a number of no bills; later no bills became scarce. Early district attorneys likely took draft indictments to grand juries for consideration, whereas their successors did not write indictments unless they knew the grand jury wanted to indict. Because that process freed some inmates of the jail and sent others to trial, newspapers described the work of the grand jury as "clearing the jail."[24]

When grand jurors agreed to return an indictment they found a true bill, and the foreman signed it. In the earliest cases the complainant's name sometimes went on the indictment as "prosecutor." Any ordinary citizen could take a case before the grand jury and push it through the system, although the district attorney tried the case. When a prosecutor lost, the court might tax him the costs of the failed prosecution. Warren County judges did not hesitate to assess costs from failed prosecutors.

The neighborhood investigation of Stephen Lewis shows the community interacting with professional law enforcers to determine who went to trial and who did not. Once Lewis went on trial the legal system showed its strength, throwing an impressive array of due process protections around defendants. Ultimately, law allowed Lewis and his lawyers to extract their case from the community where the crime occurred. The feeling against Lewis ran so deep that his lawyers persuaded the court to move the trial to Madison County. The outcome of his trial there is uncertain because records stored in the basement of the Madison County Court House in Madison became so water-damaged that they had to be discarded. Warren County records, however, reveal that Lewis soon returned home. In 1832 he could list ten slaves as assets. He soon sold his land, and the 1840 census found him living alone, apparently with no property. His neighbors may have rendered a judgment against him after all.[25]

Because Lewis won a change of venue his case differs from the norm to a considerable extent. More often, the contending parties each made their claim for community approbation before a jury, their neighbors sitting in judgment. At least as late as 1834, Mississippi sheriffs still occasionally selected "good and lawful men of the vicinage," or neighborhood where the crime occurred, to try cases. Cases tried by such local men kept justice in the hands of the neighborhood.[26]

The Lewis case deviated from the norm in that defense lawyers scored a rare success in winning a change of venue. In fact, the Lewis murder trial differed from most other cases in another important way. It involved a slave as a victim. Mississippi law kept most crime involving slaves out of court altogether. In 1822 George Poindexter wrote statutes designed both to establish a rule of law and recognize slaveowners' power over their slaves untrammeled by legal procedures. Poindexter's code, which formed the basis for all subsequent Mississippi slave codes, placed the heel of the state on the neck of slaves only when off their owners' property. Slaves could not carry guns unless their owners wanted them to. Slaves could not assemble unless their owners allowed it. And slaves could not buy or sell goods unless they had the permission of their owners.[27] Poindexter expected whites to discipline most blacks on the plantation, outside legal process. No slave could use abusive language to a white person, but no one in Mississippi or elsewhere in the slave South expected slaveowners to invoke the law against verbal abuse of whites by slaves against their own property. And planters mostly succeeded in keeping their slaves out of court all over the South. One South Carolina owner boasted that he had "never had a case in court, not even in a magistrate court."[28]

While whites bragged about their ability to punish slaves outside the law, the slaves regarded plantation sovereignty as lawless. In their narratives, escaped slaves often used the language of crime to describe their owners' conduct and slavery in general. Harriet Jacobs wrote that "no shadow of law" protected slave women from rape.[29] Elizabeth Keckly described herself as "robbed" by "cruel custom."[30] Louis Hughes accused whites of "stealing the slaves' time year after year."[31]

Despite slaves' complaints that "no shadow of law" reached the plantation, slaveowners did not punish all slave crime and did not confine their property to their plantations at all times. In Warren County, slaves had extensive access to Vicksburg.[32] Although they sometimes came back drunk, such misbehavior did not end the practice. Planters could hardly use white drivers on every wagonload of oats or cotton they dispatched to town.[33] Benjamin Wailes's diary is a catalog of the problems slaves encountered while off their owners' property. A neighboring slave attacked Wailes's "boy Gabriel" with a plank until Gabriel finally turned on him. Although Gabriel plunged his knife deep into his pursuer's groin, creating a dangerous wound, he never went to court. Wailes questioned Gabriel, who claimed he tried to get out of the way and was considerably beaten before he resorted to his knife. Wailes then contacted the victim's owner through an intermediary and learned she did not intend to prosecute. Wailes assured her that he would not attempt to screen Gabriel from punishment "if he was found to deserve it." Nothing came of the matter.[34]

A year later, another episode confirmed Wailes's doubts about the legal system. Two drunken white men whipped and stabbed Clem, a slave belonging to Wailes's son. "A most unprovoked and wanton act," Wailes fumed. He went to a justice of the peace, who agreed the attack had been "malicious and wanton." He then explained the facts of life to Wailes: "We have only negro evidence." It would be best "not to stir the matter until the next term of court." They hoped one of the guilty parties would unwittingly incriminate himself in conversation, affording evidence that could be taken to the grand jury. Neither ever did.[35]

Because slaveowners like Wailes could not or would not confine slaves to their plantations and therefore could not entirely keep them out of court, they erected a number of barriers designed to limit black access to the legal process. At the bottom, petty cases received the roughest and most informal handling; ordinary cases of serious crime made up a middle layer in circuit courts; and well-publicized cases of courtroom drama where lawmen carefully observed all the elements of due process made up the top layer.[36]

Such layering, although characteristic of all criminal justice systems past and present, took on special importance in the slave South. For whites, it meant that most crime could be punished in the neighborhood where it occurred, free from interference by higher authorities. The most informal layer blocked access to most of the protections the law offered defendants in more serious cases. Ulrich Bonnell Phillips, writing in the twentieth century but representing the thinking of the antebellum planter elite, justified the bottom layer of justice, administered by owners and slave patrols, as a "paternalistic despotism" justified by the savage nature of slaves undergoing the civilizing schooling plantation life offered.[37] The purpose, then, of the most informal layer of justice was to keep blacks out of formal processes.

Slave patrols constituted the first line of defense off the plantation. In Warren County, the Board of Police selected patrol leaders, who made a list of all persons in their districts liable to perform patrol duty. Once a month, "or oftener if necessary," the patrols assembled to search all the quarters in their respective districts. They existed as a device for punishing slaves without due process, without real law. Patrolers also made sure that slaves could not travel between plantations at night. They administered quick, informal justice, kept no records, and allowed no appeals. Although administered by the state, everyone understood that they offered an entirely different kind of "justice" from that of courts.[38]

Slave patrols existed primarily to enforce the pass system. From the beginning of slavery, Mississippi lawmakers forbade slaves from "strolling" off their owners' property without a pass.[39] Owners could not permit slaves not their own to congregate on their property for more than four hours.[40] Religious meetings posed a vexing problem. In 1822 Mississippi made it illegal for black ministers to preach, but white evangelicals howled in protest. The next year the legislature reversed course and permitted black preaching so long as two respectable white persons attended the services as well. But that brought the state onto the plantations, so eight years later the legislature acted again. Under the new law an owner could permit his slaves to preach "upon his own premises" but could not permit any other slaves to attend the services.[41] In 1842 the legislature decided that slaveowners could not quarter more than six slaves more than a mile from their own residences. In-town slaves had to be quartered on their owners' lot or on a lot adjacent to their owners' property.[42]

The way county governments administered patrols made clear that they were intended to control slaves who were off their plantations. In Warren County, the Board of Police appointed slaveowners with substantial holdings as leaders.[43] Historians have often compared slave patrols to vigilante mobs, sometimes depicting them as forerunners of the Ku Klux Klan. The comparison seems apt in Warren County, where patrol leaders had a free hand to recruit whomever they wanted. That meant that most members of the slave patrol had been rounded up informally rather than appointed by the county's governing body. Counties appointed every member of the patrol in some states, not only screening who could serve but also limiting the size of the patrols.[44]

Warren County's Board of Police expected its patrols to break up assemblies of slaves off their plantations. The board instructed slave patrols to visit all slave quarters "or other places suspected of containing unlawful assemblies." Patrols had to "disperse or dispose" of any unlawful assembles they happened upon and could whip slaves who were off their plantations without a pass or some "token of permission." The patrol could administer up to thirty-nine lashes with no judicial proceeding whatsoever.[45]

The slave patrol ignored due process. County courts, however, although less formal than circuit courts, did accord slaves a semblance of due process. In 1817 Mississippians created county courts for the explicit purpose of trying slave cases. In these courts three justices of the peace heard slave cases, including those of slaves charged with the most serious crimes of rape, arson, and murder. They shared jurisdiction with circuit courts, which also heard criminal cases involving slave perpetrators. As in magistrates' courts, county courts typically tried slaves caught stealing and off from their home plantations. Owners had to pay the costs of prosecuting the slaves for larceny, so theft from an owner resulted in nonjudicial punishment, or, if the slaveholder chose to overlook the incident, no punishment at all.[46] Magistrates often had little knowledge of law and conducted trials in the presence of the defendant's owner.

In 1833 the slave courts went out of business when the Mississippi legislature extended the jurisdiction of circuit courts and gave them the "power to hear and determine" all criminal cases "except such as may be exclusively had before a Justice of the Peace."[47] For twenty years all slave defendants either went before justices of the peace or, when charged with rape, arson, or murder, to circuit court. In 1854 the legislature created courts designed, in the words of Mississippi's High Court of Errors and Appeals, to provide a "more summary, cheaper, and more expeditious remedy for the trial of minor offences charged against slaves." The legislature intended the new courts to "secure to the slave all just protections against the errors of the Inferior Court."[48] In the new courts, two justices of the peace sat with five slaveowners when hearing slave cases. They could administer "proper corporeal punishment . . . (not extending to taking of life or member)." The new courts protected slave defendants from the errors of inferior courts but there were limits. Slaves convicted in the new courts could appeal to circuit court but no higher.[49]

The effectiveness of these lower courts can be judged by looking at their campaign to keep slaves out of the free market. Judging from the amount of energy legislators expended drafting legislation, it was an issue that mattered greatly to whites. Slaves off the plantation bought and sold goods, including liquor, forged passes, and even firearms. In 1805 legislators required that any slave buying or selling any articles must have a pass to do so, signed by the owner or overseer. An 1822 law sanctioned arrests of slavetraders by any white citizen. As an inducement, such white "apprehenders" got to keep the articles being traded or sold.

Despite these laws the problem continued, and in 1850 legislators enacted their frustrations into new law. That statute punished whites who traded with slaves and declared that district attorneys did not have to prove the kind or quantity of articles being sold, name the slave, or identify the owner of that slave. The law even went so far as to say that any slave found in any "place fitted up or kept for trading" and "seen to carry into the aforementioned place or places, any article or commodity supposed for sale, and not bring the same out" should be considered guilty. Enslaved teamsters who parked their teams near such a place for ten minutes "at any hour of the day or night" and carried goods in or out should be considered guilty as well.[50]

Even as judges and lawyers maintained order and punished crime, some ordering went on outside court. The most famous episode of this came in 1835. Gambling, drunkenness, and prostitution in a corner of town known as the Kangaroo led some Vicksburgers to organize the Vicksburg Volunteers. Claiming that popular sovereignty justified their actions, the Volunteers maintained that they represented all honest white citizens. They first passed resolutions calling on gamblers to leave town within twenty-four hours. When that did not happen, the Volunteers marched to a house known as a hangout, hoping to overcome their opponents with numbers and military discipline. Instead, the gamblers fired a volley into the crowd, killing Hugh S. Bodley. The outraged Volunteers "burst open every avenue to the building" and seized its occupants. The mob expelled some and hanged five. A year after the lynchings, travelers reported that Vicksburgers still kept a vigilant watch and eyed strangers suspiciously.[51] A Vicksburger hailed the "public spirit" that had enabled the white community to act in concert.[52]

Vicksburg's growth and commercial development represented a powerful force against such mobbing. Business needed law upon which it could depend, not order dependent on the mood of the mob. Vicksburg horses and oxen dragged wagons through streets that visitors still criticized as irregular and *"awful muddy"* in the 1840s, but new stores and warehouses appeared, and every year more strangers crowded through them.[53] The dry goods firm of Abel Fenton and Felix Turley reported sales of $51,000 annually.[54] Their rival, George Church, sold another $47,000 in dry goods each year.[55] The goods Fenton, Turley, and Church sold came, for the most part, from northern firms. To offer a wide variety of goods that would appeal to their customers, Vicksburg businessmen cultivated extensive connections with northern wholesalers. To sell the cotton their customers grew they developed close ties to New Orleans firms.

The fact that few Vicksburg merchants were native Mississippians makes it harder to argue that southern culture dictated some peculiar hostility to formal law enforcement. Oliver Woodman came to Vicksburg from Maine, and Willet Judson still had connections in Connecticut. He acted as an agent for a Connecticut firm, selling goods on commission. Isaac Sartorious was an "Italian Jew."[56] Furniture sellers Samuel and Dan Brown called themselves Samuel Brown and Company; Dan lived in Newark, New Jersey.[57] B. F. Fotterill came to Vicksburg from New York City and still found it useful to keep a partner there.[58] Few commission merchants failed to bill themselves as branches of New Orleans firms.

These merchants expected and demanded an effective legal system in Vicksburg, and lawyers played an important role in their commercial world. Merchants relied on the courts as a debt collection agency, and most of the civil suits filed in circuit court demanded payment for debts. Merchant John M. Parisot provided lawyer Perly Wallis room and board in exchange for his professional services. Although his wife thought their houseguest not worth the trouble, Parisot calculated that Wallis paid for his room and board with the many mortgages he wrote for his host and the debts he collected.[59]

Northern merchants like B. F. Fotterill or Samuel Brown and southern merchants like John Parisot could be shockingly indifferent to slavery. Saloons and brothels attracted a transient element from passing riverboats. The pressure to sell created a class of merchants who, although they often owned slaves themselves, did little to support the white solidarity necessary to maintain slavery. In 1853 a slave named Sarah allegedly put arsenic in the Charles Searles family's morning coffee. The family became ill, vomiting violently, although no one died. At Sarah's trial, authorities introduced into evidence the testimony of Randal Firber, the clerk who had sold Sarah the arsenic she had allegedly used. By law Sarah could not buy anything without a note from her owner, and she had been given no such permission. She did not even have the purchase price, 15 cents. Nonetheless, Firber had sold her the arsenic on credit. As he told the court, he "had orders from his employers to sell any thing in the store to slaves, without an order, if they had money."[60]

Ultimately, Mississippi's High Court of Errors and Appeals quashed the indictment against Sarah, and she disappeared from the legal record. But the ease with which she bought a deadly poison illustrates the changing character of Vicksburg society. Firber reflected the central tendency among local merchants. Other white Vicksburgers sold slaves guns, whiskey, and forged passes. In an increasingly urban, commercialized world, the law of the market challenged the rules of planter patriarchy.

Although merchants put profit and loss ahead of community values, plantation slaveowners aggressively asserted those values when they fought duels. The large number of Delta planters living—and dueling— in Vicksburg made the city famous for its duels. Dueling was one facet of an honor code best understood as a system of rules regulating the conduct of gentlemen. That was evident in 1842, when newspaper editor James Hagan criticized fellow Vicksburger Seargent Prentiss. Prentiss dismissed the editor as slanderous and abusive, unworthy of his attention because the public gave Hagan so little respect. T. M. Tucker, who occupied a station that gave his opinions weight in the community, publicly endorsed Hagan's writings, however. According to dueling etiquette, very precisely laid out in South Carolina Governor John Lyde Wilson's published dueling code, Prentiss should respectfully ask Tucker's meaning. He wrote a carefully crafted letter doing so and passed it to Tucker through his second, John Quitman.[61] The letter asked Tucker if he had intended to endorse Hagan's attacks on Prentiss. Tucker responded by denying Prentiss's right to inquire into his associations, public or private. A duel loomed.[62]

Adroit seconds could steer would-be duelists away from violence, however. In this case Quitman distracted the principals from their quarrel by going after Tucker himself. After delivering Prentiss's correspondence to Tucker, he wrote a letter of his own, saying that he had refused to deliver one of Tucker's letters. "Your note of yesterday," he wrote, "contains expressions which forbid its reception." Tucker used such disrespectful and offensive language, Quitman explained, that he felt insulted by it himself. Tucker expressed surprise: "I had not design[ed] . . . to offer disrespect or offense to you," he said.[63]

The focus now shifted entirely from Prentiss/Tucker to Quitman/Tucker. Quitman pronounced Tucker's response "satisfactory," but his addendum was meant to put Tucker in his place: "Of course, I consider your note as a withdrawal of your note to Mr. Prentiss." No, that was not what Tucker had in mind, and he quickly said so. The two went back and forth, with Tucker insisting that he meant no disrespect to Quitman but he would not disavow the original note. Finally, Tucker found a way out of the conundrum. On May 22 he wrote, "As you have assured me, that you consider my answer to Mr. Prentiss' note of the 17th instant offensive to you, I will for that reason withdraw that note. But as I am unconscious of having given Mr. Prentiss any ground or cause to demand, either an explanation of me or a personal conflict with me, I shall without intending any disrespect to you decline giving any other answer to Mr. Prentiss." That ended it. According to the rules, with no more communication passing between the two, there could be no duel.[64] Quitman may have manipulated the rules to guide the protagonists away from violence.

A variety of factors produced duels. The Prentiss-Tucker affair illustrates the importance of language. All three men used the power of words as a tool to assert their manhood before the public. Everyone understood that certain insults produced duels. Calling someone a "craven puppy," a "blustering rooster," or some other animal-like coward nearly guaranteed a duel.[65] Although it has almost entirely disappeared from usage today, the word *poltroon* was a favorite insult for duelists. It is not hard to see why. A poltroon is a coward, of course, but a particular kind—a wet-behind-the-ears youth hiding behind a mask of manhood. A duel might prove duelists' manhood, their coolly mature courage, or it might unmask one as unworthy. Duelists wanted to be seen as the opposite of a poltroon.[66]

Dueling came from white southern culture, a tradition that contrasted with the commercial values practiced by Vicksburg's business class. Vicksburg's commercial world sometimes actually promoted dueling, however. Advances in printing technology, the hallmark of newspaper boosterism and business, enabled men to insult social enemies with greater efficiency and impact. Newspapers allowed the lower classes to read the insults the wealthy passed back and forth. One man of honor complained that his opponent had blackened his name in newspapers "hawked about the streets of this city by the public news venders . . . *at the extremely low price of five cents per copy.*"[67] Roswell Booth wrote about the tragic history of the Vicksburg *Sentinel,* founded in 1838. The newspaper's "vindictive and vituperative utterances" on behalf of the Democratic Party led to the violent deaths of five of its editors.[68] *Sentinel* editor James A. Ryan insulted *Whig* editor Richard E. Hammett by accusing him in the columns of his newspaper of shooting a crippled man in another duel. Hammett challenged Ryan and then shot and killed him.[69] Walter Hickey of the *Sentinel* vindicated himself by killing Dr. James F. Maclin, a dentist and member of the city council who had attacked Hickey for a *Sentinel* editorial.[70] Later Hickey migrated to Texas, where he died in another duel.[71] Another editor of the *Sentinel,* James Fall, fought two duels.[72]

In 1844, when some Vicksburgers formed an anti-dueling society, the Vicksburg *Sentinel* cited the Bible to defend dueling.[73] David, after all, had fought a duel with Goliath. "This was a cool and premeditated affair," the newspaper pointed out, "the challenge having been given every day for forty days and taken up by David on the fortieth." The Lord himself had served as David's second. Joseph E. Davis also spoke on behalf of dueling. Duels could be ended, he declared, only when men "became so just and enlightened as to do away with the necessity for personal accountability." In an imperfect world an end to dueling would plunge gentlemen into a "land of insult and the abode of those closely approximating highwaymen." That could not be tolerated, Davis exclaimed. "Gross insults not properly atoned for, make it imperative for the aggrieved to stand on equal terms and fight."[74]

Defenders of dueling—including leading Vicksburg lawyers—claimed that their affairs of honor represented order rather than anarchy. But even as duelists continued to exchange shots on fields of honor, courts, judges, and lawyers proliferated, as did demands for more law and more courts. Lawyers sometimes fought duels themselves, but most understood the law as fundamentally opposed to dueling. Grand jurors regularly indicted duelists.[75] Dueling was a challenge to formal law in Warren County. Mobs, infuriated by crimes committed by slaves, also asserted themselves as better equipped to punish slaves than courts, judges, and juries. By the end of the antebellum era, however, elites resisted the siren call of the lynch mob.

In 1857 Vicksburg *Whig* readers followed the story of slaves Coleman and Henry, accused of murdering their overseer in nearby Rankin County. The *Whig* expected its readers to be shocked to learn that some Rankin County whites actually wanted to punish Coleman and Henry outside the normal process of law. A crowd the *Whig* described as "large and excited" gathered at the Rankin County courthouse in Brandon. Many in the agitated throng wanted blood, but M. M. Smith and A. G. Meyers emerged to speak against mob law, assuring the assemblage that authorities had enough evidence to convict the pair of murder. But angry men assembled to burn live human flesh do not necessarily respond to such logic, so Smith, Meyers, and other leaders had to shift tactics and adroitly channel the crowd's anger away from the two slaves. The Vicksburg *Whig* reported that a "committee was appointed to examine into and report a cure for the evils" that led to the murder. The committee quickly found the fault where slaveowners wanted it found: in "the illicit traffic with negroes here." There had to be specifics. The newspapers had been making such general complaints for years; this crowd howled for a scapegoat. If community leaders wanted to avoid a lynching they would have to deliver someone to the mob. So the committee denounced Edward Oakley for buying stolen property and selling liquor to slaves. A committee of ten went to Oakley with the news, followed by another committee of twenty assigned to make sure he left town.[76]

Community leaders had cleverly deflected the mob away from a lynching. Oakley left town, and the two slaves remained in jail. Not all expressed satisfaction with the outcome, however. Some whites griped that missing a "nigger hangin'" was like missing the circus. "I never saw such excitement," the *Whig* correspondent reported, "many of the non-slave-holders complained at the result—They 'came to see the niggers burnt[']" and were disappointed." Deeply disappointed, as it turned out. Two months later they came back, determined to seize and lynch Coleman and Henry surreptitiously. The prisoners thwarted that by sounding the alarm. Lawmen came, and the would-be lynchers disappeared. Authorities hanged Coleman in December. After a jury deadlocked on Henry's guilt he won a change of venue to Hinds County, where a jury acquitted him.[77]

In other cases crowds turned out to demand formal justice, not lawlessness. In 1857, when Cornelius McCoy shot and killed a slave on the streets of Vicksburg, escaping justice, Vicksburgers demanded that he be punished. The crowd asserted that when authorities fail to enforce the laws it is the duty of the citizenry to take prompt measures to punish delinquent officials or "derilict" citizens. McCoy had been arrested and taken to mayor's court but had escaped before he could be jailed. The assembled citizens called witnesses, heard testimony, and decided the mayor deserved no censure. But city marshal William Fagan had failed to summon a posse or call on bystanders for assistance when McCoy escaped. Although McCoy had loudly boasted he would not be taken to jail and had defied the marshal's authority, the lawman did nothing when McCoy walked away and escaped town. Under pressure, Fagan resigned his office. The crowd had gathered because a white man accused of killing a slave had been allowed to escape. Some slaveowners must have wanted to see the law better protect their property, and perhaps McCoy's victim had been a popular and well-liked slave. But the rhetoric of those assembled must not be ignored: It was, they said, the duty of citizens to see to it that officials followed the law.[78]

The McCoy case generated a spectacular scene: a mob assembled to assert law over extralegal violence. Such things did not often happen. Far more often, perhaps every day, whites displayed the contradictions in their attitudes toward constitutionalism and slavery when confronting the issue of "nominal" slavery. Unsupervised slaves challenged the prevailing notion that slaveowners should control their slaves with minimal interference by the state. They found it convenient to dispatch slaves on unsupervised errands to town.

But the problem ran deeper than a few errant slaves making occasional trips into Vicksburg. Mississippi tolerated quasi-slavery. Formally, slaves could only be freed by last will and testament and an act of the legislature. In practice, slaveowners worked out informal arrangements for favorites. That meant business arrangements allowing energetic slaves to hire themselves out or even run their own businesses.[79] Unusually energetic slaves worked on Saturdays and "moonshiney nights," accumulating property through discipline and hard work.[80] Planters sometimes paid them for corn raised outside normal working hours.[81] Some gave away injured stock or sold it at a reduced price.[82] Thomas Bradshaw's master gave him a mule so wild it had nearly killed two other slaves, but Bradshaw patiently tamed the animal and sold it for a handsome profit.[83] Slaveowner Joseph S. Acuff admitted allowing his slaves "a patch and a chance to work and make money." He bragged that some did so well that "I have even borrowed money of them myself."[84] White attorney H. F. Cook explained that he held title as trustee to two tracts of land for slave William Newman, who with his wife, Candis, operated a dairy so profitable that they owned thousands of dollars worth of property.[85] The whites willing to help such industrious blacks must have done so for a variety of reasons, including paternalism. "I raised him," one white banker proudly said of his house servant, "he was sprightly and had quite a knack of making money."[86]

Distance from supervision helped slaves feel freer; in some cases that meant arranging living quarters some distance from an ostensible owner. Jack Hyland occupied quarters eight miles from his master. Other slaves negotiated distance from their owners to pursue a trade without supervision. Barber William Hitch considered himself "free since quite a boy" because his owner did not bother to control who hired his time. Nor did he stop Hitch from using his barbering money to "lay up" funds for horse trading.[87] William Jefferson, a steward and hotel porter, described himself as only "nominally a slave of Ben Hardway," really free as he bought and sold goods without Hardway's guidance. Vicksburg's population of slave hack drivers also lived in de facto freedom. No white person could bother following the drivers of wagons and carriages around town as they chased fares.[88]

Some slaves saved thousands of dollars. In 1857 barber Oliver Garrett paid $2,500 to free himself, and Isham Lewis bought his own freedom for $1,400 eleven years before the war.[89] One slave claimed to have nearly $300 in gold when the Union army came to Vicksburg. Several slaveowners allowed their slaves not only to accumulate property but also to pass it to their heirs.[90] The most successful slaves started their own businesses, and those entrepreneurs achieved remarkable independence, buying their own stock and building stables. Whites commonly hired out surplus slave labor to other whites; in Vicksburg, however, slave entrepreneurs hired other slaves as their employees.

These slaves challenged the ideal of a well-regulated slave society. In 1841 the Board of Police, with a lone dissenter, had voted a blanket revocation of all the licenses for free black Vicksburgers. The board did not intend to eject all freed blacks from Vicksburg, planning instead to consider each case on its merits. The one dissenter, Alexander Arthur, thought freed blacks should never be allowed to stay. He knew he took the risk of being "considered inhuman and unjust" but pointed out that nothing in the law allowed Vicksburg to permit freed blacks to remain in the city. And, he argued, "the exigency of the times required their removal from among us."[91]

But the board accomplished little, and Vicksburg newspapers continued to complain bitterly about nominal slaves. In 1859 the *Citizen* declared the "class of negroes . . . now among us, who are *pretended* to be owned by white men" a "pest and annoyance of the town." The newspaper worried that such "quasi-slaves" contaminated the "bona fide" slaves, turning them into drunken gamblers.[92] The *Sun* noted that city slaves had no trouble finding liquor and forged passes. "Vicious and insolent," they owned horses, cattle, poultry, and dogs. "Depend on it," the *Whig* warned, "this state of things is eminently pernicious to the interests of our city."[93]

In some cases Warren County's circuit court moved directly against the "vicious and insolent" free and nominally free slaves so pernicious to Vicksburg. Although more slaves entered court than earlier, they still rarely entered the criminal justice system. Only forty-seven nonwhites can be identified from surviving records as defendants in Warren County's criminal justice system from 1817 through 1859, a time when the same system processed 1,856 white defendants. Yet numbers did increase in the two decades before the Civil War. There were only five nonwhite defendants in the criminal justice system before 1841 but forty-two between 1841 and 1859. Because twelve thousand slaves lived in Warren County in 1850, it could be said that only .38 percent of them entered the system; 805, or 13 percent, of the county's six thousand whites appeared in court as defendants between 1841 and 1859. The number of published appeals court decisions involving slaves rose dramatically as slaves appeared as defendants. Nonetheless, few came before the courts. Whites did not systematically use the law to control the slave population.

The circuit court moved more decisively against whites who interfered with slave property. Most of the increase in "slave" crimes involved white perpetrators associated with slaves, not the slaves themselves. Of 189 civil-order crimes recorded in extant Warren County records, 108 alleged that whites traded with slaves. In most of these cases some white grocer had sold liquor to a slave. Because blacks could not testify against whites, such cases were extremely difficult to prosecute. Authorities in the antebellum South who prosecuted sellers of alcohol had virtually no hope of finding witnesses. In Warren County, lawmen devised sting operations, one of which caught Christian Fleckenstein, who regularly sold liquor to slaves. The local reporter for the R. G. Dun and Company credit-rating agency wrote that he carried on a "low trade mostly with negroes—has been repeatedly indicted & once or twice convicted of trading with slaves."[94]

Planter John Henderson and his overseer Augustus Strong decided to do something about the troublesome Fleckenstein, and the two brought one of Henderson's slaves to Fleckenstein's store. Before sending him in, they carefully searched him so they could testify he had nothing but $3. In such sting operations the money was sometimes marked, but probably not this time. After being sent into the store "for the purpose of the experiment" the slave returned with a gun and liquor. At Fleckenstein's trial the judge instructed the jury that they must presume him guilty "unless the defendant has proved to their satisfaction that the whiskey and pistol were purchased with the permission of the owner, overseer, or employer of the negro." Fleckenstein was guilty unless he could prove himself innocent. And Fleckenstein had to produce in evidence the *"original* writing giving such consent" and had to prove that "such permission was *known* at the *time* to *the defendant.*"[95]

Mississippi's High Court of Errors and Appeals reversed Fleckenstein's conviction because his indictment had been vague and uncertain—possibly because it did not include the name of the slave. Fleckenstein continued his "low trade" with slaves, as did other merchants. In 1860 the Vicksburg *Citizen* complained that four or five "disreputable groceries" operated on Washington Street. The trade must have been lucrative, the newspaper observed, because "the dingy shanties that stood there a few years back have given place, in some instances, to brick houses of quite respectable exterior."[96] There is evidence that Vicksburg's Irish community participated in this unlawful trade with slaves. In 1859 a city officer arrested John "Red Jack" McGuiggin and charged him with selling passes to Vicksburg slaves for a dollar each. City officials had known of the trade for some time but been unable to identify the culprit because Red Jack's grateful clientele had refused to give his name to inquiring whites. Finally, in October a slave, caught with a bogus pass, had identified McGuiggin and agreed to cooperate. The city marshal then sent this slave back to McGuiggin to buy a new pass—but this time with white witnesses looking on. Caught, McGuiggin went to circuit court, where a jury found him guilty and a judge sentenced him to twenty years in prison.[97]

The *Citizen* complained that crowds of drunken blacks roamed the Washington Street neighborhood. "What liquor they want," the Vicksburg *Sun* complained, "they have no difficulty in obtaining." With "abundant liberty" they got into fights and stole to feed their horses, cattle, poultry, and dogs.[98]

The failure of some slaveowners to control their chattel had created a nuisance. Vicksburg's newspapers urged the state to act, and legislators hastened to respond. William Smedes, a local legislator and lawyer, wrote a bill making it illegal for slaveowners to keep their slaves in nominal slavery. The bill proposed making illegal any agreement between owner and slave giving the slave "the privilege of doing as he or she may please." The bill would also have made it illegal for whites to act as agents for nominally free slaves. Legislators initially supported the measure but never passed it. Perhaps they realized that such vague language would be virtually meaningless.[99] Despite the fate of the bill, its origins deserve careful attention. Slaveowners had created a nuisance, and their neighbors objected and sought police regulation to control their individual conduct for the good of the whole.

Authorities pursued these crimes in response to white citizens' complaints and to restore order. The character of the witnesses indicates that town-dwellers were the moving force behind the drive. Witnesses in slave-trading cases closely resembled defendants (table 1). Only about a third of witnesses owned slaves, about the same proportion of slaveholders as

Table 1. Slave Holdings of Defendants and Witnesses in Slave Trading Cases, 1822–59

Number of Slaves	Defendants ($N = 90$)	Witnesses ($N = 112$)
0	68.9%	64.3%
1–10	20.0	23.2
11+	11.1	12.5

Sources: Warren County Circuit Court Papers, Old Court House Museum, Vicksburg; Warren County Circuit Court Papers, Natchez Trace Collection, Center for American History, University of Texas at Austin; Warren County minute books, Circuit Clerk's Office, Vicksburg; slave schedules, Seventh U.S. Census, 1850, and Eighth U.S. Census, 1860, Warren County, Miss., microfilm, National Archives.

among defendants. Smedes's statute and a number of others seem to have been aimed at forcing owners to control their slaves. One law denied them the right to permit slaves to live off their property, and another measure sought to prevent them from allowing their slaves to preach or assemble. Nearly half of the men and women brought to trial for the offense owned more than ten slaves.

Complaints of nonslaveowners and small slaveowners often initiated slave-trading cases, but once in court legal discourse forged far from Vicksburg influenced their outcomes. To make it easier to win convictions, Mississippi—and many other states—lowered the standard of proof in illicit trading cases. In all states prosecutors faced the same problem: Illegal sales often took place in secret, with no witnesses but the parties themselves. Many northern states found they had to lower the standard of proof to win convictions in liquor cases. Vermont courts decided that merely finding a cache of liquor could be construed as evidence of intent to sell. No one need actually see the selling.[100] New Hampshire shifted the burden of proof from the state to the defendant; if the state charged someone with selling liquor without a license, the defendant had to produce a license or suffer the consequences.[101] The Massachusetts supreme court refused to require judges to caution juries against the testimony of someone drunk at the time they saw liquor sold.[102] Warren County judges instructed jurors that they needed no evidence of an actual sale to convict white merchants of trading with slaves. "If the jury believes from the evidence," one judge said, "that a negro . . . was seen to come out of the House of defendant" with goods alleged to have been sold, then "the jury ought to find the Defendant guilty."[103]

Whether the jury actually found the defendant guilty depended to a considerable extent on public opinion. That is the essence of honor, a system within which neighbors determined each individual's worth. Conscience mattered little because the public, not the self, ultimately set moral values.[104] In various ways, men made bids for public recognition of their honor. Exaggerations of honor have been used to characterize southerners: excessive touchiness, obsessive affection for guns, ambition, demagogic appeals to a fickle public, and lavish hospitality. Law and honor can coexist. The prosecution of Stephen Lewis demonstrates the importance of neighborhood opinion in criminal justice matters. But by placing such a premium on a neighborhood's judgment, honor also encouraged vigilantism, dueling, and lynching.[105]

In Mississippi, whites articulated the tension between law and mob law by fashioning a legal system designed to keep slaves out of circuit court, where defendants received the most robust protections of their due process rights. Most of the time, whites punished miscreant slaves on their plantations and farms. When slaves committed crimes off plantations, whites preferred to try them before magistrates and with minimal due process. Only slaves charged with the most serious crimes went to circuit court. And white Vicksburgers showed their periodic preference for settling disputes outside court by building a reputation for dueling and vigilante violence.

3

The Public Good and Due Process

In 1857 slaveowners across the South cheered when the Supreme Court declared that the Fifth Amendment to the U.S. Constitution protected their property. Congress, the Court said, could make no law barring southerners from taking their slaves into any western territory. The case of Dred Scott capped a long and largely successful campaign by slaveowners and their lawyers to protect their property through law.[1] The system of understandings and beliefs about law that made up whites' legal culture reserved an important place for courts in protecting property and ordering antebellum southern society. Southern whites nonetheless harbored doubts about their courts' ability to discipline blacks. The very device by which law protected the property of slaveowners, due process, also wove a web of cumbersome procedures that slaveowners found hard to manipulate. Even rules cynically created by the master class to preserve its status were still, at bottom, rules that to claim legitimacy had to appear immutable.[2]

Lawyers and judges justified due process in a way that challenged the extralegal autonomy enjoyed by slaveowners over their slaves. Lawyers claimed their regulations, while limiting the freedom of individuals, did so on behalf of the entire public. Slaveowners' property, not always carefully supervised, sometimes endangered the general welfare. Throughout the antebellum period, formal law enforcement increasingly intruded onto slaveowners' "little nations." The challenge of law and government to slaveowners' autonomy in a society that valued individual freedom for white men represented a central paradox in Warren County's slave society.

* * *

Warren County's white population feared slaves and nominal slaves; in 1831 a grand jury had warned of a threat to "our common country." The jurors reported "Authentic intelligence" that blacks in eastern states had exhibited a "dangerous insurrectionary spirit."[3] The grand jury meant the alert to put owners of slaves on notice: They would no longer be allowed to endanger the public good with unsupervised slaves and must subordinate their economic acquisitiveness to the general welfare. They had a right to make money and could use slaves to do so, but they should not forget the community's rights. But 1831 was early for grand juries to be asserting the public good, and little came of their warning.

Grand jurors' concerns about threats to the common country presaged an important shift in Vicksburg's legal culture. The intellectual world that Warren County lawyers inhabited changed in the 1830s. At least as early as the 1820s lawyers in England and North America had transformed and broadened the police power, a doctrine that justified local government intervention in neighborhood society and local economies. Published treatises, speeches, and law lectures all showed that nineteenth-century legalists conceived people as social beings and understood general happiness as best achieved by means of a well-regulated community.[4] States chartered, regulated, and subsidized social services, especially transportation. Nineteenth-century law pressed hard to promote the general welfare, curbing individual avarice when it threatened the public good or the rights enjoyed by the whole community. As Supreme Court Justice Henry Baldwin wrote, law should "make the *private* yield to the *public* interest." Common law sends its "equitable energies through all classes and ranks of men."[5]

Although the new movement threatened an old tradition—lawyers had once shielded property owners from municipal authorities' regulatory powers—judges began to conflate individual liberties with public rights. At least in part, that change in conception can be traced to the rise of a new understanding of consent and contract. Legal understandings of the rights of individuals—protected by local governments—began to emerge. One example of how that translated into more activist local government can be found in the judicial seizure of new powers to protect children. Before the 1840s, southern judges had felt compelled to return children to the custody of even the most abusive of fathers. After 1840, they assumed a new flexibility and sometimes refused to respect paternal authority. That new flexibility represented power. Government could use such new power to control nuisances, even ones created by paternal authority figures in what they saw as the exercise of their liberties.[6]

The new stress on law became apparent when Warren County built a new courthouse in 1858. Vicksburg had become the county seat in 1836, having constructed a courthouse in 1828 in anticipation of snatching the seat of government from rival Warrenton. Two stories high and with a tall cupola, the 1828 building mounted a hill overlooking the city. Twenty years after its construction, the building seemed worn out. A schoolchild described it as an old building that "does not look very well." Another observer characterized it as an ordinary-looking square brick building. Newspapers noted that the courthouse leaked badly. Nonetheless, the county government hesitated to pay for a new building. But on April 10, 1857, the old courthouse burned when sparks from a burning kitchen spread to a row of one-story houses, reaching the African Church on Grove and Cherry. The wind carried the sparks across the street to the courthouse cupola, and flames quickly engulfed the building. Supervisors had little choice but to rebuild, and the county contracted with Natchez builders, who began work in June 1858. Working with skilled slave labor, the contractors finished the job in a year. The June 1859 term of the circuit court met in the new structure.[7]

The courthouse was an imposing mass of pediments, friezes, and Ionic columns topped by a huge cupola and bell tower. The builders copied Greek architecture to erect a temple to justice. Although mounted on the same hill as the old courthouse, the new, bigger building dominated Vicksburg's skyline more impressively than the old ramshackle structure. The editor of the Vicksburg *Whig* found an "astonishing combination of beauty of strength" in the new building. Eight offices were on the first floor, and the courtroom occupied most of the top floor. The judge sat atop an iron dais, flanked by seats for the jury on his left. There was no witness box; witnesses sat in a simple chair, as did the lawyers.[8]

Two poems illustrate Vicksburgers' changing attitudes toward law. In 1844, after state lawmakers had written a confusing statute about when circuit court should meet, someone in the courthouse scribbled a bit of doggerel aimed at the legislature: "But that so num'rous were the asses in the last legislature / To have pass'd a sensible law would have gone against their nature—." Because the legislature had failed to make their meaning plain, the writer suggested the judge decide by spitting in his hand and striking the pool with his finger: "Whichever way the spittle flies, let that be the rule."[9]

That picture of judicial decision making did not match the one drawn by J. S. Byrne, a local poet, in 1858 as the county constructed its imposing monument to justice. Byrne thought that the laws to be enforced in the new courthouse came from God amid "fiery clouds" and a "fearful light":

> Which flash'd around the mountain's beauty
> When God His laws proclaimed,
> Whilst Israel's sons did humbly bow
> Before God who reigned!

Byrne promised that "quaking guilt, with horid fears" would get no solace in this temple of justice but the injured innocent would find a "guardian angel's wing." He concluded:

> To Law and Justice, Truth and Right,
> And pray Jehovah's care!
> Long as its sculptured columns stand,
> May Warren's sons uphold
> The sovereign voice of Law's command
> Which wisdom shall unfold![10]

The new emphasis on law and government led the board of police into decisions once made informally in neighborhoods, setting rates for ferry operators and deciding where roads should be placed, for example. Construction of levees to protect bottom lands along the Mississippi River from flooding constituted the biggest project for Warren County government. No single neighborhood could undertake such a massive project. Mississippi's new 1835 state constitution further shifted power from neighborhoods when it made county offices elective, which cost elite families control of local government. Voters instead placed persons in office who had no connection to leading families but rather held power by virtue of a countywide vote.[11]

Warren County proponents of law campaigned for new courts because increased police regulation and Vicksburg's growth swelled the numbers of criminal cases. In 1852 grand jurors expressed *"great mortification"* at the upsurge in crime and called for a bigger jail. Some in Vicksburg lobbied for additional courts. R. S. Buck joined the campaign, writing that "the growing importance of the city of Vicksburg both as a thoroughfare and a commercial point has greatly increased the proportion of crime from what it was some years ago when it was not so immediately connected with other large cities." The presence of transients increased crime. Persons with little stake in the social order felt freer to murder and rob than they would at home. But so many transients also meant that witnesses to major crimes often disappeared before the next court term. Residents of Ohio, Kentucky, Indiana, or other distant states could hardly be expected to wait months for the June or December circuit court. After years of lobbying, the legislature finally established a criminal court for Warren County. It would meet four times a year, in February, May, August, and November, and have the same jurisdiction over crimes as the circuit court.[12]

One sign that courts and juries had assumed a more important role can be found in renewed concern about the quality of jurors. At the same time that pressure built for more courts and more formal law enforcement, some in Mississippi campaigned for "better" grand jurors. Before 1856 Warren County defendants faced a randomly selected cross-section of white males. By law, the tax assessor had to place the name of every eligible taxpayer in a box. A clerk then drew jurors' names in open court, where, presumably, public scrutiny kept him from playing favorites. In theory, slaveowners enjoyed no special access to jury service until 1856, although somehow they still turned up more often than they should have in a purely random drawing. Nonetheless, the process produced jurors who at least crudely resembled the tax-paying population. But in 1854 the legislature discarded the random procedure in four counties, allowing the sheriff to choose grand jurors. Legislators understood that the sheriff represented the economic elite and would choose jurors more representative of the wealthier classes than the county as a whole. Two years later legislators applied the new method to the whole state, including Warren County. The next year they modified the procedure slightly, calling on the governing body in each county to select grand jurors.[13]

The new statute had an immediate impact in Warren County and led to grand juries far wealthier than the county as a whole. Before 1856 the average slaveowner serving on a grand jury had thirteen slaves, a number that grew to twenty-seven after the new law. A third of grand jurors owned no slaves before 1856, and just 12 percent had twenty or more, yet only one-fifth of jurors had no slaves and 40 percent had twenty or more after the new law.

The new emphasis on law and government that led to jury selection reforms prompted lawmakers to unprecedented interventions in the lives of ordinary citizens. At the end of the 1830s, Mississippi government dared challenge citizens' right to consume alcohol freely, an individual liberty that endangered family and community but one some imagined as unquestionably beyond the reach of government. Henry S. Foote remembered that in the 1830s Mississippians consumed "immense" quantities of liquor. He believed that plentiful alcohol, combined with a bountiful supply of firearms, accounted for Mississippi violence; two-thirds of the state's homicides resulted from drunkenness, he estimated. Even judges and lawyers tried cases under the influence of alcohol. In 1839 legislator Foote proposed a ban on the sale of alcohol in quantities of less than a gallon. According to Foote, his bill became law without public debate. Many southerners associated intemperate drinking with democracy, by which they meant the right of individuals to do as they pleased without government interference. Outraged democrats burned Foote in effigy.[14]

As part of the effort to reform the drinking habits of Mississippians, Warren County grand jurors indicted more than twice as many persons for illegal liquor sales than for assault. The effort to curb alcohol consumption represented a new direction for the criminal justice system. Foote believed that his bill, which legislators repealed in 1842, had a beneficial effect recalled years later by "thousands." Decorum returned and the criminal courts hardly had anything to do—according to Foote.[15] During the period when the gallon law remained in force, Warren County's circuit court processed 249 cases, 88 for illegal sale of liquor. Seventy liquor cases came from the gallon law, eighteen more from an old law against retailing liquor without a license. Despite grand jurors' apparently sincere efforts to enforce the new legislation, the results frustrated reformers. In Warren County, Foote's gallon law yielded just two convictions, nineteen acquittals, and forty-nine dismissals. Seventy percent of gallon law indictments did not make it to trial. The older law against retailing liquor without a license, in contrast, produced a lower rate of dismissals and a higher rate of convictions.

The problems courts encountered enforcing the gallon law did not go unnoticed. Proponents of the law blamed the failure of most prosecutions on minor technical defects in the indictments and want of evidence but primarily on the ability of defense lawyers to raise constitutional objections. "Jurors were seduced by the sophistry of counsel into the belief that . . . they were the judges of its constitutionality," one temperance advocate wrote. Jurors must be informed that they are not a *Legislature* to *make* laws."[16] The April 1841 grand jury took a more realistic position, declaring the gallon law "in advance of public opinion" and unenforceable. The law wasted tax dollars and had become an annoyance to the community.[17]

The failure of Foote's law represented a setback for those determined to protect the people's welfare through law. The broader intellectual trend could not be turned back, however. Nineteenth-century courts used the concept of nuisance to make individuals yield to the public good. People using their property for profit to the detriment of the neighbors created what lawyers called a nuisance. Pigs roaming New York soiled the streets, for example, and endangered small children. Owners profited from the freedom to keep their animals in the city, but the hogs' liberty threatened the health and safety of everyone else. Hog owners were responsible for a nuisance. Slaves roaming Vicksburg represented a similar paradox of individual versus public rights.[18]

Warren County authorities' increased efforts to police individual behavior eventually included literal nuisances. The earliest indications of this great shift in law enforcement philosophy, however, involved threats to public safety, morals, and well-being not technically called nuisances. Between 1831 and 1840 fewer than 8 percent of all indictments alleged crimes against property. But crimes against person no longer dominated the docket as they once had. Those against the moral order increased dramatically from a quarter of the cases to more than 40 percent of the total. Allegations of illegal liquor sales alone amounted to more than all the charges of assault, fighting, and homicide together. Prosecutions of gamblers increased from just one case between 1817 and 1822 to twenty-eight in the 1830s. The new pattern suggests a shift in Mississippians' understanding of law. Courts had begun to change from a place where fights could be resolved to a place where the community regulated the behavior of individuals for the good of the whole.

Abstract changes in legal discourse penetrated circuit courts and appeals courts more easily than inferior courts. That fact of life had considerable importance for slave defendants because most slave crime went to a lower court. Those charged with death penalty crimes were most likely to receive the formal justice offered by circuit courts. After 1833, only slaves accused of conspiring to rebel, arson, murder or manslaughter, preparing a poison, or rape went to circuit court.[19] But when slave crimes excited the neighborhood, lawmen proved willing to bypass due process. When slaves committed sensational crimes, centuries of common-law protections against self-incrimination vanished. In the case of murder, neighbors might rush in, force a confession, and then demand that courts accept it as evidence. In cases of alleged insurrection, slaveowners sometimes convened vigilante courts to circumvent the procedures common law required.[20] In writing of one such panic south of Vicksburg, a historian observed that in reading the transcript of a slave's "terse and jerky" confession he could almost hear the lash wrench information from the man. Planters justified torture by claiming that "the law is too tardy in its course, even if it could be effectual in its process."[21]

Some cases, even some involving the most serious criminal acts, did not excite the neighborhood. In such instances slave defendants made their way to circuit court, where they received considerable due process protection. Whites owning slaves completely controlled the circuit courts; even so, they found such courts a most imperfect medium for the control of slaves. Reuben Davis recalled that other lawyers in antebellum Mississippi "rigidly" enforced "all the technicalities of the common law." He remembered that almost any bill of indictment could be quashed "on account of some error in the organization of the court or action of the grand jury."[22] In such an environment, technicalities of due process matter more than practical crime control.

Today, lawyers distinguish procedural from substantive due process, but in slavery trials the two kinds of process merged. Procedural due process requires the government to use its power according to settled maxims of law. Legal proceedings must follow the rules and principles established to protect rights. Substantive due process protects property from legislation. A statute that has the effect of depriving people of their property without recourse to court violates the doctrine of substantive due process. An epigram explaining the difference holds that procedural due process constitutes the rules of the game whereas substantive due process is the game.[23]

The Supreme Court did not endorse substantive due process by name until 1897.[24] But property owners since the Magna Carta had looked to "the law of the land" to protect their property from governmental seizure. During the French and Indian War, James Otis argued that authorities must not seize the private property of traitors without following the forms of English law.[25] State constitutions promised not to deprive persons of their lives or liberty except by "the law of the land." Lawyers defending their clients' property rights insisted that the government navigate a thicket of detailed rules and procedures. The fundamental assumption was that the government legitimately took property when it did so after following all the esoteric rules found in common law.

Slaveowners maintained a species of property so unstable, so dangerous, that the government sometimes had to take and destroy that property for the safety of the whole. Slaveowners and their lawyers understood the maxim "use your own so as not to injure the rights of others" and almost never challenged criminal laws. Slave property could injure the rights of others. Careless or lax owners who failed to supervise their slaves properly should shoulder some of the responsibility for the conduct of that property. The state had the responsibility to protect citizens' health and welfare from dangerous slaves and lax slaveowners, but police power did not license the state to ignore property rights.

Courts protected the rights of slaveowners by refusing to destroy their property without following all the nuances of procedural due process. Trained in the common law, judges equated procedure with fairness and justice. That meant that slaves on trial for the most serious crimes could expect judges and prosecutors to follow common-law principles. Prisoners could not be tortured into a confession; defendants had to be tried by a jury and could challenge the prosecution's evidence as well as present their own. Because the common law came from England, early defense lawyers had to search English precedents for principles of law applicable to their clients; no single document codified protections for the accused. An attorney defending a client against a prosecutor wielding the prisoner's confession invoked *Rex v. Hearne* or *Rex v. Walker*, usually through one of a number of treatises summarizing common-law doctrine. One of the most popular was *A Treatise on the Law of Evidence* by Simon Greenleaf, an American, which went through sixteen editions between 1842 and 1899. These restraints on capricious governmental power have long been recognized as central to the meaning of freedom in America.[26]

After 1850 southern state courts became more sensitive to the constitutional protections surrounding all property. Local courts actually tightened procedures for slaves, affording them new protections. Jury selection constitutes a good example. Authorities almost never allowed slaves on trial to challenge prospective jurors, but in the decade before the Civil War such challenges became more common. Such changes coincide with a national trend in law toward greater protection for property.[27]

The heightened interest in property protection reached Warren County, where antebellum courts moved from little interest in property crimes to considerable interest. From 1817 through 1846 crimes against property rose above more than a quarter of the docket only once—in 1843. In thirteen years the number was fewer than 10 percent. After 1846 the proportion of property crimes fell below 25 percent only twice and went to 30 percent or higher six times. In 1848 nearly half the indictments alleged crimes against property. Nonetheless, as the nineteenth century progressed slaves seemed to accumulate more and more "rights" in southern courtrooms. At least as early as 1841, Mississippi's High Court decided that they must be tried as other persons.[28]

Ironically, the arcane rules by which law protected slaveowners' property made that same law unsuitable as a disciplinary device. Despite the protections that common-law procedures and the jury selection rules afforded them, Mississippi slaveowners sought to avoid exposure to law. They designed statutory law to keep the criminal justice system off the plantation. Slaveowning planters controlled the writing of law in Mississippi's state legislatures.[29] They could use law to structure an environment that limited slave access to circuit courts, where judges closely adhered to common-law rules. As a result, the state only reluctantly intervened in relationships between slaves and their owners. Those off the plantation had to be subject to law; they could not be allowed to become a nuisance to neighbors any more than a butcher could spew waste onto a city street without sanction.[30] But on the plantation slaves had to be shielded from the process of law. Owners expected the law to protect their sovereignty within the bounds of their property by absenting itself from the relationship as much as possible. They domesticated slavery. That is, they detached it from the public sphere, making it a private institution.[31]

Examination of the working of a particular legal procedure illustrates how the legal process could frustrate whites bent on controlling slave crime. Habeas corpus is an ancient writ issued by courts to force jailers to justify holding prisoners. In cases that did not arouse public sentiment and involved slaves, such procedures could allow lawyers to demand adherence to common-law rules of evidence. Under the common law, any confession must be shown to be voluntary before it can be received in evidence in a criminal case. "'A free and voluntary confession,'" as Simon Greenleaf quoted an English authority, "'is deserving of the highest credit.'" Greenleaf warned against confessions "forced from the mind by the flattery of hope, or by the torture of fear."[32]

According to Mississippi's High Court of Errors and Appeals, slaves never had rights similar to those enunciated in English common law and summarized by treatise writers, except in "one or two very early cases." Nonetheless, the High Court required that magistrates warn slaves accused of crimes that any statement they made might be used against them at their trial. In some ways that admonition resembles the modern Miranda warning that the Supreme Court requires all officers to recite when taking individuals into custody. The High Court thought no such caution necessary for whites because common-law principles only required such protections for suspects unusually vulnerable to coercion. Slaves, thought to be thoroughly intimidated by the entire white race, needed such special protections.

In 1844 the High Court declared that the common law's strictures against coerced confessions applied to slave as well as to white defendants. The mere presence of armed and hostile men around a prisoner made any confession suspect, especially in the case of a slave. In *State v. Peter,* before authorities took Peter before a justice of the peace for examination a crowd had extorted a confession from him with threats. Members of the same crowd, armed with guns, escorted Peter to the office of the justice of the peace, who testified later that he had told Peter he had the privilege to ask questions but gave him no further caution or charge. Peter repeated his confession, and the justice testified against him at the trial.[33]

Mississippi's High Court had read Greenleaf's treatise even if the justice of the peace who transcribed Peter's confession had not. "The general rule of law," the High Court lectured the lower court, "upon the subject of confessions, is, that when made under the influence of a sufficient threat, or at sufficient promise, they are inadmissible as evidence." The High Court went on to instruct Mississippi lawmen that "there must be very clear and strong evidence of explicit caution by the magistrate, of the consequences of confession, after the fact is known of the existence of either the influence of hope or fear superinducing confession; and it should likewise be manifest, that the prisoner understood such warning, before his subsequent confession could be given in evidence." The court observed that nothing in the circumstances attending the subsequent confession would have dispelled the fears previously created in the mind of the accused. The court announced that it would examine the confessions of slaves with special care. "Being a slave," the court declared, Peter "must be presumed to have been ignorant of the protection from sudden violence, which the presence of the justice of the peace afforded him."[34]

Once courts extended due process protections to slaves as a way of guarding their owners' property rights from arbitrary governmental interference, it became difficult to know where to draw the line. Suppose a slave confessed to his or her owner. Should the common-law principle against self-incrimination apply? In the next case, the High Court hardened its prohibition against involuntary confessions, disallowing one freely made to a slaveowner. There was no evidence that the owner had threatened or coerced the slave, but the second confession followed an earlier confession made after a whipping.

In 1852 the court protected the due process rights of Van Buren, a slave Thomas Cooper had hired and then accused of stealing two jugs of whiskey and two loaves of sugar. After a whipping, Van Buren not only confessed but also pointed out where the goods could be found. On the next morning, Cooper took him back to his owner, saying, "Van, here is your master, who has come for the things you took." And Van Buren, "without any threat made or any promise given or reward offered, voluntarily confirmed the confession he had previously made." At his trial, the circuit judge would not allow Van Buren's first confession admitted as evidence but did allow the second. The High Court condemned that as an error and reversed the conviction.[35]

Four years later the High Court seemed even more determinedly protective of slave defendants from self-incrimination. In *Jordan v. State* the justices declared that slave defendants had the right to resist with force efforts to wring a confession from them by violence. In *Jordan,* whites accused the slave of killing another slave named Aaron. After his arrest, two white men interrogated Jordan and threatened to kill him if he did not talk. After a beating, Jordan did confess. That led the High Court to reject his conviction and declare that "it is no answer to say that the confession was true—the question, and the only question which can be considered is, whether the confession was voluntary, extorted by threats or violence, or induced by the hope of reward, or immunity from punishment." Prisoners, the court added, had the right not only to maintain silence in the face of interrogation but also "to resist force by force, to compel him to act otherwise, if it had been in his power to employ such force."[36]

The stricture against involuntary confessions that prevented prosecution of a young Vicksburg slave named David illustrates how law could block punishment of an obviously guilty arsonist. Early in the morning of January 22, 1852, someone set fire to a small outbuilding in Vicksburg. Whites did not regard the fire as mysterious; they immediately identified David as the culprit. He first denied the charge but then confessed, saying he had started the fire because his master had whipped him in the same building. When authorities jailed David, his master filed a habeas corpus petition.[37]

David's master expected to use the writ of habeas corpus to return his property to slavery. Older than the Magna Carta, habeas corpus derives from the common law and has come to be associated with liberty and freedom. Supreme courts in the southern states all agreed that slaves had no right to the great writ. Persons freed by habeas corpus sometimes bypassed a jury trial. If a judge freed a slave without a trial, then the government, in essence, had taken a slaveowner's property without due process. At the same time, every southern state but one forbade owners from using the writ to recover imprisoned slave property. Alabama's high court thought using the "freedom writ" to enslave prisoners would be a perversion. The one southern state to allow such "perversions" was Mississippi.[38]

The habeas corpus petition filed on behalf of David initiated a drama involving David's owner's lawyer and the neighbors who induced David to confess. Under the common law, confessions induced by fear or hope could not be used as evidence, and the lawyer David's owner hired probed David's questioners to find out if they had coerced the confession. They first denied they had. Benjamin Harris described how he discovered the fire and then persuaded David to confess. More details emerged when James Hayes testified that his "Conversation With the Boy was Calculated to induce him to believe that I knew who done it." William C. Folsom supported Hayes, reporting that David had admitted taking "a Coal and stuck it in the House and fired it." Perhaps Folsom hoped that this new detail would persuade Judge Richards Barnett that David had confessed spontaneously, but David's lawyer pressed ahead. He called other witnesses and then recalled Folsom. The transcript records only the witness's testimony, not the questions, but this time Folsom denied that Hayes had whipped or threatened David. Clearly on the defensive, he added that he "should not think that the Boy made any Confession from any fear or favor." But Harris returned for further questioning, and the story completely unraveled: "I then took Him up into my Room and told Him that I would kill Him if he did not tell me all about—the Boy then said you will not hurt me if I tell all about it—I told him I would not." At that point the transcript ended and Barnett ordered David released. Harris had used both fear and hope to persuade David to confess. The confession was invalid.[39]

David's youth may have elicited sympathy, but authorities could not easily convict even adult slaves they thought guilty of murder. In 1851 a slave named Henry learned that his overseer had raped his "wife." Although slaves could not legally marry, whites understood that they could react with unpremeditated fury when defending a mate. Henry attacked the overseer with an axe, a choice of weapon that had legal implications. The law considered that a murderer who approached a victim with the murder weapon in hand had obviously premeditated the act. In the nineteenth century, such criminals could get the death penalty, whereas those who seized a weapon in a momentary fit of rage did not. Approaching a victim with an axe presents a more ambiguous situation than walking in with a pistol. An axe is an innocent tool, commonly found on farms. Yet a murderer might well plot to use an axe. A jury convicted Henry of manslaughter, feeling that the combination of the rape of his wife and Henry's use of the axe suggested blind fury rather than premeditation. The story suggests that a jury of white men recognized that Henry's relationship with his wife gave him a degree of justification in attacking her rapist. It also suggests whites understood that the same honor or sentiment that would legitimately drive a white man to defend his partner might also motivate a slave. But, of course, a white man would have been acquitted.[40]

An 1859 case further illustrates the ambiguity of an axe as a murder weapon in the hands of slaves. Gabriel Spence and his slave Preston had been working together, hacking out a canoe from a floating log. Preston asked Spence to specify where he should cut. While the unsuspecting slaveowner bent over the log to indicate the spot, Preston drove his axe into Spence's neck, nearly severing his head. Spence rolled into the water and Preston ran to the house, claiming an accident. After examining Spence's body, doctors doubted he could have been hit so hard without malice. His family also doubted Preston's story, asking why the slave did not try to pull his victim from the water. But Preston was acquitted. Perhaps the blow really was accidental. Or perhaps Preston had carefully plotted his crime and waited for an opportunity to murder Spence, concocting a credible story as he bided his time.[41]

Vicksburg courts could convict obviously guilty slaves, however. Doubts may persist about Preston, but without question slaves Spencer and Tarleton plotted their owner's death. Thomas Green had been resting under a beech tree, watching them deaden a sassafras when the two turned on him. In their confessions, Tarleton and Spencer each accused the other of striking Green with an axe handle. Whoever did the actual killing, the pair then arranged the scene to make it look as though the tree had fallen on Green. But they were clumsy. No blood stained the tree even though Green's head had been horribly mangled. Authorities quickly arrested the slaves, and juries convicted them.[42]

These cases probably typified the respect for due process whites accorded all defendants—even slaves—in circuit court. If every minor transgression by blacks required adherence to the common-law standards at work in such cases, slave discipline would have collapsed. But Warren County slaves rarely experienced the due process these slaves enjoyed, not because judges failed to follow procedure but because few slaves reached circuit court. In Warren County—where 70 percent of the population was slave—97 percent of circuit court defendants were white.[43] Only blacks accused of the most violent crimes appeared in circuit court, and they made up just 8 percent of defendants charged with such crimes. Whites were even less likely to charge them with morals crimes or crimes against the civil order.

The logic of common law resisted formation of a distinct "Negro law."[44] The common law was not merely a body of court decisions, a judge-made law common to the land. The common law was a logic, a way of thinking designed to solve new situations by analogy from past cases. Thus, even though slavery had not existed in England, the common law adroitly "solved" the problem of slavery. Relationships between slaveowners and slaves resembled those between parents and children or masters and apprentices. When could a slave hit a white person? No such cases existed in English common law, but there were cases where apprentices had lashed out at their masters or sons had struck fathers in self-defense. The common law did not merely offer such solutions for lawyers trained in common-law discourse, but it positively required them to reason from such precedents.[45]

Lawyers' ambitions further frustrated those bent on using the law to control slaves. Lawyers represented slaves in hopes of financial gain, of course, but they also used such cases to build their reputations. A slaveowner in another county hired two lawyers to defend his slave accused of murdering a white man, promising them not only a cash fee but also ownership of the slave if they could acquit him.[46] Another lawyer explained how the nineteenth-century tradition of gilded oratory could also motivate attorneys who defended slaves in court. He recalled that the first "jury speech" he ever heard set his very soul on fire.[47]

When litigators spoke on behalf of unpopular clients, it did not hurt their reputations. At least some observers understood that it took more skill for an attorney to get a rogue "off" than to win a verdict on behalf of a well-liked, more obviously innocent defendant. In 1858 the *Daily Vicksburg Whig* hailed Amos R. Johnson as graceful and eloquent, with "thoughts all flint and . . . words all fire." Gushing praise, the newspaper marveled that he once surmounted overwhelming testimony to free a client convicted in four previous trials of an unprovoked crime. The great Whig orator Seargent S. Prentiss illustrates the point. He built his political career on a reputation for eloquence and persuasive power established in the courtroom. His cleverly argued speech against the defendant in one criminal case drove the jury to condemn the man to death. Some later wondered if the hapless defendant really deserved that fate, but they admired Prentiss's skill nonetheless. In another case he argued on behalf of a hotel placed under quarantine because of an outbreak of smallpox there. Although he was really arguing in favor of exposing people to smallpox, his soaring oratory still impressed listeners.[48]

In addition to their oratory, lawyers also took pride in their skill at "fixing" legal problems through technicalities. Just as they competed to make the best speech, they also vied to manipulate the rules most effectively. When Reuben Davis recalled that almost any bill of indictment could be quashed on account of some error, he did not literally mean that any lawyer could quash any indictment. But he did mean that the most skillful lawyer could do so, and he obviously included himself in those ranks. "I remember," he wrote proudly, "quashing more than eighty bills of indictment at one term of the court in Tishemingo County, by one motion."[49]

That does not mean, of course, that every slave with a lawyer received a fair trial. The case of *State v. Champion* proves the contrary. In 1858 grand jurors charged that Champion had stabbed a white man, Henry Jeter. A few days after his indictment a jury convicted Champion, and the judge sentenced him to hang. But then Champion filed a plaintive affidavit. He was, he told the judge, an ignorant, illiterate Negro who knew nothing of the forms of law. Uneducated and terrified, he had not put on a proper defense. Had he done so, he could have proved he had been fetching a bundle of clothes for his wife two miles from Jeter when the stabbing occurred. Champion had affidavits from two witnesses, one a slave and the other a white man, to substantiate his story. Nonetheless, on August 12 the sheriff hanged Champion.[50] It was a quick verdict followed by a swift execution of a tongue-tied defendant who did not speak up in time to give his lawyer a chance to make an eloquent plea to a jury or find some technicality for appeal.

State v. Champion must have pleased whites hopeful that the courts could be used to discipline unruly slaves. The case shows the criminal justice system at its most expeditious. The case, or rather cases, of *State v. Sam* illustrates how legal professionals could frustrate whites bent on using law to control crime. Sam's case drifted through the courts for nine years. No one interested in crime control could take pleasure in the *State v. Sam* trials. They were more likely to point to the episode as evidence that slaves must, whenever possible, be kept out of court.

There seems little doubt that on February 25, 1848, Sam killed his master in Issaquena County. Although the victim, Absalom Barrow, owned several slaves, he worked as an overseer and lived in a one-room log shack a hundred yards from the Mississippi River. The morning after his murder, Barrow's neighbors missed him and gathered at his house, where they found a trail of blood that led to the river. When they returned to Barrow's house they found Sam. The neighbors had noticed some footprints in the bloody trail and, suspecting Sam, immediately measured his shoes. The footprints matched. A witness later testified that Sam had initially denied knowing anything about the affair, insisting he had escaped the day before and had not been home at the time of the killing.

The next day, authorities questioned another of Barrow's slaves, Jack. Jack quickly confessed his role in the killing, admitting that he had helped Sam carry the body to the river. Hearing Jack, Sam then said he would confess as well. He claimed later that the crowd fastened a chain around his neck and threatened to kill him if he did not do so. But Sam also felt guilty for involving Jack and may have confessed in hopes of exculpating his accomplice. Barrow had threatened him, he said, and he had run away the day before the killing. He returned at night and crept into the shack, where he found Barrow asleep. An axe lay nearby. He took it and struck his master as he slept, but he missed his aim with the first blow and chopped off Barrow's nose. Noseless, Barrow immediately sat up, exclaiming "Gentlemen, Sam's in the house." The "gentlemen" to whom Barrow called seem to have been his other slaves, including Jack, who slept in the same room. The second blow struck its target more squarely, killing Barrow. Sam then recruited Jack to help him throw the victim into the river. Searchers had no trouble finding Barrow's body where it had lodged on a sandbar.[51]

In April the grand jury indicted Sam for murder, and the court appointed Abraham K. Smedes and Fulton Anderson to defend him. Southern states, with the exception of Georgia, required owners to furnish counsel for slaves, and Mississippi's law of 1822 empowered judges to assign counsel "according to the circumstances of the case."[52] Sam's circumstances clearly required lawyers. In October, Smedes and Anderson won a change of venue to neighboring Warren County, and in April the sheriff summoned fifty potential jurors for the trial. Before it could begin, however, Smedes and Anderson protested and raised procedural objections that had nothing to do with the guilt or innocence of a slave accused of murdering his owner with an axe.

Outraged whites bent on vengeance must have found this legal game unbelievably, almost comically, frustrating. Smedes and Anderson claimed that Sam had been indicted in the wrong town. They pointed out that the grand jury had met in Tallula, Mississippi. Tallula had been designated county seat of Issaquena County in 1846, but after flooding had washed away the courthouse there the state legislature authorized the board of police to relocate. Judge George Coalter had insisted on holding court in Tallula anyway. Smedes and Anderson argued that the legislature's authorization of the county government to move meant that Tallula was not lawfully the county seat of Issaquena County, and, for that reason, the indictment was not legitimate.[53]

Coalter brushed aside that objection, and a jury began hearing testimony. The most damning came from Dr. Richard W. Pettway. The relationship between Sam and Pettway is not entirely clear, but Sam seems to have seen the doctor as some sort of patron. When he fled Barrow, Sam went to Pettway's house to complain that his master had threatened him. He said that he feared Barrow would whip him too much and begged Pettway to intervene on his behalf. Pettway agreed to do so. By the time he arrived at Barrow's shanty, however, neighbors had already discovered that Barrow had disappeared. From his Vicksburg jail cell Sam repeatedly sent notes to Pettway, begging him to visit. When Pettway did so, Sam blurted out a confession, expressing guilt that Jack would hang for what he, Sam, had done. According to Pettway, Sam's confession was entirely voluntary and even unwelcome.[54]

After listening to Pettway and other witnesses, jurors quickly convicted Sam. Smedes and Anderson appealed. The two compiled a bill of exceptions that detailed all the errors they thought Coalter had made, beginning with the wrong-town argument. They complained that they had not been given a true copy of the indictment two days before the trial, as required by law. And, in an exception that undoubtedly reveals Sam's version of the killing, Smedes and Anderson claimed that they had wanted to produce four defense witnesses: John Canahan, T. R. Miller, Alfred Burnley, and Jack. Coalter, however, had not granted a delay that would have allowed them to find the missing witnesses. Sam's lawyers filed a deposition claiming that the missing witnesses would prove that Barrow habitually tortured his slaves with whips and red-hot irons. Shortly before the killing, he had tried to force Sam to kill certain hogs belonging to John Fortson, who lived on a neighboring plantation. When Sam refused, Barrow had tied him down and held a red-hot iron to his chest until he agreed to kill the hogs and even Fortson himself, if necessary, to steal the hog meat. After Sam killed the hogs, Barrow ordered him to confess to Fortson that he had acted alone. When Sam refused again, Barrow flew into a rage and threatened to kill him. When Sam entered Barrow's shack two weeks later, he found him awake and armed with a gun. Only then did he swing the axe. Judge Coalter declared that he did not believe a word of the affidavit and overruled it. Sam's lawyers further alleged that the judge had erred in seating two jurors who said they were convinced of Sam's guilt even before the trial began.[55]

Sam's trial in Judge Coalter's court may well have been a due process mess. In 1849 one of Coalter's political opponents, William C. Smedes, used Sam's trial as evidence that the judge was unfit for office. Coalter's conduct, Smedes charged, "displayed . . . a wanton violation of the rights of a man, though a slave, hardly surpassed in the history of jurisprudence."[56] Smedes indulged in bombast, but it is noteworthy that he thought that Coalter's errors in the trial of a slave amounted to the worst conduct by a judge in the history of judging. Many if not most observers seem to have agreed that Coalter lacked the legal acumen necessary for competent service. In the words of one modern writer, "His mind was exceedingly slow and he did not relish intellectual novelties."[57] Coalter died in 1849, missing most of Sam's trek through the court system.[58]

Smedes and Anderson took two of their exceptions to the High Court of Errors and Appeals, where they won on both counts. The High Court agreed that the indictment had no legal standing, having been returned in a town not the county seat of Issaquena County. That finding alone, the High Court observed, would be enough to overturn the conviction. But the judges also noted that Coalter had further erred in seating two jurors who had already formed an opinion adverse to Sam.[59]

The High Court's decision quashed the original indictment. In April 1850 Issaquena County's grand jury—no doubt careful to meet in the correct town—indicted Sam again, although continuances kept him from his second trial until February 1852. Defended this time by Thomas A. Marshall and Charles L. Buck, Sam again produced an affidavit claiming that Barrow had tortured and threatened him. This time, he had a list of six witnesses he wanted to call. He expected Fortson to testify as to the extreme barbarity and cruelty Barrow manifested toward Sam; James Niblett could testify as to threats Barrow had made; Albert McCall could testify that Barrow had borrowed pistols from his neighbors for the purpose of killing Sam; Burnley could testify that he had fired Barrow as his overseer on account of cruelty; and Samuel Nelson would testify that when Sam confessed he had a chain wrapped around his neck and feared he would be killed if he did not confess.[60]

Both Marshall and Buck owned slaves, and Marshall's political opponents even insinuated that he was the rich man's candidate for political office.[61] The pair again raised objections that vengeful whites would have found perfect examples of due process wasted on a slave. Marshall and Buck objected that the list of men to be summoned as potential jurors included two names not spelled correctly. They also complained that they had only been allowed to challenge peremptorily twelve potential jurors.

Despite these objections, Judge Richards Barnett pushed ahead, and another jury convicted Sam. His lawyers again appealed, and the High Court accepted at least one of their objections. In an unpublished opinion the court again reversed Sam's conviction.[62]

At his third trial in June 1856, Sam's third team of lawyers, Horace H. Miller and James T. Rucks, made an objection at least as clever as the wrong-town argument. They complained that Mississippi's governor had illegally appointed the judge instead of calling for an election after Judge John Guion had died. They also said that one juror had already expressed the opinion that Sam was guilty.[63] Once again, the High Court reversed Sam's conviction. The judges rejected Sam's argument against his judge but agreed that he had a biased juror.[64]

Nonetheless, Sam's time was running out. The High Court reversed on December 3, and Warren County officials promptly scheduled Sam's fourth trial for December 17, 1856. His lawyers again asked for a continuance, filing the now-familiar affidavit claiming that missing witnesses prevented a fair trial.[65] Convicted for the fourth time and sentenced to hang in January, Sam again appealed. The High Court again ordered the sheriff not to hang him while they reviewed the record, but this time the judges found no errors and ordered the hanging. Sam had evaded execution for nearly ten years. In that time he had lived in the Warren County jail, where he married and fathered three children who lived with him there. All that came to an end the day before Christmas in 1857, when the sheriff carried out the sentence. Standing on the gallows, Sam explained his crime, but the newspapers did not bother to report what he said. If he claimed to be a victim of slave abuse, their silencing makes sense. The court asked leading slaveowners to appraise Sam, and the estate of his victim received half his value.[66]

A succession of lawyers defended Sam, repeatedly appealing his convictions to Mississippi's supreme court. These attorneys energetically filed motions, made exceptions, and invented ingenious stratagems to reverse Sam's convictions. They obviously did not act on behalf of Sam's owner, although Barrow's estate might have preferred to sell Sam for full value rather than receive half his value after execution. But the lawyers never produced the witnesses that would have proved Sam's assertions, and any historian reading the voluminous record of the case must feel a pang of frustration that they never attacked the issue of Barrow's brutality directly. The lawyers understood that the best way to win a reversal on appeal lay in what advocates of crime control might regard as devious circumlocutions. The contrast between Champion and Sam is illuminating on that point. The unfortunate Champion seems merely to have had the facts on his side, whereas Sam's lawyers could argue technical defects in his trials. They seem to have been little interested in pursuing Sam's argument that he had been abused and acted in self-defense. The kinds of arguments Sam's lawyers made outraged whites determined to tame the black beast through law. But they worked—at least for a while. The legal culture did not prevent authorities from hanging slaves who claimed to have been abused by their masters. Justice was not done. But arguments by a series of lawyers prevented what whites might call effective crime control.

In some ways, all the ambiguities of slavery and the law surfaced in Sam's murder trials. For Marmaduke Shannon's Vicksburg *Whig,* Sam's case was especially troubling. The *Whig* considered itself a firm champion of law and a steadfast opponent of mob rule. But the *Whig* had to admit that Sam exposed defects in the law. Putting the best face on a bad situation, Shannon insisted that "every effort for freedom has been unavailing. A faithful Executive has refused to grant a pardon . . . stern justice has at last, though long delayed, executed its inexorable penalty." But Shannon found little to cheer in Sam's execution. He called for a more "speedy and prompt enforcement of the laws" in the future. The lawyers' success in changing Sam's venue especially troubled him. The execution of an Issaquena County slave in Warren County could not have the salutary effect it should on the slaves who knew Sam. "Let it be proclaimed in Issaquena," the newspaper urged, "that the murderer of his master has been hung. . . . Let those slaves who have heard of Sam's awful crimes remember that the stern and heavy hand of the law demanded an awful retribution." Such a proclamation was a poor substitute for a hanging in the right place and at the right time. But it was the most law-and-order proponents also committed to slavery could salvage from Sam's execution.[67]

Sam's trials show that legal gamesmanship sometimes made it difficult for authorities to manipulate the law into a tool to control slaves. Even slave-owning lawyers who represented slaves filed motions that blunted the effectiveness of the criminal justice system as a mechanism for slave control.

Ironically, judges' refusal to allow slaves to be coerced into confession became one legacy of Mississippi's brutal slavery experience. In 1872 Republican Carpetbaggers published a digest of decisions made by Mississippi's supreme court that constituted a virtual road map for defense counsel seeking rights they could assert on behalf of clients and warned against involuntary confessions. What constituted a coerced confession was outlined in detail, and the section entitled "Confessions, Admissibility of" summarized decisions in fourteen cases that all involved slave defendants.[68]

Due process and the common law protected property, but law carried to the zenith of its logic would have undermined slavery as often as it protected slave property. Warren County approached the Civil War as a socially divided landscape, one that needed law to order itself. Whites approached the law understanding that ultimately it could not do what they wanted done.

At the end of the antebellum period, Vicksburgers constructed the Warren County Courthouse, a monumental temple to justice. (Author's photo)

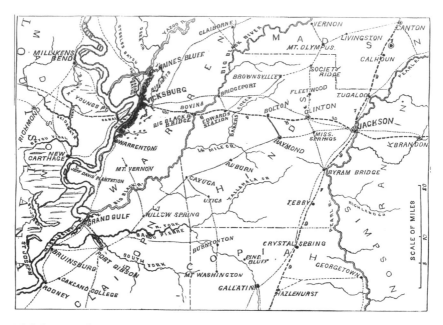

Vicksburg and vicinity. (*Harper's Magazine* 27 [July 1863]: 272)

"The City of Vicksburg Before the War." (*Harper's Weekly*, July 25, 1863, 469)

In her diary, Minerva Cook recorded her frustrations with her husband. (Old Court House Museum, Vicksburg)

T. T. Beall defended his honor by stabbing to death two men. (Old Court House Museum, Vicksburg)

After Vicksburg's surrender to Grant, women sympathetic to the Confederacy defied federal authority in various ways, including smuggling goods through the lines. Authorities arrested Emma Kline and then photographed her under guard. (Michael J. McAfee Collection)

BELOW: Vicksburg surrendered on July 4, 1863. (*Harper's Weekly,* Aug. 1, 1863, 488–89)

THE SURRENDER OF VICKSBURG—THE REBELS MARCHING OUT AND STACKING ARMS.—From a Sketch of Mr. Theodore R. Davis.—[See Page 491.]

THE SURRENDER OF VICKSBURG—VIEW OF THE CITY FROM THE RIVER BANK, SHOWING PART OF THE RIVER BATTERIES.—Sketched by Mr. Theodore R. Davis.—[See Page 491.]

The provost marshal's guard house at Vicksburg. The Union army court-martialed many of its soldiers while occupying Vicksburg. (Library of Congress)

BELOW: Jefferson Davis's elder brother, Joseph, allowed his slaves to police themselves on his Davis Bend Plantation. (Old Court House Museum, Vicksburg)

Newspaper editor William
McCardle championed white
solidarity. (Old Court House
Museum, Vicksburg)

Republican Charles Furlong
served as Warren County sheriff
during Congressional Reconstruction. (Old Court House Museum,
Vicksburg)

Marmaduke Shannon, an old-line
Whig, served as Warren County
sheriff after the Civil War. (Old
Court House Museum, Vicksburg)

The Warren County jail, ca. 1866. The Union army only reluctantly surrendered the county jail to civilian authorities. (Old Court House Museum, Vicksburg)

Vicksburg in the 1870s. (Old Court House Museum, Vicksburg)

Warren Cowan served as judge of the
Warren County Court and later as
leader of the so-called white-line
movement. (Old Court House Museum, Vicksburg)

Noah Zook. Robbers murdered
Noah and Abraham Zook of
Pennsylvania, and local officials
did little to investigate or prosecute
their murderers. (Courtesy of
James Landis)

Abraham Zook. (Courtesy of James
Landis)

After the Civil War, Warren County African Americans labored in cotton fields much as they had done before emancipation. (Old Court House Museum, Vicksburg)

4

Into the Heart of Darkness: The Civil War

The Civil War unleashed a fury on the legal order in Vicksburg and Warren County. Before the war, whites' fundamental belief that law could not effectively discipline African Americans established the roots of disorder. Vicksburg courts absorbed that insight in a structure designed to accommodate whites' extra-legal ordering within the legal system. At least by the 1850s, Warren County whites had begun to formalize in law more aspects of the slave system, and more and more cases arising out of slavery made their way into court. The Civil War disrupted that trajectory with chaos and anarchy, however. On the battlefield, military maneuver and soldiers' hunger undermined abstract legal doctrine. The Civil War crisis buffeted Vicksburg's legal culture with sectional strife, Confederate military authority, northern military power, and emancipation.

Northern soldiers came to Vicksburg, and many stayed, joined by civilians the locals condemned as carpetbaggers. They became lawyers, journalists, and community leaders. Yet they did not swerve Warren County from its course. Even with northerners in positions of leadership, Vicksburg and Warren County remained a violent place. The Civil War may even have accelerated vigilantism and lynching. Because the war strengthened racial unity, whites took a step away from the class and ethnic loyalties that had divided their society before the war. Although the Union army did not move white Vicksburgers away from their fundamental beliefs about race and law, the position of women in society did change.

They began to make new demands, insisting on the right to protection from newly freed African Americans.

*　*　*

Whites in antebellum Vicksburg learned to live in a commercial and urban world characterized by faction and division. An impoverished local Irish population lived apart from other whites, and Jews created a discrete neighborhood that recalled European patterns. Non-Jews complained about "shopkeeper Jews" engaged in disloyal profiteering. Class mattered greatly. Very likely, many poor whites in Warren County would have agreed with the bitter lament of the poor Tennessee Confederate veteran who wrote that "slave holders were the only men that could make enough money to do anything." Another complained about slaveowners who "felt their importance."[1]

Vicksburgers thought their most serious splits involved politics. Some antebellum political disputes had even led to bloodshed because political rivals regularly fought duels. Sectionalism did little to abate this. Rather than bringing political enemies together, the prewar debate over secession exacerbated political quarreling. William H. McCardle edited Marmaduke Shannon's *Vicksburg Whig* until August 1857. As sectional issues heated up, McCardle felt increasingly drawn to the Democrats, although he worked for an old-line Whig publisher. In March he claimed that the *Whig* was the organ of no party, an independent and fearless journal friendly to all. The compromise pleased no one, and McCardle published a brief valedictory in August, departing for the *True Southron*. The title of his new publication suggests that he had found a conduit better suited to his passions than the *Whig*. McCardle quickly became a leading proponent of secession, something Shannon hated. Shannon, now doing his own editing, attacked him for attempting to destroy "our glorious Union."[2] When he published a letter designed to defuse tensions over Kansas, McCardle erupted with scorn and ridicule. As editor of the *Whig*, McCardle had extended "unvarying kindness and courtesy" to "his editorial brethren of all parties."[3] Now in no mood for courtesy and brotherly feelings, he accused Shannon of cowardice, language designed to provoke a duel. Shannon sidestepped the threat, denying that he had criticized the *Southron* in his newspaper. He felt confident that the community sympathized with him rather than McCardle and even calculated that the controversy sold papers. He assured his family that at heart McCardle preferred threatening a duel over actually fighting one.[4] But Shannon had to tread carefully. One wrong step and he could have no choice but to face his former editor with a pistol, wondering just how good a shot his old friend was.

Shannon had to contend with more political enemies than just McCardle. In 1859 the Vicksburg *Sun* joined the *Southron* to warn that events had deepened northern opposition to slavery. The political success of the Republicans reflected growing numbers of South-hating abolitionists. But while the Democratic *Sun* worried, Shannon reassured readers that radical abolitionists had added no new members to their ranks. The newspaper conceded that every northern man thought slavery evil but denied that "the Black Republican organization" intended to interfere with slavery.[5] Shannon attacked Democrats as either "fire-eaters," always angry, always excited, or as "cold calculating, frigid *disunionists*" plotting to destroy the nation for personal gain.[6] He thought disunionists were self-interested factionalists, the sort who had always threatened the Republic. The conflict between disunionists and Whigs plunged the county into political tumult, and the two sides denounced each other with increasingly heated rhetoric at rival meetings.[7] Such splintering ultimately helped drive the South to civil war. Slaveowners pushed for secession because they feared that many others would be receptive to Republican overtures.[8]

Although less fully understood at the time, divisions along gender lines split Vicksburg just as surely as political fights. The Civil War weakened all these divisions—ethnic, economic, political, and gendered. But the most serious breaches in the antebellum walls separating discrete elements in Vicksburg society challenged old understandings of the role women should play.

In the antebellum era, women exerted considerable influence, although men achieved some success in keeping them subordinate. Warren County's earliest white families included few dependents, and men needed the labor wives provided. Women, in fact, were in short supply, and unmarried men had to recruit females to join them on the frontier. As slavery expanded, however, the agricultural labor of women became less essential. Coincident with their decline in economic importance, larger numbers of women migrated to Warren County, and the sex ratio evened out. In their letters, the women complained of tedium, boredom, and loneliness.[9]

Defenders of slavery repeatedly invoked the model of a husband and his faithful wife when justifying slavery. Antebellum churches preached hierarchy, with women too subordinate to influence political discourse overtly. Minerva Cook's diary suggests women's ambivalent acceptance of patriarchy. As she wrote in 1855, "The law of both Bible, God & Man, say: obey your husbands." And Cook stuck with that doctrine, even saddled with a most disagreeable mate. In 1857 an obviously depressed Cook reported that her husband brushed in and out of the house, talking only in "a rough kind of way." When she troubled him with their baby, he snapped, "Take the nasty thing away from me." She poured out her grief in the diary, writing, "I have always made it a rule to believe everything he says or tells me serious and this he did very majestically." Nonetheless, at the end of the same year she called her husband "an excellent good Pa."[10]

Cook did not divorce her husband, but in rare cases some women did. In 1822 and 1840 the legislature recognized the increasingly marginal position of women in male-dominated households and loosened divorce laws. In the five years before the Civil War, twelve women sued for divorce in Warren County, more than in the previous thirty-eight years. Ten won their cases. Nonetheless, divorce did not come easily. James Cotton, for example, clubbed his wife with a stick and whipped her with cowhide. He even tried to cut her throat with a knife. Even so, Matilda Cotton went to court only after he lost their farm, leaving her penniless. Mississippi judges tried not to intrude into family affairs. Matilda Cotton had to prove that she had done all she could to keep the household going, whereas her husband had not. In this case, the wife succeeded in meeting the difficult proof standards set by Mississippi legislators.[11]

Both men and women understood the household as a patriarchal institution. On January 6, 1861, Emma Crutcher wrote to her soldier husband Will with a warning: "I know you won't *domineer*—you love me too much for that." She promised to be mulishly stubborn, bitter, and cold *"if you ever neglect me."* But she also wrote that at the time of their marriage she had felt rebellious, having not yet decided that her husband would be the *"head* and governor, the *monarch* of our little kingdom." After marriage, Will kept his bride so "continually intoxicated with love-speeches" that she could hardly think sober thoughts. But now, on reflection, Emma Crutcher had decided to "give up the reins" to her husband and had no uneasiness in doing so.[12] Thirty-five-year-old John Ragan's marriage to seventeen-year-old Kate Boone offers another example of the prewar style of relationship. "I only hope," John's sister, Kate Stone, wrote in her diary, "he will not try to educate her according to his theories but will let her go on as Nature and her own antecedents and education would have her." But Kate Stone had misgivings. For years she had heard John talk about finding a young girl—one with an immature personality. Then, he had said, she would be tractable enough to be molded to his liking. Many southern men shared the same strategy.[13]

Although men such as John Ragan consciously tried to subordinate their wives, women participated in politics, especially after 1840 when Whigs made a concerted effort to draw women to their rallies, expecting them to bring "domestic" virtues to the public sphere. The Whigs had to overcome the revolutionary-era concept of republican wife and mother, which acclaimed the power of women to insist on civic virtue in their suitors and husbands and instill devotion to the Republic in their sons. These "true women" were supposed to be above party and to judge particular candidates according to virtue. Some remained committed to the old ideal, however, and resisted politicians' appeals. Many men continued to insist that only they could represent their households and families in the public world of politics and war. One frankly wrote that his wife was "not competent to advise the statesman or the politician—her knowledge, her advice, her ministry is in a kindlier sphere." Another woman declared that she had no political opinion but had "a peculiar dislike for all females who discuss such matters."[14]

The election for delegates to the secession convention was the last one in which women played a traditional, passive role. Male voters must have assured them that Yankees posed no serious threat to Vicksburg's way of life, and women overwhelmingly spurned McCardle and the secessionists. The voters sent Unionists to the secession convention instead.[15] One of those elected, Walker Brooke, urged the convention to submit the ordinance of secession to a referendum. When that amendment failed, he voted for secession in the hope, he explained later, that a strong vote for disunion would save the union by forcing the North to reaffirm slavery's constitutional protections.[16] After the convention voted to secede, Shannon glumly acquiesced. "We do not think," he declared in his newspaper, "that there can be any doubt as to the duty of patriots at this crisis— it is to follow the destiny of the State."[17]

After secession a martial spirit swept Vicksburg, so much so that by April 1861 most opponents of secession had fallen into line. But even that did not heal the splits in the white community. By January 1861, Vicksburg militia soldiers had occupied the strategic hill north of town. Volunteers formed companies with names such as the Southrons, the Sharpshooters, and the Dragoons and raced to the governor, hoping to be the first enrolled. By April, newspapers were describing brave soldiers boarding trains, many bound for Pensacola, with stoic resolve while women shrieked and shed tears. But raising an army did not immediately unify Vicksburgers. Various social groups organized their own military units;

the local artillery represented the commercial classes, for example. The soldiers were already considering their postbellum careers; in one meeting they considered passing resolutions calling on merchants and manufacturers to urge employees to join the army. The measure failed because members decided they should ask for no special favors or guarantees, "yet they were willing to concede, that such an act on the part of those gentlemen would influence *many* who had not yet become members of *any company.*" In Vicksburg the Irish raised their own company. According to one diarist, even gamblers and outlaws formed a unit. Kate Stone wrote that "the overseers and that class of men" roundly abused planters' sons unwilling or unable to join the army. They were too good to fight the battles of the wealthy.[18]

Apparently surrounded by happy "darkies," antebellum whites had felt little initial pressure to unite, but almost immediately after secession the earth began to shift beneath their feet. "An attempt will be made very soon to get up an insurrection on a very large scale," one Vicksburger predicted. Such reports could be alarmingly specific. One claimed that abolitionists had hidden 1,500 muskets, a thousand rifles, and 2,500 pikes in a swamp above Vicksburg for use by blacks. Large numbers of Irish, white wood choppers, railroaders, and "western men" would join this class revolt, robbing banks and distributing the arms to slaves. Free blacks in Memphis would bring flatboats loaded with arms and ammunition to Vicksburg.[19]

The fantasy reveals whites' fears of a class union of blacks and lower-class whites, especially Vicksburg's Irish population. Class mattered so much that wealthier white Vicksburgers did not consider the Irish as being fully white. In Ireland, the English had regarded Catholics as a race distinct from their own, allowing the poorest Protestant membership in the dominant race. In America, immigrant complaints about slave competition grew throughout the antebellum era. Often Irish and other immigrant laborers hated slaves rather than slavery.[20] But immigrants sometimes socialized with slaves and worked alongside them. Some Irish living in poor, integrated neighborhoods conspired with blacks in criminal gangs. Defenders of slavery inadvertently promoted such alliances when they argued that the peculiar institution happily squeezed out the "dregs of Europe." Slaveowners called the Irish "niggers turned inside out" and blacks "smoked Irish."[21] No wonder white Vicksburgers feared insurrection by both groups.

Although secession did little to unify the white South, secessionists consciously echoed the Founders' calls for republican harmony and an

end to old political quarrels. Where political parties persisted, as in Vicksburg, secession sentiment stalled. Secession appalled believers in the traditional party mechanisms. Southerners selected their president without
electioneering, and Jefferson Davis proclaimed his constituents "brethren not in name merely, but in fact—men of one flesh, of one bone, of
one interest, of one purpose." The Vicksburg *Daily Evening Citizen*
warned against "party agitations" promoted by "designing or ambitious
men, for selfish or sordid purposes." Confederates vowed not to repeat
the errors of the United States, where parties had subverted the Founders'
vision, and promoted an anti-party political culture. State and national
elections in 1861 stressed the importance of unity, and preachers and
teachers emphasized cohesion to their congregations and classes.[22]

Stirring calls for Confederate republicanism and unity promoted the
kind of socially cohesive environment in which mobs and vigilantes could
act, confident they would be supported by neighbors. In February 1861, a
mob of Vicksburgers stormed Mollie Bunch's brothel. The prostitutes had
staged a ball, much as they had done before with no trouble, but now, with
war approaching, such frivolity seemed inappropriate. This time citizens
hosed the brothel with pumpers from a fire station, destroying Bunch's
furniture and ruining the party food. The mob then stormed a saloon,
wrecked the bar, and poured the liquor into a gutter.[23]

But the Mollie Bunch riot did not signal a new regime of vigilantism.
The failure of a more formal vigilance committee, organized several
months earlier, better illustrates the state of Vicksburg society on the eve
of war. Vicksburgers had formed the committee "for the purpose of keeping order during the Holidays."[24] The committee accomplished little because white cohesion in Warren County still fell short of the rhetoric.
Alexander Arthur sniffed that vigilantes were "overzealous patriots who
did not want to go to the wars" themselves.[25] When someone reported
that the vigilantes had shot a slave, the *Daily Evening Citizen* reassured
readers that committee members were too toothless for that. No such
shooting had occurred, and the committee was not in the business of
shooting anyone, the *Citizen* said. Instead, the vigilantes merely tried to
prohibit the sale of whiskey to slaves over Christmas. They did seize a slave
named Edgar and escort him to the mayor for trial. He had suspicious
documents (the vigilantes claimed) and had corrupted at least twenty
other blacks, making them worthless to their owners.[26] In February the
Citizen reassured readers that the Vigilance Committee had not spread
terror in Vicksburg hotels. But if a visitor called Vicksburgers fools or
rebels, "He will probably pick up a quarrel which may end in his leaving

the city abruptly."[27] The failure of the vigilantes, however, became clear in May when Vicksburg newspapers again complained of the "great evil" of "idle, lounging Negroes."[28] One Vicksburger wrote, "We have too many idle, trifling, drunken, loafing, lazy, negroes about this city. Let them be looked after."[29] Those words could just as easily have been written in 1830 and probably were. Nothing had changed on that score.

The fact that vigilantes failed showed that white Vicksburgers remained divided. The war itself threatened chaos and civil disintegration. When New Orleans surrendered, sending a wave of panic (and refugees) coursing through Vicksburg, unnerved city officials provided no leadership. The circuit court met for the last time before hostilities in December 1861. Just months earlier, the district attorney had resigned to join the Confederate army. In the court's final term, the sheriff assembled a grand jury, just as he always had, which indicted three men and one woman, Mary Gibson, for attempted murder. Twenty-two defendants were dismissed and two were tried. The last trial, of Mary Gibson, resulted in a hung jury. Judge Jacob S. Yerger continued the case until the next term of court, which did not come until December 1865.[30]

As the circuit court closed, new authority arrived in the form of veteran Louisiana artillerymen promising military government. On May 1, 1862, provost marshals ceased allowing civilians to travel the roads around Vicksburg without a pass.[31] Confederate authorities also took control of the jail, much to the disgust of the sheriff. With the army policing the city, there seemed little need for civilian courts. Nonetheless, not long after the Confederates arrived, the *Daily Evening Citizen* marveled that Criminal Court Judge Harris "designs taking up the docket and going through with it." Even at the end of 1862 Harris still asserted civilian authority, granting a father's habeas corpus petition intended to get his son out of the army. Harris issued the writ and agreed when the army produced Henry Butler that he was too young for service. He ordered the young man discharged, and he was. But Harris soon gave up; his court's last antebellum session was in 1862.[32]

The county's board of supervisors met as late as April 1863. They allowed the sheriff extra time to collect the taxes "in consequence of the high water and the enemy being in the way of collecting said Taxes." At that meeting the supervisors complained that the jail was filthy and instructed the sheriff to clean the cells. In May, as Union artillery boomed overhead, only the clerk showed up for the scheduled meeting, and he scribbled a note in the minute book and hastily left. The board of supervisors did not meet again until July 1865.[33]

The Confederates centralized power just as surely as their Yankee counterparts in Washington. In Vicksburg, the Confederate army asserted its authority with increasing vigor as civil government collapsed. Confederates entrenching their big guns overlooking the Mississippi River at Vicksburg asked local planters to contribute slave labor to the effort. Some refused. Planter Charles Allen thought it unrealistic to expect slaves to dig fortifications after walking twenty-five miles, the distance from his plantation to Vicksburg. In truth, he disliked handing control of his slaves over to the government. Allen got away with refusing to contribute slaves to the war effort on that occasion, but the Confederates also challenged planter hegemony by seizing and burning cotton. The uncooperative Allen hid twenty-seven bales on a raft, which he then anchored in a swamp. When Captain W. H. Johnson found the raft and burned it, Allen expressed disappointment that the cotton, "securely hid from all eyes," had been destroyed. He wanted to know if his own slaves had tipped off the Confederates. He did not think slaves "should act as detectives." Johnson may have had his tongue firmly in cheek when he responded. "I did not for an instant suppose it was yours," the captain wrote before reassuring Allen that his slaves had not informed on him.[34]

Vicksburgers acquiesced to state power no more willingly than planters. In February 1863 a Confederate surgeon told Rowland Chambers that he must take his house for a hospital. Chambers refused. The doctor went to a general, who told Chambers he would have to move. The army first wanted all his property but "after some hard talking" allowed the civilian to keep a smaller building behind his home. A few days later, soldiers began unloading cots, and soon the sick and wounded filled the house.[35]

Jefferson Davis's brother protested that the Confederates tolerated too much dissent in Vicksburg. On May 2, 1862, Joseph complained of the confusion in town, made worse by "street talkers and . . . that malicious lying hypocrit the Revd. C K Marshall D D."[36] The Confederates probably did not arrest Marshall because he did not oppose the war effort, and during the war he aided them by ministering to casualties at several battles and organizing care for the wounded. Dissenters suspected of aiding the enemy, however, went to jail. When Henry Banks, a Vicksburg slave and hack driver, helped friends escape to the Union lines, the Confederates arrested him. His wife persuaded her husband's owner to intervene on his behalf. "I believe they had no proof," Banks said later, but "intended in the first place to whip me until I would tell." But the owner's friends persuaded the jailers to release him.[37]

Whites were jailed along with slaves. When Howell H. Goodrum cursed the Confederates in his neighborhood and tried to move his family out of the county, authorities arrested him. Like Banks, friends intervened and he was released.[38] Confederate pressure forced some dissenters from the city. Armistead Burwell, a Unionist, had campaigned for Bell and Everett in the 1860 presidential election. Loudly opposing secession, he refused to reconcile himself after the secession convention. He left Vicksburg for St. Louis on March 28, 1861, on the *Henry Ames,* the last boat to travel up the Mississippi before the war without being fired on. But Burwell could not stay away. A lawyer, he felt he had to return to Vicksburg in September to represent the business interests of clients. "I had their papers," he explained after the war, "and no one could fix them but myself." Military authorities arrested Burwell, and, when they released him, he escaped to the North through the Appalachians. He had $50,000 in assets he could not take along, so his brother-in-law converted the money into sugar and stored it in a Vicksburg warehouse, where it rested undisturbed throughout the siege.[39]

But as Vicksburgers complained about Confederate authority, they understood that a far more serious threat to their way of life approached. A massive army was headed for the city, one filled with men who had different ideas about ordering than did southerners. Vicksburgers expected the battle for their town to become a clash of cultures: localism and slavery versus federal power and abolitionism. From the beginning, they expected the war to threaten property rights. Local newspapers reported that New York robbers had been organized as a military company for the express purpose of pillaging southern cities. Anyone reading the speeches of Lincoln, Seward, and Chase, the Vicksburg *Evening Citizen* claimed, could see that such "bastard specimens of humanity" saw robbing not only as their right but also as the only sure way to reach heaven.[40]

Such propaganda obviously reveals far more about southerners' fears for their property than anything about the North. The soldiers attacking Vicksburg primarily came from the Midwest, thirty-six thousand from Illinois alone. Their society superficially resembled that found in the South. Many shared the same racial values as white southerners, and skimpy Civil War military training had done nothing to disabuse them of their hometown values.[41] Northerners, however, did come from a society that viewed property differently than southerners. In some parts of the North, a small-shop economy had produced a worldview that blended liberalism with republicanism. Northerners expressed contempt for haughty aristocrats but respect for individuals who built fortunes through skill and talent. That aspect of the northern mindset argued for the right of every person to acquire property. "Gentlemen" should expect no special favors. Some would fail through personal weakness, but there should be no governmental constraints such as slavery to trip them up. Southerners often regarded such aggressive economic acquisitiveness, where individuals put their own interests ahead of those of the community, as one of the worst elements in the Yankee character. Northerners also celebrated the ideal of sturdy freeholders who subordinated their will to that of the inclusive commonwealth, as James Harrington had urged.[42]

Northern soldiers did assault southern property rights. Grant's strategy promoted that. His long campaign through the swamps and bayous of the Mississippi Delta took his men away from their supplies and deep into enemy country. In March 1863 he began making plans that would require his army to feed itself from the property of Mississippi civilians. Grant marched his men past Vicksburg on the west side of the river, and the soldiers recrossed south of the city.[43] Once below Vicksburg, on the east side of the river, the navy could not resupply Grant's army; even if Union transports could have somehow lumbered past Vicksburg gunners, the existing road network was too meager to support the necessary traffic. The Union army would live off the land.

Resistance by Confederate soldiers and unrepentant civilians had prompted a hatred and thirst for revenge among Union soldiers. One Illinoisan compared "hungry Yankees" to "ravenous wolves among the sheep of the South."[44] An Ohio soldier pronounced himself "heartily rejoiced" at the policy, predicting that "Mississippi will be well cleaned out before Spring."[45] But Grant remained adamant that foraging did not mean pillaging. Before launching his plan, one of his subordinates cautioned against "wanton destruction of property." No one was to enter and search houses without orders.[46] Grant told the commander of the Sixteenth Corps to instruct cavalrymen to stay out of people's houses. They must live off the land and destroy anything usable in the Confederate war effort, something Grant insisted could be done "without insulting women and children or taking their clothing, jewelry, &c."[47] When William T. Sherman doubted the feasibility of continuing deeper into Mississippi without supply lines, Grant impatiently responded that he understood that the existing road network could not sustain sufficient convoys to provision such a large force. What the army did not furnish the country would.[48]

Throughout May, as the Union army maneuvered to attack Vicksburg, Grant and Sherman continued to insist that their men must respect civilians' rights yet forage for food. On May 12 Union forces vanquished the Confederates at Raymond, and two days later defeated their enemy at Mississippi's capital city, Jackson.[49] Grant now stood poised to turn west and strike at Vicksburg from its back. Union officers reiterated that foraging be done only selectively, carefully, and with respect for civilian property of no military value. The private rights of civilians, Sherman declared on May 15, should be respected.[50] On May 16 Union army units defeated rebels at Champion's Hill and the next day at the Big Black River, which formed the eastern edge of Warren County. Vicksburg was just miles away.[51]

Law and order on the battlefield would not be forged by orders from headquarters, however. Soldiers cut off from supply lines learn to trust each other more than distant commanders who do not feed them.[52] Warren County civilians faced the reality of foraging carried out by ordinary soldiers conditioned by war and starved by maneuvering away from their supply lines. For several days before the federal army crossed the Big Black those who lived west of the river waited anxiously, not knowing what to expect. They must have nervously recalled the *Daily Evening Citizen*'s report of New York thieves and cutthroats, organized as a military company specifically to pillage southern homes. They may have reminded each other that the "bastard specimens of humanity" in the Republican Party felt a religious calling to rob good southern citizens of their property. All the women stayed close to their homes.[53]

Emilie Riley McKinley, a teacher, boarded with the widow Ellen Batchelor, not far from the Big Black River. On May 18 she wrote in her diary that the previous day had been one of the saddest days in her life. Confederate forces had retreated into Vicksburg; nothing protected the civilian population outside town from Grant's army. Around 3 in the afternoon, the family met their first Union soldier but did not recognize him. Thinking him an ordinary traveler, they called out, "Any news sir?" He answered, "None." "Are you going to Vicksburg?" they innocently asked. "If I can get there," he replied. The family wondered if there were any Yankees about. "Plenty," came the answer. This first soldier searched the house, looking for guns. He also wanted horses, but the Batchelors had moved their stock into Vicksburg for safekeeping. Later a Wisconsin soldier wandered by, saying that he scorned to steal. "We did not credit all he said, by any means," McKinley wrote. Subsequent foragers searched for meal, meat, clothing, jewelry, silver, and poultry.[54]

Just as military tactics and movements led to shifts in northern soldiers' thinking about order, the fortunes of war challenged southern soldiers' ideas about ordering. When defensive lines outside the city collapsed and

Confederate soldiers retreated into the city, order broke down inside Vicksburg. As one soldier recorded in his diary, after May 18, when promised reinforcements did not appear, the Confederate rank and file lost all confidence in their officers and saw "nothing before them but death or a prison after weeks of gnawing, debilitating hunger."[55] Deserters could be seen hiding from battle behind trees and in hollows. Demoralized soldiers affronted local women. Rowland Chambers recounted one spectacular scene where a soldier chased women through their house with a club while their dog chased him. Food became scarce. Soldiers sold military stores on the black market. Provost marshals arrested a gang composed of civilians, slaves, and two provosts for looting a warehouse. Just a month before the city fell, Chambers still ate corn and strawberries from his garden while soldiers tried to subsist on a teacup of peas a day. By June 8 he was complaining of thieves, grimly writing in his diary that every night brought some new affront. Thieves took his turkey and peacock on June 9 and 10, on June 11 someone raided his bean patch, and two days later looters took his cabbage, beets, and onions. On June 19 Chambers decided to stay up all night and guard his garden. He shot at one thief. Finally, on June 30, just days before Vicksburg surrendered, he caught a party of armed "ruffians" trying to break into his stable. But when he questioned the men he discovered they had an officer and claimed to act under authority. "If so," he fumed, "it is a bad State of affairs when Robery is carried on by authority of government officers."[56]

Even with war on Vicksburg's doorstep, the tension between planters and Confederate authorities continued. By the end of June 1862, the bombardment of the city had become almost continuous. Charles Allen wrote in his plantation book that "it was a continual 'bomb, bomb, bomb'—a horrid din, so that they could not be counted," and Chambers described shot and shell falling around his house as thick as hail. Confederate soldiers had again requisitioned Allen's slaves in November. Although he liked this no more than before, Yankee artillery had focused the minds of Confederate soldiers. This time there was no stopping. Yet even with Vicksburg under an artillery barrage, Allen grumbled that the order taking his slaves was illegal. Planters conformed to it for the sake of Vicksburg, he wrote, but they "very much" disliked the Confederates' insulting and overbearing manner when they took the slaves.[57]

But Vicksburgers complained about northern soldiers, who brought anarchy and chaos, far more often than they did the Confederates. Federal troops stripped plantations around Vicksburg so bare that inhabitants had to depend on government rations for subsistence.[58] Much of the destruction represented no more than what could be expected from any invading army, however. Even Vicksburgers understood that an army in a hostile environment could be expected to cause considerable damage. As one soldier explained to Emilie McKinley, "Men d[o] things in the army, they would be ashamed to recall hereafter."[59] Vicksburg Unionists had predicted the carnage and insisted that the secessionists deserved all the blame for property losses; massive ruination was the natural consequence of secession. The devastation, one Unionist said, was "no more than he had Expected and had frequently predicted."[60]

One Vicksburg woman wrote that the soldiers "must open every door, pillage every place. . . . Ravenous as wolves," they opened her closet with a hatchet and stole clothing and keepsakes.[61] Immediately after the battles at Champion's Hill and the Big Black, Grant's army swept across the plantations of John Townsend and his son Samuel. At 3 A.M. on May 18, when John Townsend went to his gallery to investigate a noise, a Union soldier shot him. At daylight John sent a slave to tell his son the news, and Samuel Townsend hurried to his father's plantation. When he arrived, he found the place swarming with government wagons and soldiers. Samuel Townsend took his wounded father home, where he died several days later. As he left, he locked the old man's door, but when he returned later he found it broken open. Soldiers had taken axes, hoes, wagons, awnings, leather, tables, bureaus, pistols, guns, horses, oxen, mules, bedding, clothing, bacon, beef, molasses, cypress billets, fencing, books, and silver spoons from the cupboards. While occupying the Townsend plantations, Union soldiers replaced cross ties for eight miles of railroad track with wood taken from the Townsends. They also dismantled the house and barns.[62]

Union troops lost their early inhibitions against taking the property of Unionists. Property owners regularly claimed loyalty, an Iowa soldier said later, "but I never knew it to avail anything, We always took what we wanted if we could get it notwithstanding that plea."[63] Soldiers complained that they had a hard time deciding who was the worst enemy, the man with a gun, fighting face-to-face, or "the one that will stay at home to lie and swear to a lie to deceive our men and help their own."[64] One soldier remembered that "to our faces [southern] citizens seem good Union men, but behind our backs, no doubt their sentiments undergo a change."[65]

The collapse of respect for property rights even reached Warren County's slave population. Blacks hoped the soldiers would relent if it were pointed out that property seized belonged to a slave, and they often steered Yankees to the hidden property of whites. Such arguments carried no weight, however. The soldiers either brusquely dismissed them or pleaded higher orders. Sherman chastised a subordinate for allowing "a fugitive negress" to take her personal property. "The clothing & effects of a negro are the property of the master," he declared, adding, "we must not sanction theft robbing or violence." He ordered the property returned.[66]

Some black victims of army looting complained. Henry Banks, unhappy when soldiers took his hack, "said some bad words" that earned him a rebuke.[67] Slave Benjamin Stinyard complained when the Second Wisconsin Cavalry took his horse. Skeptical soldiers asked whether the horse was his "individual" property. When Stinyard insisted it was, the Yankees retorted, "It don't make a d—d bit of difference, we want it" and rode off.[68] A lieutenant took William Hitch's horse. When the slave barber protested, the officer said "he could not help it, that he must obey orders."[69] When Wisconsin soldiers took Daniel Murfee's horse he protested, only to be cursed and shoved. When Murfee "hauled off to hit him," a soldier bayonetted him. A kindly lieutenant ordered the man to stop and promised—falsely, as it turned out—that Murfee would be paid. "I just sat down and cried—I couldn't help it—myself and wife had worked nights & Sundays for what we had." It was a rough time for the freed people, Murfee thought, with rebels raiding at night and Union troops stealing their property during the day.[70] Most blacks received no more satisfaction for their protests than Murfee. Gabriel Bolger said little when cavalrymen took his horses: "What are you all doing—going to take all my horses?" "Yes we are obliged to do it," the soldiers told the crippled slave. "We are fighting for you and you doing nothing."[71]

Soldiers also took the property of the freed people they employed, the ones "doing something." Henry Watson worked as a cook for a company of Union soldiers before he joined the Pioneer Corps. Months after the fall of Vicksburg, an officer from the same company took his cow for beef. "I told him he hadn't ought to do it," Watson recalled. "The officer promised to make up a purse for me from the company," but "they never gave me a cent." Watson cooked some of his own cow. Soldiers also took his hog. "I begged them to leave [my three mules] as I purchased them to make me a living with as soon as I got the chance to do so." But that entreaty did no good. "He [the officer] said that he was sorry for it but if he didn't take them that the rebels would surely get them and took them."[72]

Some slaves had better luck than Watson and managed to save some of their property. Callie Gray remembered that Union troops "stole the corn and wheat and drove off the horses and mules and killed the hogs and sheep, and took all the chickens." But in slavery one learned to savor small victories, and Gray added that "we sho saved the turkeys." Hearing the soldiers approach, the slaves jumped into action and dropped corn under an old house. When the turkeys went after the corn, the slaves nailed boards around the house's footing, trapping the turkeys and hiding them from view. They had just finished sweeping away the tracks when the foragers arrived.[73] Another slave recalled burying food in the ground so Yankee soldiers could not find it, but often they did. "We were hungry many a time."[74]

The Union army stripped other slaves of their property, as in the case of Minerva Boyd, an astonishingly successful entrepreneur. She hired her time and made enough money to operate a draying service with her own mules and drays, employed other slaves to work in the stables she had paid for with gold and silver, and built her own house. When northern troops arrived, they seized Boyd's stock. Then they disassembled her stables and house and used the lumber to build government warehouses.[75]

After the war, soldiers spoke more frankly about their foraging and looting than did Grant and Sherman in their memoirs. One remembered being issued only three or four days' rations before beginning a long march into Confederate territory. "Union forces," he recalled, "were almost entirely dependent on the country for their supplies."[76] As a result, the army cleaned the countryside of provisions. "Our soldiers scoured the whole country for ten miles around and took everything they could eat or use."[77] A lieutenant in the Fifth Illinois Cavalry remembered taking property "in all conditions and under all circumstances when we needed it." No records were kept.[78] A hospital steward described foraging every day: "We never returned empty. . . . The whole country was stripped."[79]

Federal officers found it hard to control looting. When Union army troops marched into Vicksburg, Anne Shannon thought they "pour[ed] into town in quite an orderly manner." But she wrote later that Union soldiers had stolen clothing and blankets from a slave cabin while one officer stood on the porch to assure the family that he would permit no looting. The officer chased the looters but returned, crestfallen. "It's the meanest thing a white man can do," he said, "stealing from a nigger." Shannon observed that "all were crazy for plunder, and when officers were opposed to such wholesale thieving, they were unable to control their men." The first night after Vicksburg's surrender passed sleeplessly for Shannon. "We could hear the tearing down of fences, shooting cattle, shouting and going on."[80]

Union troops took food and often the very tools blacks needed for economic independence. When Jack Hyland lost his dray and horse to Union troops he went back to his plantation, where "I had no particular business . . . and had to go about & do the best I could for a living."[81] Losing his hack had cost Henry Banks a great deal of money. After the surrender of Vicksburg, cotton buyers flocked to the city and spent money like water. Freshly paid soldiers freely distributed their largesse as well. "They would pay anything you asked," Banks remembered, "and we asked all we thought we could get."[82] As a slave, Charles Anderson had traveled throughout Warren County, plying his trade as a carpenter. He could do so, in part, because he owned his own carpenter's tools, which he kept, along with the stock he accepted as payment, at his wife's cabin on a neighboring plantation. When Union army troops seized two chests of his tools to build fortifications and bridges, however, Anderson found himself unemployed.[83]

As Vicksburg was pillaged, residents began to understand the enormous impact Grant's army would have on society and life. During the Civil War, Union soldiers first experienced federal power. Unlike twentieth-century occupying armies, such as Israel in Lebanon, the Soviet Union in eastern Europe or Afghanistan, or the United States in Vietnam, members of the Union army would remain in Vicksburg as civilians, and they made a powerful difference in the South's social order. Some became leading newspapermen, politicians, and lawyers.

It is likely that the soldiers who attacked Vicksburg had entered the army convinced that mob justice characterized the South rather than the North. Communities in the English colonies had expelled deviants from their midst by turning out to jeer and heckle, play "rough music," and apply tar and feathers.[84] But by the time of the Civil War, such practices apparently lingered only in the South. In 1842 one northern newspaper reported that southern society seemed medieval.[85] Vicksburg had given itself a national reputation when its citizens lynched a gang of gamblers in 1835; years afterward the Boston *Liberator* still railed against "Vicksburg Lynch law."[86]

As northerners served in the army, though, they found themselves administering community justice to miscreants. The diaries and letters of Union soldiers record extralegal lashings, informal punishments, and ceremonial expulsions of soldiers from the ranks. One Illinois soldier described the ritualistic punishment of a cavalry soldier caught stealing. His former comrades shaved one side of his head clean with a razor, turned his coat wrong-side out, and posted the word *thief* on his back in large letters. A guard armed with bayonets escorted him through camp, and a drum and fife played discordant music amid the hoots and jeers of his community. Marched over a nearby hill, he disappeared, never to be seen again by his comrades.[87] The soldier's humiliation, like those played out in units all through the Union army, replicated ceremonies often considered quintessentially southern.

Foraging practices came from the bottom up, a process that resembled decision making in southern society. One newspaper articulated the view of many southerners when it declared, "The people's will is the law."[88] Similarly, Generals Sherman and Grant's foraging orders merely "gave concrete expression to the ideals of the populace."[89] The policy, practiced on both sides, of electing officers rooted them in the outlook and prejudices of the military community from which they came. Richard Yates, the governor of Illinois, formally appointed all commissioned officers, but only after volunteer regiments had held elections to indicate their choice. Officers had to maintain the good will of those they would command.[90] One captured and wounded Union soldier told Rowland Chambers that he had fought for the Constitution "and would Rather die than live with ceches [secessionists]."[91] But Yankee soldiers looked more often to their fellows for guidance than to abstract ideals or superior orders. As time passed that became more true rather than less.

Men who save each other's lives develop a cohesion impossible in civilian life. Soldiers in all wars naturally develop a devotion to their comrades and, often, an indifference or even hostility toward distant commanders and abstract authority. In the Civil War, Union soldiers fought an enemy stereotyped as obsessively clannish. As they moved south into Mississippi, midwesterners discovered that they had a capacity for what they, as civilians, had once regarded as lawless behavior. Most theft carried out by Union troops in Mississippi did not result from authorized foraging or even "bumming," individual avarice. Rather, gangs of men cultivated community-based systems of values independent of outside direction. Such groups justified the taking of civilians' chickens and other property as legitimate. They collectively decided to turn aside the pleas of southerners, even if slaves made those pleas. Any soldier in defiance of the group found himself shamed and ostracized. It is ironic that these men developed what resembled the southern system of values.[92]

Although they adopted practices that resembled features of white southern culture, many northern soldiers felt compassion for the slaves they encountered. But many also shared with southern whites a racial antipathy for blacks. One wrote home that plantation slaves "greatly amuse me with their ideas, stories, etc." He added that "they all seem pretty well satisfied, have pretty good homes to live in, and as a general thing I think this [the South] is the best place for them." Another complained, "I have slept on the soft side of a board, in the mud, and every other place that was lousey and dirty. I have drank out of goose ponds, horse tracks, etc., . . . all for the poor nigger; and I have yet to see the first one that I think has been benifited by it."[93]

That feeling is illustrated by Illinoisan Ira Batterton, who went to Vicksburg with Grant's army. Before the war he had been a self-described "black Republican" and had celebrated when "our Black regiments . . . completely *whipped*" the Confederates at Millikens Bend.[94] Batterton hated planters' "political treason." When Vicksburg fell, he described the surrendered Confederates as "dirty, ragged, sluggish and lousy."[95] He had no sympathy for them because of their "malignant hate of our government."[96] After the surrender, his superiors asked Batterton to command a black regiment. At the end of 1863 he was out of the army but still in Vicksburg, eager to make money. He thought of trading in cotton and bought an interest in a grocery store, but by June 1864 he was editing a newspaper, the *Herald*. As editor of the only Republican newspaper in Mississippi, Batterton became the voice of Unionism. He put an American flag on the masthead of every issue and published official army announcements and orders. He also crowed that "Slavery is *forever dead*."[97] Many Vicksburgers carefully read the *Herald* to discern the point of view of their conquerors, but all across the South racial bias undermined Republican newspaper editors' commitment to Reconstruction. Batterton's *Herald* was no exception. White southerners must have been delighted to learn that he was no radical. He endorsed Andrew Johnson's plan to rehabilitate Mississippi with old Whigs and, like Johnson, lacked basic compassion for former slaves. When refugee slave children streamed into Vicksburg, he remarked, for example, that they chattered like monkeys. "I have been pressed very hard by the Radicals here to advocate the policy [of black suffrage]," he wrote privately, "but I am opposed to it for the present and will not do so." A great evil of slavery, he decided, had been miscegenation. Interracial sex had defiled the white race. Perhaps the final measure of this Yankee's racial conservatism came when he hired I. M. Patridge as assistant editor of the *Herald*. Formerly the editor of the Vicksburg *Whig* and a veteran of the Volunteer Southrons, Patridge became the editor of the *Herald* after Batterton's death and turned the publication into the town's leading champion of racial conservatism.[98]

Another measure of northern soldiers' willingness to embrace the signature elements of southern society can be found in that most southern of institutions, the community-sanctioned duel. In a conscious compromise of their northern birthright, Union army officers stationed in Vicksburg embraced the same southern chivalry that had seemed so odious in 1856 when Representative Preston Brooks had caned Senator Charles Sumner. Union officers dueled with other northerners, as Captain Upton M. Young did with G. Gordon Adams in 1866. In 1874 Charles Furlong, a former Union army officer, challenged the editor of the Vicksburg *Times,* E. G. Hunt, to a duel. Following the local honor code to the letter, the two men exchanged a long series of curt notes before deciding they had to shoot at each other. Just like a generation of southern-born duelists before him, Furlong rowed across to Louisiana in a skiff. Authorities arrested Hunt, but he escaped and promptly made his way to Louisiana, where the sheriff stopped the duel. And, just like a true southern gentleman, when someone beneath his station insulted him, Furlong went after the miscreant on the streets of Vicksburg with cowhide.[99] Born in Ithaca, New York, Union army veteran Frederic Speed waived his personal prejudice against duelling when insulted by fellow Republican J. S. Morris. Speed not only accused Morris of cowardice but also published their correspondence in a newspaper, where he guessed that Morris had assumed "upon the fact that I am a Northern man . . . that I would not fight." He rushed to disabuse Morris of any such notion, however, "according to the strictest terms of the Code."[100]

Far more than the Union army, freed people would alter the nature of southern whites' legal culture. As Union forces approached, whites scrutinized the faces of servants, wanting to believe that they loyally supported the war effort against the North. As late as May 10, 1863, slaveowners around Vicksburg worked slaves just as they always had, although expecting northern troops by the hour. Some slaves encouraged that feeling of normalcy by pretending to oppose the Union, but they admitted later that they had trouble doing so with a straight face.[101] Others scarcely kept up the illusion.

Some planters complained that their slaves had been "demoralized" as early as 1861. Outside the hearing of whites, almost all favored the Union. "We talked secretly," a former slave recalled, "that is among ourselves (the colored people)—We could not have expressed our opinions public." Several former slaves reported that they feared the Confederates would have killed them had they declared support for the Union.[102] Lewis Johnson claimed that Confederates had threatened to hang him, and one soldier had thrust a gun into his stomach.[103]

In low tones, away from whites, some demonstrated that they could articulate the meaning of freedom more effectively than others. "I felt its cause to be right," Henry Banks remembered, "and told other colored people that should the Yankees succeed, we could go where, when, and how we pleased and our children would no longer be sold and that negro trading would be played out."[104] But he could only exercise his talents in secret and in nonpublic arenas. A friend recalled that he had talked with Banks "on these subjects in presence of other colored people—but not in the presence of white people—we did not dare to do that."[105]

But white people knew. In May 1861 one complained that on Sundays, when slave hack drivers took passengers to church, they collected together during the services to talk excitedly about the war. They speculated on the chances of Lincoln's success, wondering whether "old Abe" would wipe out the white folks. And, even that early, eavesdropping whites reported in the spring of 1861 that the "darkies" hoped to "be called upon to help in the wiping process."[106]

As Union forces closed in, blacks found it harder and harder to contain their excitement. On Fonsylvania Plantation south of Vicksburg, overseer Alfred Quine complained of "confusion" on May 11, 1863. "I can't tell what was done," he wrote, adding that the hands had accomplished "some Little ploughing and hoeing of corn." The next day he thought his workers manifested confusion mixed with excitement. A week later, fighting raged in Vicksburg, but Quine still managed to get some plowing done. On May 22 he complained of confusion again and admitted that his slaves did little. Freedom came just two days later. The Yankees arrived, Quine dutifully recorded in his plantation record book, "and the work all stoped." The next day he wrote, "Negros all Free. No work done." He repeated the same words, more or less, for the rest of the month. By June 5 the strike had turned celebratory. The disgusted overseer wrote that his former field hands were "all frolican," and the next day he added that it was a "holiday all the time now with the Negros."[107] In other places African Americans dated their freedom to the fall of Vicksburg. Monroe Gibson declared that when the city surrendered, "I surrendered too—I drapt my hoe."[108]

While emancipation delighted African Americans it terrified many white women. With so many of their men in the Confederate army, southern white women found themselves trying to control African Americans for the first time. They had slapped, hit, and whipped slaves but usually as a man's subaltern and proxy. As blacks became more restless and assertive, women called on male kin and neighbors, who became increasingly scarce. Emilie McKinley described how a slave had attacked her former mistress, saying, "You have had me beat enough."[109] Kate Stone's most horrifying war experience was when "a big black wretch, with the most insolent swagger" burst into a neighbor's bedroom while she was visiting. Standing on the hem of Kate's dress, he slowly looked her over, snapping his pistol. He stood there a minute—she thought it seemed like an age—then, in an instant, he laughed and left. Later Kate's mother and aunt complained that a storm had frightened them worse than anything else in the war. "They," Kate muttered, "had not had a brutal Negro man standing on their dress and fingering a pistol a few inches from their heads."[110]

Men like Alfred Quine and Charles Allen could see the effect of civil war on their slaves. It is less likely that they grasped how it would change their wives and daughters. The change in attitudes toward religion serves as a model for what happened between the sexes. The war promoted solidarity and community over individual achievement, making religious distinctions seem less important. Gentiles had always thought of Vicksburg Jews as outsiders, not really a part of the community, but the Jews surprised their neighbors by rallying to the common defense.[111] "The great benefit of this war," one southern woman wrote, is that "it allows *every one* the luxury and privilege of doing good."[112]

Just as Vicksburgers forged new alliances across religious lines, women joined men in other ways. When the first shells landed, some women wanted to flee. But the war toughened most. Emma Balfour wrote that "to think of one's sleeping with these twelve and thirteen inch shells, three inches in thickness falling and exploding all around, now and then tearing a house to pieces and knowing that yours may be the next; seems strange, but so we are constituted."[113] White males of the antebellum South had thought of themselves as soldier-citizens.[114] The Vicksburg siege made it harder for them to deny women similar status.

The war gave Emma Crutcher unprecedented opportunities to resist the domination she had claimed to welcome. By the end of January 1861, Vicksburg women had organized a free market to support the families of poorer men who had joined the army. The women advertised in a newspaper, asking planters to assist the poor by donating food, and distributed provisions, prevailing on men to assist. Marmaduke Shannon contributed the physical space they needed.[115] Emma Crutcher pitched in, although that kind of manual labor on behalf of community was not at all what Will had pictured for his wife. In one letter she related that she had distributed four barrels of flour and two hogsheads of meal *"with my own hands."* She complained that wealthy planters did not contribute as they should although they were richly endowed with surplus food crops. Some hoped to hold their potatoes until the price reached a dollar a bushel. Crutcher confided that she hoped the price would plummet to 20 cents.[116]

Class divisions made it difficult for women to forge a common identity. Upper-class white women such as Emma Crutcher did not normally associate with the poor, nor did they forget their status. But now, on Tuesday mornings after breakfast, she and her friends hurried over to the carriage room, where they took off their bonnets, furs, cloaks, and other finery before descending to the room where they distributed food. There they found the poor women, patiently lined up behind a rope. Charity creates few real bonds across class lines, but before secession Emma Crutcher would have had no contact at all with such people. Now she even started to dress like them, wearing plain clothes. One woman told her to pass the word to her husband that "I never saw his wife appear to as much advantage, or look as *pretty,* as she does today, dressed in a dark calico dress and white apron, scooping up meal for the poor women."[117] Another child of the planter class wrote that fashion had become an obsolete word. "Broadcloth," she said, "is worn only by the drones and fireside braves." Gentlemen even made social calls dressed in "Negro cloth," a cheap material made for slaves.[118]

As women rallied to the cause, reaching across class lines, the men tried to help. At first, they found it more difficult than their wives to cross class and ethnic boundaries. The Board of Police appointed Jacob Peale to take care of soldiers' families, but he quickly gave it up. "There was no use talking," he told the women of the free market, "he could *not* manage those Irish women."[119]

While men such as Jacob Peale found they could not "manage" the women, female Vicksburgers performed new kinds of work. In 1862 Crutcher reported to her husband that she had begun working at the city hospital. She clearly anticipated objections. "Now, don't you get angry and uneasy and so forth, my dear," she wrote. "This is not a voluntary affair, but the ladies *have* to do it." She described the male patients as desperately sick and not of the lowest or the highest class, either of which might be inclined toward insolence. By contrast, her patients exhibited gratitude and respect. "I am telling you all this, that you may not be uneasy at my engaging in this." She assured her husband that she faced none of the drudgery of nursing; convalescents and servants performed those chores. "I shall never take on myself anything that a servant can do as well, and never do anything that a lady may not, with perfect propriety do." Clearly Crutcher and the other married women performing hospital duty were pioneering new roles for southern women. She promised not to talk familiarly with the patients, "as most of the ladies do."[120]

Emma Crutcher and other women put unprecedented demands on their men as soldiers. Through gossip and finger-pointing, they pressured stay-at-homes to enlist. One wrote that she could hardly bridle criticism of male hold-outs, as "we are all on fire with the subject."[121] Crutcher reassured her husband that his own mother preferred his brave death to a cowardly life.[122] One group of women published and circulated a satirical broadside. "To Arms!" they cried. "There will be a meeting of the young ladies of Warren County, to be held . . . for the purpose of forming themselves into a Home Guard, for the protection of those young men who will not volunteer for the country's cause."[123]

When defeated Confederate soldiers retreated into Vicksburg, women turned out to watch. "Remember," one called encouragingly, "Mississippians never surrender!"[124] A less charitable woman cried, "Shame on you all!" Others asked plaintively, "Who shall we look to now for protection?" That question would ring in the ears of southern men for generations after Appomattox. When new troops arrived, they were made to promise never to run but to die for the women.[125]

The war exposed Vicksburg's civilian population to horrors only male soldiers had experienced in the Mexican War. Lavinia Shannon now talked of a wounded soldier taken to a field hospital in Mrs. Duff Green's house. While there, a shell took off his arm. He became so nervous that the staff moved him behind a hill for safety. But another shell found him "and tore him to pieces and the pieces just quivered for a while." Women also described how an Irish woman had rushed into her child's bedroom to find that shrapnel had cut the baby in two. The legs had been driven into a wall, where the mother found them, still kicking. Such stories traveled from woman to woman via the mail.[126]

These horrors must have prompted some Vicksburg women to question their traditional position in society. Before emancipation, southern propagandists had defended the legitimacy of slavery by calling it as natural as marriage, equating the subordination of women and slaves. Planters described slaves as being part of their extended families. All members of the household were expected to be obedient and subordinate to the patriarch; as one father instructed a daughter after her marriage, "never . . . attempt to control your husband."[127] Women exercised more influence than men cared to concede, but their subordinate status limited their power.

The available evidence makes it hard to judge, but that attitude may have begun to shift during the Civil War. After emancipation, female diarists in Vicksburg began to use a word largely absent from their antebellum writings—*protection*, which they considered an entitlement. In Vicksburg, Anne Shannon prayed for protection after watching emancipated blacks celebrate their freedom. Living on an isolated plantation with no men, Emilie McKinley moaned that "Negroes rule the land" and "poor women [are] defenseless." She prayed for "protection" just as fervently as Shannon. McKinley wanted her protection in the form of "reinforcements," by which she meant men capable of using whips to chase threatening blacks off the plantation. When white male "protectors" (as she called them) finally came to the rescue, the plantation mistress promptly directed them to the quarters, with instructions to "tell all the negroes who wished to go to the Yanks to pack up and go immediately." Yet another woman indignantly confronted Grant and his officers, demanding her "rights of protection *as a lady*."[128] Whether white women used the specter of black violence to demand protection or men used it to impose protection may be an impossible conundrum. Some Civil War–era Vicksburg females, though, did fear black violence and sometimes instructed men on how to protect them properly.

The Civil War launched a process that would ultimately unify Vicksburg's white population. It impoverished the wealthy and offered the poor opportunities to organize class revolts, but they almost never did.[129] Women did not revolt either, accepting the patriarchal system before and after the war. Where earlier they had sought the care of men as supplicants, the war encouraged them to requisition protection.[130] The racial bloc whites formed in Reconstruction would carry out the kind of vigilantism Vicksburgers had toyed with in 1861. The broad outlines of that new racial coalition could be discerned, but Jews, Irish, poor whites, Democrats, and Whigs remained disparate and not yet united in 1865.

5

Presidential Reconstruction

After Vicksburg's Confederate defenders surrendered, the Union army found whites divided on the important question of how to order their society in a world without slavery. Mississippi whites hoping to restore order through law competed with those determined to maintain order extralegally. Proponents of law wanted to use Mississippi courts to discipline and control black labor. Legislators in Mississippi and other southern states passed draconian laws that included systems of inferior courts to control freed people. The statutes these champions of formal law advocated were as discriminatory, brutal, and racist as they have been described by historians.[1] The unfair laws horrified northerners, but so did the other option whites offered. Responsible white Mississippians urged establishment of "volunteer companies" to control crime. Even after the Civil War ended, guerrilla fighters ranged over the Mississippi landscape, attacking any blacks daring to show a flicker of independence. Whites scoffed at the very idea that bestial blacks could be controlled by courts, judges, and juries. Mississippi balanced between two extremes, the rule of law and mob rule, through Presidential Reconstruction, the time between 1863 and 1867 when presidents Abraham Lincoln and Andrew Johnson regarded Reconstruction as their responsibility.

* * *

Reconstruction began in Warren County on July 4, 1863, when Vicksburg's defenders marched from behind their breastworks, stacked their arms, and watched their conquerors enter the city. Union army officers examined the town and its inhabitants with an eye to the task they faced. Idealists hoped to make the South heel to a higher law. Even before Vicksburg's defenders had surrendered, some in the Union army eagerly looked to the social revolution they thought emancipation would accomplish. One chaplain anticipated "with thrilling interest" squads of teachers and missionaries proselytizing freed slaves.[2] But most of the army officers strolling the streets of Vicksburg on July 4 thought in more practical terms. They knew they would have to occupy the city, police it, and wean a hostile population away from slavery and treason.

The slaves welcomed the northern soldiers; Independence Day in 1863 meant emancipation for black Vicksburgers. In the celebration of their freedom, some turned on their erstwhile owners. Former slaves went into the homes of the whites they once served to confiscate the property of their oppressors. Charlie Brick found "runaway" black women "rummaging around, picking up what they could find." When he ordered them to stop, they cursed him and told him they were free and had as much right there as he had. Under the slavery regime, whites had shot black "runaways" when they failed to respond to a command to stop. Now, when Brick shot one of the women in the leg, a crowd of black men gathered. They cowhided Brick and put a gun to his head, demanding that the white man call the black man "master."[3] Black resentment of property accumulated through slavery continued long after the Civil War. When one liberated slave found an account book kept by lawyer W. C. Smedes with pages listing slaves he had bought and sold before the war, she ripped out the offending leaves.[4]

Northern soldiers encouraged such behavior and sometimes seized the clothing of white Vicksburgers for redistribution to the black population. When whites refused to take an oath of allegiance, Union soldiers turned them out of their homes and installed freed blacks.[5] In some cases such incidents reflected genuine sympathy for the freed slaves, but northern troops did not often harbor any real camaraderie with the freed people. They could—and did—use them as a tool to punish slavery and secession without developing any real empathy for the blacks.

As African Americans tasted freedom, calculating whether they wanted to punish secession or not, thousands of surrendered Confederate soldiers roamed the city as well, creating a "state of wild confusion" as one visitor put it. Thirty-thousand paroled Confederates mixed with eighty thousand Yankee soldiers. Some of the northerners thought the enemy enlisted men appeared broken by the siege and glad to surrender, while the officers looked bitter and defiant.[6] Thomas Taylor, an Ohioan, could distinguish no difference in attitude between Confederate officers and enlisted men, however, and wrote to his wife that "many of them breathe defiance."[7] Another Ohio soldier asked an Irish emigrant why he would fight for the Confederacy. "Pat" conceded that "it made but little difference to me in the start which side I took" but now that he had chosen the South, "I will never desert my colors."[8]

To curious northerners, Vicksburg seemed unimpressive, dilapidated. One soldier thought it must have suffered years of neglect, as though it had been rented out. Women were everywhere. They made up a disproportionate share of the civilian population because so many male Vicksburgers served in the Confederate army. Union soldiers found the sight of threadbare Irishwomen striking, but they also noticed once-wealthy belles trying to put on airs with no more than "a rickity wagon, a poor mule, a little ragged nigger."[9]

The chaos was not confined to Vicksburg. In the surrounding countryside the Union army also struggled to establish order. Confederate guerrillas (often called "scouts") differed from common horse thieves and bandits only because they discriminated when choosing victims. They scarcely bothered with proper uniforms, but they targeted Unionists. When captured, Union army officers sometimes tried them before military commissions that differed from court martials in name only. A judge advocate would present the evidence and a jury of officers would then decide the defendant's guilt or innocence. Captured guerrillas went on trial if Union officers thought they did not belong to a Confederate army unit. Such cases were difficult to prove because civilians living outside Union lines occupied an ambiguous position, trying not to offend either the Confederates or the Yankees.[10]

In some military commission trials Union army prosecutors used black witnesses against white defendants, a first in Mississippi history. Rebecca Fields, for example, had been smuggling goods through the Union lines to her friends in Confederate territory. She and her faithful maids Eliza and Mary sewed hidden pockets on the insides of dresses. She likely never dreamed they would one day testify in court against her.[11]

Black witnesses such as Eliza and Mary came under attack from defense lawyers arguing that former slaves could not be trusted to tell the truth. Judge Richards Barnett, the lawyer for Daniel Pender, who was charged with the murder of a slave, insisted that blacks could not testify because they had no "moral or religious culture."[12] Fields's lawyer had condemned the black women arrayed against his client by claiming they had "the lowest order of intellect" and were "easily moulded."[13] Barnett orated that the policy of the U.S. government and the fortunes of war had raised Mississippi's slaves "to the condition of free men—their shackles had been broken." He then insisted that only their status had changed, asking, "Have their intellects or morals been effected[?] Are they not the same illiterate, stupid, degraded race, they were before their freedom?"[14] In one case a former slave called as a witness conceded that he did not know what an oath was and confessed he could not be trusted to tell the truth. The military commission dismissed him. More often witnesses insisted that they understood that once under oath they had to tell the truth or be punished. Commissioners allowed such witnesses to testify, over the objections of defense attorneys.

While military commissions worked to try criminals in the absence of civil authority, the Union army itself actually contributed to rural lawlessness. When Colonel Edward Siber ordered refugee slave women out of Camp Sherman near Vicksburg, the women hid in an abandoned house. A gang of Union soldiers found them and attempted to rape them. The women managed to escape, seeking safety again in the Union army camp and begging for protection. When Siber discovered them he flew into a rage even though he had been told of the attempted rape. Mounted on horseback, he herded the women out of camp ahead of his horse. That night, trapped outside camp, the freed slaves could not ward off Union army rapists.[15]

More often, the army contributed to disorder by allowing vast stretches of the countryside to go unpatroled, a practice that ran counter to the government's policy of encouraging northerners to come South and operate abandoned plantations. Brigadier General John P. Hawkins, commander of the District of Northeastern Louisiana and a West Point graduate, calculated that breaking plantations into small units for sale to blacks and loyal whites would strengthen the North's hold on the Mississippi River. For Hawkins's plan, or any other plan, to have any chance of success the Union army would have to be energetic in policing not only Vicksburg but also the countryside.[16]

The fate of Ohioan Isaac Shoemaker, a typical white adventurer attracted South by the prospect of plantation life and riches, illustrates the failure of federal policing outside Vicksburg. Leaving Cincinnati by steamboat on January 28, 1864, Shoemaker arrived in Vicksburg on February 8. There he met Charles A. Montross, an agent for the Treasury Department, which had taken over the leasing of plantations at the end of 1863. Montross assured Shoemaker that northern planters and their black laborers would be protected from Confederate guerrillas. Although ostensibly fighting for the Confederacy, neighborhood guerrillas robbed and murdered much like ordinary criminals, albeit ones sanctioned by the neighborhood. Shoemaker did not fear regular Confederates, "but it is the lawless cutthroats and robbers I dread." Nonetheless, with Montross's assurances, he rented a plantation reputed to be the best cotton producer in Warren County and contracted with former slaves to work it.[17]

In March, Shoemaker learned that the War Department had again taken over management of plantation leasing. That was encouraging news, promising better protection. No Confederate marauders had raided his plantations, but blood-curdling stories of northerners put to death horribly circulated, and Shoemaker felt isolated and alone on his plantations deep in no-man's land. For several days cavalry soldiers did stop by, and he felt safer. But then military authorities in Vicksburg shut down the cavalry post outside the town, leaving those in the countryside to fend for themselves. Crowds of freed slaves promptly fled for Vicksburg, although once in the city they faced confinement in disease-ridden contraband camps or conscription into the Union army. Shoemaker and many other northern white planters also gave up, abandoning their plantations to the brigands and ending a feeble effort to establish law and order, as well as a system of free labor run by northerners, in the countryside.[18]

Had Shoemaker chosen to stay in Vicksburg he might have faced fewer dangers, but he still would have seen conflict between Confederates and Unionists. Inside Vicksburg, Confederate sympathizers did not wage outright guerrilla warfare, as in rural areas, but a kind of war went on nonetheless, one involving women to a considerable extent. Ordinary etiquette thrust females into politics. Some Vicksburg women displayed open disdain toward northerners. One officer noticed that a woman shook her dress disgustedly after she passed him and some friends on the street, "(as if to shake off the contamination of our presence)."[19]

Some scrambled to ingratiate themselves with the northern soldiers, however. "I suppose there is not a young lady in Vicksburg that the federal officers dont visit," Anne Shannon wrote, disapprovingly. She understood the politics of etiquette. Her sister confided that "it would surprise you to see how mean some of the Vicksburgers are, a great many of them seem to be turning blue." Lucy Rawlings had once proudly worn the secession cockade, but now she told the Yankees that she had always secretly favored the Union. Some local women invited Union officers to their balls and attended parties given by Yankee women. Even so, many Yankees harbored doubts about Vicksburgers' renaissance of fealty. Chicagoan William Brown wrote to his father that they appeared to be "returning to their loyalty," but he attributed that to hunger. "It would surprise you," he reported, to see the wealthiest Vicksburgers mix with the poorest whites and with their former slaves at the commissary, all waiting for food.[20]

Throughout history, occupying military forces have encountered a variety of responses from indigenous civilian populations. Generally, civilians react in a multiplicity of ways but construct a dominant memory of their occupation. In 1945 Japanese civilians startled occupying American troops by pronouncing themselves ready to accept their fate. One Japanese civilian compared himself to a carp on the table. Like the fish, he was ready for the knife and would not even "flinch his fins." German female civilians reacted to American occupation in many ways, often resisting, but in the public memory Germans constructed of occupation sexual fraternizing with American soldiers became a symbol of acceptance of American ways.[21]

As in postwar Germany, female Vicksburgers fashioned no single response to occupation. White southerners, though, decided to remember female defiance and use it to symbolize southern resistance. And the public memory accurately captures the South's fundamental reaction to Reconstruction. Despite the fraternizing that did occur, the Union army faced a white population doubtful about national authority, especially when used to protect black rights. While some Vicksburgers thought they had no choice but to accommodate the invaders, others were truculent from the start. Young Victoria Batchelor delightedly described herself as a "stubborn traitor" who drew federal rations and laughed at authorities for "giving them to such a spirited rebel."[22] Alice Shannon lamented that only one dead Yankee lay in her yard, but "if they were all over the garden it would only make the soil richer."[23]

White Vicksburgers repeated Shannon's quip for years thereafter. They also enjoyed telling of southern girls so charming and charismatic that they could parade their Confederate sympathies before visiting Yankee officers and make them like it. When a Vicksburg minister offered a prayer for Abraham Lincoln, five women in his congregation walked out.[24] Less than a year after the surrender, such defiance had made the prospect of social change less thrilling to northern reformers stationed in Vicksburg. Whites "have little conscience where the negro's rights are concerned," one missionary wrote in March 1864.[25] By the next year the missionaries recognized that they faced an intransigent foe and described Vicksburg as "squally." "I think very little has been gained by the war unless these men are put down," one reported.[26] But Vicksburg men were only a part of the problem. Women had become a critical element of the white coalition, insisting that their men resist black rights.

More than local resistance foiled this effort to undermine the Confederacy from within. Within months of Vicksburg's surrender, Union army commanders of the occupying force began to suspect political leaders in Washington of sabotaging their efforts in Mississippi. That became clear when they tried to organize Mississippians loyal to the Union. Not all local commanders interested themselves in identifying truly loyal southerners, however. Determinedly Unionist, Lawrence Sterne Houghton complained bitterly of his shabby treatment by General N. G. T. Dana: "A large number of the army crowd," he wrote, "refuse to acknowledge any Unionism among us."[27] Nonetheless, within a month of the surrender some Yankees happily identified men true to the Union who would "exert a favorable influence over many of their wavering brethren." Some saw this as the key to victory. "If we only get the Union feeling well started," William Brown wrote to his father, "it will increase rapidly." First the Southwest and then the coastal states would give up the fight, Brown predicted, influenced by southern Unionists.[28]

Of all the Vicksburg Unionists Brown and other Yankees hoped would help end the war, Armistead Burwell could have been the most important. After Burwell returned to Vicksburg from his exile in St. Louis, he persuaded Union army generals to allow him to organize "simon-pure" Mississippi Unionists. It is likely that he had in mind a league of Mississippi whites rather than the mostly black Union League that did emerge in Vicksburg and Mississippi. Such an organization might have been useful as the basis for a civilian government of the sort Abraham Lincoln advocated in his December 8, 1863, proclamation. Lincoln's Proclamation of Amnesty and Reconstruction encouraged formation of civilian state governments in the seceded states. A lawyer-politician, Burwell would seem to have been just the sort of loyal southerner William Brown expected to exert favorable influence over his "wavering brethren." At the very least, Burwell could have served as the invaders' liaison with the civilian population. Although local commanders enthusiastically endorsed Burwell's plan, their superiors vetoed it. Perhaps they did not trust his loyalty, or they might have feared formation of a political force not under their control. But Union General J. Warren Miller placed the blame squarely on "ex-rebel and semi-rebel influence . . . with the power at Washington."[29]

It is more likely that civilian leaders in Washington objected to military interference in civil matters; Lincoln had instructed Grant to confine

negotiations with Confederates to military issues. When Sherman offend-
ed President Andrew Johnson's sensibilities on that issue by agreeing to
restore some Confederate state officials to power, Johnson accused him
of treason.[30] Moreover, the military occupation of Vicksburg occurred
during Presidential Reconstruction, when Presidents Lincoln and
Johnson failed to nurture a new elite to replace the prewar leaders. By the
time of his assassination, Lincoln had begun to move toward recognizing blacks as part of the American polity, but he died before completing
his intellectual journey. Johnson first cheered proponents of black citizenship by threatening to punish southern traitors, but then he freely
pardoned leading Confederates. Convinced that southern African Americans lacked the skills necessary to govern, or even vote, he appointed
white conservatives to offices in southern state governments. "White men
alone must manage the South," he said. Such declarations hardened
southern white resistance to Reconstruction.[31] Johnson further cheered
former Confederates by appointing Vicksburger William L. Sharkey as
provisional governor. Sharkey, a prominent Whig and antebellum Mississippi supreme court justice, was a familiar face and a representative of
the old elite willing to curry favor with Confederates. Unionists, including some who had remained true to the United States through the siege,
now fled Vicksburg for the North.[32]

As Johnson formulated his policies in Washington, military officers
stationed in Vicksburg struggled to devise a coherent strategy for the freed
people. Three weeks after the city's surrender, Union army officers still
had not produced a definite plan for governing. The provost marshal
complained that subordinate officers hesitated to act in the absence of
direction from the top, and no one made any effort to identify and encourage loyal natives.[33] Education efforts went ahead, but only as a hap-
hazard patchwork of ad hoc ventures. The freed slaves surprised the invaders with their eagerness to learn, but any passing northern woman or
missionary with access to a classroom and a willingness to teach could
set up a school.[34]

Their pupils lived in appalling conditions that the army did little to
ameliorate. Twenty thousand freed slaves in Mississippi and Louisiana fled
plantations for Vicksburg, where some died on city streets for want of
food and medical care. A visiting Catholic bishop asked northern officers
what they planned to do with the refugees but did not receive a satisfactory response. "Everyone," he recorded in his diary, "lamented that he
thinks there is no policy . . . except to deprive the masters of their services
& their belief is that . . . the race will die out." The army set up what the

soldiers called "Negro corrals," camps filled with rows of rough cabins populated with sick and dying refugees. Not all the escaped slaves went into such corrals, however. Escaped slave women also found husbands, sons, and brothers in army camps, serving in so-called colored units. Despite the terrible privation, the U.S. government refused to feed former slaves unless they came in organized groups. There was, the missionary wrote, "a great suffering."[35]

Between July 4, 1863, and July 1865, the Union army policed Vicksburg. Abraham Lincoln had suspended the writ of habeas corpus throughout the nation on September 24, 1862; six weeks earlier the secretary of war had done likewise for "all persons arrested for disloyal practices," as well as for men evading conscription. Thereafter, Union officials arrested civilians for such things as calling the war "a damned abolition war" or labeling Lincoln "a God Damn black abolition son of a bitch." Congress endorsed these arrests with the Habeas Corpus Act on March 3, 1863.[36]

Army provost marshals never indulged in wholesale arrests of southerners, but their experience in the North showed they would not hesitate to arrest troublesome civilians. In Vicksburg they imposed a curfew and forbade travel without a pass. Military authorities' records show they arrested 1,586 civilians for such crimes as theft and drunkenness, as well as for "insulting officer," "disloyalty," and "secret charges." One man went to jail for proclaiming that he "wished to God Forest would come in and kill every Yank in Vicksburg." Two-thirds of those arrested, however, were black, and most were accused of theft. Lincoln never imagined that his suspension of the great writ would authorize army arrests of apolitical civilian profiteers, but it did. When northern entrepreneurs rushed into Vicksburg, setting up saloons to soak up the salaries of Union soldiers, the provost marshal seized their billiard tables. The army then operated them, charging no more than ten cents a game. "The interests of the army must be secured before these army followers," the provost marshal declared. He also controlled rents, rolling them back as extortionate, set the price of food, and, when tipped off by detectives, seized whiskey bound for Vicksburg. With no functioning civilian government, the army collected the taxes, too.[37]

The federal government's use of black troops to occupy Vicksburg antagonized the civilian population. Arming former slaves touched whites' deepest fears and hatreds. Alice Shannon wrote that the sight of "negro soldiers marching so grand in their blue uniforms . . . with their fine swords, and their scarlet sashes, making a fine show" made her hate all blacks. For their part, black soldiers often returned the resentment.

Sergeant William Anderson and other members of the 46th U.S. Colored Infantry quarreled with planter John H. Bobb after Bobb caught Anderson and his friends picking flowers in Bobb's yard. When Anderson laughed as Bobb chastised him, Bobb became so angry that he hurled a broken brick at the soldier's head. The blow knocked Anderson down, and his worried friends thought he had been killed. As they carried their comrade away, one warned Bobb, "Your house will go up for that." But Anderson did not die. Instead, he returned to the house and shot Bobb, killing him. At his court martial Anderson argued that the blow had rendered him temporarily insane. An army surgeon supported him, and the court martial acquitted the sergeant.[38]

There were other incidents involving black troops and white civilians. In April 1865, a group of soldiers from the 52d U.S. Colored Infantry who had decided to go out after rebels sneaked out of camp, slipping between sentry posts. They knew that plantation owner Jared Reese Cook lived nearby. Hearing his dogs, Cook sprang from his bed to see his yard filled with "nigger soldiers." They acted in "a very demon like manner," he said later, "seeming to be very much infuriated from some cause." Cook, a former slaveowner, seemed genuinely puzzled—and frightened—at the wrath he saw in the faces of the former slaves.[39]

The soldiers crowded into Cook's home, demanding his pistol—they knew he had one. They also upset beds, broke locks, and threw drawers on the floor. They asked Cook if he had money, and when he said no they searched him, found some, asked why he had lied, and threatened to blow out his brains. The soldiers also confronted Minerva Cook. In her diary, she had once expressed sympathy for her slaves and worried that she could not always control her temper with them. Now she faced their anger and resentment. "Old woman," they shouted, "where's your silver?" She said there was none. The soldiers turned to Cook: "Old man, where's your silver?" Cook also denied having silver. "We'll make them tell," one of the soldiers said, knocking Minerva in the head with the butt of his musket. Another objected, pleading with his comrades to do no more harm, "You have done enough." That did not stop his fellows. "Get out of the way, God damn it, if you don't we'll shoot you." Three or four guns fired, and Minerva fell, mortally wounded. Another bullet struck Cook in the shoulder, knocking him down. "Don't kill me, oh! Lord, don't kill me," the Cooks' son, William, wailed. Eventually, the soldiers returned to their camp. In a bid to restore order, military authorities arrested twelve men and charged them with murder. A court martial convicted all the defendants, but the local commander remitted the sentence of one and Secretary of War Edwin Stanton commuted the sentences of three others. The rest went to the gallows in the largest mass formal execution carried out by the Union army during the Civil War.[40]

The killers of Minerva Cook were soldiers, but the anger many former slaves felt for former owners boiled out of the overcrowded anarchy and squalid poverty found in refugee camps. Refugees from slavery flooded into Vicksburg from the countryside, swelling the population of the city. In 1860 Vicksburg had 4,500 inhabitants; ten years later there were 12,443. Freed slaves accounted for much of the increase. In 1860 whites outnumbered blacks three to one, but by 1870 blacks made up 55 percent of Vicksburg's population.[41]

Many of Vicksburg's newest residents lived in dreadful squalor. Two years after the city's occupation by federal troops the *Herald* reported that "Negro huts" still "crowded all over the city—within and without the fortifications, each little shanty of boards or tent containing from one to half a dozen families." The *Herald*'s editor wondered how so many people could live in such circumstances and worried about smallpox and yellow fever outbreaks. If smallpox and yellow fever did not ravage the city, another kind of epidemic did. Stray gunfire, thieves, and other criminals added to the anarchic chaos Vicksburg had become. Someone suggested that an enterprising inventor should fashion a bulletproof covering for Vicksburgers and their dwellings. Thieves robbed every night and usually got away with their plunder. Even in daylight, loafers hung around the wharf with bags of stolen cotton hanging from their necks.[42]

As lawlessness threatened to rage out of control, the war ended. Grant spent the summer of 1865 touring the North and greeting enthusiastic crowds but participated little in discussions over the role of the military in the postbellum South. He did say, however, that he no longer favored military law enforcement. In fact, he favored demobilizing the army as quickly as possible. In hopes of placating southern whites, he opposed immediate enfranchisement of blacks. Grant expressed naively optimistic confidence in a southern renaissance of loyalty, choosing to overlook reports of antiblack violence. Andrew Johnson, in contrast, saw the violence as necessary to the process of reducing freed blacks to their proper subordinate status.[43]

As Grant toured the North, military authorities in Vicksburg began returning control of the criminal justice system to civilians. Governor Sharkey obviously intended county government to continue much as it had before secession. Most of the board of supervisors he appointed were men whom voters had elected before the war. But not all members of the antebellum elite were restored to office. Although Lawrence Houghton had been elected probate judge in 1860 with 74 percent of the vote against three opponents, Sharkey removed him from office and replaced him with a veteran of Confederate service. "I am bound to think," Houghton complained, "that I was removed solely because I was a Union man, and for no other reason." He speculated that Sharkey hoped to be elected to the U.S. Senate; under Johnson's regime there was "no hope of getting that but by playing into the hands of the Rebs." Houghton's removal predictably alarmed Vicksburg Unionists.[44]

Appointing a board of police amounted to a bid to reestablish civilian control of the criminal justice system. The circuit and criminal courts could not meet without a grand jury, and supervisors nominated grand jurors in public meetings. They turned their nominees over to Sheriff Marmaduke Shannon, who actually notified prospective jurors. Shannon chose his own substitutes if he could not locate persons selected by the board.[45] The board Sharkey picked, and those subsequently elected, included bankers, planters, and merchants. According to the 1870 census, one supervisor, Bovina farmer W. R. Billingslea, owned no real or personal property. The local reporter for the R. G. Dun and Company credit-rating company described Billingslea as a "reliable and progressive man" who "stands well" in the community. The Dun reporter thought him "very honest" and possessing a good character and moral habits.[46] Other board members owned more property than most Warren County whites; J. W. Goodrum, for example, owned $2,000, and Alexander Arthur had $25,000 in real estate.

On July 1 the military permitted Vicksburgers to vote for mayor, and Thomas J. Randolph won.[47] As mayor, Randolph could hold court and try persons accused of minor crimes. For a time, military and civilian law-enforcement authority overlapped, and civilians struggled to stake out limits to the military's authority. Warren County's criminal court judge, D. O. Merwin, missing an arm from his service in the Confederate army, argued that provost marshals should only arrest persons charged with military offenses. Everything else should be left to civilians. He also hoped to regain control of the courthouse, announcing that he would not hold court "in the shadow of bayonets." Merwin complained to the governor, and a few days later the army returned Warren County's courthouse to civilian control.[48]

While Merwin refused to convene circuit court, the mayor did hold his magisterial court, but he still ran into problems. Sheriff and former newspaper editor Marmaduke Shannon refused to accept prisoners on the grounds that the federal army still controlled the jail. Mayor Randolph grumbled that "the slightest effort on his part would get for the county the immediate possession of her jail." Shannon's reluctance to deal directly with Union army officers might have stemmed from their shelling during the siege, which had destroyed his home and business, and from the death of his son in Confederate service. For a time Randolph had to crowd his prisoners into one small room of the city workhouse.[49] Under pressure from the mayor and others, however, Shannon finally did approach the federal officers. But the mayor had underestimated the difficulty of getting control of the jail. Federal soldiers refused to hand it over, instead offering to keep state prisoners if the civilians would pay for feeding the inmates. Shannon first indignantly insisted that he would have nothing to do with any such scheme.[50] Nevertheless, within two weeks he had begun to place state prisoners in federal custody, complaining that doing so cost 50 percent more than state law allowed for victualing prisoners.[51] Later Shannon charged that federal soldiers had released a convicted murderer he had placed in the jail, something the army hotly denied.[52] The army did not return the jail to Sheriff Shannon until May 1, 1866.[53]

Federal soldiers further angered and alarmed local whites when they demanded that Warren County disband its white militia companies. The militia, one white Vicksburger wrote, was "the only organized *white* force at present in this county that can be relied upon for the enforcement of civil authority."[54] As an alternative, some suggested that Shannon should use federal soldiers as members of posses, and the army agreed to furnish the necessary troops. The sheriff angrily refused, however.[55] In Vicksburg, the city police were an alternative to the militia and the U.S. Army, and civilian police did begin to patrol the streets again. But when they tried to enforce order, bystanders associated the police with the Union army and intervened, knocking them down with brickbats while criminals escaped.[56]

In December 1865, while the police worked to regain control of the streets, Circuit Court Clerk George Brichett opened the same minute book that had lain idle since 1861. Much had happened since then, but when Sheriff Shannon brought the grand jury into court they resembled the type of men who had been commonly selected before the war. The board had chosen as grand jurors white men even wealthier than antebellum jurors. While the median value of real and personal property of antebellum jurors had been $500, the median value of property held by men chosen as grand jurors in the first year and a half after the Civil War was $2,850. More than a third described themselves as "planters," "farmers," "gardeners," or "fruit growers," all terms that implied considerable land holdings in Warren County.[57]

Shannon and the board of police likely picked wealthy and conservative whites as jurors to blunt the effects of emancipation. Older, wealthier men would keep things on an even keel, Warren County's white leaders may have reasoned. Shannon did not record his motives, but Mississippi's judges made it clear that they wanted to curtail the Thirteenth Amendment's impact. In one case involving a black veteran of the Union army, a circuit judge decided that emancipation had restored blacks' "natural rights" but not their "political rights." The Constitution could not restore "political rights" they never had. The judge ruled that the veteran, Wash Lowe, should be allowed to keep his gun because everyone had a right to protect their property, even non-citizens who had no political rights. Mississippi's supreme court interpreted the Thirteenth Amendment as narrowly as possible and declared the 1866 Civil Rights Act unconstitutional. The emancipation amendment had only ended slavery, its "whole and sole purpose."[58]

Vicksburg's courts expected to pick up exactly where they had left off before the war. Virtually no women appeared in courts held on the eve of the Civil War, nor in 1865 or 1866. In 1862, in one of the last criminal courts held before the siege, a slave named Harrison had been indicted for murdering another slave. He remained in jail throughout the siege until Union soldiers released him. In 1865 Sheriff Shannon rearrested Harrison, now known as Harrison Brooks, a jury convicted him, and the judge sentenced him to hang. A year later, after two respites issued by the governor had expired, Shannon executed the sentence.[59]

But things had changed. Although the 58 defendants indicted in 1861 and 1862 had included only one black man, Harrison, grand jurors in 1865 and 1866 indicted 127 blacks. In those two years blacks made up a quarter of the total charged. Court officials handled unprecedented numbers of blacks in circuit and criminal court, double the number of all defendants processed in 1861 and 1862.[60]

The sheer numbers of defendants represented another change. Grand juries in 1861 and 1862 indicted only 58 persons, but those in 1865 and 1866 indicted 462. There are gaps in the existing records, but in the extant archive of Warren County grand jury indictments the number of people indicted in 1866, 387, easily broke the prewar record of 218, set in 1856. Many more people appeared in court and were charged with a wider variety of crimes.[61]

Careful observers of the courts during 1865 and 1866 must have noticed that the kinds of felonies prosecuted had changed dramatically (table 2). Before the war, grand jurors were more likely to indict for violent crimes than for theft or some other property crime. Nearly half of the indictments returned in 1861 and 1862 claimed assault or murder. But in 1865 and 1866 grand jurors returned only eighty-seven indictments alleging violence, 18.8 percent of the total. Grand jurors in 1865 and 1866 indicted persons for violating sabbath or retailing liquor, crimes against the moral order, more often than any other category. Grand jurors at the circuit court's June 1866 term returned so many indictments for hunting on Sunday that the district attorney ordered special hunting on Sunday indictment forms printed, complete with date of term and crime, leaving only a blank for the defendant's name. But that was an aberration, for Warren County grand jurors only enforced the hunting on Sunday law in 1866 and never again. Other morals crimes faded as well. The more lasting trend came in crimes against property. Only 8 percent of indictments in the final terms before the Civil War had alleged a property crime, but in the two years immediately after the war more than a third of indictments charged larceny. That new emphasis proved enduring. Between 1865 and 1880 grand jurors indicted for property crimes far more readily than for acts of violence. A great change had occurred. Before the war grand juries strove to punish violent offenders; after emancipation they protected property (figures 1–2).[62]

Some of the new cases reflected the effects of the war. Grand jurors tried

Table 2. Categories of Crimes in Warren County, Mississippi, 1865–69

	Defendants in County Court (*N* = 168)	Defendants in Circuit Court[a] (*N* = 918)
Crimes against:		
Property	60.6	46.9
Moral order	5.5	26.7
Person	3.6	22.3
Civil order	30.3	4.1
	100.0	100.0

Sources: County court case files, criminal court case files, circuit court case files, circuit court state docket books, all in Old Court House Museum, Vicksburg, and Natchez Trace Collection, Center for American History, University of Texas at Austin.
    a. Includes criminal court.

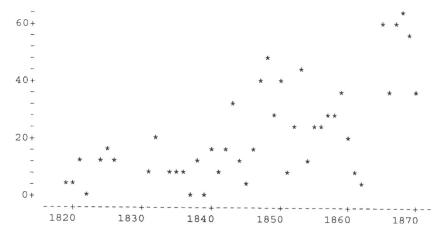

Figure 1. Warren County Grand Jury Indictments: Property Crime Indictments as a Percentage of All Indictments

Data taken from county court case files, criminal court case files; circuit court case files, and circuit court state docket books (all in Old Court House Museum, Vicksburg, and Natchez Trace Collection, Center for American History, University of Texas at Austin).

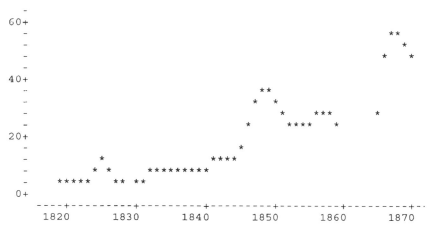

Figure 2. Warren County Grand Jury Indictments: Property Crime Indictments as a Percentage of All Indictments (Smoothed)

Data taken from county court case files, criminal court case files, circuit court case files, and circuit court state docket books (all in Old Court House Museum, Vicksburg, and Natchez Trace Collection, Center for American History, University of Texas at Austin).

to punish Union soldiers for mistreating Vicksburg civilians. They indicted Corporal Joseph Cosgrove for shooting with intent to kill a civilian
named Edward Kennedy. Cosgrove and two other corporals had sold a
pistol and then gotten drunk on the proceeds of the sale. They wandered
into the Independent saloon after Kennedy had called them "Yankee sons
of bitches" and told them to "go to hell." The soldier who had sold his
gun could only hit Kennedy with his bare hand, but Cosgrove still had
his pistol.[63]

In other cases, grand jurors sought to punish slaves who had openly
sided with the Union. They indicted for arson a former slave known to
whites as "Shanghai George." Known as "Shank" by the other slaves,
Shanghai George had set fire to Daniel Whitaker's house after William
Klein, living with Whitaker, had turned him in to Confederate guerrillas. It is not clear from the surviving record what Shank did that led to
Klein's action, but Confederate scouts seized him and another slave and
took them across the Big Black River behind Confederate lines. After
questioning the two slaves, the Confederates released them. Shank vowed
revenge and set fire to Whitaker's house—or so the state's witnesses
claimed. A jury convicted him.[64]

Such cases suggest the jurors' attitude toward Reconstruction. They
returned no indictments alleging mistreatment of Unionists or Yankee
soldiers and only rarely acted on the complaints of blacks or illiterates of
either color. Because most African Americans could neither read nor
write, that put freed people at a formidable disadvantage (table 3).

The animosities of war led authorities to ignore some cases. When two
Pennsylvanians were murdered, locals did little to apprehend their killers. In January 1866 Noah Zook left Lancaster, Pennsylvania, for Vicksburg. His brother Abraham went south in April. The two leased a plan-

Table 3. Literacy Rates by Race in Warren County,
1870

	All Black Adults (N = 7,238)	All White Adults (N = 4,080)
Literate	12.2%	93.6%
Illiterate	87.8	6.4
	100.0	100.0

Source: Manuscript population schedules, Ninth U.S. Census,
1870, Warren County, Miss., microfilm, National Archives. Adults
are defined as individuals aged 21 and older. Data comes from all
precincts and wards with the exception of Bovina and Davis Bend,
which were not coded.

tation along the Big Black and planted a crop of cotton. In October 1866 both Zooks disappeared. Locals eventually found and identified Abraham's horribly mangled body but never located Noah's remains. Warren County authorities did little to investigate the murders, and Vicksburg newspapers hardly mentioned the case. In Lancaster the murders made the front pages of the Republican *Evening Examiner,* furnishing fodder for those calling for more forceful federal Reconstruction policies. The Zook family sent an investigator to collect evidence, and the army made inquiries as well. Thaddeus Stevens, a Radical Republican member of Congress who represented Lancaster County, also intervened on behalf of his constituents. Despite the efforts of Stevens and the army, Warren County's grand jury refused to return any indictments, however. Even without help from the grand jury or the sheriff, army officers identified Cyrus Broome as the likely murderer and ordered him arrested in Texas, carried to Vicksburg, and jailed. For some months he languished in jail but then escaped.[65]

As Vicksburg's courts wrestled with lawlessness, Congress created the Bureau of Refugees, Freedmen, and Abandoned Lands. The bureau distributed clothing, food, and fuel to southern whites and former slaves and also fashioned a network of courts. The head of the Freedmen's Bureau set up courts where state authorities in the former Confederate states had made civil rights for blacks "null and void." The bureau circular envisioned the courts as a temporary expedient, authorizing them only where authorities refused to accept black testimony and limiting their jurisdiction. Federal courts adjudicating ordinary crime, after all, represented a dramatic breach of federalism, and army provost marshals retained jurisdiction over serious felonies. The new Freedmen's Bureau courts would handle cases involving punishments up to $100 or thirty days in jail.[66]

Eager for law, confronted by white state officials reluctant to give it to blacks, and politically powerless, freed slaves flocked to the Freedmen's Bureau courts, which offered, at best, paternalistic justice. Nonetheless, experience with the Freedmen's Bureau offered blacks a bridge from slavery to formal dispute resolution in regular courts. Captain E. E. Platt served as the Bureau of Refugees, Freedmen and Abandoned Lands's subassistant commissioner in Vicksburg, and hundreds of freed people came to his office with their problems. Platt's records indicate that he patiently listened to their stories and acted in a judgelike fashion, but his "court" was more informal and paternalistic than state courts. He kept a record of every complaint, summoned persons complained of, heard witnesses, and "dismissed" cases he thought trivial or unjustified.[67]

Most blacks who came to Platt complained that their white employers had failed to pay them their wages. Platt negotiated settlements. For example, when eighteen laborers from the local brickyard crowded into his office and reported that their boss had refused to pay them, Platt contacted the owner of the brickyard. The owner claimed that he did not have the money but agreed to pay the wages in bricks. Some blacks who came to Platt appeared to be trying the federal official to see what he could do for them. One farm laborer, for example, complained that his employer harassed him when he failed to pick clean cotton. Sarah Lewis complained that a justice of the peace had seized her furniture when she failed to pay her rent. Platt explained that she must pay. One man appeared "wanting rations" and "left grumbling" when Platt would not feed him.[68]

Husbands and wives brought marital problems to Platt's attention. Some of these couples had been forced together by antebellum owners and naturally had trouble getting along. When one wife complained that her husband paid too much attention to other women, Platt summoned the man to his office and decided that the woman deserved as much, or more, blame than the husband. The agent dispensed marital advice and dismissed the case. Platt generally hesitated to intervene when women complained that their husbands beat or abused them. When Kittie Stephens said her husband had threatened her life, Platt reported that she had no witnesses to support her story. He gave both parties "good advice" and sent them home. Another woman complained that the man with whom she had been living had assaulted her. Platt seemed as concerned about her failure to marry as the violence: "I have given her some good advice & dismissed the case."[69]

In some cases, Platt encouraged blacks to go to state authorities. When Thomas Simms wanted his sister's children bound to him, Platt told him to go to the probate judge. Another freedman complained that his neighbor's cattle ate his crops. Platt told the man he deserved compensation and should go to a justice of the peace. He also sent a woman wanting a divorce to state court. Platt did nothing but dispense more of his "good advice" when the brother of a man the circuit court had imprisoned for stealing $30 complained that his brother had been jailed unjustly. When blacks did go to court, Platt sometimes acted as their unofficial counselor. Several men brought contracts and other legal papers for him to examine.[70]

Platt did not just deal with freedmen; planters needed guidance from time to time as well. When one landlord complained that his hands did not fulfill their contracts, Platt wrote a letter to them "explaining things &c." Another man wanted to know "if a col'd woman has a right to bring her sick child & keep it in his qrs on his Plantation." Platt thought she "had a right to take her sick child to her house no matter where her house was." The planter left, saying "he thought it d_d strange if a man could not control his own property &c."[71]

Platt was no lawyer, but he tried to explain to both the freed people and their former owners the ways of the world in a universe governed by law rather than paternalism and slavery. In some ways Platt himself served a paternalistic function, and many African Americans saw his authority as a substitute for that of former owners. But the sub-assistant commissioner introduced many Warren Countians to lawlike solutions for their disputes and urged them to formalize interracial dispute resolution.[72]

As Platt patiently listened to the freed people crowding into his office, President Johnson worked to return prewar white elites to power that were unalterably opposed to the Freedmen's Bureau. In 1865 his policies placed former Whigs in control of Mississippi for the first time since the Jacksonian revolution swept the state in the 1830s.[73] Mississippi's postwar governors were old-line Whigs, and former Whigs dominated the August 1865 constitutional convention. White Mississippians regardless of their political affiliation agreed that the state would have to take unprecedented responsibility for disciplining African Americans.

To whites, the need for such discipline seemed all too clear. From their perspective, the Civil War had undermined authority, threatened anarchy, and created a wave of crime. Whites' overheated imaginations poisoned by racism undoubtedly exaggerated the increase in crime. In their minds, only the chains of slavery had protected white civilization from the black beast. Now those shackles lay shattered, and the brutal children of Africa prowled the landscape unrestrained. Thousands of freed slaves "fully intoxicated by the joys of freedom and mean whiskey, abandoned all pursuits of industry, and prowled at large, both day and night, over fields and forest, subsisting on game and plunder," a planter lamented. Another wrote, "Ther is a great deel of steeling a goin on in this Cuntrey and we are nearly destute of Pertection."[74] The Yazoo City mayor complained of the many murders and robberies in his city.[75] Another mayor wrote that the "negroes are troubling us constantly by committing depredations of various kinds—stealing—breaches of the peace &c and I know not what to do with them."[76] James Lusk Alcorn, who later became Mississippi's leading southern-born Republican, thought black "barbarism truly shocking."[77]

But the increase in crime was real. Confederate and Union deserters plagued the South and formed brutal bandit gangs. Even well-established citizens turned to robbery, freed by the war from communal and familial supervision. One Arkansas bandit turned out to be the local doctor. Military records confirm Vicksburg's lawlessness. Looters ravaged the city after the Confederate surrender, and Union provost marshals arrested more than 1,500 citizens in 1864 and 1865.[78] Some prisoners escaped the state penitentiary when the Union army destroyed Jackson, and doors swung open at countless local jails as well. The war impoverished some whites and turned many slaves into starving refugees. In times of want, crime—especially theft—increases. Finally, many saw the chaotic anarchy at the close of the war as an opportunity and took advantage of the temporary collapse of government to steal with impunity.

In some neighborhoods these bandits drove honest citizens into even tighter communities for protection. But when white outlaws preyed on blacks they may actually have contributed to the development of a communal culture of lawlessness. The provisional governor's answer to the crime wave promoted racial solidarity over constitutionalism. William L. Sharkey proposed formation of "Volunteer Companies" to patrol each Mississippi county. He expected these companies to pursue and apprehend criminals, whom they would then turn over to civil authorities.[79] In other words, the governor of Mississippi proposed formation of extralegal posses, gangs of white men empowered to discipline African Americans outside the law.

Crime and disorder also worried the delegates Mississippians sent to their 1865 constitutional convention, organized to abolish slavery and revoke secession. One delegate worried that "our wives and daughters dare not go from home, without an escort to protect them from being deprived of all that is precious to women."[80] Delegates regarded freed slaves as dangerous and menacing, a lawless group within society launched on a crime spree by emancipation. They also knew the Civil War had unleashed gangs of white bandits who roamed the state. Unlike the governor, the delegates thought the court system could be made to control these threats to order and directed the legislature to "provide by law for the protection and security of the person and property of the freedmen of the State, and guard them and the State against any evils that may arise from their sudden emancipation."[81] When one member advocated extending the death penalty to grand larceny, robbery, rape, arson, and burglary, others rejected that proposal.[82] They feared doing so might make juries hesitate to convict. To speed the judicial process, they agreed without recorded debate to cancel the constitutional requirement of a grand jury indictment before taking defendants to trial.[83]

While fear of crime drove convention delegates to call for draconian anti-crime efforts, others soon expressed concern about the cost of such measures and doubted that law could effectively control former slaves. After all, the governor's plan for "Volunteer Companies" would cost nothing and relied on proven extralegal methods. Proposals to create a system of county courts alarmed some. The economy-minded protested increasing taxes to create a multitude of judges, clerks, and other officials to do what had primarily been done extralegally at no cost. Slave courts had handled only crimes committed off plantations; the new courts meant to regulate blacks' behavior all the time. White critics doubted such courts would be as effective as their proponents anticipated. They thought white control of blacks could be maintained only through extralegal beatings and killings. Court opponents had a Jacksonian hostility to expanded government and the judiciary, preferring to continue the existing system of circuit courts that met only twice a year. Some championed making the criminal justice system self-sustaining by renting out the penitentiary or working convicts in chain gangs.[84] Proponents of the courts understood their opponents to advocate vigilantism. The Vicksburg *Times* warned that "a certain faction," the "force party," wanted to substitute its will for law; if the force party prevailed, passion would displace law.[85]

The legislature that wrote Mississippi's Black Code and county court law included seventeen Whigs and fourteen Democrats in the senate. Fifty-five Whigs served in the house with forty-five Democrats.[86] The chair of the Joint Select Committee on Freedmen, Whig senator J. J. Hooker, led the fight for using law to restore order. "Order and good morals can alone be restored . . . by a speedy and rigid enforcement of the criminal laws," he insisted.[87]

The Black Code that Hooker guided through the legislature required freed slaves to have written evidence of employment, forbade interracial marriages, and did not allow blacks to testify against whites in court. These statutes included provisions making it illegal for African Americans to possess guns or rent land outside cities and called for any white person to arrest freed persons who left the service of employers before the expiration of their contracts. Bidders could buy the labor of former slaves convicted and unable to pay fines at public auction. Thieves could be hanged by their thumbs.[88]

Freedmen's Bureau officials in Mississippi thought the laws unjust and overly harsh, but the head of the Mississippi office, Assistant Commissioner Samuel Thomas, refused to interfere without authorization from Washington. Oliver O. Howard, the chief of the Freedmen's Bureau, brought Thomas's objections to Secretary Stanton, who equivocated. Howard hesitated but then ordered Thomas to protect freed people's right to rent land, refusing to authorize any other interference in the Black Code. Grant later ordered his officers to protect blacks from unjust laws, but, in fact, bureau agents did little.[89]

The bureau's hesitation does not mean that officers did not find the Black Code barbaric and a cause for alarm, but they misunderstood the role of law in slavery. The Black Code was no return to slavery. It represented a dramatic innovation for white Mississippians, a sharp break with the slavery era. The Whiggish Vicksburg *Journal* expressed satisfaction that the new courts placed Mississippi blacks under law for the first time. "The negro is now protected by the civil laws of the State," the newspaper observed, "and if he does not live in strict accordance with them, the fault and consequences must be on his own head." The *Journal* "heartily rejoice[d]" that the legislature had concocted such a "happy" solution to a vexing problem.[90] One circuit court judge, James F. Trotter, hailed the county court law as a "great revolution" relieving circuit courts of jurisdiction of "the whole mass of inferior offenses." Trotter argued that restoring law would not merely reestablish order but help improve society and advance civilization.[91]

Mississippi Democrats thought it incomprehensible that the Black Codes marked a return to African American bondage. From the Democrats' perspective, the code portended too much change from the days of slavery.[92] Opponents of county courts, including many Democrats, did not believe blacks should—or could—be disciplined through courts. A white Tennessean expressed the sentiments of many when he observed that "Nigger life's cheap now" and that "when a white man feels aggrieved at anything a nigger's done, he just shoots him and puts an end to it."[93] A Mississippi planter took a position only slightly less extreme when he said, "I know niggers." They could not be punished through law, he insisted. Instead, employers must be allowed some kind of extralegal punishment. "I don't care what it is. If you'll let me tie him up by the thumbs, or keep him on bread and water, that will do. . . . All I want is just to have it so . . . the niggers . . . can't sit down and look me square in the face and do nothing." Handling blacks, such whites insisted, was like handling mules. No one used law to make a mule work.[94]

The legislature turned aside such reservations and erected a county court system for the entire state. Although historians have often ignored that new system of courts, contemporary observers did not.[95] Mississippi Republicans later condemned county courts as an integral, and particularly heinous, feature of the Black Code.[96]

The courts emphasized crime control over due process and resembled the system of county courts that Mississippi legislators had created in 1817, which, after 1824, functioned primarily to enforce the slave code. Like the postbellum version, county probate judges and two associate judges presided over antebellum county courts. Postbellum county court prosecutors brought defendants to trial without first taking them before a grand jury. In county courts, prosecuting attorneys and even county court clerks initiated prosecutions by means of an "information," just as the 1857 code allowed prosecution of slaves on "information." Informations resembled grand jury indictments in that they accused defendants of some crime. Prosecuting attorneys wrote both informations and indictments, but informations, unlike indictments, did not need grand jury approval. And when a prosecuting attorney was not around, clerks could, and often did, write informations themselves. Once a prosecuting attorney, or a clerk, wrote an information, he could go immediately to trial. Reformers had long advocated abolishing grand juries in the name of greater efficiency, and Mississippians in 1865 clearly had no objection to eliminating that facet of popular participation in the criminal justice system to control former slaves.[97]

Although nothing in the letter of the County Court Act restricted the new courts to black defendants, legislators clearly intended to use the law as an instrument to curb black lawlessness. They expected whites to govern by taking blacks to court. Because northern cities had long ordered themselves through such a system, those expectations did not seem unreasonable.[98] A newspaper explained the courts as made necessary by "the new condition of affairs." Their business would be to hear and determine cases involving "freedmen, vagrants, &c."; Mississippians called the tribunals "Freedmen's Courts."[99] Justices of the peace would continue to handle less serious crimes, but county courts met monthly to mete out the kind of immediate justice whites assumed blacks required.

Legislators tried to make county courts function like slave courts. County courts, unlike circuit courts, could impose physical punishment on convicted defendants. They could not use the lash as slave courts had, but they could impose "corporeal punishment, by suspending the party convicted by the thumbs."[100] Because probate judges ran county courts with two justices of the peace, defendants entering the courts faced a panel of judges, as had enslaved defendants.[101]

Defendants could also put their fate in the hands of an all-white jury. Antebellum lawmakers had denied slaves access to juries except in capital cases. Their postbellum counterparts did discourage jury trials for blacks but did not prohibit them. In county courts, defendants could choose trial by jury or trial by judge, but choosing trial by jury foreclosed all hope of appeal. Those choosing trial before a judge could appeal their conviction to the circuit court, which would hear the case with a jury de novo, but could go no higher. Lawmakers allowed no bill of exceptions in either court, so there would be no transcript of testimony or recorded judges' instructions. Thus, they expected county courts to create a record, but one insufficient for appeal. When county court cases did reach Mississippi's High Court of Errors and Appeals, the justices ruled that they had no jurisdiction.[102]

Critics complained that the new laws cost too much. These arguments came in two forms. Convinced that blacks could not be disciplined by courts bound to follow common-law procedures, some observers thought the courts a waste of taxpayers' money. They found galling the expense of maintaining a new network of courts in almost perpetual session to accomplish something done before with little expense. "There is a petition going round," one Mississippian noted, "recommending or instructing our representative to abolish or repeal the Freedman's court in this county as it is a verry great expense to the county with out much good arising from it." The writer calculated the court's cost at $150 each month, "which has to be raised by Taxation, the people cannot Support themselves and pay Such Taxes, particularly when there are so few benefitted."[103] Obviously the writer meant that few *whites* benefited from the new courts. He seems to have understood quite well that the courts offered an alternative to extralegal control of labor, albeit an alternative he thought too costly. Just as white conservatives would later complain that so-called carpetbagger regimes squandered the taxpayers' money, some now complained that the county court system wasted tax dollars.

Debt and the lawsuits to collect them reinforced the general hostility that such men harbored toward courts. Regardless of their feelings about race, debtors were hostile to the idea of a court constantly in session, especially when they discovered that county courts threatened poorer whites, too. In addition to criminal work, county courts had jurisdiction in all matters of debt where the principal owed did not exceed $250. They were authorized to issue attachments and garnishments to collect such debts.[104] Meeting monthly, county courts ended the respite that debtors had once enjoyed between circuit court sessions. Debtors' correspondence reveals their anger at this. One man apprehensively noted that "our circuit court comes on Monday next month" before complaining bitterly that the new "freedman's courts" met every month.[105] So many residents owed money, one Mississippian wrote, that "the Lawyers alone desire a session of the court and *not one man in fifty* desires any law for the collection of debts."[106] Another wrote that "everything I have is subject to the Law" and argued against efforts "to throw open the courts and begin a remorseless raid on the little that remains."[107] One debtor concluded, "I think our Legislators Legislated too much."[108]

The grumbling did not stop Warren's new county court from organizing in January 1866. Warren Cowan served as probate judge, which made him judge of the county court, a position he held from January 1, 1866, until his removal by military authorities on March 1, 1869. A descendant of one of the pioneer settlers of Vicksburg, Cowan had joined the Vicksburg bar in 1859 and a Confederate artillery battery two years later. The county court law required him to sit with two associate judges. All justices of the peace in Mississippi were to assemble at their respective courthouses on the first Monday in January to elect two of their number to serve as associate judges, and Warren County's justices chose Matthew Laughlin and William Brown. Although the law allowed the court to examine and cross-examine witnesses without an attorney for the state, the county could employ counsel for the state. After Warren County's justices selected associate judges, Cowan and his new assistants chose Confederate army veteran Roswell V. Booth to prosecute for the state.[109]

Legislators had designed the court over which Cowan would preside for easy access. The slave patrol no longer rode, but any citizen could bring a complaint against a former slave. The presence of Union troops likely made local officials hesitate to use their new court to punish errant blacks, however. In January, when the court first met, virtually every defendant identifiable by race was white. But officials quickly shed their reluctance to move against the freed people. In February blacks made up a larger percentage, and in March a still larger portion. By April and May most defendants were black. Passage of the Civil Rights Act broke that trend, however. A new assistant commissioner for Mississippi's Freedmen's Bureau distributed copies of the law and told his subordinates that it forbade enforcement of any discriminatory state statutes. Lawmen from all over Mississippi contacted bureau officials to ask if they could continue enforcing the Black Code. Upon being told that they faced heavy fines and imprisonment if they enforced discriminatory laws, most of these officers stopped doing so.[110] In Warren County, half of surviving case files from 1866 fall between January and April and whites again began making up an increasingly larger percentage of defendants.[111]

Legislators expected white employers to use the courts to control blacks, but a system based on popular initiation and discretion encourages a degree of popular control.[112] Whites concerned that the new courts would not be restricted to disciplining blacks realized their worst fears. Although anyone, in theory, could persuade the prosecuting attorney or court clerk to write an information, victims initiated most cases in county court, and they usually charged other whites rather than freed people. Whites made up 80 percent of victims and 60 percent of defendants. The courts became vehicles for controlling crime rather than imposing racial discipline.

Cowan and his juries seemed as willing to convict whites as blacks. Of whites accused by county court informations, only 15.6 percent won a not guilty verdict; juries and judges convicted 64.2 percent. The remainder did not go to trial, and their cases often ended when officers could not locate the accused. But 31.4 percent of black defendants won acquittals; juries and judges convicted only 49 percent. Again, the remaining defendants never made it to trial.[113] Perhaps more blacks were innocent than whites. It seems entirely likely that white accusers too quickly charged African Americans with a theft, and any prosecutor urging a white jury to convict a black defendant for a crime against another black faced white indifference.

County court judges threatened the rights of white defendants as often as those of freed slaves. On at least one occasion Judge Cowan acted as a one-man grand jury, questioning witnesses in secret session about illegal gambling in Vicksburg. When one white witness proved uncooperative, Cowan jailed him. But the prisoner filed for a writ of habeas corpus, and the criminal court judge released him.[114] County court may have been created to control blacks, but a judge acting as one-man grand jury threatened whites' prerogatives.

Had whites used county courts to control labor, their principal business would have been enforcing the law against vagrancy. Although the courts did try vagrants, they primarily went after petty thieves, whites as well as blacks. Sixty percent of defendants stood charged with some crime against property, almost always theft; another 12 percent faced vagrancy charges. Among extant cases in Warren County, all prosecutions for vagrancy came in January or April, months in which vagrants made up a majority of defendants in court. Almost 70 percent of defendants were women, although the record does not explain what they had done to be labeled "vagrants." Perhaps the court wanted to control prostitution, but that is not certain. Larceny cases appear in all but two terms for which papers survive, and two-thirds of all existing files document theft prosecutions.[115]

Part of the reason for this concentration on petty theft must be that many labor-controlling provisions of Mississippi's Black Code never went into effect or did so only briefly. The military squelched some of the code's most discriminatory provisions, and the state's attorney general issued opinions that eased some of the harsher provisions of the apprentice and vagrancy laws. But most white Mississippians seem never to have been convinced that law was the best tool to control freed black laborers. The county court law proved the most enduring element of the Black Code. It remained on the books until 1870, but local officials in some counties prevented county courts from operating effectively and insisted they had little use for them. In Lafayette County, for example, few blacks ever appeared in county court. That undoubtedly shows black skepticism of the courts and also demonstrates that local whites did not rely on the court to control blacks. In Lafayette County as in Warren County, there were few prosecutions of blacks for vagrancy, illegal meetings, or similar petty charges. Even the laws against enticing blacks away from their white employers proved dead letters in both counties.[116]

Although whites doubted that courts could effectively discipline former slaves, African Americans came out of emancipation eager to use the legal system. Trapped for years in the lawless environment of slavery, they hungered for an institution where they could resolve disputes. In his reminiscences, former slave John Roy Lynch recalled that the freed people were "determined to take advantage of the smallest and most unimportant offense to 'come to law.'" Denied access to law for so long, they now saw legal process as a "glorious privilege."[117] The Freedmen's Bureau encouraged such feelings, often advising former slaves to take complaints to court. Bureau agents offered legal advice, explaining state laws, counseling, and generally helping freed people assert their legal rights in court. When state officials seized freedmen for carrying guns in violation of state law, federal officers intervened on the side of the former slaves.[118] In at least one case, agents considered hiring lawyers to represent freed people in court although there is no evidence they actually did so.[119]

But everyone recognized county courts as bastions of prejudice. Blacks wanted to go to court, but they were not fools. African Americans could not participate in county courts as jurors or judges. In December 1865 an agent stationed in Skipworth Landing observed that the county court threw out cases initiated by blacks.[120] Another agent complained that courts administered laws "very loosely to say the least."[121] The county court judge in Port Gibson shocked a bureau agent by declaring the federal civil rights law unconstitutional.[122] The Neshoba County judge revealed his regard for the county court law by showing up for work drunk.[123] Understandably, even people eager for law hesitated to enter such courts.

While the central thrust of county court justice followed a white model, black desires did shape the margins of county court activity. African Americans initiated 20 percent of the cases in county court. (By contrast, their complaints only launched 10 percent of the cases in circuit court.) A growing number of lawyers were available to blacks or anyone else seeking to go to court. In 1860 census enumerators found twenty-one lawyers in Warren County, all southern-born except for one who was British; the 1870 census counted forty-eight lawyers. In 1865 the *Herald* observed dryly, "If we do not have an abundance of law in this city it will not be for want of lawyers."[124]

Some white lawyers rewarded the loyalty of family servants with professional services. J. W. M. Harris did so for a freedman he knew only as Charles. When Harris's own slaves fled after emancipation, Charles fortuitously appeared to take their place. Perhaps he recognized the need for a white protector. When Charles ran afoul of the law in 1866, Harris did not hesitate to represent him without charge, even petitioning the governor on his behalf.[125] Other freed slaves, caught without a white benefactor, had to rely on carpetbaggers. In the wake of the Union army, northern lawyers came to Vicksburg; by 1870 there were eight. These northerners may well have solicited black clients or at least taken their cases more readily than white southern lawyers.[126]

Warren County blacks could participate in county court trials as witnesses and thus influence their outcomes. Cowan allowed black testimony in his county court. The bureau persuaded state authorities to order other Mississippi judges to do likewise, but many outside Warren County refused. It was an especially egregious problem because former slaves regularly suffered from violence at the hands of whites.[127] In Warren County, Judges William Yerger and Josiah A. P. Campbell permitted blacks to testify as early as 1865. Campbell dismissed objections to black testimony with the argument that no black witness could hope to dupe "a jury of white men with all their knowledge of negro character."[128]

In some cases blacks accused whites of crimes. Seventeen-year-old Isaac Washington had been grazing his mule near a plum orchard when the orchard's owner, John Green, ordered some whites off his property. One of the white trespassers shouted back that he would leave the orchard only if the owner "had any gals up there." Washington laughed at the quip, and the enraged owner attacked him. Unable to open his knife to stab Washington, Green settled on flailing away at Washington's head with the knife handle. Afterward, Washington went to the nearest justice of the peace, who referred his complaint to the county court. A jury listened to Washington and Green and then convicted Green of assault.[129]

Even when county courts tried blacks, officers strove to follow proper procedures. One county attorney made his determination to adhere to the common law clear when he asked the governor if "the relation existing between the county attorney and court [is] the same as that which formerly obtained in England between the Law officer of the crown and the Court of the Kings Bench?"[130] Although the law proposed punishing blacks in ways reminiscent of slavery, most court officers expected them to do so under procedural constraints that were stricter than those of the old slave or magisterial courts.

When white lawyers adhered to the common law's procedural constraints they offered freed people less discriminatory justice. Blacks' use of habeas corpus demonstrates how opening the legal system to slaves worked to their advantage. Slaves had been released from jail through habeas corpus petitions before the war, but in that era the owners of black defendants had used habeas corpus to retrieve their property. Slaves benefited very little from the great writ; some might even have preferred jail to life on the plantation. Their owners could freely punish minor offenses with no thought of habeas corpus petitions or other legal procedures. But under the Black Codes the state prosecuted the entire range of misconduct, including the minor crimes planters had always punished outside the law. That meant that freed slaves jailed for the same kinds of crimes that once earned them an informal flogging could now challenge their imprisonment with habeas corpus petitions. Before, no argument had been possible, but the Black Codes opened a world where whites had to follow due process when disciplining laborers. For many freed slaves that must have been exhilarating, conveying the concrete reality of freedom for the first time. Earlier, they had not dared demand that owners explain why they had been imprisoned, but with emancipation blacks had the legal right to confront whites in court and insist that they justify their conduct before a judge, even if that judge was white and none too sympathetic. Stacks of habeas corpus petitions in Warren County court records give evidence of black determination to use the legal tools newly made available to them. For example, in December 1865, after the mayor had jailed his son for gambling, Charles Wright filed a habeas corpus petition to secure his release.[131] Under slavery, the son would not have been jailed for gambling; he would have been punished extralegally with no possibility for habeas corpus.

Habeas corpus could also be used to reduce unreasonable bail. In 1867 Warren County authorities set Wesley Jackson's bail at $2,000. Jackson's attorney reminded the court that his black client had no property and little prospect of raising bail money while in jail, "being dependent upon his daily labor for support." The judge lowered Jackson's bail, and he went free.[132] In 1866 a trio of former slaves identified in court documents only as "Henry, Hardy, and Richard" complained when a judge sentenced them to jail until they could pay the costs of their prosecution. In their habeas corpus petition they pointed out that they had no property and therefore no prospect of ever paying any costs while in jail. The county judge ordered them released.[133]

African Americans used the county court and other Warren County courts to challenge Mississippi's Black Code itself. Freedmen's Bureau agents encouraged them, offering legal advice where needed. Elvira Harrison, Lizzie Alexander, and Lucinda Jones forced county court prosecutor Roswell Booth to admit that he had not written an information for their arrest until after they went to jail. He also had to concede that the only evidence of their vagrancy was their failure to produce a certificate of employment. The court kept the three petitioners in custody, but three black women had forced a white man to explain himself in court. Although by 1867 Mississippi no longer enforced the code's provision that allowed whites virtually to re-enslave black children as "apprentices," Alfred Warren told the criminal court judge that a white man had illegally detained his fourteen-year-old twins. Pea Powan charged that James C. Harris had illegally detained his four minor children. Powan, an illiterate freedman, went against a former slaveowner using the Black Code to preserve slavery. In 1860 Harris, a planter, had owned forty slaves and $25,000 in real estate. The outcomes of the cases are not clear from surviving court papers, but the judge did issue the writs Warren and Powan demanded.[134]

The habeas corpus writ allowed freed people to reassemble their families and thereby build communities. Parents wanted freedom for their children to resuscitate their families, of course, but the writ helped newly freed people accumulate resources. Fathers and mothers recovered children, and husbands sought wives. A. H. Post and his wife, Milberry, had been jailed for violating miscegenation laws. But, Post asserted, they

had not done so. They were both black. In another case of a husband seeking his spouse, Albert Crump recovered his wife through the habeas corpus writ.[135] Children and wives contributed to the household economy.
Gardening, foraging, and home manufacture required the labor of the
whole family, not just adult males. Freed people used some of the proceeds
of household production to build and rebuild churches and schools.[136]

Blacks also sought legal protection for their property. Impoverished,
they had few belongings, but that made their property all the more valuable to them. Blacks charged other blacks with theft. Eliza Parker accused
George Bailey and Gus Davis of killing her hog, for example, and Caroline Green complained that John Cassidy had taken her pocketbook.[137]
Without a grand jury it is impossible to know what standards the prosecutor and clerk applied to prospective complainants. Many blacks must
have brought reports of crimes that did not result in an indictment. Un-
fortunately, no papers survive to document these rejected complaints.

Blacks entered court involuntarily, as defendants, more often than they
did as complainants. Although blacks made up 20 percent of the population of complainants in county court, 39 percent of defendants were
black. Those defendants received far more due process than they would
have had as slaves charged with minor crimes. Even though the county
court law did not require the same full record required in circuit court
cases, judges and lawyers tended to follow common-law standards rather than the letter of the statute. Defendants faced juries required to adhere to the same standards when blacks were prosecuted as they did when
whites were prosecuted.

Judge Cowan's insistence on this procedural equity contributed to the
low conviction rate for blacks. Although the county court law did not
require preservation of jury instructions, in fourteen extant county court
case files the clerk filed such instructions anyway. Some consist of nothing more than pro forma directions to acquit if jurors harbored reasonable doubt. But Cowan subjected informations to careful scrutiny even
though appellate courts had long since moved away from some of the
rigid requirements of the common law. Appeals courts usually refused to
overturn convictions on minor or technical errors in the indictment as
long as indictments accurately captured the substance of the charge.
Nonetheless, Cowan told jurors they must free defendants—even guilty
black defendants—charged with sloppily drawn informations. Jurors
acquitted one black woman after Cowan told them that any "variance"
between the evidence and the information must result in acquittal. In

Cowan's court even minor discrepancies between the information and the evidence tripped up prosecutors. One African American accused of larceny won his freedom after Cowan told jurors that "if the defendant at the bar be charged in the information as a free man of color, and the jury are satisfied that he is boy, and not a man, they must acquit."[138]

Cowan's instructions sometimes erected a standard prosecutors would have met more easily with white defendants than blacks. For example, names could be a problem for whites trying to identify newly freed slaves accurately. In 1865 the Warren County sexton's reports routinely identified whites more fully than blacks, whom they listed only by race and gender—for example, "woman, colored."[139] Even as late as 1873, the sexton sometimes gave only the first name of dead African Americans.[140] Cowan was intolerant of failures to identify defendants correctly and lectured prosecutors that they must prove the name as charged.[141] One incredulous jury asked, "If the Jury believe that the Boy is guilty—but that the state has failed to establish that his name is Philip Wiggins as charged in the information—are they bound to acquit him?" Cowan scribbled a terse answer: "Yes." Wiggins went free.[142]

Mississippi's county courts typified the South's legal response to emancipation. After the Civil War, most southern states had either created new inferior courts or enlarged existing ones to combat an expected wave of black criminality. South Carolina lawmakers called their new tribunals district courts and said frankly that the new courts would try "small and mean causes" involving black people, owners and servants, owners and apprentices, and employers and laborers.[143] Later legislatures were more discreet. They did not say, for example, that they intended Georgia's and Texas's county courts and Florida's county criminal courts to serve as black courts but mandated the tribunals to try minor criminal charges speedily.[144] Virginia did not create a new court system after the Civil War, but legislators there established special police companies authorized to search for stolen property at any time on the affidavit of anyone claiming to be a victim of theft.[145] Alabama expanded the powers of its justices of the peace to try all misdemeanor cases.[146]

Warren County courts may have been atypical in how they dealt with legal procedure because the Union army made Vicksburg its headquarters. The three-way tension between state officials, Washington, and the Mississippi Bureau greatly influenced the day-to-day operations of the county court in Warren County. But correspondence from the bureau agent in Vicksburg documents no interference in local courts whatsoever.[147] In counties where agents tried to influence county courts, they generally limited themselves to observing the proceedings. As the agent in Brookhaven recorded, "I have been present when I could at all trials where freemen were concerned, telling the court that I was there for the purpose of taking notes."[148] Often agents had little training in the law and felt powerless to influence the work of lawyers.[149]

The presence of Union troops in Vicksburg did not prevent Cowan from literally hanging some freedmen by their thumbs. Some Freedmen's Bureau agents accepted landlords' arguments that jailing black thieves unfairly punished employers by depriving them of their laborers' time. Moreover, Union soldiers had seen their own comrades hung by the thumbs, not to mention shot by firing squads and stretched on racks. Repeated exposure to such experiences hardened soldiers to military discipline, just as their commanders intended.[150]

Bureau agents came from the ranks of such men. Correspondence between one Georgia agent and his superiors illustrates army acceptance of thumb-hanging. When the agent asked his superior whether hanging freed people by their thumbs, "the punishment hitherto adopted," had been abolished, an officer assured him it had not "provided it is administered in minor cases only and with extreme caution."[151] Agents defended such corporal punishment, observing that fines punished not only the malefactor but also that person's family. Jail also punished employers by robbing them of the freed person's work. Hanging by the thumbs, this bureau agent concluded, improved the morale of black labor.[152]

Bureau agents in Warren County must have had similar feelings about this sort of torture.[153] Although Vicksburg swarmed with agents, Warren County's court regularly ordered convicted thieves to be hanged by their thumbs. The sheriff hanged Hardy Henderson by his thumbs for two hours a day for ten days after the county court convicted him of stealing blackberries valued at just 50 cents. Such sentences were hardly uncommon; the sheriff regularly hanged males convicted of theft by their thumbs. Yet Henderson was white. Normally, only blacks received ten-day sentences. Whites convicted of the same crimes were also hanged by their thumbs two hours a day but normally for five days or less. Officials jailed women thieves for ten days and fed them only bread and water.[154]

Cowan's professional self-esteem may have led him to guard defendants' rights. Judges who bypassed the law risked losing the respect of the bar, even if they cut corners in the service of white supremacy. Fragmentary evidence from other Mississippi county courts suggests that other judges ran their courts much as Cowan did.[155] The need of judges to establish their legal competence was the same everywhere. Cowan understood that he earned the respect of local lawyers by demonstrating legal acumen. That ambition, more than any desire to please note-taking northerners, may have controlled his conduct. The experiences of two Republican judges later in Reconstruction illustrate the compulsion to follow legal procedures. The Republican county court judge in Leake County confessed that he had "never spent a day in a law school, or ever slept a single night in a law office" before assuming his duties. The same judge won the respect of local lawyers by requiring them to follow the same procedures in his court as they did in circuit court, chastising those who did not.[156] In contrast, when a Republican judge in North Carolina proved himself "ignorant, *obstinate* and *unprincipled*," one lawyer accepted disbarment rather than restrain his contempt. He confided in his diary that he felt humiliated to practice law before such a man.[157]

To win the respect of the lawyers who appeared before him, Cowan proved a stickler for legal technicalities, a fact apparent in surviving county court case files. Cowan, an early and vocal "white-liner" who urged whites to unite, regardless of party, to eject blacks from power, harbored no charitable feelings toward African Americans.[158] There is no evidence from his subsequent life that Cowan was anything but a particularly committed white racist, determined to eject blacks from political influence and power. Yet despite his avowed racism and connection with the racial hardliners who eventually violently "redeemed" Warren County from Republican rule, Cowan followed the law in his court.

Ultimately, his formalism, although displeasing ordinary whites, did most blacks little good. Very few took grievances against whites to his court. Undoubtedly, most felt intimidated by a court dominated by white men and hesitated even to enter it. Moreover, it cost money to bring a grievance to court. Complainants had to make a bond for themselves to appear as witnesses, and whites could refuse to make bonds for blacks they did not like. When whites committed crimes against blacks, they could count on neighbors to protect them from authorities. One Alabama Freedmen's Bureau officer concluded, "As against freedmen the majority of whites are a unit and even honorable men, otherwise, will vouch for persons of, to say the least, doubtful character as 'high social Gentlemen.'"[159]

Using law to punish freed slaves inevitably ensnared them in due process. Small crimes that once led only to an informal flogging now produced juries, witnesses, and "technicalities." Law proved less effective than the extralegal methods many whites preferred. While county courts ultimately benefited blacks little, they had significant impact on white attitudes toward law, the legal culture. People judge their courts effective when those courts control the minor crimes people see more often than major felonies.[160] County courts were supposed to punish precisely those "quality-of-life" misdemeanors. The Black Code courts represented an experiment, an effort to use law to resume a domination previously sustained outside the law. The experiment failed.

Republicans condemned the Black Codes as a particularly heinous expression of governmental power, but white southerners understood their laws differently. They saw the codes as moving African Americans away from extralegal plantation justice and into the legal system. Terrible as the laws were, most white southerners thought the alternative was extralegal violence. In a constitutional system, even discriminatory law leaves lawyers room to maneuver and clever plaintiffs opportunities to test for inconsistencies.

6

Republican Reconstruction

Historians have often described African Americans' ascent to power after emancipation as a revolutionary event.[1] On one level, the movement of emancipated slaves from cotton fields to public office certainly did represent change in the most fundamental sense of the word. To southern whites, the sight of blacks serving in the army, in Congress, and in state legislatures made it seem as if life itself had been turned upside down, the bottom rail literally and abruptly moved to the top.

But those who have described blacks' climb to power as "revolutionary" generally cast the upheaval in class rather than ideological terms. That has the unfortunate effect of treating blacks as a nascent proletariat and obscuring how they saw themselves—as free citizens seeking assimilation into a pluralistic society. Constitutionally, African Americans pursued little change at all, buying into antebellum notions of citizenship. The notion that organic law guided by a tradition of respect for rights controlled and limited the power of authorities and individuals appealed to freed people. African Americans embraced traditional constitutional values.[2]

* * *

President Andrew Johnson himself resisted black voting and political power as too revolutionary. But by 1866 his policies were in disrepute in the North. White mob violence against blacks in states where the president had hastily returned antebellum elites to power angered many northerners. Johnson hurt himself further when he campaigned for his policies. On a speaking tour, he could not resist ill-tempered rejoinders to hecklers, incoherent tirades against critics, and stalwart defenses of former Confederates. Ulysses S. Grant grumbled privately that the speeches were a national disgrace. It sickened him to watch Johnson destroy himself or, as he put it, "make speeches on his way to his own funeral."[3] In 1866 voters showed in off-year elections that they shared Grant's disgust. Enough Republicans won seats in the House and the Senate to override any presidential veto.[4]

Once in control of Reconstruction policies, congressional Republicans moved to extend citizenship rights to African Americans. They enacted the Reconstruction Act of 1867, which would make voters of freedmen. The law divided the Confederate states, except Tennessee, into five districts commanded by generals empowered to protect life and property with military force. Seceded states could be recognized by Congress only if they wrote new constitutions allowing manhood suffrage and ratified the Fourteenth Amendment, which defined American citizenship so that black men could not be excluded.[5]

Johnson tried to thwart Congress by appointing only conservative generals to the military districts. Within weeks of the passage of the Reconstruction Act, General Edward O. C. Ord traveled to Vicksburg to take command of Military District 4, Arkansas and Mississippi. Ord, the most conservative of all the generals appointed under the act, could either remove or retain civil officials put in office under Johnson. He was to register all black men as voters while excluding certain Confederates from the rolls. That task completed, he would organize elections for delegates to state constitutional conventions that would write black political equality into organic law. To accomplish this, Ord established fifteen posts in Mississippi, garrisoned by two thousand soldiers.[6]

The Vicksburg post, once the home to tens of thousands of Union soldiers during the Civil War, now housed fewer than three hundred.[7] Many had fought through the Civil War, and some were veteran Indian fighters. They found Vicksburg a boring camp. Several entertained themselves by sneaking into town, getting drunk, and fighting with local police. In some instances they befriended whites, verbally abused leading Republicans, and, in one case, physically attacked a Republican politician.[8] And their numbers continued to shrink. By 1870 only a single company remained, and the base commander wrote to his superiors that the post served no useful purpose. The Vicksburg post closed on June 2, 1870.[9]

Such a small force meant that loyal whites wanting to win over those favoring resistance and opposition could not claim that the army gave them no choice. They had to make their case on its merits. The Vicksburg *Herald* urged whites not to boycott military-supervised registration, warning against "political hypochondria which would yield to the conqueror more than he would ask for."[10] "White people are everywhere showing their ready acquiescence in the new order of things which makes the colored people their equals before the law," the *Herald* announced. It still imagined, however, that blacks could be made to vote with their former owners.[11]

But other whites understood that a new day had dawned. William McCardle recognized that whites could resist freedmen's citizenship demands only through unprecedented unity of action. Political squabbling of the sort that characterized antebellum Warren County had become obsolete. Although once editor of the Vicksburg *Whig,* McCardle insisted that all whites must unite under the banner of the Democratic Party. Now editing the Vicksburg *Daily Times,* he saw no point in trying to placate the enemy. He denounced Ord and the other military district commanders as "infamous, cowardly, and abandoned villains, who, instead of wearing shoulder straps, and ruling millions of people, should have their heads shaved, their ears cropped, their foreheads branded, and their precious persons lodged in a penitentiary." McCardle reprinted a letter from a white conservative in Richmond, Virginia, complaining that military authorities there had rigged elections on behalf of blacks. Ord briefly jailed McCardle, bringing him before a military commission, but could not scuttle the editor's crusade for white solidarity.[12]

Ord's power to impose a new regime on Vicksburg and Mississippi came chiefly from his authority to remove local government officials.[13] In September he dismissed Vicksburg's city marshal, five of seven city council members, the sheriff, and one member of the county board of supervisors from office, replacing them with white Republican appointees.[14] The most important officer ejected was the sheriff. Traditionally the boss of the county, Mississippi sheriffs could enrich themselves through the fees they collected. For six years the man Ord appointed sheriff, former army officer Charles Furlong, had spearheaded the Republican effort to win over Warren County. He won the loyalty of black voters but was careful not to burn his bridges to white conservatives. As head of the Vicksburg Republican "ring," he hesitated to back blacks for important county offices for fear of losing all claims to legitimacy among whites. To the dismay of the local Republican newspaper, Furlong awarded the county's lucrative printing contract to the Democratic *Herald.* As a result, conservative whites sometimes defended Republican Furlong's name in the columns of their newspaper.[15]

Four years after the 1866 elections and three years after Congress voted blacks into the polity, African Americans in the Furlong government held only low-level positions. Of twenty Vicksburg police officers, nine were black. Five blacks served as constables, and the sexton and assistant jailor were both black.[16] Furlong carefully doled out enough patronage to blacks to maintain their support but not so much as to alienate whites.

The limits of Ord's commitment to extending traditional citizenship rights to freedmen became apparent on the Davis Bend Plantation once owned by Joseph and Jefferson Davis. On that isolated peninsula, Benjamin Montgomery, once a slave, worked to organize an all-black utopia. Montgomery had been a special favorite of Joseph Davis and shared his former owner's vision of an ideal community. In 1866 Davis secretly sold his plantation to Montgomery, who a year later emerged publicly as the leader of the Davis Bend community. Despite Montgomery's accomplishments, Ord tried to appoint a white carpetbagger as justice of the peace there. But when the white man could not make the required bond and crime threatened to rage out of control, Ord had no choice but to appoint Montgomery to the post. He did so on September 10, 1867, making Montgomery the first black man appointed to public office in Mississippi. He may have been the first in the entire South.[17]

Under Montgomery's leadership, blacks showed their determination to embrace a view of citizenship that whites saw as radical. But when Davis Bend residents took their annoyances with one another to court they merely pursued traditional citizenship rights, revealing a touching faith in the power of law. In one typical case, Robert Johnson made affidavit that Mary Hudson had used vulgar language toward his wife. Arthur Gales complained that Isaiah Hunter had killed his dog. A woman charged that Harvey Green had ridden her horse without permission. Montgomery and his successor, William Lewis, Jr., also heard cases of assault: roughly a third of all the cases passing before them alleged crimes of violence. Although most laborers in Davis Bend owned little, nearly a quarter of the cases in Montgomery's court involved theft. Often the thieves stole trifles; owners of watermelon patches did not hesitate to go to court with cases of watermelon larceny, for example. Instances of abusive speech made up another 18 percent of the cases, and a scattering of miscellaneous crimes filled out the docket. Montgomery and Lewis imposed small fines, usually a dollar, dismissed some cases, and negotiated solutions in others. They allowed convicted defendants who had little money to work off fines; sometimes they simply ordered the stolen goods returned, with no fine collected.[18]

Ord's reluctance to countenance Montgomery's constitutionalism was matched by his distaste for black voting. He vowed, however, to enforce the law and by fall had registered 79,176 black Mississippians.[19] In Warren County, Alston Mygatt supervised Ord's registration drive. Although he had originally come from New York, where he had gone to college with the abolitionist Gerrit Smith, Mygatt had long lived in Vicksburg. In 1856 the local R. G. Dun and Company reporter had described the transient book publisher as "a very correct worthy man of g[oo]d bus[iness] hab[it]s." But the Civil War radicalized Mygatt. He publicly opposed secession and after the fall of Vicksburg and slavery advocated breaking plantations into small farms to create a more democratic social structure. Four weeks after Vicksburg surrendered to Grant, Alston Mygatt formed the first Union League in the city—and in Mississippi. His chairmanship of the Republican State Executive Committee demonstrates the link between political activism and the Union League. On the board of registrars, Mygatt reviewed the credentials of would-be white voters. "It became my duty," he said later, "to make diligent inquiry" into the loyalty of whites wanting to vote. Unlike Furlong, Mygatt made no pretense of friendship with whites and only allowed two prewar officeholders to vote. Outraged whites ostracized him, and the Dun agent now described him as suffering from "nigger on the brain" and unworthy of credit. In 1868 newspapers condemned him as an "imbecile old wretch." Mygatt claimed his opponents tried to assassinate him and burned his property.[20]

Ord's registration drive also energized African Americans. Given the vote, they organized and politicked. One advertisement for an early black political rally called for "all persons who are interested in the reconstruction of Mississippi" to meet at the colored Baptist Church. Blacks held another meeting at Vicksburg's Apollo Hall for "those in favor of Reconstruction." Although the *Herald* wrote that "we trust we shall hear no more of such meetings" and warned against "secret political associations," blacks joined Union Leagues, with secret oaths and rituals.[21] That seemed radical to whites, but Vicksburg had a long history of such clubbing. Antebellum whites had established militia units, the Mechanics Mutual Benefit Society, Irish brotherhoods, temperance leagues, and fire-fighting companies along class lines.[22] In their secret meetings Union Leaguers pledged fealty to such conventional symbols of American political culture as the ballot box, the flag, and the Constitution.

In political meetings African Americans expressed their new citizenship through vigorous free speech. When black politicians denounced political rivals, they showed they understood the meaning of freedom and citizenship. The *Herald*'s hope that blacks would vote with former owners was as misplaced as its fear that blacks would form a solid political phalanx unblemished by dissent. Politically active freedmen began fighting among themselves in a manner characteristic of free societies everywhere. Their public debates certainly recalled the factionalism characteristic of antebellum white politics. At the time, white Republicans split in fights over spoils, putting avarice ahead of principle. Many black Republicans got into fights for the same reason, but they also fought over policy issues and who should lead Mississippi's newest citizens.[23]

The first publicly visible political divisions among black Vicksburgers came as they prepared to cast ballots for delegates to the constitutional convention. Albert Johnson and Thomas W. Stringer emerged as the city's leading black politicians. Born in Kentucky, Johnson had been a plasterer in Vicksburg, a Mississippi slave who worked his way to "nominal" status. "I was actually free," he explained later, "but under the law of Mississippi had to have a white agent, or ostensible Master." Johnson plied his trade with no white supervision. With the arrival of the Union army, Johnson served as a scout, pointing out the location of Confederate gun batteries.[24] As early as 1865 he became a leader of Mississippi blacks, serving as president of the state's black convention that met in Vicksburg.

Unlike Johnson, Stringer had not worked his way up from the depths of Mississippi slavery. Born in Maryland, he had grown up free in Ohio and served as a Methodist missionary in Ohio and Canada before the Civil War. A gifted organizer, Stringer formed black Masonic lodges, churches, and schools. Active in the Union League, he helped found the Republican Party in Mississippi and voted to disfranchise Confederates. Stringer later represented the moderate wing of the state's Republican Party. He claimed that Ku Klux Klan violence had been exaggerated, opposed establishment of Alcorn University, and served on the board of directors of the Memphis and Vicksburg Railroad, the only black man to do so. In 1873 Democrats would support his candidacy for state office.[25]

Stringer, like all African Americans of the time, took pride in his citizenship, his loyalty to flag and country. Johnson's 1867 condemnation of Stringer as "disloyal" hurt. Surviving records do not reveal why Johnson thought as he did, but Union League rhetoric stressed loyalty. Blacks typically reserved the word *disloyal* for Confederates. Johnson declared that disloyalty had caused the Civil War; white enemies of black citizenship had been Confederates. Blacks had remained true to the Union and displayed the American flag at their rallies, where they justified themselves with language taken from the Declaration of Independence.

When a white newspaper asked whether Johnson understood that "brother Stringer, colored, has as much right to his opinion, as Mr. Johnson," he retorted that he had no wish to prevent Stringer from expressing his views. Had that been the case he could have followed the course whites had so often pursued: using "cow hide, a bucket of tar, and a bag of feathers." Johnson then made his point, differentiating black political consciousness from that of white conservatives, "I don't believe it right that any of the human family should be so treated." He reminded readers that he, unlike Stringer, was no carpetbagger by signing his name "Albert Johnson, A resident of this place, for thirty-six years."[26]

The letter, published in the Vicksburg *Herald*, stung Stringer, who denounced Johnson as "one of the most perfect knaves, black or white, that can be found in the State of Mississippi." Unlike Johnson, Stringer could not invoke his long residence in Mississippi, but he claimed to have opposed slavery for thirty-four years. Reminding readers that he was a minister of the gospel of Christ, Stringer urged blacks to be controlled by the word of God and "not by the rule of Mr. A. Johnson."[27]

Congressional Reconstruction laws mandated new state constitutions, and that gave black political aspirants such as Stringer and Johnson fresh opportunities to advance. In July 1867 Republicans began meeting to organize their party.[28] In November Mississippians voted for delegates to a state convention to rewrite the constitution. Few blacks failed to vote, but only six thousand whites turned out.[29] Black political activism frightened whites. As blacks organized to vote in the November election rumors of a black insurrection swirled through the white community. Such talk even panicked Ord. After asking subordinates to report anyone making "inflamatory" speeches to freed people, Ord asked Washington for help in maintaining order. Unimpressed, Grant persuaded President Johnson to remove Ord instead.[30]

Along with three whites, Vicksburg sent both Stringer and Johnson to the convention, where they joined sixteen other black delegates. Although conservatives ridiculed the gathering as the "Black and Tan Convention," the seventy-nine white delegates outnumbered those few blacks in attendance by more than four to one. The political culture must have seemed far stranger to the former slave than to Stringer. Johnson missed few votes and served on the committee assigned to write a new bill of rights, but the official proceedings document few of his contributions. Like most delegates, he compiled an undistinguished record, offering few proposals and voting against a proposition to guarantee legal representation for poor people in court. Such a proposal was far ahead of its time. Legal representation for persons too poor to hire an attorney would have greatly evened the scales of justice in Mississippi in 1868. Johnson did not explain his vote but likely realized that his impoverished state could ill afford the luxury of hiring lawyers for poor people.[31]

Stringer, by contrast, offered an articulate voice at the convention. He served on several important committees and opposed conservative efforts to derail the gathering. When conservatives tried to make every delegate pay his own way, Stringer objected. He led the unsuccessful fight to table the conservatives' proposed ban on interracial marriages. Only ten delegates—not including Johnson—voted with him. Stringer played a key role in persuading the convention to go on record in support of congressional efforts to impeach Andrew Johnson. He was also instrumental in shaping the proposed constitution, suggesting language for the new bill of rights that eliminated racial restrictions on suffrage.[32]

Both Stringer and Johnson must have been ambivalent about the convention's most controversial issue. White Republicans proposed disfranchising white conservatives, which some thought a fitting punishment for traitors who had enslaved African Americans. Disfranchisement of whites, even former Confederates, contradicted black rhetoric promoting equality for all and universal suffrage, however. Stringer proposed allowing everyone to vote except those disfranchised by the Fourteenth Amendment or convicted for a felony.

Edward J. Castello, a white Republican delegate, introduced a far more divisive proposal, one that betrayed blacks' rhetoric of equality while seeming to affirm it. He wanted to require that anyone seeking to vote, serve on a jury, or hold office take an oath not only affirming past loyalty to the Union but also supporting the political equality of all men. Like all other Republicans and everyone else, he knew full well that few white conservatives in Mississippi could take such an oath. Republicans should have known that such a proposal would help delegitimize governments elected without white votes. Historian William Harris has condemned Castello as a cynical "ultraradical" Missouri carpetbagger. He had opposed black voting as late as 1867 and in 1879 still served as the Republican collector of customs in Natchez and backed the Exodusters. But he opportunistically abandoned the Republican Party when it proved politically expedient to do so. Moderates commanded the votes to defeat the Castello plan, but conservative opposition backfired, driving moderates

into the ranks of radicals, and the measure passed. Stringer, Johnson, and
all the other black delegates but one supported Castello's proposal. Only
native white Mississippians opposed the measure; conservative Democrats resigned from the convention in protest.[33]

The refusal of native whites, even whites acting with Republicans, to
support disfranchisement should have been a warning. During the campaign to ratify the proposed constitution the Union League's power
peaked. Blacks turned out for huge rallies in support of the document,
but white conservatives rallied as well, making the most of the disfranchisement issue. Warren County voted for the constitution, but statewide
the document went down to defeat. Congress responded by passing a law
allowing President Grant to resubmit the constitution to voters, "either
the entire constitution, or separate provisions of the same," and Grant
ordered the disfranchisement provisions to be submitted on their own.
A new military commander, Adelbert Ames, discarded the neutrality of
his predecessors and worked vigorously on behalf of the proposed constitution and the Republican Party. In hope of currying favor with Grant,
Mississippi conservatives dropped their opposition to the constitution.
As a result, fewer than a thousand voters opposed ratification in 1869, and
the proposed constitution became the organic law of Mississippi. Because
whites generally did not vote in this election, it was black voters who rejected disfranchisement of whites. Apparently, the rank and file remained
committed to equal access to the voting box. Or perhaps they just understood the likely consequences of denying the right to vote to whites.[34]

Johnson, Stringer, and other black leaders at the constitutional convention championed equality before the law, however. Such rhetoric better
characterized postbellum black discourse than the disfranchisement vote.
Black rhetoric in Mississippi is not nearly so well documented as historians would like, but in the few records that survive blacks made clear their
commitment to the language of the Declaration of Independence. The
Union League promoted "freedom and universal justice" through pam-
phlets circulated among freed people. One of these documents, popularly
known as the "Loyal League Catechism," includes a dialogue between a
fictional white Republican and a black voter. The white man explained
that the Republican Party promoted civil rights and freedom whereas
Democrats favored slavery.

Blacks invoked the language of rights and constitutionalism as a sort
of talisman. In Union League meetings, for example, members prepared
an altar with a Bible, the Declaration of Independence, the Constitution,
an American flag, a gavel, a sword, a ballot box, and such emblems of

industry as a scythe and an anvil. Recruits would pledge to uphold the principles of the Declaration of Independence, maintain liberty, and uphold labor. They also sang "Hail Columbia" or the "Star-Spangled Banner" before placing one hand on the flag, raising the other toward heaven, and, as the "fire of liberty" blazed nearby, swore loyalty to the United States and promised to elect true Union men to political office.[35]

The gavels on Union League altars symbolized equal access to court, an important component of citizenship. Although whites preferred to discipline freed slaves outside the law, blacks pressed to move punishment of all crime into court. They eagerly sought to bring complaints against other blacks into the most formal forums available. They also wanted whites to take complaints against African Americans into court rather than beat or murder violators of some informal code of conduct. As frequent victims of white crime themselves, blacks needed some recourse at law.

Freedmen's service as magistrates and on juries reveals the limits of their conception of citizenship. The presence of blacks on juries seemed revolutionary to whites. But once in power, African Americans did not freely extend active service in court to poorer citizens. In that way they adhered to the same principles that had guided antebellum whites, who had also worked within class constraints when electing magistrates or picking jurors.

Blacks determined to bring black or white malefactors into the southern criminal justice system had to persuade justices of the peace to hear their complaints and take them seriously. Virtually every prosecution in the county began before some magistrate. A justice of the peace could discourage or encourage complainants. They decided whether a victim's story sounded credible enough to order an arrest, summoned witnesses, and listened to testimony. In the case of serious felonies, they decided whether a defendant would go to jail, post bond to await the next circuit court term, or go free. They adjudicated misdemeanors, mostly small fights, themselves.[36]

The best way to encourage black crime victims to go to court was to make freedmen justices of the peace, and under the Republicans more African Americans did become magistrates. During the 1870s half of Warren County's magistrates were black, and they made a difference. Black justices dispensed more informal justice than did circuit courts. While postbellum circuit court complaints alleged theft more often than other crimes, the majority of complainants who appeared before magistrates claimed to have been assaulted. In 235 magistrate cases between 1872 and 1875, black justices of the peace heard even more assault cases than did their white counterparts. That suggests, unsurprisingly, that poorer people got into fights more often than they were robbed.[37]

Small, informal courts could open the criminal justice system to new constituencies. Nineteenth-century Americans understood going to court as a masculine activity, one that women should not have to endure. Men tried to avoid bringing women to circuit court, even as witnesses to serious felonies, but they went to magistrates' courts more freely. Although only 2.1 percent of defendants in circuit court were women, 20 percent of defendants before magistrates were women. Twelve percent of victims in circuit court were women, whereas females made up 30 percent of the complainants before magistrates. Black magistrates welcomed women even more readily. Female defendants composed 21 percent of the total in black JP courts; in their white counterparts' courts, 14 percent were female.[38]

Grand jurors served as gatekeepers for the more formal sanctums of the criminal justice system. Magistrates had the power to order defendants in felony cases to jail; grand juries decided whether or not they stayed there. The composition of grand juries signaled the level of access blacks had to law. By very visibly presenting freed slaves as preservers of law, grand jury service performed an important symbolic function. Panels had a reputation for including the better sort in the county. If former slaves could gain entry, then it would be more difficult to deny that they had attained full citizenship rights. That would help ensure that not only slavery but also its trappings would be dead for sure.

Republicans wrote no radical new law opening jury service to freedmen. Delegates to the 1868 constitutional convention understood the importance of opening jury service to blacks but did little to change the existing statutory language for petit (or trial) jurors. The 1832 constitution had said nothing about qualifications for jury duty, leaving it to the legislature to decide who could serve. On the eve of the Civil War, Mississippi law specified that jurors could be either freeholders or householders.[39]

The requirement opened jury duty to white renters and poor white landholders, but only if they were heads of households. Delegates to the 1868 constitutional convention wanted to signal the impact of emancipation on the legal system by outlawing racial discrimination in jury selection, and the convention considered language that would have made the householder restriction unconstitutional: "No qualification, except that of a good moral character, shall ever be required of a juror." The provision went down to defeat, as did a suggestion that the convention constitutionalize the existing freeholders' and householders' statute. In the end, the convention declared that "no property qualification shall ever be required of any person to become a juror," and the legislature promptly restored the language requiring that grand jurors be the heads of households. As subsequent case law confirmed, doing so marked no real advance over the antebellum statute.[40]

Delegates could have required that grand jurors be selected randomly, as had been done in Mississippi before 1856. They must have known that the 1856 law allowing white elites to pick grand jurors put rich white slaveowners in the grand jury room in numbers far beyond their proportion of the population. They could have incorporated into the constitution the jury laws of 1822 and 1830, laws that required that all jurors, grand and petit, be randomly selected from lists provided by tax assessors. Instead, the new constitution made few changes in jury selection procedures, merely extending and enlarging the old system. Mississippi's highest court declared that the Republicans' constitution had "abolish[ed] property qualifications for jury service, and impose[d] the duty on all citizens alike, who are electors."[41] The Jacksonian-era constitution had not limited service to freeholders.

Regardless of the language in the constitution, Vicksburg whites thought Republicans threatened the tradition of excluding the lower orders of society from serving on grand juries. "The difficulty," Vicksburg banker and politician Alexander H. Arthur commented, "consists in the fact that all citizens have a right to be jurors, without any reference to their intelligence or education."[42] Whites' fears seemed to take a step toward reality in 1869, when General Adelbert Ames appointed Albert Johnson as Warren County's first black supervisor. By 1871 blacks outnumbered whites on the board three to two, and from 1872 through 1874 all of the members but one were black.

Whites likely feared that black-run courts would inadequately protect their property. Before emancipation, whites had used courts primarily to settle fights. In the antebellum era more than 40 percent of all grand jury indictments initiated by white male complainants had alleged assault. After the fall of slavery, Warren County courts shifted emphasis to the protection of property (table 4). White men pushed aggressively for the change. Between 1864 and 1880, only 15 percent of white male crime victims reported an assault. Only 32 percent of antebellum white male complainants reported theft, but 65 percent of postbellum white male crime victims claimed to have been robbed. Females participated in the shift in emphasis, although perhaps less enthusiastically. Among white female

Table 4. Comparison of Types of Crime by Race,
1865–79

	Whites (N = 500)	Blacks (N = 149)
Crimes against:		
Property	71.8%	54.4%
Moral order	1.4	3.4
Person	25.2	40.9
Civil order	1.6	1.3
	100.0	100.0

Sources: County court case files, criminal court case files, circuit
court case files, circuit court state docket books, all in Old Court
House Museum, Vicksburg, and Natchez Trace Collection, Center
for American History, University of Texas at Austin.

complainants, 30 percent claimed to have been assaulted before the war
and 20 percent afterward. Before emancipation, one-quarter of female
crime victims went to court with stories of larceny, but afterward almost
60 percent made such complaints.[43] Through Reconstruction, whites
understood protecting property to be the most important job of courts.
They must have doubted that impoverished blacks would capably guard
the property of their former owners.

When black supervisors nominated grand jurors, white men attended
the meetings, loudly objecting to the choices. The Republican prosecutor lamented that the board "allowed a loose sort of practice to prevail,
and anybody could come in and talk." "Offensive and rude" people challenged the board in public meetings as it chose grand jurors. "I don't think
they appreciated the indecency of it," the prosecutor added.[44] More often than under Presidential Reconstruction, the sheriff reported that he
could not locate the persons nominated. In some cases the board failed
to nominate anyone, and then Furlong chose the jurors without direction. Between 1868 and 1875 that happened more than half of the time,
often enough to allow white conservatives to complain plausibly that
Furlong and his successor chose grand jurors not from a list but from
among their cronies.[45]

Had Furlong and the board of supervisors chosen truly representative
grand juries dominated by illiterate former slaves, white fears would have
been realized. By law, Warren County supervisors could select as grand
jurors male householders who were between twenty-one and sixty, with
the exception of state court officers, doctors, teachers, keepers of public
mills and ferries, ministers, officers of the U.S. government, and lawyers.
In 1870, 4,602 Warren County men were qualified for jury duty. Seventy-

four percent were black, 66 percent were under forty-one, 60 percent could neither read nor write, 76 percent were either laborers or farmers, and 90 percent owned no land whatsoever.[46] In other words, a grand jury really reflective of Warren County's population would have been made up primarily of young black laborers or farmers who owned no land. Barely 40 percent of those eligible for jury duty could read and write: three-quarters of white heads of household could do so, and 97 percent of eligible blacks could not. A representative jury would have been over-whelmingly illiterate and included many "country negroes," freed slaves still performing agricultural labor on rural Warren County plantations.[47]

Republicans achieved impressive gains in opening grand jury service to blacks, but Republican-selected grand juries did not represent a cross-section of Warren County society. Thirty-five percent of grand jurors were black, a vast improvement over the dismal record achieved during Pres-idential Reconstruction, when apparently no blacks served on the grand jury. But African Americans were still under-represented on grand juries; they were 70 percent of Warren County's population.[48] Eighty-eight per-cent of grand jurors were literate. The change from Presidential Recon-struction to Congressional Reconstruction had little effect on the wealth of grand jurors, however. Only 31 percent had no property recorded in the 1870 census, although 43 percent had less than $500 worth.

Looking at all grand jurors chosen between 1868 and 1875 can be mis-leading. Republican power waxed and waned, and Republicans operated more confidently during some years than in others. They could most free-ly choose the jurors they wanted between 1870 and 1873, when conserva-tive whites seemed less threatening than they would later. Nonetheless, even Republican grand jurors largely resembled the ideal to which all aspired, regardless of political affiliation. Between 1870 and 1873, sixty of 120 jurors identified in census and tax records by race were black, 85 per-cent claimed they could read and write, and almost half owned $500 or more in property. At the height of their power, Republicans chose black jurors who far better resembled the county as a whole than their white conservative predecessors. Nonetheless, Republicans showed a preference for literate white jurors who had substantial property holdings (table 5).

Republicans affirmed their commitment to traditional constitutional values through architecture, too. By seeking to turn the courthouse build-ing to their advantage, using it as a symbol of order and legitimacy, they hardly broke new ground. The courthouse, mounted on a hill dominat-ing the city, had been designed to reflect commitment to higher law in 1858. In 1868 the Republican board of supervisors put county prisoners

Table 5. Black Grand Jurors in Warren County, Mississippi, 1866–79

| Year | Black Grand Jurors | | Total Number of Grand Jurors Identified by Race |
	Percentage	Number	
1866	0	0	37
1867	0	0	66
1868	0	0	66
1869	28.0	14	50
1870	48.5	16	33
1871	46.4	13	28
1872	46.2	18	39
1873	65.0	13	20
1874	58.6	17	29
1875	39.1	9	23
1876	20.0	6	30
1877	16.7	8	48
1878	18.5	5	27
1879	23.4	11	47

Sources: Warren County Circuit Court Papers, Old Court House Museum, Vicksburg; 1870 manuscript schedules, Ninth U.S. Census, 1870, and Tenth U.S. Census, 1880, Warren County, Miss., microfilm, National Archives.

to work landscaping the grounds around the building, constructing terraces and planting shrubs. The next year the board had a brick wall built around the newly landscaped grounds. In 1871 supervisors entered into an agreement with Martin Keary to repair and paint the courthouse exterior. For $7,509 he agreed to mend the brickwork and wood trim "where the same may be broken or cracked or loose." Keary happened to be a leader of the local Irish, and hiring him delivered patronage to that community. Republicans, especially black Republicans, aspired to win the Irish to their side. Vicksburgers who hoped to lure the state capital to their city advertised the courthouse as more suitable than the dilapidated capitol in Jackson. But the supervisors intended more than that. They wanted the paint job to lend a new gravitas to the courthouse. Keary was to paint the top of the cupola sky blue and the main body of the building white, and the board carefully instructed him to repaint the columns and cornice "so as to represent Brown stone or Marble." Some of the woodwork was to look like mahogany and the base of the columns granite. The alterations changed the look of the courthouse, making the architecture call on people to respect the law's authority.[49]

The same thinking that discouraged selection of illiterate black jurors and led to an overhaul of the courthouse exterior might have prompted Republicans to choose white men as judge and prosecutor. Local blacks did not have the requisite expertise for those jobs. The 1870 census includes only one black lawyer in Warren County and lists him—surely incorrectly—as illiterate. After May 1870 George F. Brown, a carpetbagger, served as circuit judge. Before doing so, he moved to Mississippi in 1867 and had served as a delegate to the 1868 constitutional convention. He once told a congressional committee that he had no special "influence" over Warren County blacks, which perhaps explains why he failed to achieve his ambition to become the Republican candidate for Congress.[50]

District Attorney Luke Lea played a more important role in the criminal justice system. He listened to complaining citizens and encouraged or discouraged them after hearing their stories. He also wrote the indictments that specified who went to trial for what crime. For Warren County blacks interested in criminal justice, Luke Lea was the most important white man during Reconstruction. By 1870 he had lived in Mississippi for thirty years, but he still returned to his native east Tennessee when suffering with bouts of malaria. Before the war he had been an active but politically unsuccessful Whig. During the 1840s Whigs had tried to present themselves not as aristocrats but as more democratic than Democrats, and Lea must have been particularly effective at doing so. Even political opponents acknowledged his democratic credentials. After leaving office as Mississippi district attorney, Lea became U.S. attorney. He proved so lenient toward impoverished loggers poaching on public lands that the attorney general tried to fire him. Although Lea received the fatal "President has directed" telegram notifying him of his removal, he held onto his job, a measure of his considerable political skills.[51] Lea displayed the same talent as Mississippi state district attorney, carefully positioning himself between native whites, carpetbaggers, and the majority black electorate. He once told a black audience that "he had never gone among the colored men telling them how much he loved them; but can any of you . . . point to an instance where I have not been found at my post when one of you desired my assistance?"[52] It was the kind of statement designed both not to offend white conservatives and to appeal to blacks.

Lea and other Republicans carefully and deliberately refrained from turning the old system topsy-turvy. In many routine ways lawyers and juries went about their tasks just as they always had. Poor victims did not suddenly flood the courthouse with criminal charges. In 1870 the mean value of property adult males owned in Warren County was $1,224, and the median was zero. Between 1868 and 1875 the mean value of complainants' real and personal property (as recorded in the 1870 census) was $11,467, and the median was $200. During Presidential Reconstruction the mean was $7,351, and the median was again zero. Regardless of who ran the courthouse, consumers of criminal justice services tended to be wealthier than most Warren County residents.

During the Republican era, most cases involved white-on-white crime, just as during Presidential Reconstruction (tables 6–7). Between 1865 and 1867, 184 (70 percent of cases prosecuted where both parties can be identified by race) involved both white complainants and white defendants. Between 1868 and 1875, 114 (73 percent of the cases) involved such white-on-white crime. In only twenty-eight cases between 1870 and 1873 can both defendants and victims be identified by race. During this high point of Republicanism, ten cases involved white-on-white crime (about a third of the identifiable total), nine were alleged crimes by black defendants upon white victims, and six blacks charged other blacks with crimes. Only three black victims charged whites with crimes. If that tiny sample is representative, then white-on-white crime still predominated during the Republican era but not as much as at other times.[53]

One obvious possibility is that whites in Warren County committed more crimes than blacks and committed them against other whites more often than against blacks. But after emancipation many planters contin-

Table 6. Black Victims (Complainants) in Warren County, Mississippi, 1866–79

	Black Victims		Total Number of Victims Identified
Year	Percentage	Number	by Race
1865	0	0	33
1866	13.2	20	151
1867	13.1	11	84
1868	9.2	8	87
1869	13.5	5	37
1870	47.6	10	21
1871	54.2	13	24
1872	38.9	7	18
1873	41.7	10	24
1874	26.1	6	23
1875	44.4	12	27
1876	22.2	4	18
1877	31.0	13	42
1878	53.8	7	13
1879	40.0	8	20

Sources: County court case files, criminal court case files, circuit court case files, circuit court state docket books, all in Old Court House Museum, Vicksburg, and Natchez Trace Collection, Center for American History, University of Texas at Austin; manuscript population schedules, Ninth U.S. Census, 1870, and Tenth U.S. Census, 1880, Warren County, Miss., microfilm, National Archives.

Table 7. Comparison of Victims and Defendants by Race, 1865–75

	Presidential Reconstruction (1865–67)	Congressional Reconstruction (1868–75)	1870–73
White victims			
white defendants	70.2%	73.5%	35.7%
black defendants	19.5	11.1	32.1
Black victims			
white defendants	5.3	7.7	10.7
black defendants	5.0	7.7	21.5
	100.0	100.0	100.0
Total number of victims	262	155	28

Sources: County court case files, criminal court case files, circuit court case files, circuit court state docket books, all in Old Court House Museum, Vicksburg, and Natchez Trace Collection, Center for American History, University of Texas at Austin.

ued to use the same kind of violence they had used under slavery to control laborers. Landlords sometimes shot former slaves or resorted to whipping "and the most severe modes of punishment." Whites of every economic condition took advantage of the lawless environment. One observer claimed that not a day passed without some robbery or murder perpetrated against African Americans.[54]

Grand jury indictments cannot be tallied for a "crime rate." There is always a "dark figure"—crimes committed that never reached the grand jury. A study of indictments has to be understood as an examination of the system rather than of individual conduct.[55] It seems unlikely that blacks in Warren County were more law-abiding than in other localities where African Americans committed ordinary assaults and robberies at roughly the same rate as whites. Poverty may have made former slaves more prone to thieving.[56] Nor does it seem likely that criminally inclined and violent whites would have been particularly solicitous of black sensitivities. Organized lawlessness directed against blacks did not become common in Mississippi until the Black and Tan Convention in 1868, but Freedmen's Bureau records make it clear that the more casual variety between employer and employee was endemic. Only a tiny percentage of blacks took allegations against white defendants to the criminal justice system. At a time of night-riding terrorism and a daily cascade of casual violence, blacks likely were more reluctant to lodge criminal complaints against white criminals than black.[57]

During this era, African Americans made unprecedented use of the courts despite their initial reluctance to do so. Many more brought grievances than they had before. They changed the nature of criminal justice in Warren County and shifted the criminal justice system away from its heavy bias toward white-on-white crime.

The case of *State v. William Johnson* illustrates how blacks changed the character of cases moving through circuit court.[58] It was an instance of a black crime victim's using the law to fight for his property just as white people did, yet no white person would have brought such a case. In 1872 William Johnson persuaded Isaac Harris that he was, in the words of his subsequent indictment, a "great doctor & conjurer" and that Harris's wife Jane had been bewitched. Johnson convinced Harris that "a certain frog had been magically & hoo-dooishly introduced into the stomach of the said Jane Harris" and that he could remove the frog and prevent its return. (To convince Harris that his wife had a frog in her stomach would have been a relatively simple matter for a skilled conjure man. As one explained later, he would have induced the woman to vomit and then dropped a hidden frog into the bucket.)[59] To make sure the frog did not return, Johnson explained, he would need to borrow Harris's mule for two magic feedings. When he did not return with the mule, Harris went to the authorities. The Republican district attorney listened to Harris and wrote an indictment, the Republican sheriff arrested Johnson and jailed him, and the grand jury returned an indictment.

In one sense, Johnson's trial was an ordinary fraud case. In another it shows the legal system helping a crime victim new to the polity protect his property. White conservatives during Presidential Reconstruction might well have dismissed such a case as unworthy of their time. It is likely that no black would have dared to bring the matter to the attention of authorities in the first place. If any did, no record exists of it. When blacks went to court to complain of theft, they most often did so to recover stolen stock. In this case a black man fought to keep his mule, the most important "implement" a nineteenth-century farmer could own.[60]

Johnson claimed the indictment was faulty because Harris did not really own the mule until it was fully paid for. By alleging that legality, he went right to the heart of the matter, challenging Harris's property rights. Although a black man himself, he implicitly made the argument white conservatives would have endorsed: Harris was just an "uppity nigger" claiming to own a mule. Brown rejected Johnson's argument: "If Harris had made a contract for the purchase of the mule & had paid part of the purchase money & had possession of the mule under contract, then he had such a title to the mule as is sufficient to maintain this indictment." Harris kept his mule, and Johnson went to jail.[61] Encouraging men such as Harris to take to court cases like the one he brought against Johnson should have been a high priority for Warren County Republicans. It meant bringing a population excluded from participation in law under slavery within the rule of law.

Giving blacks greater access to criminal justice also changed the character of criminal justice by bringing black families into court. Slavery had corrupted the very concept of marriage, sometimes forcing couples into cohabitation. Often partners disagreed over whether to preserve a "marriage" begun in slavery. Freedom could mean walking away from a forced relationship; it could also mean fighting for a marriage by taking a reluctant partner to court. Marital disputes between former slave couples provided lawyers with a fertile field, but lawyers, judges, and juries had to agree that blacks deserved the same access to courts as whites.

Freedmen's Bureau agents failed to understand that the coercive nature of slavery extended even to sexual matters. From their perspective, the desire of many freed people to escape forced marriages showed that slavery had placed blacks into a state of marital lawlessness. Army lieutenant John D. Moore reported from Lauderdale that only "intelligent" freed people genuinely wanted to "elevate the standard of morality."[62] But he thought other blacks viewed fornication as a right. J. R. Webster complained that blacks rarely married, preferring to "cohabit for mutual good pleasure."[63] In 1868 one agent worried that slavery had taught black husbands to be tyrannical and brutal. Even the most intelligent felt free to chastise their wives in any manner they chose, he complained.[64] Another agent reported that freed people only "imperfectly observed" their marital obligations "and in many instances total[ly] disregard" them. Bigamy, he said, was common.[65] The agent stationed in Columbus, Mississippi, found little progress in marital relations since slavery and doubted there ever would be improvement.[66]

If Freedmen's Bureau agents failed to grasp how slavery poisoned marriage, they understood that white-dominated courts did little to settle blacks' marital disputes. The agents complained that antebellum whites had tried to keep black family matters out of their courts and postbellum courts did little better.[67] Although agent William H. Ross reported "very good improvement" in blacks' morality in his district, civil authorities deserved no credit, he said. Authorities held a white man in jail on a charge of adultery but ignored far more flagrant cases involving freed people.[68]

Despite white resistance, some blacks insisted on taking their marital troubles to court. When they did, and when authorities brought charges, jurors often would not convict. In one county a former slaveowner notorious for fathering children through his female slaves sat on the grand jury. Not surprisingly, that jury saw no reason to prosecute adultery or fornication in cases involving former slaves.[69]

Some black Vicksburgers, like black southerners elsewhere in the Reconstruction South, used law to protect their families. During Reconstruction poorer whites and blacks sometimes challenged prevailing attitudes and established power by charging wealthy whites with acts of sexual violence. For a brief moment Mississippi blacks literally had their day in court.[70] John Ells went to circuit court to ask for a habeas corpus petition for his daughter, Mary. Ells's wife Caroline had abandoned him in 1865. Living in "adultery" with another man, she had "abducted" Mary, according to John. The circuit court issued the writ.[71]

Other black women and men went to grand juries with complaints of spouses who had committed adultery and bigamy. In some cases jurors recognized slave marriages, which whites had always insisted had no legal standing. They charged Anna Williams with bigamy after she married Albert Watkins, who had been married to Josephine Watkins, in 1866. The court instructed the trial jury that the marriage of Albert and Josephine had legal standing only if they had been married as slaves and continued to live together after the fall of slavery.[72]

Black wives also went to authorities when their husbands beat them, and jurors sometimes returned indictments in such domestic-abuse cases. But most cases of abuse only reached authorities after abuse had turned to murder. In 1866 authorities prosecuted W. D. Chase for murdering his wife, Phillis, whom whites described as "a copper colored woman" and judged to be "tolerably good looking." The Chases lived on a thirty-yard-long alley off Cherry Street in cramped quarters crowded with poor blacks. Chase did no work, playing the guitar sometimes and drinking more often. Neighbors testified they had frequently heard the couple argue. In a typical exchange Phillis asked her husband to cut wood for her and he exploded in anger, calling her a "damned bitch" and daring her to repeat the request. The two quarreled about money. Chase once demanded the two dollars his wife had saved for food to buy whiskey. One day Kitty Washington saw Chase with a pistol and heard him and his wife arguing about that, too. When Phillis asked Chase to put his gun away, he insisted it was not loaded. "It is loaded, I know it is loaded," she retorted. At that, Chase began to threaten to shoot Phillis. But the real bone of contention did not involve the pistol. Chase had shouted "I will shoot any woman who will take a white man & leave me," and alley residents had seen a white soldier visiting the home. Shortly after that argument they heard a shot, and a crowd gathered. "You have shot your wife," someone exclaimed. "Yes and I don't care," Chase blustered. But later he wept, "Oh ma—If you die I want to die too."[73]

Such murder cases generally went to court almost automatically. For crimes less than murder, however, the decision to go to court often rested with the victim. The more firmly Republicans, especially black Republicans, controlled the courthouse, the more comfortable black crime victims felt in going to law. When the numbers of black complainants are smoothed with a running median, that of three successive values, the trend inherent in the numbers becomes clearer (figures 3–4).[74]

Blacks used courts to resolve personal disputes more than whites, perhaps because they had far less property to protect. According to the 1870 census, white property-holders in Warren County had a total of nearly $8 million in personal and real estate. African Americans, who made up a large majority of the population, had less than $1 million. Ninety percent of blacks who owned property had less than $200 worth, whereas more than 70 percent of whites had property valued at more than $800.[75] Because real estate is rarely stolen, it makes sense to focus on personal property. Here, too, whites enjoyed a staggering advantage over blacks, owning 82 percent of the personal property in Warren County. Yet the percentage of blacks who had no personal property is not much lower than the proportion of propertylessness among the white population. Seventy-nine percent of black adults had no personal property, against 71 percent of whites. Because blacks made up a larger percentage of Warren County's adult population, more black adults had personal property than white adults. Census enumerators counted 1,570 adult blacks with some, usually small, amount of personal property. Fewer white adults, 1,096, had personal property (table 8).[76]

Of course, the census drastically undercounted the property held by whites and blacks. All held property that census enumerators did not bother reporting. Stock, carriages, and farm implements were considered to be personal property, not clothing and many other small items, precisely the sorts that were commonly stolen. Even under the limited definition of personal property used in the census, the population of potential theft victims was mostly black, yet blacks reported far fewer thefts than whites. In part that must have been because whites had more valuable possessions than blacks and kept them in warehouses and stores more accessible to thieves.

With the exception of robbery, whites dominated the ranks of complainants in every category of property crime. Most cases alleged some

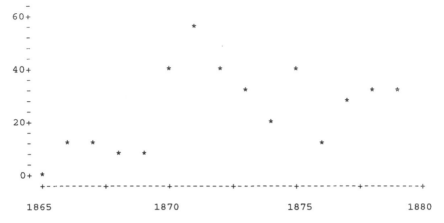

Figure 3. Black Victims as a Percentage of All Victims

Data taken from county court case files, criminal court case files, circuit court case files, and circuit court state docket books (all in Old Court House Museum, Vicksburg, and Natchez Trace Collection, Center for American History, University of Texas at Austin).

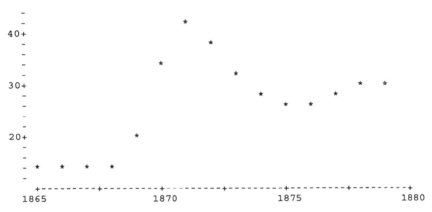

Figure 4. Black Victims as a Percentage of All Victims (Smoothed)

Data taken from county court case files, criminal court case files, circuit court case files, and circuit court state docket books (all in Old Court House Museum, Vicksburg, and Natchez Trace Collection, Center for American History, University of Texas at Austin).

Table 8. Comparison of Personal Property of Black
and White Warren County Adult Males, 1870

Value of Personal Property	Whites (N = 2,196)	Blacks (N = 3,556)
$0	61.1%	59.8%
$1–200	5.4	20.0
$201–800	14.0	18.2
$801+	19.5	2.0
	100.0	100.0

Source: Manuscript population schedules, Ninth U.S. Census,
1870, Warren County, Miss., microfilm, National Archives.

form of larceny. White-on-white crimes made up two-thirds of those in which both defendant and victim can be identified by race. White victims accused blacks of theft 25 percent of the time. Black victims initiated only 12 percent of larceny cases, and they accused whites of theft only twelve times (in 5 percent of the cases). All ten complaints of receiving stolen goods were filed by whites, and defendants were as likely to be black as white. Thirty-one victims of burglary accused white people of the crime, but only twelve blacks said their homes had been burglarized. That is not surprising. Burglars prefer to invade buildings such as stores and warehouses that are likely to be unoccupied, and whites owned such structures more often than blacks. Robbery was a crime of violence. A much larger proportion of black complainants alleged robbery than whites, but in nearly 60 percent of the cases a white person had robbed another white person. Only a quarter of robbery crimes crossed racial lines.

It is possible that blacks, more than whites, conceived of court as a place to settle personal disputes. Perhaps whites had a more absolute view of property than did former slaves. Frederick Douglass wrote that because he had been chattel he took a more ambivalent view of property than did whites.[77] The complaints blacks brought to the Freedmen's Bureau courts and to black magistrates overwhelmingly involved personal disputes. Husbands and wives complained of spouses, and employees reported problems with bosses. Twice the percentage of black complainants as white complainants charged someone with assault. Blacks rarely brought charges of rape or seduction, but neither did whites.

Blacks showed up among murder victims less often than whites. It is certainly possible that there were fewer black victims. Criminologists consider murder arrests to reflect the actual number of murders more accurately than arrests for other crimes. Grand juries indicted people for murder of whites twice as often as they did of blacks. Whites made up two-

thirds of defendants. When both the defendant and victim can be identified by race, two-thirds of murder cases involved one white person killing another white person. Just two involved black defendants and white
victims. Yet by many accounts Warren County whites did kill blacks, and
years later some still remained unapologetic. In a memoir he wrote in 1929
James Monroe Gibson confessed to no murders but did remember being fully prepared to kill any African American who interfered with his
patrols around Warren County. Gibson undoubtedly painted an exaggerated picture of himself as a tough character ready to shoot to kill, but his
narrative reveals a white man comfortable with presenting himself as
ready to kill blacks without remorse. His captain, he claimed, had ordered
him to take four or five comrades to "get" a leading African American,
but "I thought it sufficient to take only one."[78]

Although blacks did go to the courthouse with complaints, they never
made full use of the legal system. Illiterates must have felt intimidated by
the prospect of going to court. Entering the Warren County Courthouse,
designed to awe ordinary citizens who entered, would surely have been
an intimidating experience for former slaves. The judge sat on an iron
platform behind a railing in a courtroom decorated with paintings of
great white lawyers.

Little evidence suggests that the ordinary blacks who did pass between
the massive columns guarding the Warren County Courthouse abused
the privilege. Whites had worried that those who served on juries would
not convict black defendants but were surprised by the vigor with which
they did so. The probity of black men chosen as grand jurors carried over
into their service on trial juries and can be most easily documented by
the comments of whites at public trials. When asked about the willingness of "colored [petit] jurors" to convict those of their own color, one
white judge complained, "They have manifested too great an eagerness
to do so."[79]

Perhaps black jurors wanted to prove themselves capable. Perhaps they
sought to rid their community of its criminal element. Or they may have
felt they had to defer to whites. In any case, criminal lawyers with black
defendants preferred white trial jurors over blacks. Luke Lea said that
some black grand jurors shielded a few criminals but no more often than
whites, and it was "generally the other way." He also praised the fairness
of black jurors, saying, "If I were on trial as a white man, I would rather
be tried by a colored jury than by a white one."[80]

The number of black defendants convicted did not decline when Republicans put blacks on grand and petit juries. Between 1868 and 1873

juries convicted 77 percent of black defendants and 69 percent of white defendants. That conviction rate compares favorably with the prosecutors' success during Presidential Reconstruction, although Republicans seemed less likely to convict whites than their predecessors. From 1864 through 1867, juries had convicted 78 percent of white defendants and the same proportion of black defendants. It seems logical to assume that black grand jurors may have shielded blacks from unjust accusations, and black petit jurors likely voted to acquit black defendants when the evidence proved flimsy. But integrated juries convicted blacks at almost precisely the same rate as earlier all-white juries. Certainly white fears of black jurors indulging in wholesale acquittals proved unfounded.[81]

Civil rights for Warren County blacks did not generate a revolution in either legal procedures or practices. Local Republicans carefully refrained from challenging established traditions. They did not—could not—fill grand juries with illiterate field hands. Republicans consciously avoided innovation and tried desperately to preserve whatever legitimacy the circuit court enjoyed among whites. Many poor blacks did not feel free to take complaints of crime into court. Nor did blacks challenge the style of political discourse practiced in Warren County before emancipation. They formed rival factions and denounced each other in heated terms—just as whites had once done.

7

A White Republic

The Mississippi of the New South would be a land of unprecedented diversity: cotton fields and factories, planters and railroaders, professionals and reformers. In the South as well as in the North, jurists vigorously proposed law as a bulwark against disorder. But in Mississippi that
new heterogeneity and social complexity did not prevent the champions
of commerce, who sought to exclude the undeserving of either race from
citizenship, and their agrarian opponents from forging a racial coalition.[1]
Between 1871 and 1873 white Vicksburgers formed the cohesive whole that
would allow them to discipline blacks outside the law. As they became a
unified phalanx opposed to Republican rule, whites downplayed class,
ethnic, religious, and political distinctions. In a world where race trumped
every other distinction and lynchers confidently posed for photographers,
certain no white man would want to arrest them and no black man dared
challenge their authority, law mattered less than custom. After 1873 white
Vicksburgers consciously chose lawlessness.

* * *

Republicans, black or white, could do little to prevent conservative
whites from forming a racial bloc. Party leaders understood the importance of maintaining the loyalty of old-line Whigs. Only by winning them
into their ranks could they hope to establish some claim to legitimacy
among white people. But most Republican voters were black, which likely
made it impossible for old-line Whigs to be on their side. Blacks wanted

not just spots on the Republican ticket, they demanded their rights. Inveterate Whigs and some northern-born Republicans found such demands repulsive.

Republican leaders could delay formation of a white coalition against blacks only for as long as they could hold the aspirations of freed slaves in check. The first man to head the Republican "ring" that ruled Warren County, Union army veteran Charles E. Furlong, did so for six years by winning black voters without entirely alienating whites. His achievement seems all the more remarkable given that he accomplished it while looting the county treasury more successfully than any other Warren County official. Yet white conservatives defended him from criticism, and blacks loyally, some said slavishly, turned out to vote for him. He had been an organizer of the Warren County Union League, displacing Mygatt and working hard to recruit blacks into the organization. At mass meetings in the country, Furlong indulged in the antique practice of "treating," dispensing whiskey and food to voters. At least one freedman understood that he did so "to get big money."[2]

Warren County's 1871 Republican convention offered an opportunity to observe Furlong in action. At the meeting, his followers began chanting their man's name, but some black Republicans shouted objections. As he had done so often before, Furlong moved to appease the freedmen without offending his white friends. In this case, he stepped aside and allowed Charles W. Bush, a former slave, to serve in the largely ceremonial post of president of the nominating convention.[3] The move cost Furlong little but satisfied the freedmen.

Furlong's opponents challenged his sincerity. He had angered Vicksburg's Republican newspaper, the *Times,* when he awarded the county's lucrative printing contract to the rival Democratic newspaper. The *Times* retaliated through its coverage of the Republicans' meeting, describing it as chaotic, disorderly, disgraceful, and "indescribably ridiculous." It reported that Warren County blacks wanted more power in their party and had repeatedly challenged Furlong at the August meeting. By emphasizing black unrest, the newspaper hoped to encourage other African Americans to speak against Furlong; the *Times* clearly thought more freedmen *should* protest his power.[4] In September the *Times* accused Furlong of amassing a huge fortune while in office, adding that "now it is fairly the turn of the colored men to have it." It also questioned the depth of Furlong's Republicanism, observing that he owned no property in the city and paid no taxes. Instead, Sheriff Furlong kept himself ready to migrate at a moment's notice. Quite accurately, as it turned out, the

Times charged that "his aim is to make all he can out of the people of the county and then vanish from our midst."[5]

When the *Times* struck again just a week later, it touched an issue that would ultimately unite whites across ethnic and political divisions. "Furlong," the newspaper roughly demanded, "who is your candidate for Chancery Clerk of this county? We claim that a colored man must either be chancery clerk or sheriff. How is that with you? Answer." Simultaneously, the formal head of the Republican Party in Warren County, John Rankin, wrote that Furlong had "played hell becoming a Democrat." The local Republican hierarchy called on Governor James L. Alcorn to remove Furlong, and the *Times* pressured Alcorn with headlines such as "Furlong Defies the Governor." Shortly thereafter Alcorn acquiesced and removed Furlong from office.[6]

Out of office, he campaigned to win it back. The *Times* endorsed George W. Boyd, a former slave, over Furlong for the Republican nomination for sheriff, but Furlong won. His success dampened white fervor for a conservative, whites-only crusade against "black Republicanism." The convention nominated George W. Davenport for chancery clerk, Thomas W. Cardozo for circuit clerk, and Peter Crosby for treasurer, but putting those black men up for such responsible posts did not immediately inflame Warren County whites, even though nomination by the Republicans was tantamount to election. The sheriff was the boss of the county, and everyone knew it. In November Warren County's black voters loyally turned out and elected Furlong sheriff.[7]

Another party success in 1871 ultimately reminded all that many people apparently considered themselves white first and Republicans second. Republicans elected Alexander H. Arthur, a long-time Whig and banker, as city judge. Respected and wealthy, Judge Arthur was the archetypal former Whig the Republicans knew they had to win to their cause if they hoped to establish legitimacy among Mississippi whites. Born in Charlottesville, Virginia, Arthur had come to Vicksburg on horseback. He edited the Vicksburg *Whig* for a time and helped found the city's public schools, even putting up the money for the construction of one building. He had also organized Vicksburg's fire-fighting service. But Republicans may have forgotten that in 1841 he had been the only member of the board of supervisors who had favored banning free blacks from Vicksburg.[8]

On February 7, 1873, Governor Ridgley C. Powers signed into law Mississippi's civil rights bill, and black Vicksburgers did not wait long to test the legislation.[9] In March a black city official purchased a ticket for the theater and refused to sit in the colored section. Whites physically ousted him from his seat, and the Democratic *Herald* hoped local blacks had learned a lesson: "The white people of Vicksburg do not intend to tolerate such impudence." The Republican *Times* did not approve of the desegregation attempt either but sought to placate black Republicans by adding that "we have greater condemnation for the acts of those who, mob like, rushed to the assistance of the usher with drawn pistols."[10] It must have been quite a scene.

In May another black official, Justice of the Peace Sydney Brooks, challenged white Vicksburg's policy of segregating the races. He bought a ticket to hear Vermont poet John G. Saxe lecture at the YMCA and insisted on sitting in the white section. Arrested, he went before Judge Arthur. Although only a city judge and ostensibly a Republican, Arthur disappointed blacks who had voted for him by condemning the civil rights law as unconstitutional class legislation. He concluded that it did not cover private associations such as the YMCA.[11]

Arthur's actions energized some black politicians, and on the following day Cardozo, Davenport, and Crosby, leaders of Warren County's black community by virtue of the 1871 election, issued a handbill.

Hail! Republicans! Rally!

Indignation meeting! to be held at the Courthouse to-morrow night, Friday, May 2—why hallo! What's the matter now? Why there's nothing the matter—but a fresh cut, why so? Because, hallucination has taken hold of one of our most trust Judges of literary merit. Well, how do you know? Because, he has stretched back one of his far reaching roots to the very cell of usurpation, and has thrown another under the funeral pile of corruption. Yes he has twisted another around the stake of absurdity. Respectfully Yours, T. W. Cardozo, G. W. Davenport, Peter Crosby, P. C. Hall, A. W. Dorsey, W. L. Merritt, L. H. Wilson, and others.[12]

Peter Crosby spoke at the indignation meeting. The *Herald* described him as tall, intelligent-looking, and middle-aged. In a deliberate but impassioned tone he declared that "we do not intend to be satisfied until we have all the privileges belonging to all citizens. We do not intend to be satisfied in part." Reading from the Declaration of Independence, he announced, "We want the whole hog or not."[13] Democrats denounced the meeting. The Meridian *Mercury* hooted in derision at Arthur, a white man and radical, "holding his office by favor of the Radical negro party."[14] The *Herald* made the point with doggerel:

Judge Arthur is as fine a man
    As ever you did see,
Though he did decide the "civil Rights"
Unlawful for to be
And although he was censured,
    And requested to resign,
He hasn't yet forgotten how
    To law on cost and fine.
Silence in the Court!
The first man that laughs
I'll fine him.[15]

Even Republican District Attorney Luke Lea, who proclaimed himself committed to equal rights, worried that the meeting had been "unwise and impolitic" under the "circumstances."[16]

But the incident probably furthered Crosby's career. He had already served as Warren County coroner, ranger, and treasurer and seemed destined for higher office. Crosby had been born into slavery, and like so many Mississippi slaves who had become politicians he had been an artisan. In 1864 he had earned enough money by shoemaking to buy four mules and a carriage that he used to transport his family to freedom. While he served in the Union army, federal authorities seized his property. Despite that loss, in 1872 he and his wife still had money to purchase a lot in Vicksburg. Crosby traveled the county, making speeches on the political issues of the time. One observer sourly commented that the former slave had only proved himself "intellectually unable to do justice to the subject of his speech." Others, though, were more impressed.[17]

In 1873, when Warren County Republicans again met to nominate candidates for local offices, freedmen insisted on running the proceedings. Arthur's decision had convinced many blacks that they had to have their own men in Warren County's most responsible positions. The Republicans first met by wards to nominate delegates to the county meeting. Of the twenty men selected, only three were white.[18] Black men so thoroughly dominated the convention that at one point Davenport called for giving whites at least token representation.[19] Instead of pitting whites against blacks, the convention split along city-country lines. Tensions between country and city blacks ran deep; the two sides sometimes even brawled in Vicksburg saloons. Black men living in the countryside had been slaves without privilege. They had seen the peculiar institution at its worst. The population of blacks in Vicksburg included light-skinned carpetbaggers.

Even former slaves living in the city had often enjoyed privileges not available to field hands.[20]

When country folk hoped to nominate G. W. Chavis for assessor, Crosby, who had already been nominated for sheriff, induced Chavis to withdraw by offering to make him deputy sheriff. In this era men crudely sought office for profit, and Crosby promised Chavis that he could make more money as deputy sheriff than as assessor. Chavis's country supporters erupted in anger, shouting, quite accurately, that he had sold out.[21] The convention nominated Furlong for the state senate, a contest he won against a black candidate, winning every vote but seventeen. Crosby easily defeated his Democratic opponent, 2,308 to 485, and became the first elected black sheriff.[22]

During Crosby's term as sheriff whites finally achieved the unity that would allow them to turn away from formal law, terrorizing blacks outside the legal procedures and technicalities they found so cumbersome. Despite an overwhelming electoral victory, Crosby understood immediately that he confronted colossal problems. Controlling the county's wealth gave whites one immediate lever over elected blacks: they paid most of the taxes that made government possible. By law, elected officials had to make a bond, yet few blacks possessed sufficient wealth to post the large sums required. All blacks elected to office confronted this problem. In Yazoo, Mississippi, Justice of the Peace G. Morris Smith and his constable had earlier petitioned the board of supervisors to reduce their bonds. Smith explained that he was a colored man and regular member of the Union League, an organization which, he reminded supervisors, held "principles distasteful to the minds of a majority of the property holders."[23]

Crosby's election as sheriff energized white opposition to Republican rule. Even previously loyal white Republicans fled their party. Illinois-born John T. Rankin had been a party workhorse and was rewarded with such patronage jobs as deputy U.S. marshal, census enumerator, and U.S. pension agent. But he objected when blacks took control of Vicksburg's courthouse ring.[24] Judge Arthur also distanced himself from the Republicans.[25] The party appointed Frederic Speed, a New York–born former army captain, as circuit court clerk and then criminal court judge during Congressional Reconstruction, but he, too, claimed to find Republican corruption repulsive.[26] The party could ill afford to lose such community leaders.

Crosby's election as sheriff resurrected the all-white Taxpayers' League.

Dormant for years, the league sprang back to life and mutated into mili-
tia-like clubs. Although Warren County whites had been historically factionalized along political, economic, and ethnic lines, they now aspired
to the unity for which William McCardle had called since 1867. An organization known as the People's Club formed chapters in each of Vicksburg's four wards as well as in rural districts surrounding the city. People's Club officers proclaimed their intention of organizing every white
adult in the county.[27]

Reports of corruption among black political leaders further energized
People's Clubs. Taxes had gone up under Furlong's rule without exciting
such a vigorous response; nor had reports of Furlong's graft rallied opposition against him. After 1873, though, reports of corruption became
alarmingly specific and contained enough truth to resonate with many
in Warren County.

Much of the friction within Vicksburg's black community involved
tensions between former slaves and ambitious men such as Thomas W.
Cardozo who had never been slaves. Cardozo, who had come to Vicksburg for the sole purpose of making money, had been born into the free
black elite in Charleston, South Carolina, and educated in private schools
before moving to New York. At the end of the Civil War he had returned
to Charleston to supervise American Missionary Association education
efforts in that city. When the AMA fired him, his hunger for office carried him to North Carolina, but white Republicans blocked his efforts to
advance to office in that state. His ambitions thwarted elsewhere, Cardozo
came to Vicksburg. Although he was talented, his ambition, abrasive personality, and lack of moral sense made him poison on the Warren County
political scene.[28]

As circuit clerk of Warren County, Cardozo added names to lists of
witnesses to be paid out of taxes, writing the new names in a cramped
hand between the names of the original and genuine witnesses. He pock-
eted the money issued to these additional "witnesses" himself.[29] Cardozo's
successor in office, Alfred Dorsey, proved just as corrupt, failing to account
for the tax money he collected. Chancery Clerk George W. Davenport
altered the official records in his office so he could issue himself larger
checks than he deserved. Whites said Peter Crosby had similarly stolen
money when he served as treasurer and, as sheriff, covered up the crimes
committed by Cardozo, Dorsey, and Davenport.

When Cardozo's fraudulent witness certificates reached the state capital in Jackson, the state auditor refused to pay.[30] Hearing that, angry
whites demanded to examine the county's books, but black officials first

turned them away. When the board of supervisors launched an investigation of the chancery clerk's office, someone mysteriously burgled the courthouse and stole the incriminating records.[31]

Crosby had nothing to do with Cardozo's witness certificates, but the circuit clerk's graft emboldened whites to move against the sheriff anyway. Leading whites devised a stratagem that allowed them to rally whites to a direct attack on Crosby.[32] They went after his bonds as tax collector and sheriff. Mississippi's law requiring public officials to put up a bond had the effect of forcing elected officials without property of their own to find men of property to ratify their service. By law, public officials had to produce the names and signatures of property-holders willing to pledge to pay any money they might lose or steal. White planters, outvoted by their former slaves, had only the bond device available if they wished to wield any power at all. In effect, the law gave men of wealth a veto over who could serve. Blacks from outside Warren County could find no local wealthy white man to sign their bonds. As one white man explained, Warren County property-holders valued their old family servants and might sign a bond for them, but a black from outside the county would have trouble finding anyone to do so. For the sheriff, the sums involved made the problem of making a bond especially difficult. Crosby had to find men willing to stake $100,000 of their own property on his service.[33] Nonetheless, he raised a bond.

Almost immediately whites attacked the bond. The *Plain-Dealer*, a black newspaper, complained that "there is always some sly knave at work, endeavoring to give our officers in the county as much trouble as possible." George S. Yerger, who had put up $1,000, had suddenly and unexpectedly gone insolvent. Yerger wanted to notify the board of supervisors, but the *Plain-Dealer* thought the board could avoid trouble by refusing to meet. "It is simply a smear," the newspaper maintained, "a contemptible trick upon Mr. Crosby."[34]

Although Republican leaders dismissed attacks on Crosby's bond, they understood that to retain power they had to unleash the grand jury on Cardozo and other dishonest officials. Conservatives' charges of corruption offered Republicans an opportunity to demonstrate the probity of the courts under their rule. In April 1874 the circuit court convened in Warren County. By April 7 Crosby had assembled a grand jury, and George Brown, the white Republican judge, delivered a blistering charge, reminding them of Cardozo's ghost witnesses, Dorsey's failure to account for the taxes he collected, Davenport's forgeries, and the necessity of the jurors rooting out local corruption. He undoubtedly recognized the danger in allowing white conservatives to paint Republicans as corrupt. He had good reason to expect jurors to heed his instructions; African Americans had compiled a good record as jurors, indicting and convicting defendants with admirable disregard of race.

But after deliberation the grand jury refused to indict any local officials. Perhaps Crosby had carefully included jurors whom he knew would not indict his fellow Republicans, just as whites charged. Six—five white and one black—wrote a "Minority Report" to the judge and expressed sorrow and regret "that we are unable to sustain you in your noble efforts" to clean up the county. The dissenters claimed that most of the grand jury, "in the face of positive proof and direct testimony," had refused to perform its duty.[35] The Republican district attorney joined with dissenters in denouncing the grand jury for failing to indict.[36]

The Republicans' inability to clean up their own house gave political opponents a windfall. More seriously, by refusing to indict the grand jury had confirmed many whites in their conclusion that the courts could not effectively punish black criminality. The circuit court only met twice a year; it would be six months before another grand jury could indict Cardozo and the others. During those long months the idea that the law could not effectively fight Republican corruption would fester and grow. In fact, Republicans had a far better record for rooting out corruption than the Democrats, but it was a critical moment. If the Republicans could not deliver justice now, nothing else mattered. Judge George Brown told jurors that he was "astonished and shocked" by their conduct; they had shielded crime "by skulking and protecting" criminals. If crime could not be punished through the proper agencies established by law, then people would take punishment into their own hands. If that happened, the grand jury would share the blame. Brown expressed regret that he could not jail the grand jurors.[37]

Not long after the grand jury's failure to indict Warren County officials, a racial incident further inflamed white opinion in Vicksburg. In July the daughter of a wealthy Port Gibson planter married one of her father's former slaves, a state senator named Haskins Smith. The Vicksburg *Herald* shrieked that a southern lady had "eloped with a saddle-colored Fifteenth Amendment!" Whites snickered at the men in the bride's family for tolerating such a thing, questioning their manhood and honor. White outrage at the marriage and community ridicule of the Smith men prompted black leader and chancery clerk Washington Davenport to make a speech defending mixed marriages. Were he a single man, he said, and had he won the affection of a white woman and she wanted to marry him, he would take her to his heart and defend her against an army of brothers and fathers. The speech enraged whites.[38]

The circuit court's actions and Davenport's speech promoted white solidarity, and whites prepared to attack the county government. White militia companies marched on Vicksburg's streets, challenging Crosby's authority. Rioting seemed inevitable. The governor of Mississippi, carpetbagger Adelbert Ames, fretted to his wife that "I have tried to get troops, but the President refuses." Ames had heard talk that Grant hoped to win a second term with the support of southern Democrats by allowing them a free hand in the South. Violence seemed so certain that white conservatives moved their families away from Vicksburg to avoid a riot.[39]

Crosby beseeched whites not to indulge in racial tribalism. Still hoping to govern with biracial support, he called for help from whites and blacks. In a proclamation he observed that an "unwonted excitement . . . likely to lead to breaches of the peace" plagued the community. It was the duty of the sheriff, he declared, to prevent lawlessness and call on "all good men without regard to race, color, or previous condition" to promote peace. Crosby deputized sixty men and printed their names at the bottom of his proclamation. It is probable that they discovered they had been deputized only when they read the document in the newspaper.

Crosby appealed to reputable white men he thought likely to favor order, even order under a black-dominated local government. He included, for example, John A. Klein, a banker. Had Klein, a wealthy and influential Democrat, supported Crosby, more whites might have seen the sheriff's hold on office as legitimate. And Crosby probably thought it reasonable that Klein might support him. Under the slavery regime Klein had been especially sympathetic to slaves, granting several of them "nominal" status by allowing them to work as unsupervised artisans. He had also acted as Albert Johnson's agent and pretended owner. Without his help, Johnson might never have achieved the success he did in slavery and risen to a position of leadership after emancipation. Klein had even occasionally allowed slaves who had illegally bought their freedom to use his name as their ostensible "owner." But Klein did not support Crosby.[40]

With Vicksburg's voting population almost evenly divided between blacks and whites, whites could win elections only if they voted as a bloc. They did so in August city elections, ousting Republican municipal officials. White political leaders called on all white voters to rally to their color, regardless of political party. On the eve of the Civil War the worst nightmare some Vicksburgers could imagine had involved an alliance between blacks and Irish (chapter 3). In 1874 Republicans nominated Martin Keary, who was Irish, for mayor, hoping to build a coalition of Irish and black voters.[41] Vicksburg's Irish population had always held itself apart from other whites, but now they chose race over class. Irish-born Vicksburgers said that Keary had forfeited all claim he had upon the Irish "race" when he supported "negro rule." "Irishmen are *white men*," they declared.[42]

The Irish merely recited a theme common in every white mouth. Blacks had challenged whites by nominating ten blacks for thirteen city offices. Whites "must accept, like men, the issue tendered by the negroes or slink like dogs and cowards." Those unwilling to slink must "unfurl the white banner" and "plant the white standard and invite all men of the Caucasian race to rally around it. Those who stand by and protect that standard, are WHITE men. *White* in color, *white* in heart, and *white* in deed!"[42] Such rhetoric alarmed blacks, and some organized a peace meeting. Speakers called for reconciliation, and the crowd adopted resolutions naming a committee of ten to meet with a committee of whites to negotiate an armistice. But after the peace meeting tension remained high, and Vicksburgers feared their city would erupt in racial violence.[43]

As whites unified, blacks factionalized. On the eve of the election, Hannibal C. Carter attacked the Republican ticket as virtually defeated already. Born in Indiana, Carter had served in the U.S. Army during the Civil War, protesting the unequal pay of black soldiers. In Memphis, Tennessee, after the war, he became active in Republican politics. He had moved to Vicksburg after Tennessee Republicans frustrated his efforts to become a U.S. internal revenue collector. Elected to the state legislature, Carter played a key role in passing a state civil rights law. He became a political enemy of the abrasive Thomas W. Cardozo, and it was his affidavit that launched the effort to prosecute and convict Cardozo for fraud. Never at the center of the Republican Vicksburg ring, Carter implicitly criticized the strategy of Cardozo and the other party leaders when he expressed regret that the 1874 municipal election had been turned into a referendum on race. He had likely already begun planning a political future outside the Republican Party that would further divide black voters in 1875.[44]

Meanwhile, whites edged toward violence, threatening would-be black voters. White newspapers carried the names of blacks they claimed should not be allowed to vote. Registrar George R. Walton, a black Republican, saw less subtle forms of intimidation; whites tried to intimidate him with loud cursing as he registered black voters. Transient white raftsmen pushed forward, demanding to vote. In one ward rowdy whites forced him to jump out a window, shouting "kill him; catch the yellow son of a bitch and bring him back." Walton had to ask whites on the street for protection.[45]

Increased white solidarity encouraged them to more openly, heatedly, and directly excoriate the courts. They assailed Judge Brown as a "wretched old man" who had encouraged blacks to burn Vicksburg if they did not win at the polls. He wanted to run for Congress, some whites alleged, and would rig juries to protect indicted black politicians in hopes of currying their support for his own ambitions. In September the *Herald* reported that it was "perfectly apparent" that the board of supervisors intended to repeat its villainy of the last term and nominate grand jurors sympathetic to official corruption. When the board met to nominate grand jurors for the fall term of circuit court, members of the Taxpayers' League appeared to heckle the choices. The Leaguers spoke disrespectfully and cowed some supervisors into withdrawing the names of men they had nominated. The League did not dictate the names nominated, but the grand jury produced by this process proved willing to move against corrupt officials, just as the Taxpayers' League demanded.[46]

At the November term the new grand jury indicted Cardozo for forgery and embezzlement. The jurors claimed that, as circuit clerk, he had amassed $2,000 from land sold by the state for back taxes and never reported it to the state auditor. His successor in office, Dorsey, had collected $1,800 in the same fashion and also failed to report it to the state auditor, as required by law. The jurors also charged that both Cardozo and chancery clerk George Davenport had forged warrants, pocketing county money.[47]

The *Daily Vicksburger* proclaimed all the defendants guilty. "If they can't be convicted," the newspaper said, "with the testimony against them, the law is a farce." But the *Vicksburger* had already decided the jury was corrupt and had no intention of putting the courts to any test. Local whites had long since lost confidence in their court. Even white Republicans doubted a jury seated by Crosby would fairly try the sheriff's political allies.[48]

For two weeks, farms and plantations went untended as whites did little else but prepare for a war with local blacks. Throughout the fall of 1875 whites all over Warren County met in neighborhood meetings, forming companies, electing captains, and coordinating with each other and with whites in neighboring counties. Hinds County promised three hundred men. On September 6 James Madison Batchelor wrote to his brother from his plantation, Hoboken, to say that he had been so busy with "war like preparations and political organization" he scarcely had time to write. A

Confederate veteran, a survivor of Gettysburg and a Union prisoner-of-war camp, "Mad" Batchelor's neighbors had elected him captain of their company. As the inevitable showdown seemed imminent Batchelor took his company to an encampment near Baldwin's Ferry, where they posted pickets and sent out scouts. When a rumor spread that a thousand blacks intended to attack the encampment, whites cheered the news. As Batchelor wrote later, "We were overjoyed at the prospect of a good killing & prepared to give them a warm reception." But the whites missed their "good killing."[49]

Frustrated, whites decided to launch their own offensive. But when Batchelor led his men to a black gathering place, they found only tracks. Their opponents had scattered. Before going home Batchelor raided a collection of black cabins, telling the inhabitants that if they ever defied white authority again he and his men would shoot and hang them all. The whites regretted that they could not locate any of the black political leaders: "We would have made an example [of them] anyhow."[50]

William McCardle had once called on whites to unify against Warren County blacks. By 1874 Batchelor shared fully in McCardle's vision and expected united whites to wage a race war against African Americans. He had heard that blacks intended to bide their time until they could sell their crops and use the money to buy more guns. For their part, whites were euphoric about the racial solidarity they had achieved. Batchelor declared that he had never before seen a people so completely united as Warren County whites. Anything seemed possible in the heady exhilaration of such unprecedented cooperation, and the whites made plans to "get" their sheriff. In the public press they claimed that they wanted to oust Crosby on account of his faulty bond or because they believed him corrupt. Privately, though, Batchelor put his finger on Crosby's real sin. "He has considerable influence in the county among the four thousand negro votes." Eliminating Crosby would help accomplish the goal Batchelor and other whites had already set for themselves: They planned to win the 1875 elections overwhelmingly "or run every negro out of the county."[51]

Some whites made a joke out of the frustration Batchelor and others shared over their inability to find and eliminate black leaders. The *Vicksburger* published an advertisement for runaways signed BY ORDER OF THE PEOPLE that was reminiscent of antebellum slave advertisements:

> Runaways!
>   Two Niggers, Wash Davenport and Lewis Wilson!
>   The former is a high yaller nigger, about 5 feet 5 inches high. . . .[52]

McCardle and other advocates of violent action against black leaders called public meetings to confront their few remaining white critics and turn away from formal legal discourse. On November 27 and December 2 the Taxpayers' League met in Temperance Hall.[53] The *Vicksburger* justified the meetings with vigilante rhetoric: "The people felt themselves compelled to arise in their might and interpose their sovereign power between official thieves and plunderers and the interest and welfare of the city and county." Those assembled debated resolutions demanding the resignations of black county officials. When Harper Hunt objected to language hinting at violence, William H. McCardle "made an able answer to Col. Hunt's objection." The crowd decided to send a committee of ten to the courthouse to call for the resignations of Crosby, Davenport, Wilson, and Sydney Brooks.[54]

When Crosby and the other officials rebuffed the committee, the Taxpayers' League formed another committee of three lawyers and two citizens to decide whether all practicable legal remedies had been exhausted. The chair appointed lawyers Martin Marshall, Owen McGarr, and A. M. Lea and two men the *Vicksburger* identified only as Barnes and Fitzhugh. The committee met and returned with majority and minority reports. McGarr, Lea, and Fitzhugh thought all legal remedies had, in fact, not been exhausted. Davenport awaited trial, and the board of supervisors could be called on to demand sufficient bond from Crosby.[55]

But two members of the committee, Marshall and Barnes, "represented that while *in theory* the law was ample for redress, yet practically it would fail to provide a proper remedy." George Barnes had been a Warren County planter for twenty years; during the Civil War he had raised a regiment to fight the Yankees. Just twenty-four, Marshall, son of Vicksburg's top lawyer, represented a different generation.[56] He and Barnes doubted that Davenport could be convicted if Crosby picked the jury. The crowd unanimously adopted the minority report, and the whole meeting adjourned to the courthouse. When the mob spied Davenport slipping down Monroe Street they gave chase, but he escaped. Crosby, however, remained in his office to confront the crowd. "The people have resolved that you cannot be sheriff of this county one hour longer," Charles Peine declared. Crosby talked for fifteen or twenty minutes before being interrupted by Martin Marshall, who leaped atop a desk and whooped, "We have six hundred men; have we come to parley with this man? We came here for business." The appeal broke Crosby's resistance, and he signed a letter of resignation.[57]

To their credit, these events troubled local lawyers. The bar met at the courthouse to discuss the situation, and Martin Marshall's father, Thomas A. Marshall, chaired the meeting. The lawyers agreed that Crosby was corrupt, or at least passively the instrument of corrupt men, but conceded that "there could be no question but that Crosby was still the legal sheriff." Trained in the common law, some lawyers still believed in a law that even transcended race. Fearing Crosby would be lynched and knowing his killers would be guilty of murder, the lawyers proposed a compromise. Crosby would continue to serve as sheriff but would appoint someone satisfactory to the Taxpayers' League as deputy. He would be a figurehead, with his deputy performing the real work of sheriff.[58] But at least for the moment the proposal went nowhere. Few whites had patience for legal stratagems devised by attorneys.

When whites ejected Crosby from office they shocked Republicans, leaving them reeling in confusion. The evening he resigned, Crosby escaped Vicksburg on horseback. In Bovina he caught a freight train to Jackson, where the governor assembled a sort of kitchen cabinet of advisors to discuss how to react to the forced resignation. The attorney general thought Crosby should demand admission to his office and, if refused, call upon a posse to reclaim it. But others thought Crosby should not return to Vicksburg unaccompanied by a military force. Governor Ames, who had asked for U.S. Army troops before and been rebuffed, stated positively that he would not again call for federal help.[59] Some of the white Republicans in attendance regarded Crosby as incompetent and worthless. Ames himself made it clear that he thought black leaders in Vicksburg needed to stand up for themselves. He lectured Crosby and other black Vicksburgers who had come to Jackson for help that he and other white men had faced bullets to free them. Now, he insisted, they should fight to maintain the freedom given them by whites or be exposed as unworthy of that freedom.[60] The meeting ended inconclusively, but a U.S. Army captain named A. W. Allyn, who claimed to have blundered into the meeting by accident, said later that had he been Crosby he would have considered himself instructed by the governor to seize his office by force.[61]

Conservative white Mississippians later scrutinized Crosby's actions in Jackson, looking for evidence that he incited violence. They thought they found it in a proclamation he prepared in the offices of the *Plain Dealer,* in which he claimed to have been forced from office "in open violation of the Constitution. . . . because I have . . . tried to deal out justice equally to all." The document proposed no specific course of action; instead, Crosby called on his friends to "fight the cause out on its merit, by any and all means known to the constitution." The proclamation ended in melodramatic cadences: "Citizens, shall we submit to such violent and lawless infringements on our rights? No; let us with united strength oppose this common enemy." Crosby said later that he did not order his proclamation published in handbill form, but it was. On Saturday, December 5, newsboys distributed it in Vicksburg, and the next day black ministers read it from their pulpits.[62]

Ames claimed later that he tried to head off trouble by dispatching his adjutant general to Vicksburg. A. G. Packer met with members of the Taxpayers' League, who insisted that their only complaint with Crosby was his bad bond. Meeting with Crosby, Packer found the sheriff insisting that he could make a good bond. Apparently failing to comprehend the deep racial animus in Vicksburg, Packer genuinely thought that a compromise bond might defuse the situation. He urged Crosby to make a new bond. On the street, local white leaders advised him that they believed Crosby planned to take his job back by force. Packer promised to try to halt such a plan if he could, and when he next saw Crosby he told him, "This thing has got to stop." Crosby willingly agreed to send couriers into the country to stop his forces from approaching the city.[63]

Nonetheless, blacks continued to approach Vicksburg, and more and more whites set aside political and ethnic differences to defend their city. At 4:30 A.M. on December 7, Erasmus R. Richardson, a Republican turned conservative, rang the courthouse bell as an alarm to whites. It proved to be a false alarm, but it signaled the unity whites had achieved. Former Confederates turned out to stand alongside their former Yankee enemies, and former Republicans joined with conservatives.

At 8:00 A.M. Richardson rang the bell again. This time it was no false alarm.[64] Led by Andrew Owen, an army friend of Crosby's from the Civil War, blacks approached the city. On Crosby's instructions Owen had assembled 120 men at a church twelve miles from Vicksburg. Fewer than half had guns—old muskets, shotguns, and a few pistols. As Owen's force marched toward Vicksburg in a long line, a white Vicksburger intercepted them. "Owen, go home," Harper Hunt said. Hunt, who had earlier spoken against violence to Vicksburg whites, perhaps still hoped to avoid bloodshed. Having failed to dissuade whites, he now tried his luck with the freedmen. Owen insisted that he could not turn back without talking to Crosby first. Hunt acquiesced, and the pair rode toward Vicksburg together for some time. But as they approached the city Hunt must have decided that he could not face other whites in the company of the blacks. Having failed to block their approach, he had a racial duty to warn the others. Spurring his horse, Hunt galloped into town, leaving Owen behind.[65]

Alerted by Hunt, H. H. Miller hastily assembled his informally organized white militia to defend Vicksburg. As the mayor explained later, there was no military organization, "They were just called out on the spur of the moment." For several tense minutes, Miller and his men confronted Owen's force. Miller and Owen exchanged angry words, Owen again insisting that he wanted to see Crosby. The whites agreed and escorted him to the courthouse, where Crosby told Owen to disband his men. Owen came out of the meeting cursing Crosby as "the cause of all this trouble."[66]

As Owen surveyed the white men arrayed against him, what he saw must have alarmed him. Historians have undoubtedly exaggerated the reconciliation that occurred among Union and Confederate veterans after the Civil War, but scanning the white men behind Miller, Owen could see former Union men alongside former Confederates and Republicans and Whigs mixed with Democrats. Furlong asserted later that "every" white Union army veteran in Vicksburg had turned out to repulse the blacks that day. The Irish turned out as well, using the impending riot as an opportunity to prove themselves.[67]

Returning to his men, Owen told them to disperse, but some stubbornly refused. Miller later reported that blacks shouted and flourished their hats. He could not say who fired first, it seemed simultaneous. Owen remembered the event differently. His men began to disperse, and the whites fired on them as they tried to escape. Much the same happened when two other columns of blacks approached the city. No one knows how many men died that day. The city sexton buried sixteen men, all but two of them black. The mayor reported twenty-five to thirty killed at a fight on Cherry Street, another thirty to forty killed near the Pemberton monument, and fifteen to twenty killed on Grove Street.[68]

After the riot, whites claimed that law had triumphed over lawlessness. The people of the city, the *Vicksburger* proclaimed, had vindicated the law and rebuked mob violence.[69] But it was "people's law," not the statutes printed in law books. Whites believed that their unity legitimized their actions, making them "lawful." But few whites thought deeply about what they had done. Most, such as James Madison Batchelor, marveled that the cost had been so low. Batchelor assured relatives that his side had suffered only mental anxiety—and, in fact, only women and old men had suffered much from that. All the younger men who had been "on the '*war path*' *with me*," he wrote, rather enjoyed the excitement.[70]

For several days after the riot whites continued to enforce their popular, extralegal "law." In the days immediately after, they disarmed local blacks, searching their homes for arms. On Tuesday night rampaging white men went door to door in the black part of Vicksburg.[71] Furlong, the former sheriff now firmly allied with white conservatives, went to William Wood's house to demand his gun. Wood's wife refused to give it to them, but later whites challenged Wood on the street and warned him that he would be shot if he did not produce the gun, a musket he had "got new to save my own life." He turned it over.[72] Seven or eight white men crashed into John McPherson's house, turning over beds. His wife, confined to her bed "in a delicate condition," miscarried in terror.[73] When Tom Bidderman, perhaps too crazy to understand the necessity of deference to white authority, admitted having a gun but refused to turn it over, whites shot and killed him.[74] When twenty whites with fixed bayonets burst into Lusinda Henry's home, they ripped up the floor, broke down the bed, tore open the mattress, and threw clothing on the floor. They found the gun her husband had concealed under the house and also stole $45 he had hidden.[75] Whites arrested former deputy sheriff Charles H. Smith.[76] Crosby remained in town as the battle unfolded, but whites quickly arrested him and forced him to resign again.[77]

Whites worked to make permanent the unity they had achieved in the riot. U.S. Army troops returned Crosby to office, but their presence reinforced local white cohesion.[78] But these dangers did threaten whites' newfound solidarity. Some advocated war against blacks. Men such as James Madison Batchelor grumbled that "the *conservation* element among us checked us from punishing them as we *should have done.*" He predicted that whites would yet regret not having killed many more blacks. "Had we done our *duty,* we would have taught them a lesson which would have lasted a life time." The previous fall, planter Batchelor had talked of running all blacks out of Warren County, and although frustrated by his fellow whites he still liked that idea. But he gave it up for racial solidarity. Searching for a solution all whites could endorse, he proposed asking the federal government to take "charge of Sambo" and colonize him "(the sooner the better)."[79]

A new threat to white unity appeared when Crosby produced a new bond, his third, with white bondsmen. Many whites feared that some of their fellows had defected from the white coalition. U.S. Army troops still patrolled the streets and occupied the courthouse, but angry whites erupted in a storm of indignation, demanding to know who among them had signed Crosby's bond. Knots of men could be seen on the streets, talking about the latest development. From their perspective, those who had stepped forward to defend their "city and families from outraged and the threatened torch and turpentine of the brutal negroes" had been outmaneuvered by the man who had ordered their homes outraged. White Vicksburgers confronted and demanded an explanation from every man on Crosby's bond, who all denied that they meant their names to appear. They had understood that the lawyers' compromise would take effect. Crosby would remain as a figurehead, but a deputy would perform his duties. The Vicksburg *Herald* took pains not to disturb the new unity among whites. "We were glad," the *Herald* wrote, "to find some of the bondsmen expressing a determination not to qualify." The *Herald* reassured readers that the bond had been prepared from good motives and therefore no one should be reproached. The newspaper even announced its regret for the initial feeling of outrage that some had expostulated on learning that some white men had apparently deserted to Crosby: "We are all engaged in a common cause and struggling together to get out of the present trouble."[80]

Pressure on whites not to cooperate with Crosby likely forced the sheriff to make yet another bond, his fourth, using outsiders as bondsmen. By now he clearly recognized that he could not personally act as sheriff. J. P. Gilmer, a former Confederate turned Republican from Kemper County, arranged the bond, intending to act as de facto sheriff himself. Crosby's deputy and political rival, G. W. Chavis, would continue in office and take charge of the jail. All twenty-three bondsmen came from outside Warren County; almost all were Kemper County Republicans. Whites regarded Gilmer as a "radical Radical" but accepted his assurances that he intended to pour oil on troubled waters. "The white people of this county have never asked anything but a fair show," the *Herald* said, "and if Mr. Gilmer gives them that . . . he will receive their encouragement and support." A deal had been struck. Crosby and Gilmer would share the proceeds of the office, with Crosby continuing as sheriff but Gilmer performing the duties. Crosby even signed a formal contract with Gilmer.[81]

Even as whites remained nearly unanimous in their determination to rid their county of "negro rule," Warren County's black population further factionalized. Some felt betrayed by Crosby's deal with Gilmer. In the face of white intimidation they had elected their first black sheriff in 1873, and many had been willing to lay down their lives for him the following year. By 1875 he had traded away his authority to a white man. Black Republicans convened an indignation meeting in the courthouse. The black president of the board of supervisors, George Walton, denounced Crosby, who sat and listened as Walton reprimanded him for signing away his rights and betraying the black voters who had placed him in office. Walton even claimed that he would prefer a Democrat to a mercenary like Gilmer. Crosby defended himself by lashing out at his black deputies, the organizers of the protest against him. He claimed the sheriff's office functioned better under Gilmer than it had six months earlier and predicted that Gilmer would stand by him and not crawl into cellars in times of danger. Deputy Sheriff Chavis, the leading critic of the arrangement with Gilmer, had been noticeably absent when Crosby faced the white mob alone on December 7.[82]

Under pressure from whites, the deal between Gilmer, Crosby, and certain leading whites unraveled throughout the spring of 1875, and in March the Taxpayers' League met and vowed to pay no taxes to either man. A few days later Chavis filed suit against Crosby, claiming the sheriff owed him $500 from his days as deputy. Crosby searched Vicksburg to confront Chavis, but when Chavis flourished a gun the sheriff backed away.[83]

In the end, Gilmer's mercenary lusts brought him down. He had been speculating in county warrants to supplement his income as deputy sheriff. A local pawnbroker named Rothschild sold him some warrants that turned out to be the fraudulent warrants Davenport had circulated. Gilmer chastised the pawnbroker and even threatened to whip him with cowhide. Arrested, Gilmer appeared before the mayor. But the mayor's authority carried little weight with the angry deputy, and upon release Gilmer immediately returned to Rothschild's shop with more threats and, this time, a pistol.[84]

On June 7 Peter Crosby accused Gilmer of shooting him in a Vicksburg saloon. The pair had fallen out, Crosby said later, over the appointment of deputies. More likely, they fought over the spoils of office. The shot fired into his head did not immediately kill Crosby, but newspapers reported that the wound would certainly prove fatal. Apparently dying, Crosby swore out a warrant against Gilmer, accusing him of attempted murder. Vicksburg's black newspaper interviewed Crosby and reported that he had declared that Gilmer "had it done or did it himself."[85] But Crosby lived and retreated from his original accusations at Gilmer's hearing before a justice of the peace. He and Gilmer had gone into the saloon together after clearing up whatever bad feelings had existed between the two. Although he had once been positive that Gilmer had either shot him or ordered it done, he now admitted that he could only see the perpetrator's arm and elbow. The justice dismissed the charges against Gilmer.[86]

Despite his testimony, Crosby's quarrel with Gilmer had been worked out after the shooting, not before. He had fired Gilmer on June 5, but the deputy had refused to vacate the office. By July, Crosby had located a new white man, Thomas C. Bedford, to serve as his chief deputy. Gilmer returned to Kemper County, where a mob would murder him in 1877.[87] The conservative *Herald* praised Bedford as an old Vicksburger of unquestioned integrity. He would, the newspaper reassured readers, have full charge of the office. His bond included H. H. Miller, the same man who had led the military-style attack on Crosby's followers on December 7. When Crosby resigned for the third and final time on October 28, 1875, Reconstruction had been effectively ended in Warren County, Mississippi.[88]

After ousting Crosby, white conservatives turned to the black president of the board of supervisors, George Walton. Unlike Davenport or even Crosby, Walton had no reputation among whites for corruption. Instead, the white candidate he had defeated at the polls, J. Fred Baum, challenged Walton's election in circuit court. Republicans had once hoped to recruit the German-born Baum into their ranks, but now he served as president of the white conservative Taxpayers' League. Baum conceded that Walton had badly beaten him at three of the four voting places, but in one precinct he had received twice as many votes as Walton. He lost, he said, only because officials had thrown out many of the votes in his favor. The official inspectors insisted that the rejected ballots had been illegal because they had the wrong district marked on them. Although whites insisted they had no confidence in the courts and claimed Brown too biased to give them a fair trial, in the end Walton, not Baum, cried foul. Just as the trial began, his white Republican lawyer abandoned him to face the trial unrepresented by counsel. Perhaps as a result, Baum triumphed. The Republican judge ordered Walton to step down in favor of Baum.[89]

White Vicksburgers came away from their triumphs over Crosby and Walton determined to carry the 1875 election against all hazards.[90] Such language suggested the use of extralegal, vigilante tactics. Working-class Democrats formed a vigilante organization called the Modocs, named for an Indian tribe. One Warren Countian remembered the atmosphere in 1875 as "pregnant . . . with intimidation." Bodies of armed white men marched through Warren County, firing cannons every three or four hundred yards.[91] At night, bands of white men patrolled the county, stopping blacks on the highway and ordering them back to their homes. Blacks planned to celebrate July 4 with speeches and a ceremonial reading of the Declaration of Independence in the circuit courtroom, but whites armed with pistols marched into the chamber. A scuffle broke out, and one of the invading whites fired. In a confusion of shooting and shouting voices, someone yelled, "Get out of here, you radical sons-of-bitches!" The crowd rushed for doors and windows. After the blacks had fled, more whites came into the courtroom, found Ben Allen on the floor, and beat him unmercifully. White boys threw spittoons at his head. Questioned afterward, they insisted they had no objection to celebrating the Fourth but objected to the presence of Cardozo, Davenport, and Crosby.[92] Blacks stopped holding public political meetings and gathered instead in swamps.[93] Some whites were not satisfied to drive black political activity underground; they meant to extinguish it entirely. The night before the Republican nominating convention, whites invaded the Davenports' house. They could not find him but satisfied themselves with killing his brother-in-law and burning the body.[94]

The violence destroyed Republican influence over criminal justice in Warren County, even as Republicans continued formally to control the machinery of criminal justice. After 1874 the percentage of black grand jurors sharply declined to 25 percent of the county's total black population. Throughout the remainder of the decade white conservatives kept that number at nearly the same level. These mostly white grand juries resisted returning many indictments based on black complaints and were rarely receptive to the testimony of illiterates. Only 14 percent of complainants could not read or write. Whites "redeemed" criminal justice even before they seized political power.

The conservatives' success in reducing black participation on grand juries matched their political triumph throughout the state. They so completely rallied whites to their cause that the Republican governor felt he had to agree to white demands that black militia units be disbanded. In Vicksburg the blacks' total political defeat became apparent when Republican state officials appointed John Beaird, a white militia major and one of the leaders in the ouster of Crosby in December, to take charge of the mustering-out. Black soldiers had to surrender their state arms to Beaird, their sworn enemy. To make sure former black militiamen did not rearm, whites guarded the riverfront, seizing a shipment of arms intended for the militia in September.[95]

Whites could seize the arms because of their unified political power. That same political strength allowed them to choose to control blacks through vigilante violence in 1875. They neutralized blacks' political ambitions, suppressing public black political meetings. In the secret nocturnal meetings African Americans held instead, some argued against voting at all. Others thought—mistakenly—that they could wield some modicum of political power by nominating a white Democrat. Crosby's white deputy, Bedford, for example, was a good citizen inclined to enforce the laws impartially. When white conservatives heard of the blacks' plan, they shot Bedford's supporters, wounding at least two and killing one. Whites calling themselves Modocs invaded Republican meetings to force an endorsement of the white conservative candidate. When Republicans started to leave one meeting without endorsing any candidate the Modocs fingered their pistols and announced that no one could leave until someone was either nominated or endorsed for sheriff. Some tried to jump out windows, but in the end they endorsed the white conservative candidate, A. J. Flanagan.[96]

Other politically ambitious blacks tried to cope by running as independents but could not honestly win a significant number of votes. Ham Carter and W. W. Edwards announced themselves as independent candidates for the Mississippi house of representatives. One Republican later claimed that "I don't suppose there was twenty-five republicans in the whole county had read" his announcement. In the nineteenth century, parties ran elections and printed their own ballots, which party workers handed out to prospective voters. In 1875 Warren County Republicans prepared ballots on blue paper, shorter than the Democratic tickets. Martin Keary and Edwards went to New Orleans, where they had so-called bogus tickets printed on blue paper the same size and shape as the Republican ballots but with the names of Carter and Edwards substituted for the regular Republican legislative candidates.

Whites cheated, too. Democrats used violence and intimidation to drive some Republicans from the polls. They also refused to count the ballots of those black voters who did pick up Republican ballots. Although D. J. Foreman, a black candidate for justice of the peace, handed out three hundred ballots to supporters in one precinct, the next day white officials told him he had received only forty-seven votes.[97] Democrats not only threw out genuine Republican ballots but also inserted handfuls of the bogus Republican tickets Carter and Edwards had prepared into ballot boxes. A. C. Knadler, who counted the votes in one precinct, reported "a devilish sight of bogus tickets in all the boxes." As contemporaries phrased it, Edwards and Carter had been "counted in" by corrupt Democrats, and the regular Republican candidates "counted out."[98]

After the riot on December 7, 1874, white Vicksburgers saw themselves as a solid unit, a racially defined community. Lawyer Roswell V. Booth described what happened as a "civic revolution," one that "swept the last vestige of carpetbag, negroe-Republican rule from Mississippi." That was an overstatement. As Booth himself wrote elsewhere, Republicans, both black and white, remained a force long after 1875. Their presence in the body politic prompted whites to rewrite the state constitution in 1890 to eliminate black voting.

Yet something dramatic had happened at the end of 1874 and continued through 1875: Whites had forged a new coalition that severely reduced political, economic, and social differences within their community.[99] Law played a reduced role. When Roswell Booth wrote a historical sketch of the city, he conceded that the conduct of the outraged Vicksburgers who had lynched five gamblers in the 1835 gambling riots had been indefensible morally. Booth, after all, had decided to become a lawyer in the 1850s, a time when Vicksburgers had moved toward police regulation and away from extralegal collective action such as the gambling riots. But now, he added, "It must be remembered that 'desperate diseases require desperate remedies.'" Right or wrong, Booth thought, the lynchers "taught a salutary lesson," and he observed approvingly that professional gamblers had never dared return to Vicksburg after 1835.[100] Booth's writing recalled the vigilante spirit that Vicksburgers had begun to move away from by the Civil War but in 1875 stood ready to embrace once again.

Conclusion

In the twentieth century, legal historians have proven that judges and lawyers do not "discover" law. They make it—usually to suit their own ends. Many scholars have looked at the statutes and the state and federal Supreme Court decisions where the elite articulate their understandings of law and its place in society. Scholars seeking hegemony rarely examine popular attitudes toward legal institutions.

The network of local attitudes and understandings toward law that makes up a locality's legal culture plays an important role in law. In the absence of a proactive police force, such non-elites as grand jurors, justices of the peace, and witnesses control which crimes go to court and which do not. The attitudes of these people toward law shift and evolve over time. In Warren County, for example, law became more protective of property after the Civil War than it had been before. At the very least, that shift had to be ratified by non-elite participants in the legal system.

Some elite rhetoric about law circumscribed and curbed elite power. Leading lawyers and judges of the nineteenth century said they believed in higher law, a law beyond human manipulation. As one New Orleans newspaper explained, law existed "independent of human will." Naturally, it followed that "no man has ever created law. Governments can only ascertain and declare it."[1] We cannot go back and interview people in the past. If we could, it is likely that nineteenth-century jurors would have repeated some of the same rhetoric: People cannot make law, they only discover it. So long as lawyers mythologized law as ultimate, organic, and beyond the grasp of mortal men, even the most discriminatory statutes could never fully be trusted to control African Americans.

The idea that law lay beyond the control of political leaders was a myth. To understand that such beliefs constituted a myth does not diminish their importance. Students of society dismiss myth at their peril. Commonly shared beliefs about the epistemology of law or any societal function help legitimize—or delegitimize—those functions. The fictions people make "true" reveal the kind of society they have constructed.

Another myth important in shaping attitudes toward law involved understandings of community. People able to sustain myths of strong community can see formal law as less necessary than do folk in more atomistic societies. When James Madison Batchelor exulted in the new unity he found among his white neighbors in 1874, he understood that the new solidarity made abstract, higher law less necessary, even an obstacle, to racial discipline.[2] The nature of community life shaped the forms of justice, defining the kind of law whites wanted enforced. White southerners preferred a kind of law where they could pull the strings, shaping outcomes to their immediate needs. And intense racial solidarity and community made it possible to indulge their preferences. Lawyers did become more important in southern society at the end of the nineteenth century, but truly immutable law did not. Lawyers proved quite willing to evade formal law when disciplining black people. One judge frankly admitted that public defenders often persuaded black clients to plead guilty. They did so to spare white taxpayers the expense of trials.

Legislators crafted a variety of anti-enticement laws, vagrancy laws, and convict-lease statutes to serve whites.[3] The young lawyers who emerged to lead southern society after Reconstruction endorsed lynching. Whites governed the Deep South not so much through written law as by unwritable conduct codes, complex rituals, and etiquette.[4] They betrayed a lack of confidence in the rule of law but considerable faith in the informal "law" meted out by their own communities. Such was certainly the case in and around Vicksburg. Between 1880 and 1931 regional newspapers reported nineteen lynchings in Warren County.[5]

In nineteenth-century America, society always balanced informal, extralegal justice against constitutionalism. Americans undeniably believed in their constitution. As revolutionaries they rejected English rule in part because England had no "fixed" constitution to limit and control governmental power or public passion. Free to govern themselves, Americans wrote a constitution that guaranteed due process. Just as undeniably, they

believed that some times, in some instances, the crowd could more effectively control crime than rule-bound courts.

During and after the Civil War, white southerners shifted the balance
between law and extralegal justice and learned to rely less on higher, immutable law. Instead, they reconfigured what they "knew" about law. It
became something more plastic, more easily circumvented or manipulated, and not so much guided by abstract principles as shaped by social
forces. But even this new understanding could not make law malleable
enough. The common law remained too stubbornly autonomous to be
fully effective in controlling blacks. As before the war, the real punishing
of black criminality took place outside court when masters simply
whipped misbehaving slaves.

While law can be used to control people it naturally implies rights. At
the end of the twentieth century, after sophisticated studies of the role
elites play in manipulating law-making and law-enforcing, immutable,
higher law can seem a myth, an impossible ideal. For southern whites at
the end of the nineteenth century, it was all too real. In his private journal, Roswell Booth described the principles of law as necessarily eternal
and immutable. Perhaps he struggled to work out his understanding of
law for himself. "No legislation," he mused, "can be passed that will operate harshly on the blacks, that will not act with equal hardship, and
oppression, on the white."[6] Just ten years earlier, of course, Booth had
worked to enforce Mississippi's cruelly discriminatory Black Code as
prosecutor in county court. By 1876 he had learned that common-law
doctrines promoted equality. Lawyers committed to the common-law
mentalité reflexively transferred perquisites and penalties from one class
of plaintiff or defendant to another.

Blacks' embrace of objective justice may have made it easier for whites
to reject that paragon. When African Americans displayed the Constitution, the Declaration of Independence, and the American flag at their
gatherings, they made a bid for the higher-law ideal. Many blacks in
Warren County understood that they needed fair justice meted out according to immutable principles. They had no chance in a courtroom
where elites openly controlled the proceedings. For Vicksburg's black
population, the extent to which even the illusion of higher law penetrated the white consciousness had real consequences. Abstract principles,
uniformly applied, curtailed the usefulness of law as a tool of oppression.
If white lawyers occasionally paid homage to higher law, that helped black
defendants and crime victims. For most ordinary whites, law controlled

by immutable principles and due process "technicalities" was unworkable for precisely the reasons blacks needed such law.

The white community, unified to deny the autonomous power of law, understood that no matter how it rigged the rules it still had to appear neutral to have any legitimacy at all and that pretense could be exploited by the subordinate group. Whites understood that this constrained their power to manipulate the law. Any rules whites imposed through law inevitably included rights that could be claimed by those subject to law. Such attitudes toward law set the stage for the extralegal violence that characterized New South life in Vicksburg. On December 7, 1874, in the streets of Vicksburg, a crowd consciously chose lawlessness over law. Whites had learned something from their experiences in slavery, Civil War, and Reconstruction: Law could never be made oppressive enough to effectively control African Americans.

Appendix

Table A-1. Wealth of Justices of the Peace Compared with Male Heads of Households in 1860

	Male Heads of Household (N = 1,188)	Justices of the Peace (N = 17)	
Number of slaves owned			
0	57.2%	52.9%	(N = 9)
1–19	31.4	35.3	(N = 6)
20+	11.4	11.8	(N = 2)
	100.0	100.0	
Value of real estate			
$0	48.7%	35.3%	(N = 6)
$1–10,000	39.3	52.9	(N = 9)
$10,001+	12.0	11.8	(N = 2)
	100.0	100.0	
Value of personal estate			
$0	41.7%	35.3%	(N = 6)
$1–10,000	38.0	29.4	(N = 5)
$10,001+	20.3	35.3	(N = 6)
	100.0	100.0	

Sources: Magistrates were identified in the Natchez Trace Collection, Center for American History, University of Texas at Austin. Wealth has been calculated from the manuscript population census schedules, Eighth U.S. Census, 1860, Warren County, Miss., microfilm, National Archives.

Table A-2. Comparison of Types of Crimes before and after the Civil War

	1822–59	1865–79
Crimes against:		
Property	18.7%	39.7%
Moral order	27.3	25.2
Person	32.8	24.3
Civil order	21.2	10.8
	100.0	100.0
Total crimes committed	1,898	2,078

Source: Warren County Circuit and Criminal Court Papers.

Table A-3. Comparison of Types of Crimes during and Immediately after the Civil War

	1861–62	1865–66
Crimes against:		
Property	8.6%	34.7%
Moral order	22.4	42.4
Person	44.9	18.8
Civil order	24.1	4.1
	100.0	100.0
Total crimes committed	58	462

Sources: Warren County Circuit and Criminal Court Papers. No civil courts met in 1863 and 1864.

Table A-4. Participation in Warren County Courts by Race

	County, 1865–69		Circuit,[a] 1865–69		Military,[b] 1864–65	
	%	N	%	N	%	N
Defendants						
Black	38.7	53	18.0	93	33.9	538
White	61.3	84	82.0	425	66.1	1,048
	100.0	137	100.0	518	100.0	1,586
Victims						
Black	20.3	12	10.1	18	—	—
White	79.7	47	89.9	161	—	—
	100.0	59	100.0	179		

Sources: County court cases files, criminal court case files, circuit court case files, circuit court state docket book, Old Court House Museum, Vicksburg, and Natchez Trace Collection, Center for American History, University of Texas at Austin; Gordon A. Cotton and Ralph C. Mason, *With Malice Toward Some: The Military Occupation of Vicksburg, 1864–1865* (Vicksburg: Warren County Historical Society, 1991), 22–55.

a. Includes criminal court, a court created for Warren County in 1860 that followed the same rules and procedures as circuit court but met quarterly.

b. Record of arrests by military authorities.

Table A-5. Comparison of Literacy by Race of Crime Victims

	Presidential Reconstruction (1865–67)	Congressional Reconstruction (1868–74)	Conservative Era (1875–79)
White victims	($N = 21$)	($N = 79$)	($N = 42$)
Literate	100.0%	83.5%	88.1%
Illiterate	—	16.5	11.9
	100.0	100.0	100.0
Black victims	($N = 8$)	($N = 67$)	($N = 34$)
Literate	37.5	14.9	23.5
Illiterate	62.5	85.1	76.5
	100.0	100.0	100.0

Sources: Warren County Circuit Court Papers, Old Court House Museum, Vicksburg; manuscript population schedules, Ninth U.S. Census, 1870, Warren County, Miss., microfilm, National Archives.

Table A-6. Literacy Rates for Grand Jurors in Warren County

	Presidential Reconstruction ($N = 91$)	Congressional Reconstruction ($N = 224$)	Conservative Era ($N = 102$)
Literate	97.8%	88.4%	90.2%
Illiterate	2.2	11.6	9.8
	100.0	100.0	100.0

Sources: Warren County Circuit Court Papers, Old Court House Museum, Vicksburg; manuscript population schedules, Ninth U.S. Census, 1870, and Tenth U.S. Census, 1880, Warren County, Miss., microfilm, National Archives.

Table A-7. Comparison of Grand Juror Property Holdings in Warren County

Value of Property	Presidential Reconstruction ($N = 89$)	Congressional Reconstruction ($N = 222$)	Conservative Era ($N = 94$)
$0	24.7%	30.6%	29.8%
$1–500	4.5	12.2	10.6
$501–10,000	48.3	40.1	42.5
$10,001+	22.5	17.1	17.1
	100.0	100.0	100.0

Sources: Warren County Circuit Court Papers, Old Court House Museum, Vicksburg; manuscript population schedules, Ninth U.S. Census, 1870, Warren County, Miss., microfilm, National Archives.

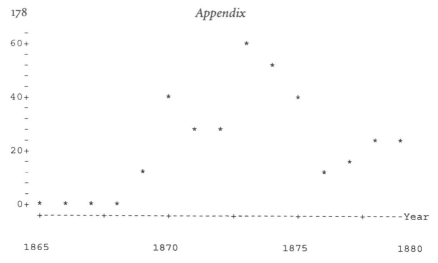

Figure A-1. Black Grand Jurors as a Percentage of All Grand Jurors
    Data taken from Warren County Circuit Court Papers, Old Court House Mu-
seum, Vicksburg, and manuscript population schedules, Seventh U.S. Census,
1870, Warren County, Miss., microfilm, National Archives.

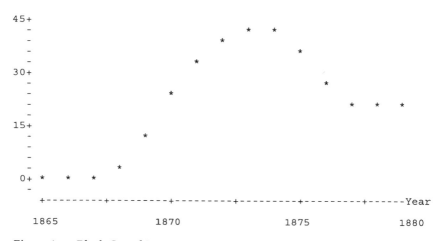

Figure A-2. Black Grand Jurors as a Percentage of All Grand Jurors (Smoothed)
    Data taken from Warren County Circuit Court Papers, Old Court House Mu-
seum, Vicksburg, and manuscript population schedules, Seventh U.S. Census,
1870, Warren County, Miss., microfilm, National Archives.

Notes

Introduction

1. Tom O'Connor, "Portrait of a Lynch Town: 'Best People' Blamed as Much as 'Crackers': PM Reporter in Georgia Town Just after Four Slayings Describes People," Aug. 5, 1946, Papers of the NAACP, ser. A, pt. 7, reel 28, microfilm, Library of Congress.

2. Eugene D. Genovese, *Roll, Jordan, Roll: The World the Slaves Made* (New York: Random House, 1974), 25–49; Douglas Hay, "Property, Authority, and the Criminal Law," in *Albion's Fatal Tree: Crime and Society in Eighteenth-Century England,* ed. Douglas Hay et al. (New York: Parthenon, 1975), 17ff.

3. For recent statements of this argument, see Mark Tushnet, *The American Law of Slavery, 1810–1860: Considerations of Humanity and Interest* (Princeton: Princeton University Press, 1981); and Christopher Tomlins, *Law, Labor, and Ideology in the Early American Republic* (New York: Cambridge University Press, 1993). Stewart E. Tolnay and E. M. Beck, *A Festival of Violence: An Analysis of Southern Lynchings, 1882–1930* (Urbana: University of Illinois Press, 1992), 105–65, argue that ordinary people's attitudes toward law had little influence on lynching violence. They look to economic variables. More persuasively, Fitzhugh Brundage, considering regional variation within and between Georgia and Virginia, has found that Virginians had a deeper faith in law as a social control mechanism than did Georgians. They "devised a 'web of restrictive legislation'" and depended on it. White Virginians lynched less than Georgians because they believed they could use law as an instrument to achieve control of labor. W. Fitzhugh Brundage, *Lynching in the New South: Georgia and Virginia, 1880–1930* (Urbana: University of Illinois Press, 1993), 1–16.

4. Lawrence Friedman, "Legal Culture and Social Development," *Law and Society Review* 4 (1969): 29–44; Richard Hamm, *Shaping the Eighteenth Amendment: Tem-*

perance Reform, Legal Culture, and the Polity, 1880–1920 (Chapel Hill: University of North Carolina Press, 1995), 11–15; Norman L. Rosenberg, *Protecting the Best Men: An Interpretive History of the Law of Libel* (Chapel Hill: University of North Carolina Press, 1986), 21–28; John Phillip Reid, *Law for the Elephant: Property and Social Behavior on the Overland Trail* (San Marino: Huntington Library, 1980), 19–30.

5. Linda O. McMurry, *Recorder of the Black Experience: A Biography of Monroe Nathan Work* (Baton Rouge: Louisiana State University Press, 1985), 125; Merrill W. Smith to George Fort Milton, Sept. 21, 1930, Association of Southern Women for the Prevention of Lynching Papers, 1930–1942, reel 1, microfilm, Atlanta University.

6. The South Carolina prototype of American vigilante movements used violence to build communities, punishing bandit gangs, and hunters. These backcountry regulators shared terrible secrets, committed murders together, forging bonds that made a society safe for slavery. Rachel N. Klein, *Unification of a Slave State: The Rise of the Planter Class in the South Carolina Backcountry, 1760–1808* (Chapel Hill: University of North Carolina Press, 1990), 1–108; James P. Whittenburg, "Planters, Merchants, and Lawyers: Social Change and the Origins of the North Carolina Regulation," *William and Mary Quarterly* 34 (April 1977): 215–38; Rachel N. Klein, "Ordering the Backcountry: The South Carolina Regulation," *William and Mary Quarterly* 38 (Oct. 1981): 661–80; Richard Maxwell Brown, *The South Carolina Regulators* (Cambridge: Harvard University Press, 1963), 53–63.

7. Jerold S. Auerbach, *Justice without Law? Resolving Disputes without Lawyers* (New York: Oxford University Press, 1983), 3–46; Christine B. Harrington, *Shadow Justice: The Ideology and Institutionalization of Alternatives to Court* (Westport: Greenwood Press, 1985), 9–39; Dan Fenno Henderson, *Conciliation and Japanese Law: Tokugawa and Modern* (Seattle: University of Washington Press, n.d.), 173–81; John Henry Wigmore, *A Panorama of the World's Legal Systems* (St. Paul: West, 1928), vol. 2, 491–503; Maxwell Bloomfield, *American Lawyers in a Changing Society, 1776–1876* (Cambridge: Harvard University Press, 1976), 32–58; Henry Sumner Maine, *Ancient Law: Its Connection with the Early History of Society and Its Relation to Modern Ideas* (1861, repr. London: Henry Holt, 1864); Roscoe Pound, *The Spirit of the Common Law* (Boston: Marshall Jones, 1921), 139–65; Lawrence M. Friedman, *The Republic of Choice: Law, Authority, and Culture* (Cambridge: Harvard University Press, 1990), 18–50.

8. Benedict O'Gorman Anderson, *Imagined Communities: Reflections on the Origin and Spread of Nationalism* (New York: Verso, 1991); Darrett B. Rutman and Anita H. Rutman, *Small Worlds, Large Questions: Explorations in Early American Social History, 1600–1850* (Charlottesville: University of Virginia Press, 1994), 34–54; Bryant Simon, "The Appeal of Cole Blease of South Carolina: Race, Class, and Sex in the New South," *Journal of Southern History* 62 (Feb. 1996): 57–61; Thomas Bender, *Community and Social Change in America* (New Brunswick: Rutgers University Press, 1978), 3–14.

9. Fractured, competitive societies experience a kind of extralegal violence quite different from that found in cohesive societies, more violent and individualistic. For the transition, see Paul A. Gilje, *The Road to Mobocracy: Popular Disorder in New York City, 1763–1834* (Chapel Hill: University of North Carolina Press, 1987), 121–282; and Iver Bernstein, *The New York City Draft Riots: Their Significance for American Society*

and Politics in the Age of the Civil War (New York: Oxford University Press, 1990), 4–8. Altina Waller makes this point for Memphis in "Community, Class, and Race in the Memphis Draft Riot of 1866," *Journal of Social History* 18 (Winter 1984): 233–46.

10. Edward L. Ayers, *The Promise of the New South: Life after Reconstruction* (New York: Oxford University Press, 1992), 155–59; Jacquelyn Dowd Hall, *Revolt against Chivalry: Jessie Daniel Ames and the Women's Campaign against Lynching* (1979, repr. New York: Columbia University Press, 1993), 139; Simon, "The Appeal of Cole Blease," 57–86; Stephen J. Whitfield, *A Death in the Delta: The Story of Emmett Till* (New York: Free Press, 1988), 28–31. In both this book and his earlier work, Ayers, as well as W. Fitzhugh Brundage and Roberta Senechal de la Roche, note the tendency of lynchers to prey on outsiders. See Edward Ayers, *Vengeance and Justice: Crime and Punishment in the Nineteenth-Century American South* (New York: Oxford University Press, 1984), 252–53; Brundage, *Lynching in the New South*, 81–84; and Roberta Senechal de la Roche, "Collective Violence as Social Control," *Sociological Forum* 11 (1996): 97–128. For outside pressure on community, see Jessie Shirley Bernard, *The Sociology of Community* (Glenview: Scott, Foresman, 1973), 149–62.

11. Auerbach, *Justice without Law?* 5.

12. J. William Harris, "Etiquette, Lynching, and Racial Boundaries in Southern History: A Mississippi Example," *American Historical Review* 100 (April 1995): 387–410; Tolnay and Beck, *A Festival of Violence*, figure 2–6. I am indebted to Terry Finnegan for sharing his database of Mississippi lynchings. See Terence Robert Finnegan, "'At the Hands of Parties Unknown': Lynching in Mississippi and South Carolina, 1881–1940," Ph.D. diss., University of Illinois at Urbana-Champaign, 1993.

13. The North also saw considerable vigilante activity. In Revolutionary Boston, whole neighborhoods turned out to challenge hapless British officers. John Phillip Reid, *In a Defiant Stance: The Conditions of Law in Massachusetts Bay, the Irish Comparison, and the Coming of the American Revolution* (University Park: Pennsylvania State University Press, 1977). Not long thereafter, however, a new ethic took hold in many parts of the North that cracked the old communitarianism, encouraging commercial competition and the growth of individual fortunes. See John L. Brooke, *The Heart of the Commonwealth: Society and Political Culture in Worcester County, Massachusetts, 1713–1861* (Amherst: University of Massachusetts Press, 1989); Alexander Keyssar, *Out of Work: The First Century of Unemployment in Massachusetts* (New York: Cambridge University Press, 1986), 9–38; and David A. Gerber, *The Making of American Populism: Buffalo, New York, 1825–1860* (Urbana: University of Illinois Press, 1989), 113–409.

14. Kristin Bumiller, *The Civil Rights Society: The Social Construction of Victims* (Baltimore: Johns Hopkins University Press, 1988); R. Emerson Dobash and Russell P. Dobash, *Women, Violence, and Social Change* (New York: Routledge, 1992); Myra C. Glenn, *Campaigns against Corporal Punishment: Prisoners, Sailors, Women, and Children in Antebellum America* (Albany: State University of New York, 1984).

15. On this point, see Herbert Shapiro, *White Violence and Black Response: From Reconstruction to Montgomery* (Amherst: University of Massachusetts Press, 1988), xi–xvi and passim.

Chapter 1: The Setting

1. The classic statement of this remains Kai Erikson, *Wayward Puritans: A Study in the Sociology of Deviance* (New York: Wiley and Son, 1966).

2. Christopher Morris, *Becoming Southern: The Evolution of a Way of Life, Warren County and Vicksburg, Mississippi, 1770–1860* (New York: Oxford University Press, 1995), 3–22; John Hebron Moore, *The Emergence of the Cotton Kingdom in the Old Southwest: Mississippi, 1770–1860* (Baton Rouge: Louisiana State University Press, 1988), 1–17; Robin F. A. Fabel, "An Eighteenth Colony: Dreams for Mississippi on the Eve of the Revolution," *Journal of Southern History* 59 (Nov. 1993): 647–72; Bradley G. Bond, *Political Culture in the Nineteenth-Century South: Mississippi, 1830–1900* (Baton Rouge: Louisiana State University Press, 1995), 14–214; James C. Cobb, *The Most Southern Place on Earth: The Mississippi Delta and the Roots of Regional Identity* (New York: Oxford University Press, 1992), 19–33; Pamela Lea Grillis, *Vicksburg and Warren County: A History of People and Place* (Vicksburg: Dancing Rabbit, 1992), 19–33.

3. Morris, *Becoming Southern*, 3–22; Cobb, *The Most Southern Place on Earth*, 7–28.

4. Jacob Perry Welch, *Welch Journal: An Autobiography Commenced January 1, 1857*, ed. Edwin Shields and Ann Flynt (Meridian, Miss.: privately printed, 1996), 23.

5. Joan E. Cashin, *A Family Venture: Men and Women on the Southern Frontier* (New York: Oxford University Press, 1991), 32–118, 36 (first quotation), 103 (second quotation). James Oakes and Jane Turner Censer argue against this interpretation, finding that materialism motivated southern pioneers. James Oakes, *The Ruling Race: A History of American Slaveholders* (New York: Knopf, 1982), ch. 3; Jane Turner Censer, "Southwestern Migration among North Carolina Planter Families: 'The Disposition to Emigrate,'" *Journal of Southern History* 57 (Aug. 1991): 407–26.

6. Morris, *Becoming Southern*, 114–31.

7. Gertrude Philippsborn, *The History of the Jewish Community of Vicksburg from 1820 to 1968* (Vicksburg: privately printed, 1969), 9–12.

8. Morris, *Becoming Southern*, 151.

9. James Burns Wallace Diary, Jan. 13, 1836, Special Collections, Hill Memorial Library, Louisiana State University, Baton Rouge (first quotation); James Morris Perrin, comp., *Reverend Newit Vick: Founder of Vicksburg, Mississippi. His Ancestry, Relatives, and Descendants* (Hammond, La.: privately printed, 1990), 9–14; Bond, *Political Culture in the Nineteenth-Century South*, 55; Morris, *Becoming Southern*, 103–13; James T. McIntosh, Haskell M. Monroe, Jr., and Lynda Lasswell Crist, eds., *The Papers of Jefferson Davis* (Baton Rouge: Louisiana State University Press, 1974–), vol. 2, 11n1; John Quitman to Eliza, Dec. 5, 1829, Quitman Family Papers, Southern Historical Collection, Wilson Library, University of North Carolina, Chapel Hill (second and third quotations).

10. 1824 Tax List, Warren County, microfilm, Mississippi Department of Archives and History, Jackson (hereafter cited as MDAH); Morris, *Becoming Southern*, 27–28.

11. Through the antebellum era, the top slaveholders became an ever more select group. The slaveowning proportion of Warren County's taxpaying population shrank. In 1830, 40 percent of taxpayers owned slaves. By 1860 only a quarter of the

taxpaying population did. Because tax lists include the sons of planters among the propertyless, a better measure of the distribution of wealth can be found by looking at the heads of households. The percentage of household heads owning slaves remained stable between 1830 and 1850 but shrank in the 1850s; meanwhile, the slave population exploded.

12. 1830 Tax List, Warren County, microfilm, MDAH; manuscript population schedules, Eighth U.S. Census, 1860, Warren County, Mississippi, microfilm, National Archives (hereafter cited as NA); Morris, *Becoming Southern,* table 4-4, 159.

13. Morris, *Becoming Southern,* 23–41, 156–68; Bond, *Political Culture in the Nineteenth-Century South,* 14–80; John Hebron Moore, *Agriculture in Ante-Bellum Mississippi* (New York: Bookman, 1958), 13–68. Warren County's slaveholding elite did not form a closed club. Of 648 slaveowners in the 1860 census, only about a third, or 237, had been slaveowners in the county ten years earlier. Those who did poorly often disappeared. Of the 588 heads of household in 1860 who had appeared in the 1850 census, about half gained slaves; 33 percent (193) owned the same number of slaves as they had ten years before. Just 15 percent lost slaves, and very few (only 5 percent) lost ten or more slaves; 20 percent (121) did very well, gaining ten or more slaves. People moved into Warren County's slaveholding elite. In 1860, in fact, a majority of the wealthiest slaveowners in Warren County were born in states other than Mississippi. Manuscript population schedules, Seventh U.S. Census, 1850, and Eighth U.S. Census, 1860, Warren County, Mississippi, microfilm, NA. On this point, see Randolph B. Campbell, "Intermittent Slave Ownership: Texas as a Test Case," *Journal of Southern History* 51 (Feb. 1985): 15–23; and James Oakes, "A Response," *Journal of Southern History* 51 (Feb. 1985): 23–28.

14. Janet Sharp Hermann, *The Pursuit of a Dream* (New York: Oxford University Press, 1981), 3–14. For Robert Owen and the communitarian movement generally, see Carl J. Guarneri, "Reconstructing the Antebellum Communitarian Movement: Oneida and Fourierism," *Journal of the Early Republic* 16 (Fall 1996): 463–88; and Arthur Bestor, *Backwoods Utopias: The Sectarian Origins and Owenite Phase of Communitarian Socialism in America, 1663–1829* (1950, rev. ed. Philadelphia: University of Pennsylvania Press, 1970), 44–59.

15. Genovese, *Roll, Jordan, Roll,* 3–7; Peter Kolchin, *American Slavery, 1619–1877* (New York: Harvard University Press, 1993), 111–35.

16. Moore, *Emergence of the Cotton Kingdom,* 78–83; Michael Tadman, *Speculators and Slaves: Masters, Traders, and Slaves in the Old South* (Madison: University of Wisconsin Press, 1989); Herbert Aptheker, *American Negro Slave Revolts* (New York: Columbia University Press, 1943); Vincent Harding, *There Is a River: The Black Struggle for Freedom in America* (New York: Harcourt Brace Jovanovich, 1981); Norrece T. Jones, Jr., *Born a Child of Freedom, Yet a Slave: Mechanisms of Control and Strategies of Resistance in Antebellum South Carolina* (Hanover: Wesleyan University Press, 1990), 10–12, 19, 58, 205, 213; James C. Scott, *Weapons of the Weak: Everyday Forms of Peasant Resistance* (New Haven: Yale University Press, 1985); Raymond and Alice Bauer, "Day to Day Resistance to Slavery," *Journal of Negro History* 27 (1942): 388–419; Mary Ellison, "Resistance to Oppression: Black Women's Response to Slavery in the United States," *Slavery and Abolition* 4 (1983): 56–63; Leslie Howard Owens,

This Species of Property: Slave Life and Culture in the Old South (New York: Oxford University Press, 1976).

17. Minerva Cook Diary, 40, typescript, Old Court House Museum, Vicksburg (hereafter cited as OCHM).

18. Minerva Cook Diary, 31, OCHM; Michael P. Johnson, "Smothered Slave Infants: Were Slave Mothers at Fault?" *Journal of Southern History* 47 (Nov. 1981): 493–520; Richard H. Steckel, "A Dreadful Childhood: The Excess Mortality of American Slaves," *Social Science History* 10 (1986): 427–66.

19. Minerva Cook Diary, 42, 43, OCHM; Dickson D. Bruce, Jr., *Violence and Culture in the Antebellum South* (Austin: University of Texas Press, 1979), 3–20, 31; Michael Les Benedict, "Victorian Moralism and Civil Liberty in the Nineteenth-Century United States," in *The Constitution, Law, and American Life: Critical Aspects of the Nineteenth-Century Experience,* ed. Donald G. Nieman (Athens: University of Georgia Press, 1992), 91–122.

20. *State v. Joseph Wade,* Warren County Circuit Court Papers, Natchez Trace Collection, Center for American History, University of Texas at Austin (hereafter cited as NTC).

21. *State v. Arthur Jordan et al.,* Warren County Circuit Court Papers, OCHM.

22. Francis Jefferson Coleman probate file, Chancery Clerk's Office, Vicksburg; Vicksburg *Whig,* Jan. 28, 1857.

23. Bond, *Political Culture in the Nineteenth-Century South,* 28–42.

Chapter 2: Law and Mob Law

1. Boston *Liberator,* Oct. 5, 1849. A Florida judge referred to "Vicksburg Justice"; see James M. Denham, *"A Rogue's Paradise": Crime and Punishment in Antebellum Florida, 1821–1861* (Tuscaloosa: University of Alabama Press, 1997), 100.

2. David M. Oshinsky, in *Worse Than Slavery: Parchman Farm and the Ordeal of Jim Crow Justice* (New York: Free Press, 1996), 4, describes the South as "a place of violent moods and minimal restraint, where passion took precedence over law." Oshinsky merely summarizes the stereotype. The great historian of southern culture Bertram Wyatt-Brown insisted that local opinion was the dominant force in southern society, shaping attitudes toward law, the legal culture. Bertram Wyatt-Brown, *Southern Honor: Ethics and Behavior in the Old South* (New York: Oxford University Press, 1982), 363–64. His student, Christopher Morris, finds an evolution away from public opinion as a governing force, but he, too, argues that a "mesh of kinship ties," not government, gave structure to rural neighborhoods. See Morris, *Becoming Southern,* 84–85. Bradley Bond writes that Mississippians generated a social ethic that defined liberty as freedom from government. Bond, *Political Culture in the Nineteenth-Century South,* 2–42.

3. Frederick Douglass, *My Bondage and My Freedom* (1855, repr. New York: Dover, 1969), 64.

4. Shapiro, *White Violence and Black Response,* xii–xiii.

5. This is the major point of Morris in *Becoming Southern,* ch. 8.

6. William Faulkner, *The Hamlet* (New York: Random House, 1931), 5.

7. A search of Warren County records in the Natchez Trace Collection, Center for American History, University of Texas at Austin, revealed the names of seventeen justices of the peace identifiable in the 1860 census. Nine, or about half, owned no slaves. Among all male heads of households in the 1860 census, 57 percent had no slaves. The magistrates' holdings of slaves averaged six, whereas the mean for all male heads of households in Warren County was eight. About a third of the justices had no land, whereas just under half of the male household heads had no real estate. Forty-one percent of male household heads had no personal estate recorded in the 1860 census, and 35 percent of the magistrates reported no such property (table A-1 in the appendix).

8. Manuscript population schedules, Eighth U.S. Census, 1860, Warren County, Mississippi, microfilm, NA; for Townsend, see Mary G. Wright deposition, Dec. 10, 1872, John Townsend, claim 4220, box 212, record group 217, Settled Case Files for Claims Approved by the Southern Claims Commission, Records of the Accounting Officers of the Department of the Treasury, NA (hereafter cited as SCC).

9. JPs had a long history as the primary peacekeepers of the community. Coke once praised English magistrates for keeping the realm tranquil and quiet. In the seventeenth and eighteenth centuries, magistrates had possessed impressive powers to order summary punishment of the "idle, lewd, and disorderly." In decentralized colonial Virginia, the General Assembly had placed local government in the hands of magistrates. Most Virginia magistrates owned considerable land. They often monopolized county offices, served in the House of Burgesses, and won seats on the council. Nineteenth-century legislators curbed many of the arbitrary powers associated with magistrates in earlier times, and the JPs developed a more democratic function. A study of Philadelphia found that inferior courts carried out much of the governing in that city. Warren M. Billings, "The Growth of Political Institutions in Virginia, 1634 to 1676," *William and Mary Quarterly* 31 (April 1974): 225–42; James Willard Hurst, *The Growth of American Law: The Lawmakers* (Boston: Little, Brown, 1950), 147 (quotation); Thomas D. Morris, *Southern Slavery and the Law, 1619–1860* (Chapel Hill: University of North Carolina Press, 1995), 210–15; Jack P. Greene, ed., *The Diary of Landon Carter of Sabine Hall, 1752–1778*, 2 vols. (1965, repr. Richmond: University of Virginia Press, 1987), vol. 2, 845; Alan F. Cirket, ed., *Samuel Whitbread's Notebooks, 1810–11, 1813–14* (Bedfordshire: Bedfordshire Historical Record Society, 1971), 9–27; Allen Steinberg, *The Transformation of Criminal Justice: Philadelphia, 1800–1880* (Chapel Hill: University of North Carolina Press, 1989), 5–78; John R. Wunder, *Inferior Courts, Superior Justice: A History of the Justices of the Peace on the Northwest Frontier, 1853–1889* (Westport: Greenwood Press, 1979), 19–50; Paul M. McCain, "Magistrates Courts in Early North Carolina," *North Carolina Historical Review* 48 (Jan. 1971): 23–30; James Griffith Harris, "The Background and Development of Early Missouri Trial Courts," Ph.D. diss., University of Missouri, 1949, 229–70.

10. Frank E. Everett, Jr., *Vicksburg Lawyers prior to the Civil War* (Vicksburg: privately printed, n.d.), 86.

11. Everett, *Vicksburg Lawyers prior to the Civil War,* 34.

12. Lawrence Sterne Houghton to Cousin, Dec. 28, 1859, and April 27, 1861, typescript, Houghton Papers, OCHM.

13. *The Revised Code of the Statute Laws of the State of Mississippi* (Jackson: E. Barksdale, 1857), 404–13.

14. *The Revised Code of the Statute Laws of the State of Mississippi* (1857), 626–29.

15. In 1823 the legislature ordered justices of the peace to determine, in the cases of free persons of color charged with insolent language, whether the language was aggravated. If not, the defendant was to pay a fine rather than be whipped.

16. *The Revised Code of the Statute Laws of the State of Mississippi* (1857), 626–29.

17. Superior Court Minute Book B, OCHM.

18. Lewis owned six slaves and five hundred acres. Warren County Tax Rolls, 1827, 1830, 1831, reel B-1125, MDAH.

19. In the colonial South, some states had lightened their homicide laws for owners accused of killing their slaves. Both Virginia and South Carolina wrote laws excusing murder of recalcitrant slaves. Maryland and Delaware did not tinker with the common law of homicide, so presumably murderers of slaves faced the same justice as the murderers of whites. Georgia passed a law against murder, dismemberment, and cruelty toward slaves, but few defendants in such cases went to the gallows. After the Revolution some legislatures toughened laws against the willful murder of slaves. Nonetheless, in 1821 Mississippi's supreme court declared that "it would be a stigma upon the character of the state" to tolerate the murder of slaves, recognizing it as a common-law crime. Just as in the colonial era, however, southern states executed few defendants charged with slave murder. Morris, *Southern Slavery and the Law,* 161–81.

20. Wylin Bohannon testimony, March 17, 1831, examination of Stephen Lewis, *State v. Stephen Lewis,* Warren County Circuit Court Papers, NTC; Ariela Gross, "Pandora's Box: Slave Character on Trial in the Antebellum Deep South," *Yale Journal of Law and the Humanities* 7 (Summer 1995): 267–316; Judith Kelleher Schafer, *Slavery, the Civil Law, and the Supreme Court of Louisiana* (Baton Rouge: Louisiana State University Press, 1994), 127–48; Andrew Fede, "Legal Protection for Slave Buyers in the U.S. South: A Caveat Concerning *Caveat Emptor*," *American Journal of Legal History* 31 (Oct. 1987): 342. On this point, see also Pound, *The Spirit of the Common Law,* 18–20; and Morris, *Southern Slavery and the Law,* 104–13.

21. Wylin Bohannon testimony, March 17, 1831, examination of Stephen Lewis, *State v. Stephen Lewis,* Warren County Circuit Court Papers, NTC.

22. John Slater testimony, March 17, 1831, examination of Stephen Lewis, *State v. Stephen Lewis,* and John Slater affidavit, March 12, 1831, Warren County Circuit Court Papers, NTC.

23. Robert Brown testimony, March 17, 1831, examination of Stephen Lewis, *State v. Stephen Lewis,* Warren County Circuit Court Papers, NTC.

24. Luke Lea testimony, in U.S. Congress, House, Select Committee to Visit Vicksburgh, *Vicksburgh Troubles,* House Report 265, 43d Cong., 2d sess., 310 (hereafter cited as *Vicksburgh Troubles*).

25. *State v. Stephen Lewis,* Warren County Circuit Court Papers, NTC; Minute Book C, 36, 54, Warren Circuit Court Clerk's Office, Vicksburg; Warren County Tax Rolls, 1827, 1830, 1831, 1835, 1836, microfilm, reel B-1124, MDAH; Warren County Deed Book F, Chancery Clerk's Office, Vicksburg; manuscript population schedule, Sixth U.S. Census, 1840, microfilm, NA.

26. *Byrd v. State,* 1 Howard 164 (1834); Thomas Andrew Green, *Verdict According to Conscience: Perspectives on the English Criminal Trial Jury, 1200–1800* (Chicago: University of Chicago Press, 1985), 4–150; Keith Wrightson, "Two Concepts of Order: Justices, Constables, and Jurymen in Seventeenth-Century England," in *An Ungovernable People: The English and Their Law in the Seventeenth and Eighteenth Centuries,* ed. John Brewer and John Styles (New Brunswick: Rutgers University Press, 1980), 21–46.

27. For Poindexter's Code see 1822 Mississippi 179 ff.

28. Phillip N. Racine, ed., *Piedmont Farmer: The Journals of David Golightly Harris, 1855–1870* (Knoxville: University of Tennessee Press, 1990), 239.

29. Harriet Jacobs [Linda Brent], *Incidents in the Life of a Slave Girl,* edited by L. Maria Child (1861; New York: Harcourt Brace Jovanovich, 1973), 36,

30. Elizabeth Keckley, *Behind the Scenes; Or, Thirty Years a Slave, and Four Years in the White House* (1868, repr. New York: Arno, 1988), xii. See also Peter Randolph, *Sketches of Slave Life; Or, Illustrations of the "Peculiar Institution"* (Boston: privately printed, 1855), 12, for similar language.

31. Louis Hughes, *Thirty Years a Slave: From Bondage to Freedom, The Institution of Slavery as Seen on the Plantation and in the Home of the Planter* (Milwaukee: South Side, 1897), 20.

32. Morris, *Becoming Southern,* 118.

33. John Quitman to Eliza Quitman, June 6, 1830, Quitman Family Papers, Southern Historical Collection, Wilson Library, University of North Carolina, Chapel Hill; Henry Frederick Shugart account book/diary, MDAH.

34. B. L. C. Wailes Diary, June 1, 2, 1856, Special Collections Library, Duke University, Durham, N.C.

35. B. L. C. Wailes Diary, Sept. 8, 9, 1857, Special Collections Library, Duke University, Durham, N.C.

36. In some ways the structure of slave discipline resembled the many overlapping layers Lawrence Friedman and Robert Percival found in their study of the criminal justice system in Alameda County, California. Lawrence M. Friedman and Robert V. Percival, *The Roots of Justice: Crime and Punishment in Alameda County, California, 1870–1910* (Chapel Hill: University of North Carolina Press, 1981), 259–62. For Mississippi courts, see Michael H. Hoffheimer, "Mississippi Courts: 1790–1868," *Mississippi Law Journal* 65 (Fall 1995): 99–170.

37. Ulrich Bonnell Phillips, "Racial Problems, Adjustments, and Disturbances," in *Political History of the Southern States,* ed. Franklin L. Riley (Richmond: Southern Historical Publication Society, 1909), 194–241, esp. 200; Ulrich Bonnell Phillips, *American Negro Slavery: A Survey of the Supply, Employment, and Control of Negro Labor as Determined by the Plantation Regime* (New York: D. Appleton, 1918), 454–514; Ulrich Bonnell Phillips, "The Plantation as a Civilizing Factor," *Sewanee Review* 12 (July 1904), 257–67; Ulrich B. Phillips, *Life and Labor in the Old South* (1929, repr. Boston: Little, Brown, 1963), 198–201.

38. E. Russ Williams, "Slave Patrol Ordinances of St. Tammany Parish, Louisiana, 1835–1838," *Louisiana History* 13 (Fall 1962): 399–412; H. M. Henry, *The Police Control of the Slave in South Carolina* (1914, rpr. New York: Negro Universities Press, 1968),

28–45; Philip J. Schwarz, *Twice Condemned: Slaves and the Criminal Laws of Virginia, 1705–1865* (Baton Rouge: Louisiana State University Press, 1988), 12–13.

39. John Wunder, "American Law and Order Comes to Mississippi Territory: The Making of Sargent's Code, 1798–1800," *Journal of Mississippi History* 38 (May 1976): 151.

40. 1823 Mississippi Acts 61.

41. Randy J. Sparks, *On Jordan's Stormy Banks: Evangelicalism in Mississippi, 1773–1876* (Athens: University of Georgia Press, 1994), 70; 1822 Mississippi Acts 184; 1823 Mississippi Acts 22; A. Hutchinson, comp., *Code of Mississippi: Being an Analytical Compilation of the Public and General Statutes of the Territory and State with Tabular References to the Local and Private Acts, from 1798 to 1848* (Jackson: A. Hutchinson, 1848), ch. 37, art. 10, sec. 6, p. 534.

42. Hutchinson, comp., *Code of Mississippi*, ch. 37, art. 17, sec. 7, p. 539.

43. Rules and Regulations Adopted for the Appointment and Organization of Patrol, n.d., NTC.

44. See, for example, C. S. Morehead and Mason Brown, *A Digest of the Statute Laws of Kentucky*, 2 vols. (Frankfort, 1834), vol. 2, 1257, which held that county courts would "appoint in each district a company of patrollers." *The Code of Virginia. . . .* (Richmond: William F. Ritchie, 1849), 445.

45. Warren County Slave Patrol Rules and Regulations, not dated, Board of Police Papers, NTC.

46. 1817 Mississippi Acts 58–68; Hoffheimer, "Mississippi Courts," 127–29. For a master who countenanced food theft, see Theodore Rosengarten, ed., *Tombee: Portrait of a Cotton Planter* (New York: Morrow, 1986), 157–61; Michael Stephen Hindus, *Prison and Plantation: Crime, Justice, and Authority in Massachusetts and South Carolina, 1767–1878* (Chapel Hill: University of North Carolina Press, 1980), 137–61; William C. Henderson, "The Slave Court System in Spartanburg County," *Proceedings of the South Carolina Historical Association* (1976), 24–38; Yao Foli Modey, "Black Justice under White Law: Criminal Prosecutions of Blacks in Antebellum North Carolina," M.A. thesis, Wake Forest University, 1978, 50–64; and Alan D. Watson, "North Carolina Slave Courts, 1715–1785," *North Carolina Historical Review* 60 (Jan. 1983), 24–36.

47. Hutchinson, comp., *Code of Mississippi*, 738–39.

48. *Bob Minor, a Slave v. State*, 36 Mississippi 631.

49. 1854 Mississippi Acts 126–30; Hoffheimer, "Mississippi Courts," 159.

50. 1850 Mississippi Acts 100.

51. James Burns Wallace Diary, Jan. 13, 1836, Special Collections, Hill Memorial Library, Louisiana State University, Baton Rouge; Vicksburg *Register*, July 9, 1835 (quotation); G. W. Featherstonhaugh, *Excursion through the Slave States, from Washington on the Potomac to the Frontier of Mexico; with Sketches of Popular Manners and Geological Notices*, 2 vols. (London: Murray, 1844), vol. 1, 250–55; Harriet Martineau, *Retrospect of Western Travel*, 2 vols. (New York: Harper, 1838), vol. 1, 17–18; Vicksburg *Herald*, Dec. 27, 1912; Morris, *Becoming Southern*, 121; Kenneth S. Greenberg, *Honor and Slavery: Lies, Duels, Noses, Masks, Dressing as a Woman, Gifts, Strangers, Humanitarianism, Death, Slave Rebellions, the Proslavery Argument, Baseball, Hunting, and Gambling in the Old South* (Princeton: Princeton University Press, 1996), 136–37.

52. *Niles' Register,* Aug. 8, 1835.

53. Edward Gilbert Messinger, "Journal of a Visit to Mississippi," Nov. 20, 1844, OCHM.

54. "Mississippi," vol. 21, 7, R. G. Dun and Co. Papers, Baker Library, Harvard University Graduate School of Business Administration, Cambridge, Mass.

55. Ibid.

56. Ibid., 9, 11.

57. Ibid., 11.

58. Ibid., 29, 15.

59. James J. Higgins deposition, Sept. 26, 1826, *Perly Wallis v. John M. Parisot,* box 34, Warren County Superior Court Papers, attic, Warren County Court House, Vicksburg.

60. *State v. Sarah,* Warren County Circuit Court Papers, OCHM. A New York City sales clerk, in contrast, told a court, "We are always in the habit of refusing to sell arsenic to strangers and others." Andie Tucher, *Froth and Scum: Truth, Beauty, Goodness, and the Ax Murder in America's First Mass Medium* (Chapel Hill: University of North Carolina Press, 1994), 23.

61. *Code Duello: Letters Concerning the Prentiss-Tucker Duel of 1842* (Dallas: Book Club of Texas, 1931); Steven M. Stowe, *Intimacy and Power in the Old South: Ritual in the Lives of the Planters* (Baltimore: Johns Hopkins University Press, 1987), 5–49; Greenberg, *Honor and Slavery,* 53–69.

62. *Code Duello.*

63. *Code Duello.*

64. *Code Duello.*

65. Stowe, *Intimacy and Power in the Old South,* 5–49; Monroe F. Cockrell, "The Duelling Editors of Vicksburg, 1841–1860, a Study from Contemporary Newspapers," May 10, 1956, unpublished manuscript, MDAH; Bruce, *Violence and Culture,* 21–43. This was true in the North as well. See Joanne B. Freeman, "Aristocratic Murder and Democratic Fury: Honor and Politics in Early National New England," delivered to the Society for the History of the Early American Republic, Nashville, July 20, 1996, 7. For animal analogies as insults, see Keith Thomas, *Man and the Natural World: Changing Attitudes in England, 1500–1800* (London: Lane, 1983), 36–50.

66. Greenberg, *Honor and Slavery,* 8–9, 24–62; Stowe, *Intimacy and Power in the Old South,* 5–49.

67. Vicksburg *Times,* Aug. 25, 1869.

68. R. V. Booth, "Historic Vicksburg," Aug. 18, 1906, Private Memoranda, vol. 5, 107, MDAH.

69. Henry S. Foote, *Casket of Reminiscences* (Washington, D.C.: Chronicle, 1874, repr. New York: Negro Universities Press, 1968), 385; Vicksburg *Sentinel,* Nov. 6, 1843.

70. Vicksburg *Sentinel,* June 17, 1844; McIntosh, Monroe, and Crist, eds., *The Papers of Jefferson Davis,* vol. 2, 25n8.

71. Vicksburg *Sentinel,* May 23, 1849.

72. McIntosh, Monroe, and Crist, eds., *The Papers of Jefferson Davis,* vol. 2, 114n122.

73. Vicksburg *Constitutionalist,* May 11, 1844; McIntosh, Monroe, and Crist, eds., *The Papers of Jefferson Davis,* vol. 2, 142–65.

74. Vicksburg *Sentinel,* June 5, 1844.

75. Extant records show antebellum grand jurors returned forty indictments charging dueling or aiding in a duel. In 1842 the Circuit Court jailed Richard E. Hammett because Judge George Coalter thought he might fight a duel with James Fall. Coalter required Hammett to enter into a recognizance for $1,000, which he would forfeit should he fight the threatened duel. (Warren County Minute Book L, 386, Circuit Clerk's Office, Vicksburg.) But the outcomes of these dueling indictments reveal the ambiguity in authorities' feelings about the practice. Lawyers had no qualms about dueling. Horace H. Miller made himself a recognized authority on the rituals and rules of the *code duello,* much as other lawyers established themselves as experts on property law or probate. (R. V. Booth, "The Story of My Life," vol. 3, ch. 4, MDAH.) With two exceptions, the gentlemen charged with dueling never had to suffer the indignity of a trial; judges and district attorneys found a way to dismiss the charges. And the two exceptions both ended in acquittals. On January 25, 1867, the *Daily Herald* said in print what many Vicksburgers must have been saying privately for years. All dueling cases should be dismissed, the paper urged, "for where public opinion recognizes the *duello,* laws against it will be certainly violated."

76. Vicksburg *Weekly Whig,* July 22, 29, Sept. 9, 1857.

77. Vicksburg *Weekly Whig,* July 22, 29, Sept. 9, Nov. 18, Dec. 9, 1857. Robert Ingalls finds the attitudes of local elites the critical factor in lynchings. Ingalls, "Lynchings and Establishment Violence in Tampa, 1858–1935," *Journal of Southern History* 53 (Nov. 1987): 613–44.

78. Vicksburg *Weekly Whig,* July 1, 8, 1857.

79. This "problem" was widespread in the South, and some states tried to stamp out such quasi-emancipation. In 1827 North Carolina's high court warned that "collections of slaves, having nothing but the name, and working for their own benefit," would excite in other slaves' discontent, encouraging idleness and disobedience. The North Carolina court worried that permitting the quasi-emancipated to roam loose could even lead to servile insurrection. But banning the practice meant the government would tell slaveowners how to use their property. South Carolina blanched at that. How much control an owner must exercise over a slave before the slave could be called free, one judge declared, must be decided by that owner, not the government. Morris, *Southern Slavery and the Law,* 400–404.

80. Henry Watson deposition, Oct. 11, 1873, Henry Watson, claim 16555, box 212, SCC; Loren Schweninger, *Black Property Owners in the South, 1790–1915* (Urbana: University of Illinois Press, 1990), 44–57; Betty Wood, *Women's Work and Men's Work: The Informal Slave Economies of Lowcountry Georgia* (Athens: University of Georgia Press, 1995); Roderick A. McDonald, *The Economy and Material Culture of Slaves: Goods and Chattels on the Sugar Plantations of Jamaica and Louisiana* (Baton Rouge: Louisiana State University Press, 1993); John Hope Franklin, "Slaves Virtually Free in Antebellum North Carolina," *Journal of Negro History* 28 (July 1943): 284–310; Philip D. Morgan, "Work and Culture: The Task System and the World of Lowcountry Blacks, 1700–1880," *William and Mary Quarterly* 39 (Oct. 1982): 563–600; Philip D. Morgan, "The Ownership of Property by Slaves in the Mid-Nineteenth-Century Low Country," *Journal of Southern History* 49 (Aug. 1983): 399–420; Lawrence T.

McDonnell, "Money Knows No Master: Market Relations and the American Slave Community," in *Developing Dixie: Modernization in a Traditional Society,* ed. Winfred B. Moore, Jr., et al. (Westport: Greenwood Press, 1988), 31–44; Morris, *Southern Slavery and the Law,* 351–53; Michael P. Johnson, "Work, Culture, and the Slave Community: Slave Occupations in the Cotton Belt in 1860," *Labor History* 27 (Summer 1986): 325–55; Jonathan Beasley, "Blacks—Slave and Free—Vicksburg, 1850–1860," *Journal of Mississippi History* 38 (Feb. 1976): 1–32.

81. Henry Watson deposition, Oct. 11, 1873, Henry Watson, claim 16555, box 212, SCC.

82. Daniel Murfee deposition, July 21, 1873, Daniel Murfee, claim 18062, box 211, SCC.

83. Thomas Bradshaw, claim 11363, box 207, SCC.

84. Peter Jackson deposition, Peter Jackson, claim 14295, box 210, SCC; Joseph S. Acuff deposition, Peter Jackson, claim 14295, box 210, SCC; Moore, *Emergence of the Cotton Kingdom,* 100–103.

85. Candis Newman, claim 10385, box 211, SCC; see also Morris, *Becoming Southern,* 176–77.

86. John A. Klein deposition, May 20, 1873, John Cole, claim 116558, 208, SCC.

87. William Hitch deposition, Feb. 28, 1879, William Hitch, claim 22092, box 210, SCC.

88. William Jefferson deposition, May 5, 1877, William Jefferson, claim 2606, box 210, SCC; see also Ira Berlin et al., eds., *The Wartime Genesis of Free Labor: The Lower South* (New York: Cambridge University Press, 1990), 633–34, 650–64.

89. Oliver Garrett deposition, June 28, 1873, Oliver Garrett, claim 22093, box 210, SCC; Henry Watson deposition, Oct. 11, 1873, Henry Watson, claim 16555, box 212, SCC.

90. Benjamin Stinyard petition, claim 6999, box 211, SCC.

91. "Minutes of the Board of Police," 1838–45, Aug. 1841, Chancery Clerk's Office, Vicksburg; Moore, *Emergence of the Cotton Kingdom,* 257–84.

92. Vicksburg *Citizen,* Oct. 31, 1859.

93. Vicksburg *Sun,* quoted in the Vicksburg *Whig,* June 15, 1859; Vicksburg *Whig,* Sept. 30, 1858.

94. "Mississippi," vol. 21, R. G. Dun and Co. credit ledgers, Historical Records Department, Baker Library, Harvard University Graduate School of Business Administration, Cambridge, Mass.

95. *State v. Fleckenstein,* Warren County Circuit Court Papers, OCHM.

96. *Vicksburg Weekly Citizen,* April 2, 1860.

97. Grand jury indictment, Dec. 20, 1859, *State v. John McGuiggin,* Warren County Circuit Court Papers, NTC; *Vicksburg Weekly Citizen,* Oct. 31, 1859. The Union army freed McGuiggin from prison, but he died in Vicksburg during the war, an army employee. Blanche Terry to author, Aug. 1, 1995.

98. Vicksburg *Sun,* quoted in Vicksburg *Whig,* June 15, 1859; Vicksburg *Citizen,* April 2, May 21, 1860.

99. Vicksburg *Whig,* Dec. 7, 1859.

100. *Lincoln v. Smith* (1855), 27 Vermont 328.

101. *State v. Simmons* (1845), 17 New Hampshire 83.

102. *Commonwealth v. Whitcomb* (1858), 78 Massachusetts 126.

103. *State v. Pat Lynch,* Warren County Circuit Court Papers, OCHM.

104. Ayers, *Vengeance and Justice,* 13.

105. Wyatt-Brown, *Southern Honor,* 3–114; Ayers, *Vengeance and Justice,* 9–33; David Hackett Fischer, *Albion's Seed: Four British Folkways in America* (New York: Oxford University Press, 1989), 398–418, 765–82.

Chapter 3: The Public Good and Due Process

1. Jenny B. Wahl, "American Slavery and the Path of the Law," *Social Science History* 20 (Summer 1996): 281–316.

2. *Dred Scott v. Sandford,* 60 U.S. (19 Howard) 393 (1857); Daniel J. Flanigan, "Criminal Procedure in Slave Trials in the Antebellum South," *Journal of Southern History* 40 (Nov. 1974): 544–45. A. E. Keir Nash has made this point in a series of articles. See "Fairness and Formalism in the Trials of Blacks in the State Supreme Courts of the Old South," *Virginia Law Review* 56 (1970): 64–100; "A More Equitable Past? Southern Supreme Courts and the Protection of the Antebellum Negro," *North Carolina Law Review* 48 (1970): 197–241; "Negro Rights, Unionism, and Greatness on the South Carolina Court of Appeals: The Extraordinary Chief Justice John Belton O'Neall," *South Carolina Law Review* 21 (1969): 141–90; "Reason of Slavery: Understanding the Judicial Role of the Peculiar Institution," *Vanderbilt Law Review* 32 (Jan. 1979): 7–218; and "The Texas Supreme Court and the Trial Rights of Blacks, 1845–1860," *Journal of American History* 58 (Dec. 1971): 622–42.

3. Vicksburg *Advocate and Register,* Nov. 18, 1831.

4. William J. Novak, *The People's Welfare: Law and Regulation in Nineteenth-Century America* (Chapel Hill: University of North Carolina Press, 1996), 1–50; Morris, *Southern Slavery and the Law,* 337–53.

5. Robert A. Lively, "The American System," *Business History Review* 29 (March 1955): 81–96; Baldwin quoted in Novak, *People's Welfare,* 41; *Commonwealth v. Alger,* 7 Cushing 53 (Mass. 1851).

6. Hendrik Hartog, *Public Property and Private Power: The Corporation of the City of New York in American Law, 1730–1870* (Ithaca: Cornell University Press, 1983), 184–220; John C. Weaver, *Crime, Constables, and Courts: Order and Transgression in a Canadian City, 1816–1970* (Montreal: McGill-Queens University Press, 1995), 16–50; Eric H. Monkkonen, *America Becomes Urban: The Development of U.S. Cities and Towns, 1780–1980* (Berkeley: University of California Press, 1988), 93–105; Wilbur R. Miller, *Cops and Bobbies: Police Authority in New York and London, 1830–1870* (Chicago: University of Chicago Press, 1977), 2–4; Perry Miller, *The Life of the Mind in America: From the Revolution to the Civil War* (New York: Harcourt, Brace, World, 1965), 99–116; Robert A. Ferguson, *Law and Letters in American Culture* (Cambridge: Harvard University Press, 1984), 199–304; Alfred Zabtzinger Reed, *Training for the Public Profession of the Law: Historical Development and Principal Contemporary Problems of Legal Education in the United States with Some Account of Conditions in England and Canada* (New York: Merrymount, 1921), 35–46; Peter W. Bardaglio, *Recon-*

structing the Household: Families, Sex, and the Law in the Nineteenth-Century South (Chapel Hill: University of North Carolina Press, 1995), 79–112; Kermit Hall, *The Magic Mirror: Law in American History* (New York: Oxford University Press, 1989), 106–28; Michael Grossberg, *Governing the Hearth: Law and the Family in Nineteenth-Century America* (Chapel Hill: University of North Carolina Press, 1985), 19–27.

7. Gordon Cotton, *The Old Court House* (Raymond, Miss.: Keith Printing, 1982), 9–13.

8. Cotton, *The Old Court House,* 9–13; Joseph D. Shields, *The Life and Times of Seargent Smith Prentiss* (Philadelphia: Lippincott, 1883), 45.

9. Anonymous, May 28, 1844, OCHM.

10. Cotton, *The Old Court House,* 16.

11. Morris, *Becoming Southern,* 132–55.

12. Grand Jury Report, Feb. 24, 1852, Warren County Circuit Court Papers, NTC; R. S. Buck to John J. Pettus, Jan. 10, 1860, Governors' Papers, box 35, record group 27, MDAH; *Daily Vicksburg Whig,* Dec. 28, 1855, Jan. 1, 1856; 1859 Mississippi Acts, 181–88; Hoffheimer, "Mississippi Courts," 156–57.

13. *The Revised Code of the Laws of Mississippi. . . .* (Natchez: Poindexter, 1824), 133–34; 1854 Mississippi Acts 428–29; 1856 Mississippi Acts 26; Morris, *Southern Slavery and the Law,* 220.

14. Foote, *Casket,* 264–74; Douglas Wiley Carlson, "Temperance Reform in the Cotton Kingdom," Ph.D. diss., University of Illinois, 1982, 171–79; Daniel Dupre, "Barbecues and Pledges: Electioneering and the Rise of Democratic Politics in Antebellum Alabama," *Journal of Southern History* 60 (Aug. 1994): 479–512.

15. Foote, *Casket,* 272. But see William Graham Davis, "Attacking 'The Matchless Evil': Temperance and Prohibition in Mississippi, 1817–1908," Ph.D. diss., Mississippi State University, 1975, 10–20.

16. Vicksburg *Sentinel,* May 18, 1841.

17. Vicksburg *Sentinel,* May 14, 1841.

18. Hartog, *Public Property and Private Power,* 184–220.

19. *The Revised Code of the Statute Laws of the State of Mississippi* (1857), 248–50.

20. Foote, *Casket,* 250–63.

21. Winthrop D. Jordan, *Tumult and Silence at Second Creek: An Inquiry into a Civil War Slave Conspiracy* (Baton Rouge: Louisiana State University Press, 1993), 168, 76 (quotation); Melton A. McLaurin, *Celia, a Slave* (Athens: University of Georgia Press, 1991), 33–103; for an excellent discussion of nineteenth-century confession law and due process generally, see David J. Bodenhamer, *Fair Trial: Rights of the Accused in American History* (New York: Oxford University Press, 1992), 53–54.

22. Davis, *Recollections,* 103–4.

23. Melvin I. Urofsky, *A March of Liberty: A Constitutional History of the United States* (New York: Knopf, 1988), 496–502; Henry Campbell Black, *Black's Law Dictionary,* abridged 5th ed. (St. Paul: West, 1983), 261–62; Morris, *Southern Slavery and the Law,* 207–48.

24. *Allgeyer v. Louisiana,* 165 U.S. 578 (1897); Edward S. Corwin, "The Doctrine of Due Process of Law Before the Civil War," *Harvard Law Review* 24 (1911): 366–85; Howard Jay Graham, "Procedure to Substance—Extra-Judicial Rise of Due Process, 1830–1860,"

California Law Review 40 (Winter 1952–53): 483–500; Wallace Mendelson, "A Missing Link in the Evolution of Due Process," *Vanderbilt Law Review* 10 (Dec. 1956): 125–37; Lowell J. Howe, "The Meaning of 'Due Process of Law' prior to the Adoption of the Fourteenth Amendment," *California Law Review* 18 (Sept. 1930): 583–610.

25. Rodney L. Mott, *Due Process of Law: A Historical and Analytical Treatise of the Principles and Methods Followed by the Courts in the Application of the Concept of the "Law of the Land"* (Indianapolis: Bobbs-Merrill, 1926), 111–42.

26. Bodenhamer, *Fair Trial,* 4; Morris, *Southern Slavery and the Law,* 37–57.

27. Thomas Morris quite rightly corrects Mark Tushnet on this point. Tushnet argued that whites dared not relax procedures for slaves for fear that such relaxed standards would reach whites on trial as well. Morris, *Southern Slavery and the Law,* 215–25; Tushnet, *The American Law of Slavery,* 121–22; Morton J. Horwitz, "The Rise of Legal Formalism," *American Journal of Legal History* 19 (1975): 251; *Dred Scott v. Sandford,* 60 U.S. (19 Howard) 393 (1857); Don E. Fehrenbacher, *The Dred Scott Case: Its Significance in Law and Politics* (New York: Oxford University Press, 1978), 379–84. Historians often regard Dred Scott as a calamitous peculiarity in the law, but some now regard it as an expression of antebellum legal discourse. See William M. Wiecek, "Slavery and Abolition before the United States Supreme Court, 1820–1860," *Journal of American History* 65 (June 1978): 34–59. For the earlier view of Dred Scott, see Graham, "Procedure to Substance," 494. Fehrenbacher calls Taney's use of substantive due process "meager and somewhat obscure." Fehrenbacher, *The Dred Scott Case,* 382.

28. *Isham, a Slave v. State,* 6 How. Miss. See Helen Tunncliff Catterhall, *Judicial Cases Concerning American Slavery and the Negro,* 5 vols. (1932, repr. New York: Octagon, 1968), vol. 3, 293. James Oakes traces the mentality that underlay such decisions to the eighteenth century, when the Enlightenment generated a rights discourse so powerful that it even permeated southern courtrooms. Oakes thinks such rhetoric undermined slavery, but Bertram Wyatt-Brown finds the institutionalization of slavery through law a natural development in the life-cycle of slavery, one destined to make the peculiar institution permanent. James Oakes, *Slavery and Freedom: An Interpretation of the Old South* (New York: Knopf, 1990), 162–64; Bertram Wyatt-Brown, "Modernizing Southern Slavery: The Proslavery Argument Revisited," in *Region, Race, and Reconstruction,* ed. J. Morgan Kousser and James M. McPherson (New York: Oxford University Press, 1982), 27–49; Joyce E. Chaplin, "Slavery and the Principle of Humanity: A Modern Idea in the Early Lower South," *Journal of Social History* 24 (Winter 1990): 299–311.

29. The Mississippi legislature published broadsides listing legislators and their occupations. In the antebellum era, these broadsides survive in MDAH for 1850, 1856, and 1861. In 1850, eighty-three legislators described themselves as planters or farmers. That includes those who said they were planters and merchants or farmers and merchants; just thirty gave their occupations as lawyer or merchant. In 1856, 90 of 130 legislators claimed to be farmers or planters, and in 1861, 105 of 133 with identifiable occupations said they were farmers or planters. Thus of all the legislators in these three years, about 70 percent claimed to be farmers or planters. Of course such self-descriptions are crude, but almost certainly these farmer-planters represented the

slaveholding class. The handful of merchants and lawyers in the legislature may well have owned slaves as well. See Legislative Papers, vol. 659, record group 47, MDAH.

30. William Novak, "The Road to *Slaughterhouse:* The Regulation of Noxious Trades, 1830–1872," delivered at the annual meeting of the American Society for Legal History, Memphis, 1993. Novak's argument that local authorities regulated nuisances holds up in Warren County. From 1832 through 1859, Warren County grand juries indicted twenty-three individuals for maintaining a nuisance. If two other kinds of nuisance are added, disorderly houses and disorderly persons, the number rises to thirty-two. Warren County Circuit Court Papers, NTC: Warren County Circuit Court Papers, OCHM; Warren County Circuit Court Minute Books C, D, G, I, II, K, L, M, N, Circuit Court Clerk's Office, Vicksburg.

31. Jan Lewis, "The Problem of Slavery in Southern Political Discourse," in *Devising Liberty: Preserving and Creating Freedom in the New American Republic,* ed. David Thomas Konig (Stanford: Stanford University Press, 1995), 283–89; Willie Lee Rose, *Slavery and Freedom,* ed. William W. Freehling (New York: Oxford University Press, 1982), 18–36.

32. Morris, *Southern Slavery and the Law,* 239–46.

33. *Peter, a Slave v. State,* 4 Smedes and Marshall 31.

34. Ibid., 38.

35. *Van Buren, a Slave v. State,* 24 Miss. 512.

36. *Jordan, a Slave v. State,* 32 Miss. 382.

37. David (a slave), habeas corpus petition, January 1852, Warren County Circuit Court Papers, OCHM. For arson generally, see Morris, *Southern Slavery and the Law,* 330–35.

38. Dallin H. Oaks, "Habeas Corpus in the States," *University of Chicago Law Review* 32 (Winter 1965): 243–88; Milton Cantor, "The Writ of Habeas Corpus: Early American Origins and Development," in *Freedom and Reform: Essays in Honor of Henry Steele Commager,* ed. Harold Hyman and Leonard W. Levy (New York: Harper and Row, 1967), 55–77.

39. David (a slave), habeas corpus petition, Jan. 1852, Warren County Circuit Court Papers, OCHM.

40. *State v. Henry, a Slave,* Warren County Circuit Court Papers, OCHM.

41. *State v. Preston, a Slave,* Warren County Circuit Court Papers, NTC.

42. *State v. Tarleton and Spencer, Slaves,* Warren County Circuit Court Papers, OCHM.

43. This is calculated from a series of intact bundles of Warren County Circuit Court case files, 1850–54, OCHM.

44. Neil R. McMillen, *Dark Journey: Black Mississippians in the Age of Jim Crow* (Urbana: University of Illinois Press, 1989), 201–17, writes about "Negro law" for the period after 1890 and concludes that blacks then had fewer procedural safeguards than had slaves. Tushnet, *The American Law of Slavery,* 100–121; Morris, *Southern Slavery and the Law,* 37–57.

45. For analogical reasoning, see Morton J. Horwitz, *Transformation of American Law, 1870–1960: The Crisis of Legal Orthodoxy* (Cambridge: Harvard University Press, 1992), 202–3.

46. Mrs. Ed Joiner interview with Henry Gibbs, n.d., in *American Slave*, ed. George Rawick, supplement, ser. 1, vol. 8, pt. 3, 834.

47. Reuben Davis, *Recollections of Mississippi and Mississippians* (Boston: Houghton Mifflin, 1890), 36.

48. *Daily Vicksburg Whig*, Feb. 18, 1858; Shields, *The Life and Times of Seargent Smith Prentiss*, 44–49; Dallas C. Dickey, *Seargent S. Prentiss: Whig Orator of the Old South* (Gloucester: Smith, 1970), 45–70; Joseph G. Baldwin, *The Flush Times of Alabama and Mississippi: A Series of Sketches* (New York: Sagamore, 1957), 144–62.

49. Davis, *Recollections*, 104.

50. *State v. Champion*, Warren County Circuit Court Papers, NTC.

51. Testimony of S. Y. Whitehead, *State v. Sam*, Warren County Circuit Court Papers, OCHM. On the mutability of evidence, including footprint evidence, see Robert Penn Warren, *World Enough and Time* (New York: Random House, 1950), 253.

52. Morris, *Southern Slavery and the Law*, 252–53. Mississippi was one of the earliest states to do so. Virginia passed a counsel law in 1792, but Kentucky did not require counsel until 1834. Alabama, Tennessee, and South Carolina came still later.

53. "Transcript from the Minutes of the April and October Terms," *State v. Sam*, Warren County Circuit Court Papers, NTC; *Sam, a Slave, vs. the State*, 21 Mississippi 189.

54. Testimony of Dr. Richard Pettway, *State v. Sam*, Warren County Circuit Court Papers, OCHM.

55. *Sam, a Slave v. State*, case 2823, High Court of Errors and Appeals Papers, record group 32, MDAH; 21 Mississippi 189; Vicksburg *Weekly Whig*, Aug. 28, 1849.

56. Vicksburg *Weekly Whig*, Aug. 28, 1849.

57. Everett, *Vicksburg Lawyers prior to the Civil War*, 25–29.

58. Vicksburg *Weekly Whig*, Sept. 15, 1849.

59. 21 Mississippi 189.

60. *State v. Sam*, case 5378, High Court of Errors and Appeals Papers, record group 32, MDAH.

61. Vicksburg *Whig*, June 12, 1849.

62. *State v. Sam*, case 5378, High Court of Errors and Appeals Papers, record group 32, MDAH. Morris writes that slave defendants did not commonly challenge jurors. Morris, *Southern Slavery and the Law*, 222–26.

63. *Sam v. State*, case 7687, High Court of Errors and Appeals Papers, record group 32, MDAH.

64. 31 Mississippi 480.

65. *State v. Sam*, Warren County Circuit Court Papers, OCHM.

66. *Sam v. State*, case 7910, High Court of Errors and Appeals Papers, MDAH; Vicksburg *Weekly Whig*, Dec. 30, 1857. On compensation of the owners of executed slaves, see Morris, *Southern Slavery and the Law*, 253–57.

67. Vicksburg *Weekly Whig*, Dec. 30, 1857.

68. James Z. George, *A Digest of the Reports of the Decisions of the Supreme Court and of the High Court of Errors and Appeals of the State of Mississippi from the Organization of the State to the Present Time* (Philadelphia: T. and J. W. Johnson, 1872), sec. 22.

Chapter 4: Into the Heart of Darkness

1. Peter F. Walker, *Vicksburg: A People at War, 1860–1865* (1960, repr. Wilmington: Broadfoot, 1987), 77; Fred Arthur Bailey, *Class and Tennessee's Confederate Generation* (Chapel Hill: University of North Carolina Press, 1987), 25, 38.

2. Vicksburg *Weekly Whig*, April 21, 188.

3. Vicksburg *Weekly Whig*, March 11, 1857.

4. Marmaduke Shannon to Daughter, April 20, 1858, Crutcher-Shannon Papers, NTC.

5. Vicksburg *Weekly Whig*, Oct. 19, 1859.

6. Vicksburg *Whig*, Jan. 11, 1860.

7. Vicksburg *Whig*, Aug. 22, Nov. 21, Dec. 12, 1860.

8. Michael P. Johnson, *Toward a Patriarchal Republic: The Secession of Georgia* (Baton Rouge: Louisiana State University Press, 1977). For decades, historians quarrelled over class conflict in the antebellum South. Frank L. Owsley, *Plain Folk of the Old South* (Baton Rouge: Louisiana State University Press, 1949), 1–22, became the scholar most closely identified with the argument that the South did not suffer social divisions, a view that has been discredited. See, for example, James C. Bonner, "Profile of a Late Ante-Bellum Community," *American Historical Review* 49 (July 1944): 663–80; Fabian Linden, "Economic Democracy in the Slave South," *Journal of Negro History* 32 (April 1946): 140–89; Randolph B. Campbell, "Planters and Plain Folk: Harrison County, Texas, as a Test Case, 1850–1860," *Journal of Southern History* 40 (Aug. 1974): 369–92; Eugene D. Genovese, "Yeoman Farmers in a Slaveholders' Democracy," *Agricultural History* 49 (April 1975): 331–42; Gavin Wright, "'Economic Democracy' and the Concentration of Agricultural Wealth in the Cotton South, 1850–1860," *Agricultural History* 44 (Jan. 1970): 83–93; and Bailey, *Class and Tennessee's Confederate Generation*, 20–76.

9. Morris, *Becoming Southern*, 42–62.

10. Minerva Cook Diary, OCHM.

11. Morris, *Becoming Southern*, 55–60.

12. Emma Crutcher to Will Crutcher, Jan. 6, 1861, Crutcher-Shannon Papers, NTC.

13. Kate Stone, *Brokenburn: The Journal of Kate Stone, 1861–1868*, ed. John Q. Anderson (1955, repr. Baton Rouge: Louisiana State University Press, 1995), 74; Suzanne Lebsock, *The Free Women of Petersburg: Status and Culture in a Southern Town, 1784–1860* (New York: Norton, 1984), 33. Lee Ann Whites, in *The Civil War as a Crisis in Gender: Augusta, Georgia, 1860–1890* (Athens: University of Georgia Press, 1995), 41–63, argues that men and women assumed increasingly similar roles in the Civil War as women became important economically and combat reduced the significance of men to their bodies. George C. Rable, in *Civil Wars: Women and the Crisis of Southern Nationalism* (Urbana: University of Illinois Press, 1989), 45–153, argues that the war politicized women, making them more aggressive in the public sphere. Stephen V. Ash, however, argues that "women struggled to preserve the patriarchal world they had known." See Ash, *When the Yankees Came: Conflict and Chaos in the Occupied South, 1861–1865* (Chapel Hill: University of North Carolina Press, 1995), 197–203.

14. Jan Lewis, "The Republican Wife: Virtue and Seduction in the Early Repub-

lic," *William and Mary Quarterly* 44 (Oct. 1987): 689–721; Jacob Katz Cogan, "The Reynolds Affair and the Politics of Character," *Journal of the Early Republic* 16 (Fall 1996): 389–418; Elizabeth R. Varon, "Tippecanoe and the Ladies, Too: White Women and Party Politics in Antebellum Virginia," *Journal of American History* 82 (Sept. 1995): 494–521; Linda Kerber, *Women of the Republic: Intellect and Ideology in Revolutionary America* (Chapel Hill: University of North Carolina Press, 1980); Paula C. Baker, "The Domestication of Politics: Women and American Political Society, 1780–1920," *American Historical Review* 89 (June 1984): 627–32; Mary P. Ryan, *Women in Public: Between Banners and Ballots, 1825–1880* (Baltimore: Johns Hopkins University Press, 1990); Elizabeth Fox-Genovese, *Within the Plantation Household: Black and White Women of the Old South* (Chapel Hill: University of North Carolina Press, 1988), 195 (first quotation); Drew Gilpin Faust, *Mothers of Invention: Women of the Slaveholding South in the American Civil War* (Chapel Hill: University of North Carolina Press, 1996), 10 (second quotation); Michael McGerr, "Political Style and Women's Power, 1830–1930," *Journal of American History* 77 (Dec. 1990): 866–67; John Quitman to Eliza Quitman, Aug. 29, 1836, John Quitman to Henry Quitman, July 31, 1836, Quitman Family Papers, Southern Historical Collection, Wilson Library, University of North Carolina, Chapel Hill; Jefferson Davis to Varina Howell Davis, Oct. 5, Dec. 10, 1846, Feb. 8, 25, 1847, all in *The Papers of Jefferson Davis*, ed. McIntosh, Monroe, and Crist, vol. 3, 54–55, 93–95, 118, 122–23.

15. Vicksburg *Weekly Whig*, Dec. 26, 1860.

16. Vicksburg *Weekly Whig*, Jan. 16, 1861.

17. Vicksburg *Weekly Whig*, Jan. 23, 1861.

18. Lawrence Houghton to Cousin, April 27, 1861, typescript, Houghton Papers, OCHM; Vicksburg *Daily Evening Citizen*, Jan. 14, March 13, April 12, 1861; Stone, *Brokenburn*, 95, 113.

19. "An Abolitionist" to Governor John J. Pettus, Nov. 30, 1859, Governors' Papers, box 35, record group 27, MDAH.

20. Noel Ignatiev, *How the Irish Became White* (New York: Routledge, 1995), 35–111.

21. Ira Berlin and Herbert G. Gutman, "Natives and Immigrants, Free Men and Slaves: Urban Workingmen in the Antebellum American South," *American Historical Review* 88 (Dec. 1983): 1195–1200; Ignatiev, *How the Irish Became White*, 35–111 (quotations).

22. Vicksburg *Daily Evening Citizen*, March 30, 1861; George C. Rable, *The Confederate Republic: A Revolution against Politics* (Chapel Hill: University of North Carolina Press, 1994), 30–89; Donald Nieman, "Republicanism, the Confederate Constitution, and the American Constitutional Tradition," in *An Uncertain Tradition: Constitutionalism and the History of the South*, ed. Kermit Hall and James W. Ely, Jr. (Athens: University of Georgia Press, 1989), 201–24.

23. Walker, *Vicksburg*, 41.

24. Vicksburg *Daily Evening Citizen*, Jan. 3, 1861.

25. Walker, *Vicksburg*, 55–56.

26. Vicksburg *Daily Evening Citizen*, Jan. 22, 1861.

27. Vicksburg *Daily Evening Citizen*, Feb. 2, 1861.

28. Vicksburg *Daily Evening Citizen*, May 21, 1861.

29. Vicksburg *Daily Evening Citizen,* May 28, 1861.

30. Supervisors' Minutes, Chancery Clerk's Office, Vicksburg; Warren County Circuit Court Minute Book U, 1860–1866, Warren County Circuit Clerk's Office, Vicksburg.

31. Walker, *Vicksburg,* 78–81; Jesse W. Beale deposition, claim 3423, box 207, SCC.

32. Vicksburg *Daily Evening Citizen,* May 13 (quotation), 14, 28, 1861; Joseph Butler, habeas corpus petition, Nov. 11, 1862, NTC.

33. Supervisors' Minutes, Chancery Clerk's Office, Vicksburg.

34. Charles Allen Plantation Book, MDAH. Allen resisted centralization of authority. See Richard Franklin Bensel, *Yankee Leviathan: The Origins of Central State Authority in America, 1859–1877* (New York: Cambridge University Press, 1990), 94–237.

35. Rowland Chambers Diary, Feb. 10, 27, March 3, May 17, 1863, Special Collections, Hill Memorial Library, Louisiana State University, Baton Rouge.

36. Joseph Davis to Jefferson Davis, May 2, 1862, in *The Papers of Jefferson Davis,* ed. McIntosh, Monroe, and Crist, vol. 8, 160.

37. Charles Allen Plantation Book, MDAH; Henry Banks deposition, June 24, 1873, claim 14443, box 207, SCC.

38. Alexander H. Arthur deposition, May 6, 1876, Howell H. Goodrum, claim 8519, box 209, SCC.

39. Armistead Burwell deposition, April 18, 1871, claim 111, box 207, SCC.

40. Vicksburg *Daily Evening Citizen,* May 13, 1861.

41. Albert O. Marshall, *Army Life; From a Soldier's Journal: Incidents, Sketches and Record of a Union Soldier's Army Life, in Camp and Field, 1861–64* (Joliet: privately printed, 1883), 15–18; Wales W. Wood, *A History of the Ninety-fifth Regiment Illinois Infantry Volunteers: From Its Organization in the Fall of 1862, until Its Final Discharge from the United States Service in 1865* (Chicago: Tribune, 1865), 15, 18, 25–26; R. L. Howard, *History of the 124th Regiment, Illinois Infantry Volunteers, Otherwise Known as the "Hundred and Two Dozen," from August, 1862, to August, 1865* (Springfield: H. W. Rokker, 1880), 8, 16 18.

42. Brooke, *The Heart of the Commonwealth,* 353–97; Gordon Wood, *The Radicalism of the American Revolution* (New York: Knopf, 1992), 229–369; J. Mills Thornton III, *Politics and Power in a Slave Society: Alabama, 1800–1860* (Baton Rouge: Louisiana State University Press, 1978), 3–162; Harry L. Watson, *Jacksonian Politics and Community Conflict: The Emergence of the Second American Party System in Cumberland County, North Carolina* (Baton Rouge: Louisiana State University Press, 1981), 17–59; Grady McWhiney, *Cracker Culture: Celtic Ways in the Old South* (Tuscaloosa: University of Alabama Press, 1988), 245–71.

43. Grant to David Porter, March 29, 1863, and Porter to Grant, March 29, 1863, both in U.S. War Department, *The War of the Rebellion: A Compilation of the Official Records of the Union and Confederate Armies,* 70 vols. (Washington, D.C.: Government Printing Office, 1880–1901), ser. 1, vol. 24, pt. 3, 151–52 (hereafter cited as *OR*); James McPherson, *Battle Cry of Freedom: The Civil War Era* (New York: Oxford University Press, 1988), 576–79, 586–88, 627–36; Mark Grimsley, *Hard Hand of War: Union Military Policy Toward Southern Civilians, 1861–1865* (New York: Cambridge University Press, 1995), 151–62.

44. William F. Norris Diary, Nov. 30, 1862, Robert Sterling Collection, Charleston, Ill.

45. DeWitt Clinton Loudon to Hannah, Jan. 1, 1863, Dewitt Clinton Loudon Papers, Ohio Historical Society, Columbus.

46. *OR*, ser. 1, vol. 24, pt. 3, 212–14; Grimsley, *Hard Hand of War*, 96–105; Ash, *When the Yankees Came*, 38–75.

47. Grant to Stephen A. Hurlbut, May 5, 1863, *OR*, ser. 1, vol. 24, pt. 3, 264–75.

48. Grant to William T. Sherman, May 9, 1863, *OR*, ser. 1, vol. 24, pt. 3, 285–86.

49. Henry W. Halleck report, Nov. 15, 1863, *OR*, ser. 1, vol. 24, pt. 1, 5. In 1856 Sherman had commanded an effort to quell vigilantes in San Francisco. John S. Hittell, *A History of the City of San Francisco and Incidentally of the State of California* (San Francisco: Bancroft, 1878), 250–66.

50. William T. Sherman to Joseph G. Mower, May 15, 1863, *OR*, ser. 1, vol. 24, pt. 3, 315.

51. G. D. Molineaux Diary, May 16, 1863, Special Collections, Augustana College Library, Rock Island, Ill.; Halleck report, Nov. 15, 1863, *OR*, ser. 1, vol. 24, pt. 1, 5–6.

52. Joseph Allan Frank and George A. Reaves, *"Seeing the Elephant": Raw Recruits at the Battle of Shiloh* (New York: Greenwood Press, 1989), 40–44.

53. Vicksburg *Daily Evening Citizen*, March 30, 1861; Mary Jenkins, claim 43533, box 210, SCC.

54. Emilie Riley McKinley Diary, May 18, 1863, Missouri Historical Society Library, St. Louis.

55. William Pitt Chambers, in *Blood and Sacrifice: The Civil War Journal of a Confederate Soldier*, ed. Richard A. Baumgarter (Huntington: Blue Acorn, 1994), 80.

56. Walker, *Vicksburg*, 139, 141, 154, 158; Rowland Chambers Diary, June 8, 9, 10, 11, 13, 14, 16, 17, 18, 19, 23, 30, 1863, Special Collections, Hill Memorial Library, Louisiana State University, Baton Rouge; Chambers, *Blood and Sacrifice*, 70–85.

57. Charles Allen Plantation Book, MDAH; Rowland Chambers Diary, June 28, 1862, Special Collections, Hill Memorial Library, Louisiana State University, Baton Rouge.

58. Daniel Pender, claim 6933, box 211, SCC.

59. Emilie Riley McKinley Diary, June 11, 1863, Missouri Historical Society Library, St. Louis; Grimsley, *Hard Hand of War*, 40–41.

60. Newton J. Hall deposition, Thomas J. Jones claim, Tamsey Jones administrator, 2291, box 210, SCC.

61. W. Maury Darst, "The Vicksburg Diary of Mrs. Alfred Ingraham," *Journal of Mississippi History* 44 (May 1982): 151–52.

62. John Townsend, claim 4220, and Samuel Townsend, claim 14278, box 212, SCC.

63. Dr. E. W. Gray deposition, James Warnes, claim 4896, box 212, SCC.

64. Kennedy to Wife, Dec. 21, 1862, William J. Kennedy Papers, Illinois State Historical Library, Springfield.

65. Osborn Oldroyd, *A Soldier's Story of the Siege of Vicksburg from the Diary of Osborn H. Oldroyd* (Springfield: privately printed, 1885), 10.

66. Darst, "The Vicksburg Diary of Mrs. Alfred Ingraham," 171; Morris, *Southern Slavery and the Law*, 350.

67. Henry Banks, claim 14443, box 207, SCC.

68. Benjamin Stinyard petition, claim 6999, box 211, SCC.

69. William Hitch deposition, Feb. 28, 1879, William Hitch, claim 22092, box 210, SCC.

70. Daniel Murfee deposition, July 21, 1863, Daniel Murfee, claim 18062, box 211, SCC.

71. Gabriel Bolger, claim 6940, box 207, SCC.

72. Henry Watson, claim 16555, box 212, SCC.

73. Netty Fant Thompson interview with Callie Gray, n.d., in *American Slave,* ed. Rawick, supplement, ser. 1, vol. 8, pt. 3, 867.

74. Netty Fant Thompson interview with Emma Johnson, n.d., in *American Slave,* ed. Rawick, supplement, ser. 1, vol. 8, pt. 3, 1155.

75. Minerva Boyd, claim 6942, box 207, SCC. For slaves' entrepreneurial activity and property-holding, see McDonald, *The Economy and Material Culture of Slaves;* Schweninger, *Black Property Owners,* 29–60; and Joseph P. Reidy, *From Slavery to Agrarian Capitalism in the Cotton Plantation South, Central Georgia, 1800–1880* (Chapel Hill: University of North Carolina Press, 1992), 58–81, 102–6.

76. Joseph W. Fifer deposition, May 18, 1874, James Warnes, claim 4896, box 212, SCC.

77. John Stanefirth deposition, James Warnes, claim 4896, box 212, SCC.

78. Thadeus B. Packard deposition, James Warnes, claim 4896, box 212, SCC.

79. Samuel P. Shannon deposition, James Warnes, claim 4896, box 212, SCC.

80. Anne Shannon to Emma, June, July, 1863, Crutcher-Shannon Papers, MDAH.

81. Jack Hyland deposition, April 2, 1874, Jack Hyland, claim 19956, box 210, SCC.

82. Henry Banks deposition, June 24, 1873, Henry Banks, claim 14443, box 207, SCC.

83. Matilda Anderson deposition, May 20, 1873, Mrs. M. Steigelman deposition, May 3, 1877, and Matilda Anderson, claim 6935, all in box 207, SCC.

84. Wyatt-Brown, *Southern Honor,* 7–8.

85. *Liberator,* Nov. 18, 1842.

86. *Liberator,* Oct. 5, 1849.

87. Marshall, *Army Life,* 83–84; Linderman, *Embattled Courage,* 56–57; Frank and Reaves, *"Seeing the Elephant,"* 29.

88. Thornton, *Politics and Power,* 74 (quotation); Grimsley, *Hard Hand of War,* 39–46; Frank and Reaves, *"Seeing the Elephant,"* 48–54.

89. Thornton, *Politics and Power,* 60.

90. Marshall, *Army Life,* 77–78.

91. Rowland Chambers Diary, May 24, 1863, Special Collections, Hill Memorial Library, Louisiana State University, Baton Rouge.

92. James M. McPherson, *For Cause and Comrades: Why Men Fought in the Civil War* (New York: Oxford University Press, 1997), 77–89.

93. W. L. Brown to Father, April 7, 1863, and Dick Puffer to Sister, Feb. 12, 1863, both in Leo M. Kaiser, ed., "Beleaguered City: The Vicksburg Campaign as Seen in Unpublished Letters," *Southern Studies* 17 (Spring 1978): 77, 76.

94. Ira Batterton to Mary Batterton, June 13, 1863, Ira A. Batterton Papers, Illinois State Historical Library, Springfield.

95. Ira Batterton to Sister, July 14, 1863, Ira A. Batterton Papers, Illinois State Historical Library, Springfield.

96. Ibid.

97. Ira Batterton to Father and Mother, June 30, 1865, Ira A. Batterton Papers, Illinois State Historical Library, Springfield.

98. Ibid.; Richard Abbott, "The Republican Party Press in Reconstruction Georgia, 1867–1874," *Journal of Southern History* 61 (Nov. 1995): 725–60. For Patridge's Civil Service, see Vicksburg *Daily Evening Citizen,* May 29, 1861; James Bolls, comp., *A Complete Roster of the Soldiers and Sailors of Warren County during the Civil War* (n.p., n.d.).

99. Th. J. Wood to Benjamin Humphreys, Jan. 9, 1867, Governor Humphrey's Correspondence, Governors' Papers, box 67, record group 27, MDAH; Vicksburg *Herald,* Aug. 23, 1874.

100. Vicksburg *Times,* Aug. 25, 1869.

101. Fonsylvania Plantation Diary, May 10, 1863, MDAH; Louise Lattimer deposition, Andrew Black, claim 10361, box 207, SCC.

102. Stone, *Brokenburn,* 33, 35; William Green deposition, Dick Green, claim 6963, box 210, SCC.

103. Lewis Johnson deposition, Lewis Johnson, claim 10684, box 210, SCC.

104. Henry Banks deposition, June 24, 1873, Henry Banks, claim 14443, box 207, SCC.

105. Joseph McFields deposition, June 24, 1873, Henry Banks, claim 14443, box 207, SCC.

106. Vicksburg *Daily Evening Citizen,* May 28, 1861.

107. Fonsylvania Plantation Diary, MDAH.

108. Monroe Gibson deposition, William L. Fortner, claim 8528, box 209, SCC.

109. Emilie Riley McKinley Diary, May 22, 1863, Missouri Historical Society Library, St. Louis.

110. Faust, *Mothers of Invention,* 62–65; Stone, *Brokenburn,* 196, 202.

111. Emma Crutcher to Will Crutcher, Nov. 18, 1861, Crutcher-Shannon Papers, NTC.

112. Faust, *Mothers of Invention,* 179–95.

113. Rowland Chambers Diary, May 26, 1862, Special Collections, Hill Memorial Library, Louisiana State University, Baton Rouge; Emma Balfour, *Diary of Emma Balfour, May 16, 1863–June 2, 1863: The Historic Vicksburg Siege,* ed. Fred Swaney (n.p.: 1979), May 27, 1863; Rable, *Civil Wars,* 162–80.

114. Thornton, *Politics and Power,* 163–461.

115. Rowland Chambers Diary, May 26, 1862, Special Collections, Hill Memorial Library, Louisiana State University, Baton Rouge; Rable, *Civil Wars,* 63–153; Catherine Clinton, *Tara Revisited: Women, War, and the Plantation Legend* (New York: Abbeville Press, 1995), 79–159; Lori D. Ginzberg, *Women and the Work of Benevolence: Morality, Politics, and Class in the Nineteenth-Century United States* (New Haven: Yale University Press, 1990); Emma Crutcher to Will Crutcher, Dec. 23, 1861, Crutcher-Shannon Papers, NTC.

116. Emma Crutcher to Will Crutcher, Jan. 20, 1861, Crutcher-Shannon Papers,

NTC. For the persistence of class divisions through the war, see Whites, *The Civil War as a Crisis in Gender,* 64–95; Rable, *Civil Wars,* 106–11.

117. Emma Crutcher to Will Crutcher, Dec. 23, 1861, Crutcher-Shannon Papers, NTC. On this point, see Faust, *Mothers of Invention,* 220–33.

118. Stone, *Brokenburn,* 109–10; Walker, *Vicksburg,* 95–96.

119. Emma Crutcher to Will Crutcher, Dec. 23, 1861, Crutcher-Shannon Papers, NTC.

120. Emma Crutcher to Will Crutcher, March 21, 1862, Crutcher-Shannon Papers, NTC; Faust, *Mothers of Invention,* 92–113.

121. Stone, *Brokenburn,* 96.

122. Emma Crutcher to Will Crutcher, April 10, 1862, Crutcher-Shannon Papers, NTC.

123. Walker, *Vicksburg,* 104–5.

124. Chambers, *Blood and Sacrifice,* 72.

125. [Mary Webster Loughborough], *My Cave Life in Vicksburg* (1864, repr. Vicksburg: Vicksburg and Warren County Historical Society, 1990), 40–47; Whites, *The Civil War as a Crisis in Gender,* 160–98.

126. Lavinia Shannon to Emmie, July 13, 1863, Crutcher-Shannon Papers, NTC. Balfour described this in her diary as well; see *Diary,* May 24, 1863. Faust, *Mothers of Invention,* 118.

127. Michael P. Johnson, "Planters and Patriarchy: Charleston, 1800–1860," *Journal of Southern History* 46 (Feb. 1980): 45–72 (quotation); Stephanie McCurry, "The Two Faces of Republicanism: Gender and Proslavery Politics in Antebellum South Carolina," *Journal of American History* 78 (March 1992): 1245–64.

128. Anne to Emma, June, July, 1863, Crutcher-Shannon Papers, MDAH; Emilie Riley McKinley Diary, May 21 (first quotation), 22 (second quotation), 23 (third quotation), 1863, Missouri Historical Society Library, St. Louis.

129. Ash, *When the Yankees Came,* 170–94.

130. Faust, *Mothers of Invention,* 114–23.

Chapter 5: Presidential Reconstruction

1. For Presidential Reconstruction in Mississippi, see William C. Harris, *Presidential Reconstruction in Mississippi* (Baton Rouge: Louisiana State University Press, 1967), which is still the standard work. The role of inferior courts in Presidential Reconstruction has been obscure for many years. In part this may be because in 1867 Major General Oliver Otis Howard's staff prepared a collection of the racially discriminatory laws southern state legislatures had passed immediately after the Civil War that ignored the new courts. See U.S. Congress, Senate, Committee on Military Affairs and the Militia, "Synopsis of Laws Respecting Persons of Color in the Late Slave States," 39th Cong., 2d sess. Senate Ex. Doc. 6, 170–230.

Subsequent historians have followed Howard's lead in overlooking Black Code–era lower courts. Howard did include the district courts created by South Carolina. For the new inferior courts, see 1864–65 South Carolina Laws 278; 1865 Florida Acts 20; 1865 Georgia Acts 64; 1866 Texas Laws 43; and 1865 Mississippi Laws 66. Alabama did not create a new court system but authorized justices of the peace to take cognizance and try all cases of misdemeanor, except gaming and revenue law cases (1865 Alabama Acts 119). Virginia already had a system of county courts but authorized the appointment of companies of special police empowered to search for stolen property at any time on the affidavit of anyone willing to make a complaint (1865–66 Virginia Acts 82). Historians have for decades viewed the South's postbellum Black Codes as an economic effort by whites to control newly freed black labor rather than a bid to control crime. Vernon Lane Wharton, *The Negro in Mississippi, 1865–1890* (1947, repr. New York: Harper and Row, 1965), 80–96; Kenneth M. Stampp, *The Era of Reconstruction, 1865–1877* (New York: Knopf, 1966), 79–81; Charles L. Flynn, Jr., *White Land, Black Labor: Caste and Class in Late Nineteenth-Century Georgia* (Baton Rouge: Louisiana State University Press, 1983), 35–37; and Eric Foner, *Reconstruction: America's Unfinished Revolution, 1863–1877* (New York: Harper and Row, 1988), 199–201. Yet contemporaries regarded the new inferior courts as central to southern whites' efforts to use law to control black behavior.

2. John Eaton to G. Whipple, June 29, 1863, American Missionary Association Papers, Amistad Research Center, New Orleans (hereafter cited as AMA).

3. Anne Shannon and Grace or Alice Shannon to Emma, June, July, 1863, Crutcher-Shannon Papers, MDAH.

4. W. C. Smedes, personal account book, W. C. Smedes Papers, OCHM.

5. Lavinia Shannon to Emmie, July 13, 1863, Crutcher-Shannon Papers, NTC.

6. Charles B. Burwell deposition, April 19, 1871 (quotation), Armistead Burwell claim, April 18, 1871, 111, box 207, SCC; Charles A. Dana, *Recollections of the Civil War,* ed. Paul M. Angle (1898, repr. New York: Collier Books, 1963), 99–105; W. L. Brown to Father, July 4, 1863, in "Beleaguered City," ed. Kaiser, 85.

7. Thomas T. Taylor to Netta Taylor, July 4, 1863, Thomas T. Taylor Papers, Ohio Historical Society, Columbus.

8. Undated document, text of speech to soldiers, DeWitt Clinton Loudon Papers, Ohio Historical Society, Columbus.

9. Seneca B. Thrall to Wife, Aug. 2, 6 (quotation), 1863, in Mildred Throne, ed., "An Iowa Doctor in Blue: The Letters of Seneca B. Thrall, 1862–1864," *Iowa Journal of History* 58 (April 1960): 165–66.

10. See, for example, *United States v. Robert Turnbull,* file MM 1615, box 1034, Records of the Office of the Judge Advocate General (Army), record group 153, NA.

11. *United States v. Rebecca Fields,* file LL 3117, box 868, Records of the Judge Advocate General (Army), record group 153, NA.

12. *United States v. Daniel Pender,* file MM 2409, box 722, Records of the Judge Advocate General (Army), record group 153, NA. Turnbull's lawyer made the same argument. See *United States v. Robert Turnbull.*

13. *United States v. Rebecca Fields.*

14. Richards Barnett, brief and argument, *United States v. Daniel Pender.*

15. Thomas T. Taylor to Netta Taylor, Aug. 19, 1863, Thomas T. Taylor Papers, Ohio Historical Society, Columbus.

16. Berlin et al., eds., *The Wartime Genesis of Free Labor,* 725, 742.

17. Isaac Shoemaker Diary, Special Collections Library, Duke University, Durham,

N.C., see April 28, 1864, for quotation; Berlin et al., eds., *The Wartime Genesis of Free Labor,* 621–900, see esp. 826n for Montross.

18. Isaac Shoemaker Diary.

19. Seneca B. Thrall to Wife, Aug. 6, 1863, in "An Iowa Doctor in Blue," ed. Throne, 166.

20. Annie Shannon to Emmie, Aug. 8, 1863, Crutcher-Shannon Papers, NTC; Alice Shannon to Emma, Nov. 19, 1863, Crutcher-Shannon Papers, MDAH; W. L. Brown to Father, Aug. 16, 1863, in "Beleaguered City," ed. Kaiser, 89; Faust, *Mothers of Invention,* 207–19; Elizabeth Heineman, "The Hour of the Woman: Memories of Germany's 'Crisis Years' and West German National Identity," *American Historical Review* 101 (April 1996): 380–95.

21. Tokyo *Nippon Times,* Dec. 16, 1945; Heineman, "The Hour of the Woman," 354–95; Atina Grossmann, "German Women Doctors from Berlin to New York: Maternity and Modernity in Weimar and in Exile," *Feminist Studies* 19 (Spring 1993): 65–86.

22. Emilie Riley McKinley Diary, Nov. 10, 1863, Missouri Historical Society Library, St. Louis.

23. Allice Shannon to Emma Crutcher, Nov. 19, 1863, Crutcher-Shannon Papers, MDAH.

24. Emilie Riley McKinley Diary, July 22, Nov. 10, 1863, Jan. 6, 1864, Missouri Historical Society Library, St. Louis.

25. Samuel F. Porter to George Whipple, March 5, 1864, microfilm frame no. 71605, AMA.

26. J. P. Bardwell to M. E. Strickby, Oct. 14, 1865, microfilm frame no. 71817, AMA.

27. Lawrence Sterne Houghton to Lizzie Tupper, Feb. 29, 1865, typescript, Houghton Papers, OCHM.

28. W. L. Brown to Father, Aug. 16, 1863, in "Beleagured City," ed. Kaiser, 90.

29. J. Warren Miller deposition, March 20, 1868, Armistead Burwell claim, April 18, 1871, 111, box 207, SCC.

30. Brooks D. Simpson, *Let Us Have Peace: Ulysses S. Grant and the Politics of War and Reconstruction, 1861–1868* (Chapel Hill: University of North Carolina Press, 1991), 95–99.

31. Foner, *Reconstruction,* 176–227.

32. Lawrence Houghton to Lizzie Tupper, Feb. 29, 1865, typescript, Houghton Papers, OCHM; James W. Garner, *Reconstruction in Mississippi* (1901, repr. Baton Rouge: Louisiana State University Press, 1968), 77.

33. S. Kent to T. S. Bowers, July 25, 1863, letter 64, Letters Sent by the Provost Marshal, Army of the Tennessee, U.S. Army Continental Commands, book 36A, record group 393, NA.

34. Fannie J. Scott to George Whipple, Oct. 10, 1864, 71686, AMA; L. A. Eberhart to C. H. Fowler, Feb. 1, 1864, 71589, AMA; John Eaton, *Grant, Lincoln, and the Freedmen: Reminiscences of the Civil War, with Special Reference to the Work for the Contrabands and Freedmen of the Mississippi Valley* (1907, repr. New York: New American Library, 1970), 66–67.

35. Eaton, *Grant, Lincoln, and the Freedmen,* 104–6; James T. Currie, *Enclave: Vicks-*

burg and Her Plantations, 1863–1870 (Jackson: University Press of Mississippi, 1980), 33–35; L. A. Eberhart to C. H. Fowler, Feb. 1, 1864, 71589, AMA; Bishop William Henry Elder, *Civil War Diary (1862–1865) of Bishop William Henry Elder Bishop of Natchez* (n.p.: Most Reverend R. O. Gerow, n.d.), 56–60.

36. Mark E. Neely, Jr., *The Fate of Liberty: Abraham Lincoln and Civil Liberties* (New York: Oxford University Press, 1991), 52–68.

37. Neely, *The Fate of Liberty,* 75–92; Ash, *When the Yankees Came,* 82–91; Gordon A. Cotton and Ralph C. Mason, *With Malice toward Some: The Military Occupation of Vicksburg, 1864–1865* (Vicksburg: Vicksburg and Warren County Historical Society, 1991), 19–55; L. Kent to James Wilson, Aug. 30, 1863 (quotation), L. Kent to James Wilson, Sept. 1, 1863, and L. Kent to William Porterfield, Sept. 27, 1863, all in Letters Sent by the Provost Marshal, Headquarters Military Division of the Mississippi, vol. 36A, E-2516, record group 393, NA.

38. *United States v. William Anderson,* file LL 2278, box 700, Records of the Judge Advocate General (Army), record group 153, NA.

39. Alice Shannon to Emma Crutcher, Nov. 19, 1863, Crutcher-Shannon Papers, MDAH; Thomas Richardson testimony, William Cook testimony, and Jared Reese Cook testimony, all from court martial of Thomas Fore and others, Records of the Judge Advocate General (Army), Court Martial Case Files, 1809–1938, record group 153, NA.

40. Jared Reese Cook testimony, court martial of Thomas Fore and others; Robert I. Alotta, *Civil War Justice: Union Army Executions under Lincoln* (Shippensburg, Pa.: White Mane, 1989), 168; Gordon A. Cotton, *Horrible Outrage: The Murder of Minerva Cook* (Vicksburg: privately printed, 1993), 28–38.

41. Bureau of the Census, *Ninth Census of the United States: Statistics of Population* (Washington, D.C.: Government Printing Office, 1872), 186.

42. Vicksburg *Daily Herald,* Jan. 18, March 8 (quotation), April 6, May 26, 27, Aug. 15, Sept. 6, 8, 1865.

43. Simpson, *Let Us Have Peace,* 112–16.

44. Lawrence Houghton to Cousin, Aug. 22, 1865, typescript, Houghton Papers, OCHM; Board of Police Minute Book, 1853–1866, Chancery Clerk's Office, Vicksburg.

45. Boards of supervisors were called boards of police before the 1868 constitution. For antebellum grand jury selection, see *The Revised Code of the Statute Laws of the State of Mississippi* (1857), ch. 61, sec. 11, 498. For procedures under the Republican code, see *The Revised Code of the Statute Laws of the State of Mississippi, as Adopted at January Session, A.D., 1871, and Published by Authority of the Legislature* (Jackson: Alcorn and Fisher, 1871), ch. 8, sec. 724–25, 150.

46. "Mississippi," vol. 21, 64, R. G. Dun and Co. credit ledgers, Historical Collections Department, Baker Library, Harvard University Graduate School of Business Administration, Cambridge, Mass.

47. Marmaduke Shannon to Governor Sharkey, July 1, 1865, Governors' Papers, box 61B, record group 27, MDAH.

48. D. O. Merwin to Governor Sharkey, June 30, 1865, Governors' Papers, box 61A, record group 27, MDAH; W. L. Sharkey to P. J. Osterhaus, July 2, 1865, Letters Received,

Department of the Mississippi, U.S. Army Continental Commands, box 2, record group 393, NA.

49. T. Randolph to Governor Sharkey, Sept. 17, 1865, Governors' Papers, box 62, record group 27, MDAH.

50. Marmaduke Shannon to Governor Sharkey, Oct. 5, 1865, Governors' Papers, box 62, record group 27, MDAH.

51. Marmaduke Shannon to Governor Humphreys, Oct. 18, 1865, Governors' Papers, box 65, record group 27, MDAH.

52. Thomas J. Wood to Governor Humphreys, March 14, 1866, Governors' Papers, box 65, record group 27, MDAH.

53. T. J. Wood to H. Lieb, April 25, 1866, Letters Received, Department of the Mississippi, U.S. Army Continental Commands, box 61B, record group 393, NA.

54. L. M. Hall to Governor Sharkey, July 25, 1865, Governors' Papers, box 35, record group 27, MDAH.

55. Thomas J. Wood to Governor Humphreys, March 14, 1866, and D. O. Merwin to Governor Humphreys, March 15, 1865, both in Governors' Papers, box 65, record group 27, MDAH.

56. Vicksburg *Herald,* Jan. 18, Feb. 24, March 8, April 7, May 26, 27, Aug. 15, Sept. 6, 7, 8, 14, 1865.

57. Manuscript population schedule, Ninth U.S. Census, 1870, Warren County, Mississippi, microfilm, NA.

58. The New York *Times* published the text of these decisions on Oct. 26, 1866.

59. *State v. Harrison,* Warren County Circuit Court Papers, OCHM.

60. Warren County Circuit Court and Criminal Court Papers; see the appendix.

61. Ibid.

62. See the appendix.

63. *State v. Joseph Cosgrove,* Warren County Circuit Court Papers, OCHM.

64. *State v. Shanghai George,* Warren County Circuit Court Papers, NTC.

65. New York *Times,* March 17, 1867; Lancaster *Daily Evening Express,* Nov. 26, 27, 30, 1866, Jan. 5, 10, 12, 15, Feb. 5, 7, 8, 9, 15, 23, 25, March 16, 18, 19, 21, April 2, 6, 10, 13, 1867; Vicksburg *Herald,* March 5, 1867.

66. Donald G. Nieman, *To Set the Law in Motion: The Freedmen's Bureau and the Legal Rights of Blacks, 1865–1868* (Millwood, N.Y.: KTO Press, 1979), 4–28; Foner, *Reconstruction,* 68–70; James Oakes, "A Failure of Vision: The Collapse of the Freedmen's Bureau Courts," *Civil War History* 25 (March 1979): 66–76.

67. E. E. Platt, Monthly Report of Complaints Made by Freedmen at Hd Qrs Bureau Refugees Freedmen and Abandoned Lands, September 1867, microfilm publication M-826, roll 30, NA. Other Freedmen's Bureau courts had similar experiences. See John Richard Dennett, *The South as It Is, 1865–1866* (1965, repr. Baton Rouge: Louisiana State University Press, 1995), 52, 55, 75, 110, 124.

68. E. E. Platt, Monthly Report of Complaints Made by Freedmen at Hd Qrs Bureau Refugees Freedmen and Abandoned Lands, September 1867, microfilm publication M-826, roll 30, NA.

69. Ibid.

70. Ibid.

71. Ibid.

72. For paternalism, see Genovese, *Roll, Jordan, Roll.* For extra-legal violence against slaves, see Judith K. Schafer, "'Details of a Most Revolting Character': Cruelty to Slaves as Seen in Appeals to the Supreme Court of Louisiana," *Chicago-Kent Law Review* 68 (1993): 1283.

73. Dan T. Carter, *When the War Was Over: The Failure of Self-Reconstruction in the South, 1865–1867* (Baton Rouge: Louisiana State University Press, 1985), 61–95; Reidy, *From Slavery to Agrarian Capitalism,* 150–63.

74. P. L. Rainwater, ed., "The Autobiography of Benjamin Grubb Humphreys, August 26, 1808–December 20, 1882," *Mississippi Valley Historical Review* 21 (Sept. 1934): 247 (first quotation); Jeptaha Evans to William L. Sharkey, Sept. 3, 1865, box 62, Governors' Papers, box 35, record group 27, MDAH.

75. W. S. Epperson to Sharkey, n.d., box 62, Governors' Papers, box 35, record group 27, MDAH.

76. R. D. McLean to William Sharkey, Aug. 1, 1865 (quotation), box 62, Governors' Papers, box 35, record group 27, MDAH.

77. Garner, *Reconstruction in Mississippi,* 118, 288.

78. Stephen V. Ash writes that bandits with a "propensity for brutal violence against innocent, unarmed civilians" deluged parts of the South. Ash, *When the Yankees Came,* 205–11; Cotton and Mason, *With Malice Toward Some,* 22–55.

79. W. L. Sharkey, proclamation, Sept. 18, 1865, Letters Received, Department of the Mississippi, U.S. Army Continental Commands, box 2, record group 393, NA.

80. *Journal of the Proceedings and Debates in the Constitutional Convention of the State of Mississippi, August, 1865* (Jackson: E. M. Yerger, 1865), 252; Harris, *Presidential Reconstruction in Mississippi,* 47–60.

81. *Journal of the Proceedings and Debates,* 165.

82. Ibid., 23, 258–62.

83. Ibid., 165–66.

84. Natchez *Democrat* quoted in the Jackson *Clarion,* Oct. 18, 1866; see also William Banks Taylor, *Brokered Justice: Race, Politics, and Mississippi Prisons, 1798–1992* (Columbus: Ohio State University Press, 1993), 1–54. For the persistence of Jacksonian values into the Reconstruction Era, see Samuel L. Webb, "A Jacksonian Democrat in Postbellum Alabama: The Ideology and Influence of Journalist Robert McKee, 1869–1896," *Journal of Southern History* 62 (May 1996): 239–74.

85. Vicksburg *Times,* Dec. 13, 1866.

86. "Tabular View of the Mississippi Legislature," Legislative Papers, vol. 659, record group 47, MDAH.

87. *Journal of the Senate of the State of Mississippi, 1866* (Jackson: Shannon, 1866), 121.

88. For Mississippi's Black Code, see Act to Confer Civil Rights on Freedmen, and for Other Purposes (1865 Mississippi Acts 82), Act to Regulate the Relation of Master and Apprentice, as Relates to Freedmen, Free Negroes, and Mulattoes (1865 Mississippi Acts 86), Act to Amend the Vagrant Laws of the State (1865 Mississippi Acts 90), Act to Punish Certain Offences Therein Named, and for Other Purposes (1865 Mississippi Acts 165), and Act to Establish County Courts, 1865 Mississippi Acts 66.

Mississippi was not the only southern state to create inferior courts to handle increased crime after emancipation. For Florida, see Joe M. Richardson, "Florida Black Codes," *Florida Historical Quarterly* 47 (Spring 1969): 373; for Georgia, see Jonathan M. Bryant, *How Curious a Land: Conflict and Change in Greene County, Georgia, 1850–1885* (Chapel Hill: University of North Carolina Press, 1996), 108–11. States such as North Carolina that already had a functioning system of inferior courts created no new tribunals.

89. Nieman, *To Set the Law in Motion*, 76–83.

90. Vicksburg *Journal*, Nov. 25, 1865.

91. James F. Trotter, charge to the DeSoto County grand jury, 1866, Southern Historical Collection, University of North Carolina Library, Chapel Hill.

92. Carter, *When the War Was Over*, 221.

93. Leon F. Litwack, *Been in the Storm So Long: The Aftermath of Slavery* (New York: Vintage Books, 1979), 275.

94. Litwack, *Been in the Storm So Long*, 371.

95. An exception is Richardson, "Florida Black Codes," 373–74, who likens Florida's county courts to planters' "household tribunals." Harris discusses county courts in *Presidential Reconstruction in Mississippi*, 139–49.

96. Jackson, Miss., *Daily Pilot*, Oct. 13, 1875.

97. 1817 Mississippi Acts 58–68; Hoffheimer, "Mississippi Courts," 127–70; David J. Bodenhamer, "Criminal Justice and Democratic Theory in Antebellum America: The Grand Jury Debate in Indiana," *Journal of the Early Republic* 5 (Winter 1985): 481–502; Richard D. Younger, *The People's Panel: The Grand Jury in the United States, 1634–1941* (Providence: Brown University Press, 1963), ch. 5.

98. Steinberg, *The Transformation of Criminal Justice*, 1–33.

99. Vicksburg *Daily Herald*, Nov. 19, 1865.

100. 1865 Mississippi Acts 68.

101. 1865 Mississippi Acts 71.

102. *Daniel Dawkins v. the State of Mississippi*, 42 Miss. 631 (1869); *James M. Lyles v. Richard Barnes*, 40 Miss. 608 (1866).

103. Duncan McKenzie to Duncan McLaurin, Sept. 9, 1866, Duncan McLaurin Papers, Special Collections Library, Duke University, Durham, N.C.

104. 1865 Mississippi Acts 79–80.

105. Duncan McKenzie to Duncan McLaurin, Sept. 9, 1866, Duncan McLaurin Papers, Special Collections Library, Duke University, Durham, N.C.

106. Thomas J. Hudson to Benjamin Humphreys, March 13, 1866, Governors' Papers, box 65, record group 27, MDAH.

107. [Signature missing] to Benjamin Humphreys, May 10, 1866, Governors' Papers, box 66, record group 27, MDAH.

108. George Torrey to Benjamin G. Humphreys, March 29, 1866, Governors' Papers, box 65, record group 27, MDAH.

109. 1865 Mississippi Acts, 66–81; Vicksburg *Daily Herald*, January 9, 1866; Everett, *Vicksburg Lawyers prior to the Civil War*, 100; Bolls, *A Complete Roster*. Cowan favored enfranchising women in 1890 as a way of canceling out the black majority among male voters. Bond, *Political Culture in the Nineteenth-Century South*, 249.

110. Donald Nieman, "The Freedmen's Bureau and the Mississippi Black Code," *Journal of Mississippi History* 40 (May 1978): 108–18.

111. Determining the racial bias of any court is always problematic. Court documents rarely indicate defendants' race, and matching transient defendants with tax and census records can be nearly impossible. But the county court in Warren County carefully described defendants as "free women of color," "free men of color," "free boys of color," or as a "citizen" (white). Sixty-four percent of the defendants passing through Warren County's county court were "citizens."

112. Steinberg, *The Transformation of Criminal Justice,* 76–91.

113. Warren County Court case files, OCHM.

114. "Questions Propounded to Samuel Brown by County Court of Warren County April Term A.D. 1866 in Secret Session," Habeas Corpus Petition, *S. W. Brown v. State,* Warren County Criminal Court Papers, OCHM.

115. Warren County Court case files, OCHM and NTC.

116. Vicksburg *Daily Times,* Oct. 21, 1866; Debbielee Landi, "Best Evidence: A Social History of the County Court of Lafayette County, 1865–1870," M.A. thesis, University of Mississippi, 1992, passim, but see 38 for the Oxford *Falcon*'s objection to the courts.

117. John Roy Lynch, *Reminiscenses of an Active Life: The Autobiography of John Roy Lynch,* ed. John Hope Franklin (Chicago: University of Chicago Press, 1970), 61.

118. See, for example, Fielding Neale to Robert G. Burrows, Sept. 25, 1866, vol. 282, Mississippi Records, Bureau of Refugees, Freedmen, and Abandoned Lands, vol. 282, record group 105, NA. For federal protection of former slaves' right to bear arms, see Leonard Miles deposition, Feb. 14, 1867, Vicksburg District Narrative Reports, Mississippi Records, Bureau of Refugees, Freedmen, and Abandoned Lands, box 54-A, record group 105, NA.

119. James M. Babcock to Major, Jan. 2, 1866, Letters Sent, District of Natchez and Sub Districts, Mississippi Records, Bureau of Refugees, Freedmen, and Abandoned Lands, vol. 249, record group 105, NA.

120. Lt. O. B. Foster to Major [?], Dec. 15, 1865, Narrative Reports from Subordinate Officers, Aug. 1865–Oct. 1867, Records of the Assistant Commissioner for the State of Mississippi, Bureau of Refugees, Freedmen, and Abandoned Lands, 1865–69, roll 30, microfilm publication M-826, NA (hereafter cited as Narrative Reports from Subordinate Officers).

121. William H. Ross to Lt. Col. H. W. Smith, Sept. 4, 1867, Narrative Reports from Subordinate Officers.

122. A. Sid Alden to Lt. J. F. Canynham, Sept. 1, 1867, Narrative Reports from Subordinate Officers.

123. Robert P. Gardner to Capt. J. W. Sunderland, Sept. 30, 1867, Narrative Reports from Subordinate Officers.

124. Manuscript population schedules, Eighth U.S. Census, 1860, and Ninth U.S. Census, 1870, Warren County, Mississippi, microfilm, NA; Vicksburg *Daily Herald,* May 17, 1865.

125. J. W. M. Harris to Benjamin Humphreys, Jan. 2, 1867, Governors' Papers, box 67, record group 27, MDAH.

126. E. E. Platt, Monthly Report of Complaints Made by Freedmen at Hd Qrs Bureau Refugees Freedmen and Abandoned Lands, Sept. 1867, microfilm publication M-826, roll 30, NA.

127. Nieman, "The Freedmen's Bureau," 92–93; James T. Currie, "From Slavery to Freedom in Mississippi's Legal System," *Journal of Negro History* 65 (Spring 1980): 112–25.

128. Currie, "From Slavery to Freedom," 122; Garner, *Reconstruction in Mississippi*, 117n1; J. T. Trowbridge, *The South: A Tour of Its Battle-Fields and Ruined Cities* (1866, repr. New York: Arno, 1969), 373.

129. Transcript of testimony, *State v. John Green*, June 1866.

130. H. Bonner to Benjamin Humphreys, June 26, 1866, Governors' Papers, box 66, record group 27, MDAH. Bonner wanted to know if he could initiate informations when court was not in session.

131. Majer Lewis, petition, Dec. 1865, Case of Charles Wright, Warren County Criminal Court Papers, OCHM. For a discussion of gaming and race, see Ann Vincent Fabian, *Card Sharps, Dream Books, and Bucket Shops: Gambling in Nineteenth-Century America* (Ithaca: Cornell University Press, 1990), 120–28. Fabian argues that gambling offered the possibility of not working—an offensive prospect for people in the business of making people work.

132. Wesley Jackson, habeas corpus petition, Feb. 2, 1867, *State v. Wesly Jackson*, Warren County Criminal Court Papers, OCHM.

133. Habeas corpus petition, June 5, 1866, *State v. Henry, Hardy, Richard*, Warren County Criminal Court Papers, OCHM.

134. Roswell V. Booth, habeas corpus return, Jan. 16, 1866, NTC; habeas corpus petition, Jan. 26, 1867, *State v. Alfred Warren*, Warren County Criminal Court Papers, OCHM; Pea Powan, habeas corpus petition, July 11, 1868, NTC. For James C. Harris, see manuscript population schedule, Eighth U.S. Census, 1860, Warren County, Mississippi, microfilm, NA.

135. John Ells, habeas corpus petition, Oct. 11, 1870, A. H. Post, habeas corpus petition, Aug. 27, 1866, and Albert Crump, habeas corpus petition, Oct. 13, 1866, all in NTC.

136. Sharon Ann Holt, "Making Freedom Pay: Freedpeople Working for Themselves, North Carolina, 1865–1900," *Journal of Southern History* 60 (May 1994): 229–62; Laura F. Edwards, "'The Marriage Covenant Is at the Foundation of All Our Rights': The Politics of Slave Marriages in North Carolina after Emancipation," *Law and History Review* 14 (Spring 1996): 81–124.

137. *State v. George Bailey and Gus Davis*, and *State v. John Cassidy*, Warren County Court Papers, OCHM.

138. *State v. Ephraim Moore*, Warren County Court Papers, OCHM; Bodenhamer, *Fair Trial*, 51–53.

139. Vicksburg *Journal*, Dec. 19, 1865.

140. Vicksburg *Herald*, April 8, 1873.

141. *State v. James Gordon*, Warren County Circuit Court Papers, OCHM.

142. Jury note, April 1864, *State v. Philip Wiggins*, Warren County Court Papers, OCHM. It is impossible to say what became of black defendants released into the

community by legal "technicalities." Vigilantes may have targeted them, although surviving newspapers and other sources contain no evidence to support such a supposition until the 1870s. The presence of Union army troops may well have prevented such terrorism.

143. 1864–65 South Carolina Acts 281.

144. 1866 Georgia Acts 69; 1865 Florida Acts 21; 1866 Texas Laws 44.

145. 1865–66 Virginia Acts 82.

146. 1865–66 Alabama 119.

147. Letter Book, vol. 1, Office of the Sub-Commissioner, Vicksburg District, entry 2359, record group 105, NA; Correspondence and Reports, District of Vicksburg, Bureau of Refugees, Freedmen, and Abandoned Lands, box 54–A, entry 2368, record group 105, NA; Records of the Assistant Commissioner for the State of Mississippi, Bureau of Refugees, Freedmen, and Abandoned Lands, 1865–1869, roll 30, microfilm publication M-826, record group 105, NA.

148. Captain Z. B. Chatfield to Major, Oct. 29, 1865, Narrative Reports from Subordinate Officers.

149. Howard C. Westwood, "Getting Justice for the Freedman," *Howard Law Journal* 16 (Spring 1971): 505–6; Oakes, "A Failure of Vision," 66–76.

150. Gerald F. Linderman, *Embattled Courage: The Experience of Combat in the American Civil War* (New York: Free Press, 1987), 172–73.

151. Joseph Taylor to Lt. T. F. Forbes, Sept. 1, 1866, and T. F. Forbes to Joseph H. Taylor, Sept. 5, 1866, both in Records of the Assistant Commissioner for the State of Georgia, Bureau of Refugees, Freedmen, and Abandoned Lands, 1865–1869, roll 19, record group 105, microfilm publication 798, NA. See William L. Richter, "'The Revolver Rules the Day!': Colonel DeWitt C. Brown and the Freedmen's Bureau in Paris, Texas, 1867–1868," *Southwestern Historical Quarterly* 93 (Jan. 1990): 306n5.

152. F. A. H. Gaebel to W. W. Deane, Sept. 22, 1866, Records of the Assistant Commissioner for the State of Georgia, Bureau of Refugees, Freedmen, and Abandoned Lands, 1865–1869, record group 105, microfilm publication 798, roll 19, NA.

153. For nineteenth-century attitudes toward corporal punishment generally, see Glenn, *Campaigns against Corporal Punishment,* and George Ryley Scott, *The History of Corporal Punishment: A Survey of Flagellation in Its Historical, Anthropological and Sociological Aspects* (London: Torchstream, 1950), 33–107.

154. The Eighth Amendment's sanctions against cruel and unusual punishment did not apply to the states in the nineteenth century. See *Pervear v. Commonwealth* 72 US 475; *Baron v. Baltimore* 7 Peters 243 (1833); and *Barker v. People* 3 Cow. 686.

155. Landi, "Best Evidence," 16–29; H. Bonner to Benjamin Humphreys, June 26, 1866, Governors' Papers, box 65, record group 27, MDAH; Henry W. Warren, *Reminiscences of a Mississippi Carpetbagger* (Holden, Mass.: Davis Press, 1914), 50, 83. But Bryant, in *How Curious a Land,* 108–11, finds that in Georgia's Greene County the county court judge dealt unfairly with black defendants.

156. Warren, *Reminiscences of a Mississippi Carpetbagger,* 50, 83.

157. David Schenck Diary, David Schenck Papers, Southern Historical Collection, University of North Carolina Library, Chapel Hill.

158. For Cowan's role as an organizer of the first Tax-Payers League in Mississip-

pi, see Vicksburg *Times*, Feb. 2, 1868. See also *Origin and Progress of the Vicksburg Troubles as Reported Daily in the Columns of the* Vicksburg Herald (Vicksburg: *Vicksburg Herald*, 1874), 5, 15; *Vicksburgh Troubles*, 328.

159. Litwack, *Been in the Storm So Long*, 285.

160. Michael R. Gottfredson and Travis Hirschi, "National Crime Control Policies," *Society* 32 (Jan.–Feb. 1995): 30; Marcus Felson, *Crime and Everyday Life* (Thousand Oaks: Pine Forge Press, 1994).

Chapter 6: Republican Reconstruction

1. Genovese, *Roll, Jordan, Roll*, 158. The most recent work on Reconstruction has continued this old tradition. In *Reconstruction*, Eric Foner describes black politicization as "the most radical development of the Reconstruction years, a massive experiment." See *Reconstruction*, xxv. Joel Williamson has described white racists at the end of the nineteenth century as "radicals." See *The Crucible of Race: Black and White Relations in the American South since Emancipation* (New York: Oxford University Press, 1984).

2. Some historians have argued that the Republicans pursued an essentially conservative course through Reconstruction, struggling to preserve the existing balance of power between the states and the national government, for example. See Michael Les Benedict, "Preserving the Constitution: The Conservative Basis of Radical Reconstruction," *Journal of American History* 61 (June 1974): 65–90; Harold M. Hyman, *A More Perfect Union: The Impact of the Civil War and Reconstruction on the Constitution* (New York: Knopf, 1973); and Donald Nieman, "The Language of Liberation: African Americans and Egalitarian Constitutionalism, 1830–1950," in *The Constitution, Law, and American Life: Critical Aspects of the Nineteenth-Century Experience*, ed. Donald G. Nieman (Athens: University of Georgia Press, 1992), 67–90.

3. Simpson, *Let Us Have Peace*, 150–51.

4. Foner, *Reconstruction*, 228–68; Paul Moreno, "Racial Classification and Reconstruction Legislation," *Journal of Southern History* 61 (May 1995): 271–304.

5. 14 Stat. 428; Foner, *Reconstruction*, 271–80.

6. William C. Harris, *The Day of the Carpetbagger: Republican Reconstruction in Mississippi* (Baton Rouge: Louisiana State University Press, 1979), 1–33.

7. See Weekly Stations Reports, post of Vicksburg, April, May, June, July, Aug. 1867, all in Department of Mississippi Records, U.S. Army Continental Commands, record group 393, NA.

8. W. P. Carlin to C. D. Langdon, July 8, 1869, Letters Sent by the Post of Vicksburg, Department of Mississippi Records, U.S. Army Continental Command, vol. 115, record group 393, NA; *United States v. Joseph Powers, United States v. Phillip Meagher*, and *United States v. Patrick Kane*, all in file OO 3371, box 1492, Records of the Judge Advocate General (Army), record group 153, NA; *United States v. David Quill*, file OO 3101, box 1519, *United States v. Thomas McMurry*, file OO 2683, box 1445, and *United States v. Riley McIntosh*, file OO 2211, box 1402, all in Records of the Judge Advocate General (Army), record group 152, NA.

9. W. P. Carlin to Edward Davis, May 3, 1870, W. P. Carlin to R. P. Hughes, May 21,

1870, and W. P. Carlin to Adjutant General, June 2, 1870, all in Letters Sent by the Post of Vicksburg, Department of Mississippi Records, U.S. Army Continental Commands, vol. 115, record group 393, NA.

10. Vicksburg *Daily Herald,* March 28, 1867.

11. Vicksburg *Daily Herald,* May 8, 1867.

12. Vicksburg *Daily Times,* Jan. 1, 1868, Nov. 6, 1867 (quotation); *Ex Parte McCardle,* 6 Wallace 320 (1867), *Ex Parte McCardle,* file 5105, box 636, U.S. Supreme Court Appellate Case Files, record group 267, NA. McCardle appealed his case to the Supreme Court, which heard arguments but did not proceed after Congress revised the Habeas Corpus Act to take away the Court's jurisdiction in cases such as McCardle's.

13. Federal officials at the highest levels disagreed over the role generals such as Ord should play in state politics. Grant viewed such removals as essential to the success of Reconstruction, but President Johnson disagreed. Phil Sheridan, commander of Louisiana and Texas, discovered that when he removed from office the mayor of New Orleans, Louisiana's attorney general, a judge, twenty-two members of the New Orleans city council, and the governor of Texas. Simpson, *Let Us Have Peace,* 179–93.

14. Currie, *Enclave,* 195.

15. Garner, *Reconstruction in Mississippi,* 208; Harris, *Day of the Carpetbagger,* 178–79.

16. Some of these people later moved on to bigger and better things. The assistant jailor, G. W. Davenport, became chancery court clerk in 1872. Governor Alcorn appointed William H. Mallory, a police officer in 1870, an alderman in 1871, and he served in the state's house of representatives in 1872 and 1873. Eric Foner, *Freedom's Lawmakers: A Directory of Black Officeholders during Reconstruction* (New York: Oxford University Press, 1993), 141.

17. Hermann, *Pursuit of a Dream,* 109–31.

18. Davis Bend magistrates' book, OCHM; Benjamin Montgomery, Report of Fines Collected, NTC.

19. Harris, *Day of the Carpetbagger,* ch. 3, 67.

20. Michael W. Fitzgerald, *The Union League Movement in the Deep South: Politics and Agricultural Change during Reconstruction* (Baton Rouge: Louisiana State University Press, 1989), 54; Alston Mygatt deposition, Dec. 10, 1872, Henry Banks, claim 14442, box 207, SCC; Alston Mygatt deposition, Mary E. Acuff, claim 6934, box 207, SCC (second quotation); "Mississippi," vol. 21, 57, R. G. Dun and Co. Papers, Baker Library, Harvard University Graduate School of Business Administration, Cambridge, Mass. (first and third quotations); Vicksburg *Daily Herald,* Feb. 26, 27, 1867, April 2, 1868 (fourth quotation).

21. Vicksburg *Daily Herald,* April 13, 19, 20, 21, 1867.

22. See Articles of Agreement, Mechanics Mutual Benefit Society of Vicksburg and Phoenix Engine Company, Sept. 19, 1845, NTC.

23. For Republican factionalism, see Lawrence N. Powell, "The Politics of Livelihood: Carpetbaggers in the Deep South," in *Region, Race, and Reconstruction: Essays in Honor of C. Vann Woodward,* ed. J. Morgan Kousser and James M. McPherson (New York: Oxford University Press, 1982), 315. Perhaps the most prominent statement of the view that black political leaders pursued an essentially conservative course came

from John Hope Franklin, *Reconstruction: After the Civil War* (Chicago: University of Chicago Press, 1961), 86–92, 133–38. See also Wharton, *The Negro in Mississippi*, 157–80. The most important work on grass-roots postbellum black leadership has been completed by Eric Foner; see "Black Reconstruction Leaders at the Grass Roots" in *Black Leaders of the Nineteenth Century*, ed. Leon Litwack and August Meier (Urbana: University of Illinois Press, 1988), 219–34; and Foner, *Freedom's Lawmakers*, xi–xxxi. But see also Nieman, "The Language of Liberation," 67–90; Howard Rabinowitz, ed., *Southern Black Leaders of the Reconstruction Era* (Urbana: University of Illinois Press, 1982); and Philip S. Foner and George Walker, eds., *Proceedings of the Black National and State Conventions. 1840–1865*, 2 vols. (Philadelphia: Temple University Press, 1986).

24. Albert Johnson deposition, April 29, 1875, Albert Johnson, claim 43532, box 210, SCC.

25. Foner, *Freedom's Lawmakers*, 206; Fitzgerald, *Union League Movement*, 87; Wharton, *The Negro in Mississippi*, 150; Thomas W. Stringer testimony, "Condition of Affairs in Mississippi: Evidence Taken by the Committee on Reconstruction," 40th Cong., 3d sess., House mis. doc. 53, 26–29, 140–43; Thomas Holt, *Black over White: Negro Political Leadership in South Carolina during Reconstruction* (Urbana: University of Illinois Press, 1977), 152–70; Edmund L. Drago, *Black Politicians and Reconstruction in Georgia: A Splendid Failure* (Baton Rouge: Louisiana State University Press, 1982), 161–63.

26. Vicksburg *Daily Herald*, May 28, 1867.

27. Vicksburg *Daily Herald*, June 4, 1867.

28. Harris, *Day of the Carpetbagger*, 103–4.

29. Currie, *Enclave*, 197; Harris, *Day of the Carpetbagger*, 108.

30. Harris, *Day of the Carpetbagger*, 27–28; Currie, *Enclave*, 169–70; Orville Hickman Browning, *The Diary of Orville Hickman Browning*, ed. Theodore Calvin Pease (Springfield: Illinois State Historical Society, 1933), vol. 2, 170–71.

31. *Journal of the Constitutional Convention of 1868*, 436. But in Peru the government did provide lawyers for slaves, the Defenson de Menores. Carlos Aquirre, "Working the System: Black Slaves and the Courts in Lima, Peru, 1821–1854," presented at "The History of Black People in Diaspora," a conference at East Lansing, Mich., April 1995.

32. *Journal of the Constitutional Convention of 1868*, 7, 9, 46, 133, 134, 178, 199, 264.

33. Harris, *Day of the Carpetbagger*, 116–48; Nell Irvin Painter, *Exodusters: Black Migration to Kansas after Reconstruction* (New York: Knopf, 1977), 199n51; *Journal of the Constitutional Convention of 1868*, 519.

34. Harris, *Day of the Carpetbagger*, 160–263; *An Act Authorizing the Submission of the Constitutions of Virginia, Mississippi, and Texas to a Vote of the People*, Statutes at Large, 16, ch. 17, 40.

35. "Union League Ritual" and the "Loyal League Catechism," both in Walter L. Fleming, *Documentary History of Reconstruction: Political, Military, Social, Religious, and Industrial, 1865 to the Present Time* (Cleveland: Arthur Clark, 1907), vol. 2, 7–19; Peter Crosby, "Proclamation to the Citizens of Warren County" (1874), *Vicksburgh Troubles*, 10; unsigned resolution (G. W. Walton?), NTC.

36. *The Revised Code of the Statute Laws of the State of Mississippi* (1871), 612–14.

37. The following are all in the NTC: Seaborn Jones, Report of Fines Collected, March 30, 1872; G. M. Smith, Report of Fines Collected, April 6, 1872; E. Hunt, Report of Fines Collected, April 8, 1872; Sydney Brooks, Report of Fines Collected, April 13, 1872; George W. Stith, Report of Fines Collected, April 13, 1872; Sydney Brooks, Report of Fines Collected, May 27, 1872; Sydney Brooks, Report of Fines Collected, Dec. 16, 1872; B. T. Montgomery, Report of Fines Collected, Dec. 30, 1872; J. Adler, Report of Fines Collected, Jan. 1, 1873; E. Hunt, Report of Fines Collected, Jan. 1, 1873; Seaborn Jones, Report of Fines Collected, Jan. 6, 1873; David Hebron, Report of Fines Collected, Jan. 6, 1873; Pleasant Crosby, Report of Fines Collected, May 31, 1873; William Foreman, Report of Fines Collected, July 17, 1873; J. Adler, Report of Fines Collected, Aug. 9, 1873; H. K. Thomas, Report of Fines Collected, Sept. 17, 1873; E. Hunt, Report of Fines Collected, Sept. 22, 1873; Cooley Mann, Report of Fines Collected, Sept. 23, 1873; L. M. Lowenberg, Report of Fines Collected, March 20, 1874; Cooley Mann, Report of Fines Collected, March 28, 1874; and B. T. Montgomery, Report of Fines Collected, Nov. 22, 1875.

38. For the accessibility of smaller courts to women, see Cornelia Hughes Dayton, *Women before the Bar: Gender, Law, and Society in Connecticut, 1639–1789* (Chapel Hill: University of North Carolina Press, 1995), 8–14.

39. *The Revised Code of the Statute Laws of the State of Mississippi* (1857), ch. 61, art. 126, sec. 11, 497; Taylor, *Brokered Justice*, ch. 1.

40. *Journal of the Proceedings in the Constitutional Convention of the State of Mississippi (1868)* (Jackson: E. Stafford, 1871), 229–31; *The Revised Code of the Statute Laws of the State of Mississippi as Adopted at January Session, A.D. 1871, and Published by Authority of the Legislature* (Jackson: Alcorn and Fisher, 1871), ch. 8, art. 9, sec. 724–25, 150.

41. *James W. Head v. the State*, 44 Miss. 749 (quotation). In 1879, under the influence of conservatives, Mississippi's highest court explained that the householder language, in fact, meant that not all electors had been called to service. To qualify as a grand juror, a Mississippian must be "the head, master, or person who has the charge of and provides for a family"; this excluded persons who were "subordinate members or inmates of the household." *Presley W. Nelson v. the State*, 57 Miss. 286. Republicans emphasized how inclusive the constitutional language was; the Redeemers pointed out that it allowed some limitations.

42. A. H. Arthur testimony, *Vicksburgh Troubles*, 327.

43. Warren County Circuit Court, County Court, and Criminal Court indictments.

44. Luke Lea testimony, *Report of the Joint Committee Appointed to Investigate the Late Insurrection in the City of Vicksburg, Warren County* (Jackson, 1875), 28

45. *Vicksburgh Troubles*, 30.

46. Manuscript population schedule, Ninth U.S. Census, 1870, Warren County, Mississippi, microfilm, NA. Literacy data comes from all precincts and wards with the exception of Bovina and Davis Bend, which were not coded. All other data comes from the entire county.

47. Manuscript population schedules, Ninth U.S. Census, 1870, Warren County, Mississippi, microfilm, NA.

48. But in Greene County, Georgia, they did even worse; not one black man served on a jury in that black-majority county. See Bryant, *How Curious a Land,* 126.

49. Articles of Agreement between Martin Keary and the Warren County Board of Supervisors, July 22, 1871, NTC; Cotton, *The Old Court House,* 27–34.

50. *Vicksburgh Troubles,* 494, 511–12; William Harris describes Brown as a moderate, see *Day of the Carpetbagger,* 121, 209.

51. Vicksburg *Sentinel,* March 5, 1845, Sept. 20, 1849; Sydney Nathans, *Daniel Webster and Jacksonian Democracy* (Baltimore: Johns Hopkins University Press, 1973), 141–44; Charles Devens to Luke Lea, June 11, 1878, Instructions to U.S. Attorneys and Marshals, 1867–1904, book H at 141, Letters Sent by the Department of Justice, microfilm, M-701, roll 8, NA. Incredibly, even after receiving a letter firing him, Lea kept his job.

52. Vicksburg *Times,* Aug. 16, 1871.

53. Calculated from Warren County Circuit court papers in OCHM and Circuit Clerk's Office, Vicksburg.

54. Nieman, *To Set the Law in Motion,* 44.

55. The most important work in trial records has been carried out by students working in periods before the publication of appeals court opinions. These scholars warn about the "dark figure." See J. M. Beattie, "Towards a Study of Crime in Eighteenth-Century England: A Note on Indictments," in *The Triumph of Culture: Eighteenth-Century Perspectives,* ed. Paul Fritz and David Williams (Toronto: A. M. Hakkert, 1972), 299–314; V. A. C. Gatrell and T. B. Hadden, "Criminal Statistics and Their Interpretation," in *Nineteenth-Century Society: Essays in the Use of Quantitative Methods for the Study of Social Data,* ed. E. A. Wrigley (New York: Cambridge University Press, 1972), 350–51; John I. Kitsuse and Aaron V. Cicourel, "A Note on the Uses of Official Statistics," *Social Problems* 2 (1963): 137; Michael S. Hindus and Douglas L. Jones, "Quantitative Methods or Quantum Meruit: Tactics for Early American Legal History," *Historical Methods* 13 (Winter 1980): 63–74; Michael S. Hindus and Douglas L. Jones, "Quantitative and Theoretical Approaches to the History of Crime and Law" in *The Newberry Papers in Family and Community History* (1977): 26; Peter C. Hoffer, "Counting Crime in Premodern England and America: A Review Essay," *Historical Methods* 14 (Fall 1981): 187–93; and Eric Monkkonen, "Systematic Criminal Justice History: Some Suggestions," *Journal of Interdisciplinary History* 9 (Winter 1979): 456.

56. This seems to have been the case in Texas. See Donald Nieman, "Black Political Power and Criminal Justice: Washington County, Texas, 1868–1884," *Journal of Southern History* 55 (Aug. 1989): 391.

57. For postbellum white violence, see George C. Rable, *But There Was No Peace: The Role of Violence in the Politics of Reconstruction* (Athens: University of Georgia Press, 1984); and George C. Wright, *Racial Violence in Kentucky, 1865–1940: Lynchings, Mob Rule, and "Legal Lynchings"* (Baton Rouge: Louisiana State University Press, 1990).

58. *State v. William Johnson,* Nov. 1872, case 337, Warren County Circuit Court Papers, OCHM.

59. Richard Mercer Dorson, *American Negro Folktales* (Greenwich: Fawcett, 1967), 193–95; Owens, *This Species of Property,* 42–43.

60. *State v. William Johnson,* Nov. 1872, case 337, Warren County Circuit Court Papers, OCHM.

61. Judge's Instructions, *State v. William Johnson.*

62. John D. Moore to J. F. Conygham, Sept. 21, 1867, Narrative Reports from Subordinate Officers.

63. J. R. Webster to M. Barber, Nov. 19, 1867, and George S. Smith to Barber Merritt, Nov. 9, 1867, both in Narrative Reports from Subordinate Officers.

64. Allen Huggins to S. C. Greene, July 31, 1868, Narrative Reports from Subordinate Officers.

65. "Report of Operations in the Sub-District of Woodville, Mississippi from the First of August to the 31st of August 1868, Inclusive," Narrative Reports from Subordinate Officers.

66. W. H. Bartholomew to S. C. Greene, Aug. 8, 1868, Narrative Reports from Subordinate Officers.

67. Edwards, "'The Marriage Covenant,'" 81–124; Herbert G. Gutman, *The Black Family in Slavery and Freedom, 1750–1925* (New York: Vintage, 1976); Ira Berlin, Steven F. Miller, and Leslie S. Rowland, "Afro-American Families in the Transition from Slavery to Freedom," *Radical History Review* 42 (Fall 1988): 89–121.

68. Bardaglio, *Reconstructing the Household,* 48–64; William H. Ross to H. W. Smith, Sept. 4, 1867, Narrative Reports from Subordinate Officers.

69. J. R. Webster to M. Barber, Nov. 19, 1867, Narrative Reports from Subordinate Officers.

70. Bardaglio, *Reconstructing the Household,* 132; Laura Edwards, "Sexual Violence, Gender, Reconstruction, and the Extension of Patriarchy in Granville County, North Carolina," *North Carolina Historical Review* 68 (July 1991): 237–60.

71. John Ells, habeas corpus petition, Oct. 11, 1870, Warren County Circuit Court Papers, NTC.

72. Jury instructions, not dated, *State v. Anna Williams,* OCHM. On this issue, see Edwards, "'The Marriage Covenant,'" 81–124.

73. Testimony in *State v. W. D. Chase,* May 1866 term, Warren County Circuit Court Papers, OCHM.

74. John W. Tukey, *Exploratory Data Analysis* (Reading, Mass.: Addison-Wesley, 1977), ch. 7.

75. Calculated from manuscript population schedule, Ninth U.S. Census, 1870, Warren County, Mississippi, microfilm, NA. White wealth totaled $7,817,997 and black wealth totaled $778,473. There were 897 blacks with real or personal property and 1,107 whites. The median for blacks was $200; the white median was $2,500.

76. Calculated from manuscript population schedule, Ninth U.S. Census, 1870, Warren County, Mississippi, microfilm, NA.

77. Frederick Douglass, *My Bondage and My Freedom* (1855, repr. New York: Dover, 1969), 189–91; see also Patricia J. Williams, *The Alchemy of Race and Rights* (Cambridge: Harvard University Press, 1991), 146–65.

78. J. M. Gibson, *Memoirs of J. M. Gibson: Terrors of the Civil War and Reconstruction Days,* ed. James Gibson Alverson and James Gibson Alverson, Jr. (n.p.: privately printed, 1966), 70–75.

79. G. F. Brown testimony, *Vicksburgh Troubles.*

80. Luke Lea testimony, *Report of the Joint Special Committee Appointed to Investigate the Late Insurrection in the City of Vicksburg, Warren County* (Jackson, 1875), 29.

81. During the slavery era, juries found 63 percent of white defendants guilty and 67 percent of slaves.

Chapter 7: A White Republic

1. C. Vann Woodward, *Origins of the New South, 1877–1913* (Baton Rouge: Louisiana State University Press, 1951), 75–106; Bond, *Political Culture in the Nineteenth-Century South*, 183–295; Albert D. Kirwan, *Revolt of the Rednecks: Mississippi Politics, 1876–1925* (1951, repr. New York: Harper, 1965); Bardaglio, *Reconstructing the Household*, 214–28; Arnold Paul, *Conservative Crisis and the Rule of Law: Attitudes of Bar and Bench, 1887–1895* (Ithaca: Cornell University Press, 1960).

2. Fitzgerald, *Union League Movement*, 97; Harris, *Day of the Carpetbagger*, 37.

3. Vicksburg *Times*, Aug. 13, 16, 1871.

4. Ibid. (quotation from Aug. 16, 1871).

5. Vicksburg *Times*, Sept. 12, 1871.

6. Vicksburg *Times and Republican*, Sept. 16, 17, 1871.

7. Vicksburg *Times and Republican*, Sept. 24, 27, Nov. 10, 1871.

8. See chapter 2, p. 32; New Orleans *Picayune*, Jan. 30, 1885.

9. 1873 Mississippi Acts 66; Harris, *Day of the Carpetbagger*, 446.

10. Vicksburg *Times and Republican*, March 3, 1873.

11. Vicksburg *Daily Herald*, May 1, 1873.

12. Vicksburg *Daily Herald*, May 3, 1873.

13. Ibid.

14. Meridian *Mercury*, quoted in Vicksburg *Daily Herald*, May 8, 1873.

15. Vicksburg *Daily Herald*, May 13, 1873.

16. Vicksburg *Daily Herald*, May 3, 1873.

17. Hermann, *Pursuit of a Dream*, 187; Warren County deed book MM, 250–52, Chancery Clerk's Office, Vicksburg.

18. Vicksburg *Daily Herald*, Aug. 13, 1873.

19. Vicksburg *Daily Herald*, Aug. 16, 1873.

20. Vicksburg *Daily Herald*, April 14, 1875.

21. Vicksburg *Daily Herald*, Aug. 16, 1873.

22. Vicksburg *Daily Herald*, Nov. 6, 1873.

23. G. Morris Smith petition to Board of Supervisors, Board of Supervisors Papers, NTC.

24. J. T. Rankin testimony, *Mississippi in 1875*, Report of the Select Committee to Inquire into the Mississippi Election of 1875, 44th Cong., 1st sess., senate report 527, pt. 2, 1417.

25. Alexander H. Arthur testimony, *Vicksburgh Troubles*, 249–51.

26. Frederic Speed testimony, *Vicksburgh Troubles*, 215–16. For Speed's background, see Jerry O. Potter, *The* Sultana *Tragedy: America's Greatest Maritime Disaster* (Gretna: Pelican, 1992), 30–33.

27. John E. Hogan testimony, Moses Kellaby testimony, and Warren Cowan testimony, *Vicksburgh Troubles*, 153, 197, 342.

28. Euline W. Brock, "Thomas W. Cardozo: Fallible Black Reconstruction Leader," *Journal of Southern History* 47 (May 1981): 183–206.

29. Brock, "Thomas W. Cardozo," 183–206; Alexander H. Arthur testimony, *Vicksburgh Troubles*, 256–57.

30. Alexander H. Arthur testimony, *Vicksburgh Troubles*, 259.

31. Ibid., 265–67.

32. Although they claimed Crosby was as guilty of corruption as Cardozo or Davenport, his critics could never make a specific charge of corruption stick against the sheriff. Hard evidence of venality never surfaced. Luke Lea testimony, *Report of the Joint Special Committee Appointed to Investigate the Late Insurrection in the City of Vicksburg, Warren County* (Jackson, 1875), 16.

33. Luke Lea testimony, *Vicksburgh Troubles*, 308.

34. Vicksburg *Plain-Dealer*, quoted in the *Vicksburger*, Nov. 15, 1874.

35. "Minority Report," *Vicksburgh Troubles*, 461.

36. L. W. McGruder testimony, *Vicksburgh Troubles*, 462.

37. Ibid., 462–63.

38. Vicksburg *Herald*, July 1 (quotation), 9, 14, Oct. 15, 1874.

39. Adelbert Ames to Blanche Ames, July 31 (quotation), Aug. 2, 1874, in *Chronicles from the Nineteenth Century: Family Letters of Blanche Butler and Adelbert Ames*, ed. Blanche Butler Ames, 2 vols. (Clinton, Mass.: privately printed, 1957), vol. 1, 692–95.

40. Andrew Black, claim 10362, box 207, SCC; John Cole, claim 116558, box 208, SCC; Albert Johnson, claim 43532, box 210, SCC; Vicksburg *Herald*, July 12, 1874.

41. Vicksburg *Herald*, July 28, 1874.

42. Vicksburg *Herald*, July 4, 1874.

43. Vicksburg *Herald*, July 14, 17, 1874.

44. Foner, *Freedom's Lawmakers*, 42; Brock, "Thomas W. Cardozo," 199; Vicksburg *Herald*, July 31, 1984.

45. L. W. McGruder testimony and George R. Walton testimony, *Vicksburgh Troubles*, 463, 361–63; Vicksburg *Herald*, July 31, 1874.

46. Vicksburg *Herald*, July 18, 19, Sept. 23, 1874, March 23, 27, April 17, 1875; Luke Lea testimony, *Report of the Joint Special Committee Appointed to Investigate the Late Insurrection in the City of Vicksburg, Warren County* (Jackson, 1875), 28–29.

47. The following grand jury indictments (all from November 1874) are in the Warren County Circuit Court Papers, OCHM: *State v. Thomas W. Cardozo* (case 528), *State v. Thomas W. Cardozo* (case 529), *State v. Thomas W. Cardozo* (case 531), *State v. Thomas W. Cardozo* (case 532), *State v. Thomas W. Cardozo* (case 533), *State v. Alfred W. Dorsey* (case 543), *State v. Alfred W. Dorsey* (case 544), *State v. Alfred W. Dorsey* (case 545), *State v. Alfred W. Dorsey and E. E. Perkins* (case 550), *State v. George W. Davenport* (case 526), *State v. George W. Davenport* (case 527), and *State v. George W. Davenport* (case 534). See also Luke Lea testimony, *Report of the Joint Special Committee Appointed to Investigate the Late Insurrection in the City of Vicksburg, Warren County* (Jackson, 1875), 17.

48. *Daily Vicksburger,* Oct. 17, 1874; Alexander H. Arthur testimony, *Vicksburgh Troubles,* 273; *Daily Vicksburger,* Nov. 3, 1874; Luke Lea testimony, *Vicksburgh Troubles,* 306.

49. James Madison Batchelor to Albert A. Batchelor, Sept. 6, 1874, box 5, folder 36, Albert A. Batchelor Papers, Special Collections, Hill Memorial Library, Louisiana State University, Baton Rouge.

50. James Madison Batchelor to Albert A. Batchelor, Sept. 6, 1874.

51. Ibid.

52. *Daily Vicksburger,* Dec. 3, 1874.

53. *Daily Vicksburger,* Nov. 28, 1874.

54. *Daily Vicksburger,* Dec. 3, 1874.

55. *Daily Vicksburger,* Dec. 3, 1874.

56. Vicksburg *Daily Herald,* July 22, 1875.

57. Peter Crosby testimony, *Vicksburgh Troubles,* 400–401; *Daily Vicksburger,* Dec. 3, 1874.

58. *Daily Vicksburger,* Dec. 4, 1874.

59. W. W. Dedrick testimony, "Proceedings of Special [Mississippi House] Committee Appointed to Investigate Conduct of Gov. Ames, 1876," vol. 51, record group 47, Mississippi Department of Archives and History, Jackson (hereafter cited as Ames Investigation).

60. G. E. Harris testimony, Ames Investigation.

61. A. W. Allyn testimony, Ames Investigation.

62. Peter Crosby testimony, *Vicksburgh Troubles,* 402; the proclamation appears on 10.

63. A. G. Packer testimony, Ames Investigation; Peter Crosby testimony, *Vicksburgh Troubles,* 404–5.

64. A. G. Packer testimony, Ames Investigation.

65. Andrew Owen testimony, *Vicksburgh Troubles,* 108–26; For excellent accounts of the riot, see Rable, *But There Was No Peace,* ch. 9; Harris, *Day of the Carpetbagger,* 645–49.

66. R. O'Leary testimony, John D. Beaird testimony, H. H. Miller testimony, and James M. Hunt testimony, *Vicksburgh Troubles,* 8, 126–28, 16, 93.

67. Charles Furlong testimony, *Vicksburgh Troubles,* 99–100. It had happened elsewhere. In Philadelphia during the 1830s, impoverished Irish had learned they could define themselves as white by rioting against abolitionists. Thereafter, the Irish rose to responsible positions in municipal government. The "Irish cop" emerged as a symbol of Irish ascension to the rights of white men. Amy J. Kinsel, "American Identity, National Reconciliation, and the Memory of the Civil War," paper presented at the Organization of American Historians, March 29, 1996, Chicago; Ignatiev, *How the Irish Became White,* 124–76. For race as socially constructed, see Barbara J. Fields, "Ideology and Race in American History," in *Region, Race, and Reconstruction,* ed. J. Morgan Kousser and James M. McPherson (New York: Oxford University Press, 1982), 143–77; Theodore W. Allen, *The Invention of the White Race,* vol. 1: *Racial Oppression and Social Control* (New York: Verso, 1994); Alexander Saxon, *The Rise and Fall of the White Republic: Class, Politics and Mass Culture in Nineteenth-Century America* (New

York: Verso, 1990); and David Roediger, *The Wages of Whiteness: Race and the Making of the American Working Class* (New York: Verso, 1991).

68. H. H. Miller testimony, Andrew Owen testimony, J. Q. Arnold testimony, and R. O'Leary testimony, *Vicksburgh Troubles*, 16–17, 108–10, 460, 4–5; Rable, *But There Was No Peace*, 148–49.

69. *Daily Vicksburger*, Dec. 11, 1874.

70. James Madison Batchelor to Albert A. Batchelor, Jan. 4, 1875, box 5, folder 39, Albert A. Batchelor Papers, Special Collections, Hill Memorial Library, Louisiana State University, Baton Rouge.

71. In addition to the other testimony cited, see Harriet Gray testimony and Thomas Brogden testimony, *Vicksburgh Troubles*, 488, 398.

72. William Wood testimony, *Vicksburgh Troubles*, 175.

73. John McPherson testimony, *Vicksburgh Troubles*, 275.

74. Lucinda Mitchell testimony, *Vicksburgh Troubles*, 317.

75. Lusinda Henry testimony, *Vicksburgh Troubles*, 351.

76. Charles H. Smith testimony, *Vicksburgh Troubles*, 180.

77. A. G. Packer testimony, Ames Investigation.

78. Vicksburg *Herald*, Jan. 19, 1875; A. J. Flanagan testimony, Ames Investigation.

79. James Madison Batchelor to Albert A. Batchelor, Jan. 4, 1875, box 5, folder 39, Albert A. Batchelor Papers, Special Collections, Hill Memorial Library, Louisiana State University, Baton Rouge.

80. Vicksburg *Herald*, Jan. 26, 1875.

81. Vicksburg *Herald*, Feb. 9, 1875.

82. Vicksburg *Herald*, Feb. 17, 1875.

83. Vicksburg *Herald*, March 23, 27, April 27, 1875.

84. Vicksburg *Herald*, April 28, 1875.

85. Vicksburg *Plain-Dealer*, June 11, 1875.

86. Vicksburg *Herald*, June 27, 1875.

87. G. K. Chase to Charles Devens, April 29, 1877, Letters Received by the Department of Justice from Mississippi, Source Chronological File, southern Mississippi, microfilm publication M-970, NA.

88. Peter Crosby to Adelbert Ames, Oct. 28, 1875, Governors' Papers, box 99, record group 27, MDAH; Vicksburg *Herald*, July 13, 14, 1875.

89. *J. F. Baum v. G. W. Walton*, Warren County Circuit Court Papers (civil), attic, Warren County Court House, Vicksburg; Vicksburg *Herald*, April 18, 1875. For Baum's political inclinations, see Joseph Butler to Baum, July 15, 1871, Jacob F. Baum Papers, NTC. For Baum's commercial activities, see his papers generally and *In and About Vicksburg: An Illustrated Guide Book to the City of Vicksburg, Miss., Its History; Its Appearance; Its Business Houses* (Vicksburg: Gibralter Publishing, 1890), 181–82.

90. G. M. Barber testimony, *Mississippi in 1875*, 1340.

91. W. F. Fitzgerald testimony, *Mississippi in 1875*, 1292.

92. W. W. Edwards testimony, J. C. Embry testimony, M. G. Bennett testimony, George W. Stith testimony, and J. T. Tankin testimony, *Mississippi in 1875*, 1351–53, 1304–7, 1386–87, 1394–97, 1407–12.

93. D. J. Foreman testimony, *Mississippi in 1875*, 1379.

94. W. F. Fitzgerald testimony, *Mississippi in 1875*, 1286–87.

95. John D. Beaird testimony and Harris Wilkerson testimony, *Mississippi in 1875*, 1405, 1277–85.

96. S. H. Scott testimony, D. J. Foreman testimony, and E. D. Richardson testimony, *Mississippi in 1875*, 1322–23, 1380, 1422.

97. D. J. Foreman testimony, *Mississippi in 1875*, 1381.

98. J. T. Rankin testimony, W. W. Edwards testimony, A. C. Knadler testimony, E. D. Richardson testimony, S. H. Scott testimony, W. F. Fitzgerald testimony, and Cornelius Axelson textimony, *Mississippi in 1875*, 1414–15, 1358, 1372–73, 1427, 1325, 1332–34, 1289, 1348–49.

99. R. V. Booth, "Glimpsing Backward," June 16, 1913, Private Memoranda, vol. 8, 91, MDAH.

100. R. V. Booth, "Historic Vicksburg," Aug. 18, 1906, Private Memoranda, vol. 5, 165–84, MDAH.

Conclusion

1. New Orleans *Daily Picayune,* Feb. 14, 1885.

2. Seventy-six years later, Delta journalist Hodding Carter praised the "unity that fuses families and clans and, spreading out, brings together whole peoples" as a central feature of the South. Hodding Carter, *Southern Legacy* (Baton Rouge: Louisiana State University Press, 1950), 1–15.

3. Bryant, *How Curious a Land*, 166–82; David M. Oshinsky, *Worse Than Slavery: Parchman Farm and the Ordeal of Jim Crow Justice* (New York: Free Press, 1996), 202; William Cohen, "Negro Involuntary Servitude in the South, 1865–1940: A Preliminary Analysis," *Journal of Southern History* 42 (Feb. 1976): 33–34; Pete Daniel, *The Shadow of Slavery: Peonage in the South, 1901–1969* (Urbana: University of Illinois Press, 1972), 22; Daniel A. Novak, *The Wheel of Servitude: Black Forced Labor after Slavery* (Lexington: University Press of Kentucky, 1978), 1–43.

4. David L. Cohn, *The Mississippi Delta and the World: The Memoirs of David L. Cohn,* ed. James C. Cobb (Baton Rouge: Louisiana State University Press, 1995), 6, 67–68; William Alexander Percy, *Lanterns on the Levee: Recollections of a Planter's Son* (Baton Rouge: Louisiana State University Press, 1974), 286, 307.

5. Terence Finnegan has compiled a data base of Mississippi lynchings and kindly provided me with a list of such incidents for Warren County. See Finnegan, "'At the Hands of Parties Unknown.'"

6. Roswell Valentine Booth journal, April 30, May 19, 1876, microfilm, MDAH.

Bibliography

Primary Sources

Atlanta University
    Association of Southern Women for the Prevention of Lynching Papers (microfilm)
Library of Congress
    Papers of the NAACP (microfilm)
Louisiana State University
    Albert A. Batchelor Papers
    Rowland Chambers Diary
    James Burns Wallace Diary
Southern Historical Collection, University of North Carolina, Chapel Hill
    Samuel A. Agnew Papers. Diary, 1865–66
    David Alexander Barnes Papers
    J. F. H. Claiborne Papers
    Thomas D. S. McDowell Papers
    Jason Niles Papers
    Josiah A. Patterson Collection
    James P. Roach Diary
    David Schenck Papers
    James F. Trotter Papers
Missouri Historical Society
    Emilie Riley McKinley Diary
Mississippi Department of Archives and History
    Administration of Governor Benjamin G. Humphreys
        Claiborne Collection

    Crutcher-Shannon Papers
    High Court of Errors and Appeals. Record Book, 1848–53
    High Court of Errors and Appeals. Index to Decided Cases, 1834–52
    High Court of Errors and Appeals. Docket Book B, 1834–46
    High Court of Errors and Appeals. Docket Book D, 1842–44
    High Court of Errors and Appeals. Record Book, 1853–54
    High Court of Errors and Appeals. General Docket D, 1852–57
    High Court of Errors and Appeals. Docket Book E, 1858–60
    High Court of Errors and Appeals. Minute Book J, 1858–60
    High Court of Errors and Appeals. Index of Decided Cases, Book 1, 1834–54
    Mississippi Legislative Papers. Bills and Petitions, 1840–49
    Mississippi Legislative Papers. Bills Relating to Slavery
    Sharkey Papers
    Henry Frederick Shugart Account Book/Diary (microfilm), 1835–36, 1839–40, 1866
    Timberlake Papers
University of Texas at Austin
    G. Gordon Adams Papers
    Archer Family Papers
    Jacob Baum Papers
    Chamerlain-Hyland-Gould Family Papers
    Crutcher-Shannon Papers
    John Dutton Papers
    Kiger Family Papers
    Natchez Trace Collection legal records
    Winchester Papers
Duke University
    Duncan McLaurin Papers
    Diary of Isaac Shoemaker
    Diary of B. L. C. Wailes
Illinois State Historical Society
    Francis R. Baker Papers
    Ira A. Batterton Papers
    Thomas B. Beggs Papers
    James P. Boyd Diary
    Martin Van Buren Coder Papers
    John P. Davis Diary
    Lucy Ann Eberhard Papers
    John B. Fletcher Diary
    Andrew Flick Diary
    John G. Given Papers
    Samuel Gordon Papers
    John A. Griffin Papers
    William J. Kennedy Papers
    George Read Lee Diary

Thaddeus B. Packard Papers
Joseph B. Williamson Diary
Joseph M. Willson Papers
Ohio Historical Society
Hugh Boyle Ewing Papers
DeWitt Clinton Loudon Papers
McCausland Family Papers
Robert K. Scott Papers
Thomas T. Taylor Papers
Old Court House Museum, Vicksburg
Mrs. J. R. Cook's Journal. Bovina, Mississippi (typescript)
Executions from Warren County Criminal Court, Aug. 1860–Jan. 1868
Flower Hill Church Book
Minutes of the Board of Police, 1838–45
Minutes of the Superior Court of Warren County. Book B, Sept. 1818–March 1821
C. E. Mount, Justice of the Peace, District 1. Docket Book, 1876–77
Smedes and Marshall Legal Cases Register
State Docket. May 1856–Feb. 1870
Warren County Account Book, November 1837–39. "List of Warrants Issued by
the Board of Police, October 1865–August 1870"
Warren County Circuit Court. Docket, 1839
Warren County Grand Jury Docket Book, 1882–87
National Archives
Department of the Treasury
Settled Case Files for Claims Approved by the Southern Claims Commission,
1871–80, Records of the Lands, Files, and Miscellaneous Division, Records
of the Accounting Officers of the Department of the Treasury. RG 217
U.S. Army
Department of Mississippi. U.S. Army Continental Commands. RG 393
Letters Sent by Provost Marshal General, June 1863–Feb. 1864. Division of Mis-
sissippi. Old Book 36A E-2516, RG 393
Records of the Judge Advocate General (Army). Court martial files, RG 153
Registers of Letters Received, Office of Civil Affairs. Vols. 28–33, RG 393, entry 384
Wilkinson, W. S. M. *Trial of E. M. Yerger, before a Military Commission for the Killing
of Bv't-Col. Joseph G. Crane, at Jackson, Miss., June 8th, 1869.* Jackson: Clarion,
1869.
U.S. Department of Justice
Letters Received by the Department of Justice from Mississippi
Letters Sent by the Department of Justice: Instructions to U.S. Attorneys and
Marshals, 1867–1904. National Archives Microfilm, M701, roll 7, vol. G, Aug.
25, 1876–March 28, 1878
Letters Sent by the Department of Justice: Instructions to U.S. Attorneys and
Marshals, 1867–1904. National Archives Microfilm, M701, roll 8, vol. H, March
28, 1878–Feb. 27, 1879
Letters Sent by the Department of Justice: Instructions to U.S. Attorneys and

Marshals, 1867–1904. National Archives Microfilm, M701, roll 9, vol. I, Feb. 28, 1879–March 11, 1880

Source Chronological file southern Mississippi, Nov. 1877–Aug. 1881 and Misc. correspondence, 1877–82. National Archives Microfilm, M970, rolls 3, 4

Mississippi Official Records

Alden, T. J. Fox, and J. A. Van Huesen. *A Digest of the Laws of Mississippi, Comprising All the Laws of a General Nature, Including the Acts of the Session of 1839.* New York: Alexander S. Gould, 1839.

Bridewell, Lemuel Owens. *The Mississippi Justice of the Peace.* Jackson: Clarion, 1877.

Digest of the Statutes of the Mississippi Territory. N.p.: Toulmin, 1807.

George, James Z. *A Digest of the Reports of the Decisions of the Supreme Court and of the High Court of Errors and Appeals of the State of Mississippi from the Organization of the State, to the Present Time.* Philadelphia: T. and J. W. Johnson, 1872.

Hutchinson, A., comp. *Code of Mississippi: Being an Analytical Compilation of the Public and General Statutes of the Territory and State with Tabular References to the Local and Private Acts, from 1798 to 1848.* Jackson: A. Hutchinson, 1848.

Journal of the Proceedings in the Constitutional Convention of the State of Mississippi, 1868. Jackson: E. Stafford, 1871.

Journal of the Proceedings and Debates in the Constitutional Convention of the State of Mississippi, August, 1865. Jackson: E. M. Yerger, 1865.

Journal of the Senate of the State of Mississippi, 1866. Jackson: Shannon, 1866.

Laws of the State of Mississippi; Embracing All Acts of a Public Nature from January Session, 1824, to January Session 1838, Inclusive. Jackson: State of Mississippi, 1838.

Mississippi Justice and Constables' Guide. 1839

[Poindexter, George]. *The Revised Code of the Laws of Mississippi in Which Are Comprised All Such Acts of the General Assembly of a Public Nature; as Were in Force at the End of the Year 1823; with a General Index.* Natchez: Baker, 1824.

Report of the Joint Special Committee Appointed to Investigate the Late Insurrection in the City of Vicksburg, Warren County. Jackson: n.p., 1875.

The Revised Code of the Statute Laws of the State of Mississippi. Jackson: E. Barksdale, 1857.

The Revised Code of the Statute Laws of the State of Mississippi, as Adopted at January Session, A.D. 1871, and Published by Authority of the Legislature. Jackson: Alcorn and Fisher, 1871.

Sargent's Code [1799–1800]. Jackson: Historical Records Survey, 1939.

Statutes of the Mississippi Territory. Natchez: Peter Isler, 1816.

The Statutes of the State of Mississippi of a Public and General Nature with the Constitutions of the United States and This State and an Appendix Containing Acts of Congress Affecting Land Titles, Naturalization, &c., and a Manual for Clerks, Sheriffs and Justices of the Peace. New Orleans: E. John, 1840.

Winter, William, ed. "The Journal of the Constitutional Convention of 1817." *Journal of Mississippi History* 29 (Nov. 1967): 443–504.

U.S. Congress

Mississippi in 1875: Report of the Select Committee to Inquire into the Mississippi Election of 1875, with the Testimony and Documentary Evidence. 2 vols. Washington, D.C.: Government Printing Office, 1876 [Boutwell Report].

Sen. Docs. 1st sess., 39th Cong., no. 2, 1–106. [Schurz's report after visiting Vicksburg and other places in Mississippi].

Senate Report 41, U.S. Serial Set 1494 and 1495.

U.S. Congress, House, Committee on Reconstruction. *Evidence Taken Before the Committee on Reconstruction,* House Misc. Doc. 53. 40th Cong., 3d sess.

U.S. Cong., House, Joint Committee on Reconstruction. *Report of the Joint Committee on Reconstruction,* House Report 30, 39th Cong., 1st sess.

U.S. Congress, House, Select Committee to Visit Vicksburgh. *Vicksburgh Troubles,* House Report 265, 43d Cong., 2d sess.

U.S. Congress, Senate, Committee on Military Affairs and the Militia. *Synopsis of Laws Respecting Persons of Color in the Late Slave States,* Senate Ex. Doc. 6, 170–230, 39 Cong., 2d sess.

U.S. Congress, Senate. *Testimony Taken by the Joint Select Committee to Inquire into the Affairs of the Late Insurrectionary States,* 42d Cong., 2d sess. Washington, D.C.: Government Printing Office, 1872 [13-vol. KKK report].

Warren County Circuit Clerk

Warren County Circuit Court Minute Book A, 1823–26

Warren County Circuit Court Minute Book C, 1831–34

Warren County Circuit Court Minute Book D, 1835–37

Warren County Circuit Court Minute Book F, 1837–38

Warren County Record Book 2, 1838–40

Warren County Circuit Court Minute Book I, 1840–41

Warren County Circuit Court Minute Book K, 1841–43

Warren County Circuit Court Minute Book L, 1842–43

Warren County Circuit Court Minute Book M, 1843–44

Warren County Circuit Court Minute Book N, 1845–46

Warren County Circuit Court Minute Book R, 1853–56

Warren County Circuit Court Minute Book S, 1856–58

Warren County Circuit Court Minute Book T, 1858–60

Warren County Circuit Court Minute Book U, 1860–66

Warren County Circuit Court Minute Book V, 1866–68

Warren County Circuit Court Minute Book W, 1868–69

Warren County Circuit Court Minute Book X, 1869–71

Warren County Circuit Court Minute Book Y, 1872

Warren County Circuit Court Minute Book Z, 1873–75

Warren County Circuit Court Minute Book A-A, 1875–77

Warren County Circuit Court Minute Book B-B, 1877

Warren County Circuit Court Minute Book C-C, 1878–81

Warren County Chancery Clerk

Warren County Board of Police Minutes, 1845–53

Warren County Board of Police Minutes, 1858–67

Warren County Board of Police Minutes, 1867–70
Warren County Supervisors Minute Book A, 1870–80

Contemporary Accounts

Ames, Blanche Butler, ed. *Chronicles of the Nineteenth-Century: Family Letters of Blanche Butler and Adelbert Ames.* 2 vols. Clinton, Mass.: privately printed, 1957.

Avey, Michael Garland, ed. *The Civil War Letters of John Avey, 2/4/1822–1/31/1911.* [Fort Steilacoom, Wash.]: Department of Anthropology, Fort Steilacoom Community College, 1986.

Bailey, Thomas J. *Prohibition in Mississippi.* Jackson: Hederman Bros., 1917.

Balfour, Emma. *Diary of Emma Balfour, May 16, 1863–June 2, 1863: The Historic Vicksburg Siege.* Edited by Fred Swaney. N.p.: 1979.

Beck, Stephen C. *A True Sketch of His Army Life.* [Edgard, Neb.]: n.d.

Bentley, W. H. *History of the 77th Illinois Volunteer Infantry, September 2, 1862–July 10, 1865.* Peoria: Edward Hine, 1883.

Browning, Orville Hickman. *The Diary of Orville Hickman Browning.* 2 vols. Edited by Theodore Calvin Pease. Springfield: Illinois State Historical Society, 1933.

Bureau of the Census. *Ninth Census of the United States: Statistics of Population.* Washington, D.C.: Government Printing Office, 1872.

Chambers, William Pitt. *Blood and Sacrifice: The Civil War Journal of a Confederate Soldier.* Edited by Richard A. Baumgartner. Huntington: Blue Acorn, 1994.

Chaplin, Thomas B. *Tombee: Portrait of a Cotton Planter.* Edited by Theodore Rosengarten. New York: Morrow, 1986.

Cirket, Alan F., ed. *Samuel Whitbread's Notebooks, 1810–11, 1813—14.* Bedfordshire: Bedfordshire Historical Record Society, 1971.

Clarke, Norman E., Sr., ed. *Warfare along the Mississippi: The Letters of Lieutenant Colonel George E. Currie.* Mount Pleasant: Clarke Historical Collection, 1961.

The Code of Virginia: with the Declaration of Independence and the Constitution of the United States, and the Declaration of Rights and Constitution of Virginia. Richmond: William F. Ritchie, 1849.

Dana, Charles A. *Recollections of the Civil War.* Edited by Paul M. Angle. 1898. New York: Collier Books, 1963.

Darst, W. Maury. "The Vicksburg Diary of Mrs. Alfred Ingraham." *Journal of Mississippi History* 44 (May 1982): 151–52.

David, Reuben. *Recollections of Mississippi and Mississippians.* Boston: Houghton Mifflin, 1890.

Dennett, John Richard. *The South as It Is, 1865–1866.* 1965. Reprint. Baton Rouge: Louisiana State University Press, 1995.

Douglass, Frederick. *My Bondage and My Freedom.* 1855. Reprint. New York: Dover, 1969.

Eaton, John. *Grant, Lincoln, and the Freedmen: Reminiscences of the Civil War, with Special Reference to the Work for the Contrabands and Freedmen of the Mississippi Valley.* 1907. Reprint. New York: New American Library, 1970.

Elder, Bishop William Henry. *Civil War Diary (1862–1865) of Bishop William Henry Elder Bishop of Natchez.* N.p.: Most Reverend R. O. Gerow, n.d.

Featherstonhaugh, G. W. *Excursion through the Slave States, from Washington on the Potomac to the Frontier of Mexico; with Sketches of Popular Manners and Geological Notices.* 2 vols. London: Murray, 1844.

Fleming, Walter L. *Documentary History of Reconstruction: Political, Military, Social, Religious, Educational, and Industrial, 1865 to the Present Time.* 2 vols. Cleveland: Arthur H. Clark, 1906, 1907.

Foner, Philip S., and George Walker, eds. *Proceedings of the Black National and State Conventions, 1840–1865.* Philadelphia: Temple University Press, 1986.

Foote, Henry S. *Casket of Reminiscences.* 1874. Reprint. New York: Negro Universities Press, 1968.

Gibson, J. M. *Memoirs of J. M. Gibson: Terrors of the Civil War and Reconstruction Days.* Edited by James Gibson Alverson and James Gibson Alverson, Jr. N.p.: 1966.

Grant, Julia Dent. *The Personal Memoirs of Julia Dent Grant.* Edited by John Y. Simon. New York: G. P. Putnam's Sons, 1975.

Grant, Ulysses S. *The Papers of Ulysses S. Grant.* Edited by John Y. Simon. Carbondale: Southern Illinois University Press, 1967– .

Greene, Jack P., ed. *The Diary of Landon Carter of Sabine Hall, 1752–1778.* 2 vols. 1965. Reprint. Richmond: University of Virginia Press, 1987.

Hamilton, Mary. *Trials of the Earth.* Jackson: University Press of Mississippi, 1992.

Harris, Luther William. *Soldiering on Foot and on Horseback during the Civil War: Interesting Experiences during the War of the Rebellion.* Augusta, Ill., n.d.

Heaford, George H. *Chevrons and Shoulder Straps.* Chicago: Poole Brothers, 1895.

Henry, R. H. *Editors I Have Known since the Civil War.* New Orleans: Privately printed, 1922.

Hogan, William Ransom, and Edwin Adams Davis, eds. *William Johnson's Natchez: The Antebellum Diary of a Free Negro.* 1951. 2 vols. Reprint. Port Washington, N.Y.: Kennikat Press, 1968.

Howard, Richard L. *History of the 124th Regiment Illinois Infantry Volunteers, Otherwise Known as the "Hundred and Two Dozen," from August, 1862, to August, 1865.* Springfield, Ill.: H. W. Rokker, 1880.

Hughes, Louis. *Thirty Years a Slave: From Bondage to Freedom, the Institution of Slavery as Seen on the Plantation and in the Home of the Planter.* Milwaukee: South Side, 1897.

In and About Vicksburg: An Illustrated Guide Book to the City of Vicksburg, Miss., Its History; Its Appearance; Its Business Houses. Vicksburg: Gibralter Publishing, 1890.

Jacobs, Harriet [Linda Brent]. *Incidents in the Life of a Slave Girl.* Edited by L. Maria Child. New York: Harcourt Brace Jovanovich, 1973.

Johnson, Charles Beneulyn. *Muskets and Medicine; or, Army Life in the Sixties.* Philadelphia: F. A. Davis, 1917.

Johnson, William. *William Johnson's Natchez: The Antebellum Diary of a Free Negro.* Edited by William Ransom Hogan and Edwin Adams Davis. Baton Rouge: Louisiana State University Press, 1951, 1979.

Kaiser, Leo M., ed. "Beleaguered City: The Vicksburg Campaign as Seen in Published Letters." *Southern Studies* 17 (Spring 1978): 76–77.

Keckley, Elizabeth. *Behind the Scenes of Thirty Years a Slave and Four Years in the White House*. 1868. Reprint. New York: Arno, 1968.

[Kuner, Max]. "Vicksburg, and After: Being the Experience of a Southern Merchant and Non-Combatant during the Sixties." *Sewanee Review* 15 (Oct. 1907): 485–96.

[Loughborough, Mary Webster]. *My Cave Life in Vicksburg*. 1864. Reprint. Vicksburg: Vicksburg and Warren County Historical Society, 1990.

Lynch, John Roy. *Reminiscenses of an Active Life: The Autobiography of John Roy Lynch*. Edited by John Hope Franklin. Chicago: University of Chicago Press, 1970.

Marshall, Albert O. *Army Life; from a Soldier's Journal: Incidents, Sketches and Record of a Union Soldier's Army Life, in Camp and Field, 1861–64*. Joliet: privately printed, 1883.

Martineau, Harriet. *Retrospect of Western Travel*. 2 vols. New York: Harper, 1838.

McIntosh, James T., Haskell M. Monroe, Jr., and Linda Crist, eds. *The Papers of Jefferson Davis*. Baton Rouge: Louisiana State University Press, 1974– .

Montgomery, Frank A. *Reminiscences of a Mississippian in Peace and War*. Cincinnati: Robert Clarke, 1901.

Morgan, A. T. *Yazoo; or, On the Picket Line of Freedom in the South*. 1884. Reprint. New York: Russell and Russell, 1968.

Oldroyd, Osborn. *A Soldier's Story of the Siege of Vicksburg from the Diary of Osborn H. Oldroyd*. Springfield: privately printed, 1885.

Olmstead, Frederick Law. *A Journey in the Back Country, 1853–1854*. 1860. Reprint. New York: Schocken Books, 1970.

Origins and Progress of the Vicksburg Troubles as Reported Daily in the Columns of the Vicksburg Herald. Vicksburg: Vicksburg Herald, 1875.

Powell, J. C. *The American Siberia*. 1891. Reprint. Gainesville: University of Florida Press, 1976.

Proceedings of the Black National and State Conventions. 2 vols. Edited by Phillip S. Foner and George E. Walker. Philadelphia: Temple University Press, 1986.

Proceedings of the 124th Regimental Veteran Association, in Reunion, at Kewanee, Illinois, September 4th, 1889. N.p., n.d.

Racine, Phillip, ed. *Piedmont Farmer: The Journals of David Golightly Harris, 1855–1870*. Knoxville: University of Tennessee Press, 1990.

Rawick, George P. *The American Negro Slave: A Composite Autobiography*. Westport: Greenwood Press, 1977–79.

Rainwater, P. L., ed. "The Autobiography of Benjamin Grubb Humphreys, August 26, 1808–December 20, 1882." *Mississippi Valley Historical Review* 21 (Sept. 1934): 231–55.

Randall, James G. *The Diary of Orville Hickman Browning*. 2 vols. Springfield: Illinois State Historical Library, 1933.

Randolph, Peter. *Sketches of Slave Life; or, Illustrations of the Peculiar Institution*. Boston: privately printed, 1855.

Royall, William L. *A Reply to "A Fool's Errand by One of the Fools."* New York: E. J. Hale and Son, 1881.

Society Re-Union of the Seventy-Second Reg't. Illinois Infantry, Crosby's Music Hall, Tuesday, November 30th, 1869, Chicago. Chicago: Spalding and La Montes, n.d.

Stockton, Joseph. *War Diary (1862–5) of Brevet Brigadier General Joseph Stockton, First*

Lieutenant. Captain, Major and Lieutenant-Colonel 72d Illinois Infantry Volunteers (First Board of Trade Regiment). Chicago: John T. Stockton, 1910.

Stone, Kate. *Brokenburn: The Journal of Kate Stone, 1861–1868.* Edited by John Q. Anderson. Baton Rouge: Louisiana State University Press, 1972.

Street, James H. *Look Away! A Dixie Notebook.* New York: Viking, 1936.

Taylor, Alma, comp. *Major David Gavin's Horseback Ride: St. George, S.C. to Mississippi and Return, 1843.* Meridian, Miss.: Lauderdale County Department of Archives and History, n.d.

Throne, Mildred, ed. "An Iowa Doctor in Blue: The Letters of Seneca B. Thrall, 1862–1864." *Iowa Journal of History* 58 (April 1960): 165–66.

Trowbridge, J. T. *The South: A Tour of Its Battle-Fields and Ruined Cities.* 1866. Reprint. New York: Arno, 1969.

Walton, Augustus Q. *A History of the Detection, Conviction, Life and Designs of John A. Murel, the Great Western Land Pirate; Together with His System of Villany and Plan of Exciting a Negro Rebellion and a Catalogue of the Names of Four Hundred and Forty-Five of His Mystic Clan Fellows and Followers, and Their Efforts for the Destruction of Mr. Virgil A. Stewart to Which Is Added a Biographical Sketch of Mr. Virgil A. Stewart.* N.p., 1835.

The War of the Rebellion: A Compilation of the Official Records of the Union and Confederate Armies. Washington, D.C.: Government Printing Office, 1880–1901.

Warren, Henry W. *Reminiscences of a Mississippi Carpetbagger.* Holden, Mass.: Davis Press, 1914.

Welch, Jacob Perry. *Welch Journal: An Autobiography Commenced January 1, 1857.* Edited by Edwin Shields and Ann Flynt. Meridian, Miss.: privately printed, 1996.

Whitbread, Samuel. *Samuel Whitbread's Notebook, 1810–11, 1813–14.* Edited by Alan F. Cirket. Ampthill: Bedfordshire Historical Record Society, 1971.

Wilson, John Lyde. *The Code of Honor; or, Rules for the Government of Principals and Seconds in Duelling.* 1838. Reprint. Charleston: J. Phinney, 1858.

Wood, Wales W. *A History of the Ninety-Fifth Regiment Illinois Infantry Volunteers: From Its Organization in the Fall of 1862, until its Final Discharge from the United States Service, in 1865.* Chicago: Tribune, 1865.

Newspapers

Chicago *Tribune; Daily Vicksburg Whig; Daily Vicksburger; Lancaster* [Pa.] *Daily Evening Examiner;* Mississippi *Daily Pilot;* Mississippi *Weekly Pilot;* New York *Times;* Vicksburg *Daily Evening Citizen;* Vicksburg *Herald;* Vicksburg *Plain-Dealer;* Vicksburg *Sentinel;* Vicksburg *Times;* Vicksburg *Times and Republican;* Vicksburg *Weekly Citizen.*

Secondary Sources

BOOKS

Abramson, Jeffrey. *We, the Jury: The Jury System and the Ideal of Democracy.* New York: Basic Books, 1994.

Adams, Charles Hansford. *"The Guardian of the Law": Authority and Identity in James Fenimore Cooper.* University Park: Pennsylvania State University Press, 1990.

Allen, Theodore W. *The Invention of the White Race,* vol. 1: *Racial Oppression and Social Control.* New York: Verso, 1994.

Alotta, Robert I. *Civil War Justice: Union Army Executions under Lincoln.* Shippensburg, Pa.: White Mane, 1989.

Ames, Blanche. *Adelbert Ames, 1835–1933: General, Senator, Governor.* New York: Argosy-Antiquarian, 1964.

Anderson, Benedict O'Gorman. *Imagined Communities: Reflections on the Origin and Spread of Nationalism.* London: Verso, 1983.

Anderson, Eric, and Alfred A. Moss, Jr. *The Facts of Reconstruction: Essays in Honor of John Hope Franklin.* Baton Rouge: Louisiana State University Press, 1991.

Aptheker, Herbert. *American Negro Slave Revolts.* New York: Columbia University Press, 1943.

Ash, Stephen V. *When the Yankees Came: Conflict and Chaos in the Occupied South, 1861–1865.* Chapel Hill: University of North Carolina Press, 1995.

Ashworth, John. *"Agrarians" and "Aristocrats": Party Political Ideology in the United States, 1837–1846.* New York: Cambridge University Press, 1987.

Auerbach, Jerold S. *Justice without Law? Resolving Disputes without Lawyers.* New York: Oxford University Press, 1983.

Ayers, Edward L. *The Promise of the New South: Life after Reconstruction.* New York: Oxford University Press, 1992.

———. *Vengeance and Justice: Crime and Punishment in the Nineteenth-century American South.* New York: Oxford University Press, 1984.

Bailey, Fred Arthur. *Class and Tennessee's Confederate Generation.* Chapel Hill: University of North Carolina Press, 1987.

Baker, Lewis. *The Percys of Mississippi: Politics and Literature in the New South.* Baton Rouge: Louisiana State University Press, 1983.

Baldwin, Joseph G. *The Flush Times of Alabama and Mississippi: A Series of Sketches.* New York: Sagamore, 1957.

Bardaglio, Peter W. *Reconstructing the Household: Families, Sex, and the Law in the Nineteenth-century South.* Chapel Hill: University of North Carolina Press, 1995.

Barney, William L. *The Secessionist Impulse: Alabama and Mississippi in 1860.* Princeton: Princeton University Press, 1974.

Barton, Michael. *Goodmen: The Character of Civil War Soldiers.* University Park: Pennsylvania University Press, 1981.

Bender, Thomas. *Community and Social Change in America.* New Brunswick: Rutgers University Press, 1978.

Belknap, Michal R. *Federal Law and Southern Order: Racial Violence and Constitutional Conflict in the Post-Brown South.* Athens: University of Georgia Press, 1987.

Benedict, Michael Les. *A Compromise of Principle: Congressional Republicans and Reconstruction, 1863–1869.* New York: Norton, 1974.

Bensel, Richard Franklin. *Yankee Leviathan: The Origins of Central State Authority in America, 1859–1877.* New York: Cambridge University Press, 1990.

Berger, Peter L., and Thomas Luckman. *The Social Construction of Reality: A Treatise in the Sociology of Knowledge.* New York: Doubleday, 1966.

Berlin, Ira, and Philip D. Morgan. *The Slaves' Economy: Independent Production by Slaves in the Americas.* London: Frank Cass, 1991.

Berlin, Ira, Joseph P. Reidy, and Leslie S. Rowland. *The Black Military Experience.* New York: Cambridge University Press, 1982.

Berlin, Ira, Barbara J. Fields, Thavolia Glymph, Joseph P. Reidy, and Leslie S. Rowland, eds. *The Destruction of Slavery.* New York: Cambridge University Press, 1985.

Berlin, Ira, Travolia Glymph, Steven F. Miller, Joseph P. Reidy, Leslie S. Rowland, and Julie Saville, eds. *The Wartime Genesis of Free Labor: The Lower South.* New York: Cambridge University Press, 1990.

Bernard, Jessie Shirley. *The Sociology of Community.* Glenview: Scott, Foresman, 1973.

Bernstein, Iver. *The New York City Draft Riots: Their Significance for American Society and Politics in the Age of the Civil War.* New York: Oxford University Press, 1990.

Berry, Mary Frances. *Military Necessity and Civil Rights Policy: Black Citizenship and the Constitution, 1861–1868.* Port Washington, N.Y.: Kennikat Press, 1977.

Bestor, Arthur. *Backwoods Utopias: The Sectarian Origins and Owenite Phase of Communitarian Socialism in America, 1663–1829.* 1950. Revised. Philadephia: University of Pennsylvania Press, 1970.

Biographical and Historical Memoirs of Mississippi Embracing an Authentic and Comprehensive Account of the Chief Events in the History of the State, and a Record of the Lives of Many of the Most Worthy and Illustrious Families and Individuals. 2 vols. Chicago: Goodspeed Publishing, 1891.

Black, Henry Campbell. *Black's Law Dictionary.* Abridged 5th ed. St. Paul: West, 1983.

Blassingame, John W. *The Slave Community: Plantation Life in the Antebellum South.* New York: Oxford University Press, 1972.

Bloomfield, Maxwell. *American Lawyers in a Changing Society, 1776–1876.* Cambridge: Harvard University Press, 1976.

Bodenhamer, David J. *Fair Trial: Rights of the Accused in American History.* New York: Oxford University Press, 1992.

———. *The Pursuit of Justice: Crime and Law in Antebellum Indiana.* New York: Garland, 1986.

Boles, John B., and Evelyn Thomas Nolen. *Interpreting Southern History: Historiographical Essays in Honor of Sanford W. Higginbotham.* Baton Rouge: Louisiana State University Press, 1987.

Bolls, James, comp. *A Complete Roster of the Soldiers and Sailors of Warren County during the Civil War.* N.p.: n.d.

Bond, Bradley G. *Political Culture in the Nineteenth-century South: Mississippi, 1830–1900.* Baton Rouge: Louisiana State University Press, 1995.

Botkin, B. A. *A Treasury of Mississippi River Folklore: Stories, Ballads, Traditions, and Folkways of the Mid-American River Country.* New York: Crown, 1955.

Bowen, David Warren. *Andrew Johnson and the Negro.* Knoxville: University of Tennessee Press, 1989.

Braithwaite, John. *Crime, Shame, and Reintegration.* New York: Cambridge University Press, 1989.

Brewer, John, and John Styles, eds. *An Ungovernable People: The English and their Law in the Seventeenth and Eighteenth Centuries.* New Brunswick: Rutgers University Press, 1980.

Brock, William R. *Parties and Political Conscience: American Dilemmas, 1840–1850.* Millwood, N.Y.: KTO Press, 1979.

Brooke, John L. *The Heart of the Commonwealth: Society and Political Culture in Worcester County, Massachusetts, 1713–1861.* Amherst: University of Massachusetts Press, 1989.

Brown, Richard Maxwell. *No Duty to Retreat: Violence and Values in American History and Society.* New York: Oxford University Press, 1991.

———. *South Carolina Regulators.* Cambridge: Harvard University Press, 1963.

———. *Strain of Violence: Historical Studies of American Violence and Vigilantism.* New York: Oxford University Press, 1975.

Bruce, Dickson D., Jr. *Violence and Culture in the Antebellum South.* Austin: University of Texas Press, 1979.

Brundage, W. Fitzhugh. *Lynching in the New South: Georgia and Virginia, 1880–1930.* Urbana: University of Illinois Press, 1993.

Bumiller, Kristin. *The Civil Rights Society: The Social Construction of Victims.* Baltimore: Johns Hopkins University Press, 1988.

Burton, Orville Vernon. *In My Father's House Are Many Mansions: Family and Community in Edgefield, South Carolina.* Chapel Hill: University of North Carolina Press, 1985.

Burton, Orville Vernon, and Robert C. McMath, Jr., eds. *Toward a New South? Studies in Post–Civil War Southern Communities.* Westport: Greenwood Press, 1982.

Butterfield, Fox. *All God's Children: The Bosket Family and the American Tradition of Violence.* New York: Knopf, 1995.

Bynum, Victoria E. *Unruly Women: The Politics of Social and Sexual Control in the Old South.* Chapel Hill: University of North Carolina Press, 1992.

Bryant, Jonathan M. *How Curious a Land: Conflict and Change in Greene County, Georgia, 1850–1885.* Chapel Hill: University of North Carolina Press, 1996.

Calhoun, Daniel H. *Professional Lives in America: Structure and Aspiration, 1750–1850.* Cambridge: Harvard University Press, 1965.

Carpenter, John A. *Sword and Olive Branch.* Pittsburgh: University of Pittsburgh Press, 1964.

Carter, Dan T. *When the War Was Over: The Failure of Self-Reconstruction in the South, 1865–1867.* Baton Rouge: Louisiana State University Press, 1985.

Carter, Hodding. *Southern Legacy.* Baton Rouge: Louisiana State University Press, 1950.

Cashin, Joan E. *A Family Venture: Men and Women on the Southern Frontier.* New York: Oxford University Press, 1991.

Catterall, Helen Tunnicliff. *Judicial Cases Concerning American Slavery and the Negro.* 5 vols. 1937. Reprint. New York: Octagon, 1968.

Chadbourn, James Harmon. *Lynching and the Law.* Chapel Hill: University of North Carolina Press, 1933.

Clark, Thomas D., and John D. Guice. *Frontiers in Conflict: The Old Southwest, 1795–1830.* Albuquerque: University of New Mexico Press, 1989.

Clinton, Catherine, and Nina Silber, eds. *Divided Houses: Gender and the Civil War.* New York: Oxford University Press, 1992.

Clinton, Catherine, ed. *Half Sisters of History: Southern Women and the American Past.* Durham: Duke University Press, 1994.

———. *Tara Revisited: Women, War, and the Plantation Legend.* New York: Abbeville Press, 1995.

Cobb, James C. *The Most Southern Place on Earth: The Mississippi Delta and the Roots of Regional Identity.* New York: Oxford University Press, 1992.

Cobb, Thomas R. R. *An Inquiry into the Law of Negro Slavery in the United States of America.* 1858. Reprint. New York: Negro Universities Press, 1968.

Cockburn, J. S., and Thomas A. Green. *Twelve Good Men and True: The Criminal Trial Jury in England, 1200–1800.* Princeton: Princeton University Press, 1988.

Code Duello: Letters Concerning the Prentiss-Tucker Duel of 1842. Dallas: Book Club of Texas, 1931.

Cohen, William. *At Freedom's Edge: Black Mobility and the Southern White Quest for Racial Control, 1861–1915.* Baton Rouge: Louisiana State University Press, 1991.

Cohn, David L. *The Mississippi Delta and the World: The Memoirs of David L. Cohn.* Edited by James C. Cobb. Baton Rouge: Louisiana State University Press, 1995.

———. *Where I Was Born and Raised.* Boston: Houghton Mifflin, 1948.

Cornelius, Janet Duitsman. *"When I Can Read My Title Clear": Literacy, Slavery, and Religion in the Antebellum South.* Columbia: University of South Carolina Press, 1991.

Cotton, Gordon A. *Asbury: A History.* Vicksburg: privately printed, 1994.

———. *Horrible Outrage: The Murder of Minerva Cook.* Vicksburg: privately printed, 1993.

———. *The Old Court House.* Raymond, Miss.: Keith Printing, 1982.

Cotton, Gordon A., and Ralph C. Mason. *With Malice Toward Some: The Military Occupation of Vicksburg, 1864–1865.* Vicksburg: Vicksburg and Warren County Historical Society, 1991.

Cronin, William. *Nature's Metropolis: Chicago and the Great West.* New York: Norton, 1991.

Currie, James T. *Enclave: Vicksburg and Her Plantations.* Jackson: University Press of Mississippi, 1980.

Cutler, James Elbert. *Lynch-Law: An Investigation into the History of Lynching in the United States.* 1905. Reprint. New York: Negro Universities Press, 1969.

Daniel, Pete. *The Shadow of Slavery: Peonage in the South, 1901–1969.* Urbana: University of Illinois Press, 1972.

Darden, Christopher, and Jess Walter. *In Contempt.* New York: HarperCollins, 1996.

Davis, Ronald L. F. *Good and Faithful Labor: From Slavery to Sharecropping in the Natchez District, 1860–1890.* Westport: Greenwood Press, 1982.

Davis, S. F. *Mississippi Negro Lore.* Indianola, Miss.: privately printed, 1914.

Dayton, Cornelia Hughes. *Women before the Bar: Gender, Law, and Society in Connecticut, 1639–1789.* Chapel Hill: University of North Carolina Press, 1995.

Denham, James M. *"A Rogue's Paradise": Crime and Punishment in Antebellum Florida, 1821–1861.* Tuscaloosa: University of Alabama Press, 1997.

Dickey, Dallas C. *Seargent S. Prentiss: Whig Orator of the Old South.* Baton Rouge: Louisiana State University Press, 1945.

Dobash, R. Emerson, and Russell P. Dobash. *Women, Violence, and Social Change.* New York: Routledge, 1992.

Dorson, Richard Mercer. *American Negro Folktales.* Greenwich: Fawcett, 1967.

Drago, Edmund L. *Black Politicians and Reconstruction in Georgia: A Splendid Failure.* Baton Rouge: Louisiana State University Press, 1982.

Du Bois, W. E. B. *Black Reconstruction in America, 1860–1880.* 1935. Reprint. New York: Atheneum, 1969.

Dunning, William A. *Reconstruction, Political and Economic, 1865–1877.* New York: Harper and Brothers, 1907.

Erikson, Kai T. *Wayward Puritans: A Study in the Sociology of Deviance.* New York: Wiley and Son, 1966.

Escott, Paul D. *Many Excellent People: Power and Privilege in North Carolina, 1850–1900.* Chapel Hill: University of North Carolina Press, 1985.

Evans, W. McKee. *Ballots and Fence Rails: Reconstruction on the Lower Cape Fear.* New York: Norton, 1967.

Everett, Frank, Jr. *Vicksburg Lawyers prior to the Civil War.* Vicksburg: privately printed, n.d.

Fabian, Ann Vincent. *Card Sharps, Dream Books, and Bucket Shops: Gambling in Nineteenth-century America.* Ithaca: Cornell University Press, 1990.

Farrell, Harry. *Swift Justice: Murder and Vengeance in a California Town.* New York: St. Martin's Press, 1992.

Faulkner, William. *The Hamlet.* New York: Random House, 1931.

Faust, Drew Gilpin. *Mothers of Invention: Women of the Slaveholding South.* Chapel Hill: University of North Carolina Press, 1996.

Fehrenbacher, Don E. *The Dred Scott Case: Its Significance in American Law and Politics.* New York: Oxford University Press, 1978.

Felson, Marcus. *Crime and Everyday Life.* Thousand Oaks, Calif.: Pine Forge Press, 1994.

Ferguson, Robert A. *Law and Letters in American Culture.* Cambridge: Harvard University Press, 1984.

Finkelman, Paul. *The Law of Freedom and Bondage: A Casebook.* New York: Oceana, 1986.

Fischer, David Hackett. *Albion's Seed: Four British Folkways in America.* New York: Oxford University Press, 1989.

———. *Paul Revere's Ride.* New York: Oxford University Press, 1994.

Fitzgerald, Michael W. *The Union League Movement in the Deep South: Politics and Agricultural Change during Reconstruction.* Baton Rouge: Louisiana State University Press, 1989.

Flynn, Charles L., Jr. *White Land, Black Labor: Caste and Class in Late Nineteenth-century Georgia.* Baton Rouge: Louisiana State University Press, 1983.

Foner, Eric. *Freedom's Lawmakers: A Directory of Black Officeholders during Reconstruction.* New York: Oxford University Press, 1993.

———. *Free Soil, Free Labor, Free Men: The Ideology of the Republican Party before the Civil War.* New York: Oxford University Press, 1970.

———. *Reconstruction: America's Unfinished Revolution, 1863–1877.* New York: Harper and Row, 1988.

Forbath, William E. *Law and the Shaping of the American Labor Movement.* New York: Cambridge University Press, 1991.

Ford, Lacy K., Jr. *Origins of Southern Radicalism: The South Carolina Upcountry, 1800–1860.* New York: Oxford University Press, 1988.

Forsyth, William. *History of Trial by Jury.* 1875. Reprint. New York: Burt Franklin, 1971.

Foster, Gaines M. *Ghosts of the Confederacy: Defeat, the Lost Cause, and the Emergence of the New South.* New York: Oxford University Press, 1987.

Fox-Genovese, Elizabeth. *Within the Plantation Household: Black and White Women of the Old South.* Chapel Hill: University of North Carolina Press, 1988.

Fox-Genovese, Elizabeth, and Eugene D. Genovese. *Fruits of Merchant Capital: Slavery and Bourgeois Property in the Rise and Expansion of Capitalism.* New York: Oxford University Press, 1983.

Frank, Joseph Allan, and George A. Reaves. *"Seeing the Elephant": Raw Recruits at the Battle of Shiloh.* Westport: Greenwood Press, 1989.

Franklin, John Hope. *Reconstruction: After the Civil War.* Chicago: University of Chicago Press, 1961.

Fraser, Walter J., Jr., R. Frank Saunders, Jr., and Jon L. Wakelyn, eds., *The Web of Southern Social Relations: Women, Family, and Education.* Athens: University of Georgia Press, 1985.

Friedman, Lawrence M. *Crime and Punishment in American History.* New York: Basic Books, 1993.

———. *A History of American Law.* 2d ed. New York: Simon and Schuster, 1985.

———. *A Republic of Choice: Law, Authority, and Culture.* Cambridge: Harvard University Press, 1990.

———. *Total Justice.* New York: Russell Sage, 1985.

Friedman, Lawrence M., and Robert V. Percival. *The Roots of Justice: Crime and Punishment in Alameda County, California, 1870–1910.* Chapel Hill: University of North Carolina Press, 1981.

Fritz, Paul et al., eds. *The Triumph of Culture: Eighteenth-Century Perspectives.* Toronto: A. M. Hakkert, 1972.

Garner, James W. *Reconstruction in Mississippi.* 1901. Reprint. Baton Rouge: Louisiana State University Press, 1968.

Genovese, Eugene D. *The Political Economy of Slavery: Studies in the Economy and Society of the Slave South.* New York: Random House, 1965.

———. *Roll, Jordan, Roll: The World the Slaves Made.* New York: Random House, 1974.

Gerber, David A. *The Making of American Populism: Buffalo, New York, 1825–1860.* Urbana: University of Illinois Press, 1989.

Gilje, Paul A. *The Road to Mobocracy: Popular Disorder in New York City, 1763–1834.* Chapel Hill: University of North Carolina Press, 1987.

Gillette, William. *Retreat from Reconstruction, 1869–1879.* Baton Rouge: Louisiana State University Press, 1979.

Ginzberg, Lori D. *Women and the Work of Benevolence: Morality, Politics, and Class in the Nineteenth-century United States.* New Haven: Yale University Press, 1990.

Glenn, Myra C. *Campaigns against Corporal Punishment: Prisoners, Sailors, Women, and Children in Antebellum America.* Albany: State University of New York Press, 1984.

Green, Thomas Andrew. *Verdict According to Conscience: Perspectives on the English Criminal Trial Jury, 1200–1800.* Chicago: University of Chicago Press, 1985.

Greenberg, Kenneth S. *Honor and Slavery: Lies, Duels, Noses, Dressing as a Woman, Gifts, Strangers, Humanitarianism, Death, Slave Rebellions, the Proslavery Argument, Baseball, Hunting, and Gambling in the Old South.* Princeton: Princeton University Press, 1996.

Grillis, Pamela Lea. *Vicksburg and Warren County: A History of People and Place.* Vicksburg: Dancing Rabbit, 1992.

Grimsley, Mark. *The Hard Hand of War: Union Military Policy toward Southern Civilians, 1861–1865.* New York: Cambridge University Press, 1995.

Grossberg, Michael. *Governing the Hearth: Law and the Family in Nineteenth-Century America.* Chapel Hill: University of North Carolina Press, 1985.

Guinther, John. *The Jury in America.* New York: Facts on File, 1988.

Gutman, Herbert. *The Black Family in Slavery and Freedom, 1750–1925.* New York: Vintage, 1976.

Hahn, Steven. *The Roots of Southern Populism: Yeoman Farmers and the Transformation of the Georgia Upcountry, 1850–1890.* New York: Oxford University Press, 1983.

Haines, Charles Grove. *The American Doctrine of Judicial Supremacy.* New York: Russell and Russell, 1959.

Hall, Jacquelyn Dowd. *Revolt against Chivalry: Jessie Daniel Ames and the Women's Campaign against Lynching.* 1979. Reprint. New York: Columbia University Press, 1993.

Hall, Kermit. *The Magic Mirror: Law in American History.* New York: Oxford University Press, 1989.

Hamm, Richard F. *Shaping the Eighteenth Amendment: Temperance Reform, Legal Culture, and the Polity, 1880–1920.* Chapel Hill: University of North Carolina Press, 1995.

Harding, Vincent. *There Is a River: The Black Struggle for Freedom in America.* New York: Harcourt Brace Jovanovich, 1981.

Harrington, Christine B. *Shadow Justice: The Ideology and Institutionalization of Alternatives to Court.* Westport: Greenwood Press, 1985.

Harris, Trudier. *Exorcising Blackness: Historical and Literary Lynching and Burning Rituals.* Bloomington: Indiana University Press, 1984.

Harris, William C. *The Day of the Carpetbagger: Republican Reconstruction in Mississippi.* Baton Rouge: Louisiana State University Press, 1979.

———. *Presidential Reconstruction in Mississippi.* Baton Rouge: Louisiana State University Press, 1967.

Harrison, Robert W. *Levee District and Levee Building in Mississippi: A Study of State and Local Efforts to Control Mississippi River Floods.* Stoneville: Mississippi Agricultural Experiment Station, 1951.

Hartog, Hendrik. *Public Property and Private Power: The Corporation of the City of New York in American Law, 1730–1870.* Ithaca: Cornell University Press, 1983.

Hay, Douglas et al., eds. *Albion's Fatal Tree: Crime and Society in Eighteenth-century England.* London: A. Lane, 1975.

Henderson, Dan Fenno. *Conciliation and Japanese Law: Tokugawa and Modern.* Seattle: University of Washington Press, n.d.

Henry, H. M. *The Police Control of the Slave in South Carolina.* 1914. Reprint. New York: Negro Universities Press, 1968.

Hermann, Janet Sharp. *Joseph E. Davis: Pioneer Patriarch.* Jackson: University Press of Mississippi, 1990.

———. *The Pursuit of a Dream.* New York: Oxford University Press, 1981.

Hindus, Michael Stephen. *Prison and Plantation: Crime, Justice, and Authority in Massachusetts and South Carolina, 1767–1878.* Chapel Hill: University of North Carolina Press, 1980.

Hine, Darlene Clark. *The State of Afro-American History: Past, Present, and Future.* Baton Rouge: Louisiana State University Press, 1986.

Hittell, John S. *A History of the City of San Francisco, and Incidentally of the State of California.* San Francisco: Bancroft, 1878.

Holt, Thomas. *Black over White: Negro Political Leadership in South Carolina during Reconstruction.* Urbana: University of Illinois Press, 1977.

Horwitz, Morton J. *The Transformation of American Law, 1780–1860.* Cambridge: Harvard University Press, 1977.

———. *The Transformation of American Law, 1870–1960: The Crisis of Legal Orthodoxy.* New York: Oxford University Press, 1992.

Howard, Gene L. *Death at Cross Plains: An Alabama Reconstruction Tragedy.* University: University of Alabama Press, 1984.

Howe, Daniel Walker. *The Political Culture of the American Whigs.* Chicago: University of Chicago Press, 1979.

Hurd, John Codman. *The Law of Freedom and Bondage in the United States.* 2 vols. Boston: Little, Brown, 1858.

Hurst, James Willard. *The Growth of American Law: The Lawmakers.* Boston: Little, Brown, 1950.

———. *Law and the Conditions of Freedom in the Nineteenth-century United States.* 1956. Reprint. Madison: University of Wisconsin Press, 1967.

Hyman, Harold, and Leonard W. Levy, eds. *Freedom and Reform: Essays in Honor of Henry Steele Commager.* New York: Harper and Row, 1967.

Hyman, Harold. *A More Perfect Union: The Impact of the Civil War and Reconstruction on the Constitution.* New York: Knopf, 1973.

Ignatiev, Noel. *How the Irish Became White.* New York: Routledge, 1995.

Johnson, Charles S. *Shadow of the Plantation.* 1934. Reprint. Chicago: University of Chicago Press, 1966.

Johnson, Michael P. *Toward a Patriarchal Republic: The Secession of Georgia.* Baton Rouge: Louisiana State University Press, 1977.

Jones, Alan R. *The Constitutional Conservatism of Thomas McIntyre Cooley: A Study in the History of Ideas.* New York: Garland, 1987.

Jones, Norrece T., Jr. *Born a Child of Freedom, Yet a Slave: Mechanisms of Control and Strategies of Resistance in Antebellum South Carolina.* Hanover: Wesleyan University Press, 1990.

Jordan, Winthrop D. *Tumult and Silence at Second Creek: An Inquiry into a Civil War Slave Conspiracy.* Baton Rouge: Louisiana State University Press, 1993.

———. *White over Black: American Attitudes toward the Negro, 1550–1812.* Chapel Hill: University of North Carolina Press, 1968.

Joyner, Charles. *Down by the Riverside: A South Carolina Slave Community.* Urbana: University of Illinois Press, 1984.

Kaczorowski, Robert J. *The Politics of Judicial Interpretation: The Federal Courts, Department of Justice and Civil Rights, 1866–1876.* New York: Oceana, 1985.

Karamanski, Theodore J. *Rally 'Round the Flag: Chicago and the Civil War.* Chicago: Nelson-Hall Publishers, 1993.

Kerber, Linda. *Women of the Republic: Intellect and Ideology in Revolutionary America.* Chapel Hill: University of North Carolina Press, 1980.

Kettner, James H. *The Development of American Citizenship, 1608–1870.* Chapel Hill: University of North Carolina Press, 1978.

Keyssar, Alexander. *Out of Work: The First Century of Unemployment in Massachusetts.* New York: Cambridge University Press, 1986.

Kirwan, Albert D. *Revolt of the Rednecks: Mississippi Politics, 1876–1925.* 1951. Reprint. New York: Harper, 1965.

Klein, Rachel N. *Unification of a Slave State: The Rise of the Planter Class in the South Carolina Backcountry, 1760–1808.* Chapel Hill: University of North Carolina Press, 1990.

Kolchin, Peter. *American Slavery, 1619–1877.* Cambridge: Harvard University Press, 1993.

———. *First Freedom: The Responses of Alabama's Blacks to Emancipation and Reconstruction.* Westport: Greenwood Press, 1972.

———. *Unfree Labor: American Slavery and Russian Serfdom.* Cambridge: Harvard University Press, 1987.

Konig, David Thomas, ed. *Devising Liberty: Preserving and Creating Freedom in the New American Republic.* Stanford: Stanford University Press, 1995.

Kousser, J. Morgan, and James M. McPherson, eds. *Region, Race, and Reconstruction: Essays in Honor of C. Vann Woodward.* New York: Oxford University Press, 1982.

Kruman, Marc W. *Parties and Politics in North Carolina, 1836–1865.* Baton Rouge: Louisiana State University Press, 1983.

Kulikoff, Allan. *The Agrarian Origins of American Capitalism.* Charlottesville: University Press of Virginia, 1992.

Lang, Meredith. *Defender of the Faith: The High Court of Mississippi, 1817–1875.* Jackson: University Press of Mississippi, 1977.

Lazarus-Black, Mindie, and Susan F. Hirsch, eds. *Contested States: Law, Hegemony and Resistance.* New York: Routledge, 1994.

Lebsock, Suzanne. *The Free Women of Petersburg: Status and Culture in a Southern Town, 1784–1860.* New York: Norton, 1984.

Lichtenstein, Alex. *Twice the Work of Free Labor: The Political Economy of Convict Labor in the New South.* New York: Verso, 1996.

Linderman, Gerald F. *Embattled Courage: The Experience of Combat in the American Civil War.* New York: Free Press, 1987.

Litwack, Leon. *Been in the Storm so Long: The Aftermath of Slavery.* New York: Vintage, 1979.

Litwack, Leon, and August Meier, eds. *Black Leaders of the Nineteenth Century.* Urbana: University of Illinois Press, 1988.

Lofgren, Charles A. *The* Plessy *Case: A Legal-Historical Interpretation.* New York: Oxford University Press, 1987.

Lynch, James D. *The Bench and Bar of Mississippi.* New York: E. J. Hale and Son, 1881.

———. *Kemper County Vindicated, and a Peep at Radical Rule in Mississippi.* 1879. Reprint. New York: Negro Universities Press, 1969.

Maine, Henry Sumner. *Ancient Law: Its Connection with the Early History of Society and Its Relation to Modern Ideas.* 1861. Reprint. New York: Henry Holt, 1864.

Malone, Ann Patton. *Sweet Chariot: Slave Family and Household Structure in Nineteenth-century Louisiana.* Chapel Hill: University of North Carolina Press, 1992.

Masur, Louis P. *Rites of Execution: Capital Punishment and the Transformation of American Culture, 1776–1865.* New York: Oxford University Press, 1989.

McCaslin, Richard B. *Tainted Breeze: The Great Hanging at Gainesville, Texas, 1862.* Baton Rouge: Louisiana State University Press, 1994.

McCurry, Stephanie. *Masters of Small Worlds: Yeoman Households, Gender Relations, and the Political Culture of the Antebellum South Carolina Low Country.* New York: Oxford University Press, 1995.

McDonald, Roderick A. *The Economy and Material Culture of Slaves: Goods and Chattels on the Sugar Plantations of Jamaica and Louisiana.* Baton Rouge: Louisiana State University Press, 1993.

McLaurin, Melton A. *Celia: A Slave.* Athens: University of Georgia Press, 1991.

McMillen, Neil R. *Dark Journey: Black Mississippians in the Age of Jim Crow.* Urbana: University of Illinois Press, 1989.

McMurry, Linda O. *Recorder of the Black Experience: A Biography of Monroe Nathan Work.* Baton Rouge: Louisiana State University Press, 1985.

McPherson, James M. *Battle Cry of Freedom: The Civil War Era.* New York: Oxford University Press, 1988.

———. *For Cause and Comrades: Why Men Fought in the Civil War.* New York: Oxford University Press, 1997.

———. *The Struggle for Equality: Abolitionists and the Negro in the Civil War and Reconstruction.* Princeton: Princeton University Press, 1964.

———. *What They Fought For, 1861–1865.* Baton Rouge: Louisiana State University Press, 1994.

McWhiney, Grady. *Cracker Culture: Celtic Ways in the Old South.* Tuscaloosa: University of Alabama Press, 1988.

Miers, Earl Schenck. *The Web of Victory: Grant at Vicksburg.* 1955. Reprint. Baton Rouge: Louisiana State University Press, 1983.

Miles, Edwin Arthur. *Jacksonian Democracy in Mississippi.* Chapel Hill: University of North Carolina Press, 1960.

Miller, Perry. *The Life of the Mind in America: From the Revolution to the Civil War.* New York: Harcourt, Brace and World, 1965.

Miller, Wilbur R. *Cops and Bobbies: Police Authority in New York and London, 1830–1870.* Chicago: University of Chicago Press, 1977.

Monkkonen, Eric H. *America Becomes Urban: The Development of U.S. Cities and Towns, 1780–1980.* Berkeley: University of California Press, 1988.

Moore, John Hebron. *Agriculture in Ante-Bellum Mississippi.* New York: Bookman, 1958.

―――. *The Emergence of the Cotton Kingdom in the Old Southwest: Mississippi, 1770–1860.* Baton Rouge: Louisiana State University Press, 1988.

Morris, Christopher. *Becoming Southern: The Evolution of a Way of Life, Warren County and Vicksburg, Mississippi, 1770–1860.* New York: Oxford University Press, 1995.

Morris, Thomas D. *Southern Slavery and the Law, 1619–1860.* Chapel Hill: University of North Carolina Press, 1996.

Mott, Rodney L. *Due Process of Law: A Historical and Analytical Treatise of the Principles and Methods Followed by the Courts in the Application of the Concept of the "Law of the Land."* Indianapolis: Bobbs-Merrill, 1926.

Nathans, Sydney. *Daniel Webster and Jacksonian Democracy.* Baltimore: Johns Hopkins University Press, 1973.

Neely, Mark E., Jr. *Confederate Bastille: Jefferson Davis and Civil Liberties.* Milwaukee: Marquette University Press, 1993.

―――. *The Fate of Liberty: Abraham Lincoln and Civil Liberties.* New York: Oxford University Press, 1991.

―――. *The Last Best Hope of Earth: Abraham Lincoln and the Promise of America.* Cambridge: Harvard University Press, 1993.

Nieman, Donald G. *To Set the Law in Motion: The Freedmen's Bureau and the Legal Rights of Blacks, 1865–1868.* Millwood, N.Y.: KTO Press, 1979.

Novak, William J. *The People's Welfare: Law and Regulation in Nineteenth-century America.* Chapel Hill: University of North Carolina Press, 1996.

Oakes, James. *The Ruling Race: A History of American Slaveholders.* New York: Knopf, 1982.

―――. *Slavery and Freedom: An Interpretation of the Old South.* New York: Knopf, 1990.

Oshinsky, David M. *Worse than Slavery: Parchman Farm and the Ordeal of Jim Crow Justice.* New York: Free Press, 1996.

Owens, Leslie Howard. *This Species of Property: Slave Life and Culture in the Old South.* New York: Oxford University Press, 1976.

Ownby, Ted. *Subduing Satan: Religion, Recreation, and Manhood in the Rural South, 1865–1920.* Chapel Hill: University of North Carolina Press, 1990.

Owsley, Frank. *Plain Folk of the Old South.* Baton Rouge: Louisiana State University Press, 1949.

Painter, Nell Irvin. *Exodusters: Black Migration to Kansas after Reconstruction.* New York: Knopf, 1977.

Paludan, Phillip S. *A Covenant with Death: The Constitution, Law, and Equality in the Civil War Era.* Urbana: University of Illinois Press, 1975.

―――. *"A People's Contest": The Union and the Civil War, 1861–1865.* New York: Harper and Row, 1988.

Paul, Arnold. *Conservative Crisis and the Rule of Law: Attitudes of Bar and Bench, 1887–1895.* Ithaca: Cornell University Press, 1960.

Patterson, Orlando. *Slavery and Social Death: A Comparative Study.* Cambridge: Harvard University Press, 1982.

Pereyra, Lillian A. *James Lusk Alcorn: Persistent Whig.* Baton Rouge: Louisiana State University Press, 1966.

Percy, William Alexander. *Lanterns on the Levee: Reflections of a Planter's Son*. New York: Knopf, 1953.

Perman, Michael. *Reunion without Compromise: The South and Reconstruction, 1865–1868*. New York: Cambridge University Press, 1973.

———. *The Road to Redemption: Southern Politics, 1869–1879*. Chapel Hill: University of North Carolina Press, 1984.

Perrin, James Morris, comp. *Reverend Newit Vick: Founder of Vicksburg, Mississippi. His Ancestry, Relatives, and Descendants*. Hammond, La.: J. M. Perrin, 1990.

Philippsbourn, Gertrude. *The History of the Jewish Community of Vicksburg from 1820 to 1968*. Vicksburg: privately printed, 1969.

Phillips, Ulrich B. *American Negro Slavery: A Survey of the Supply, Employment, and Control of Negro Labor as Determined by the Plantation Regime*. New York: D. Appleton, 1918.

———. *Life and Labor in the Old South*. 1929. Reprint. Boston: Little, Brown, 1963.

Pole, J. R. *The Pursuit of Equality in American History*. Berkeley: University of California Press, 1978.

Posner, Richard A. *The Problems of Jurisprudence*. Cambridge: Harvard University Press, 1990.

Potter, Jerry O. *The* Sultana *Tragedy: America's Greatest Maritime Disaster*. Gretna: Pelican, 1992.

Pound, Roscoe. *The Spirit of the Common Law*. Boston: Marshall Jones, 1921.

Rabinowitz, Howard N. *Race Relations in the Urban South, 1865–1890*. New York: Oxford University Press, 1978.

———, ed. *Southern Black Leaders of the Reconstruction Era*. Urbana: University of Illinois Press, 1982.

Rable, George C. *But There Was No Peace: The Role of Violence in the Politics of Reconstruction*. Athens: University of Georgia Press, 1984.

———. *Civil Wars: Women and the Crisis of Southern Nationalism*. Urbana: University of Illinois Press, 1989.

———. *The Confederate Republic: A Revolution against Politics*. Chapel Hill: University of North Carolina Press, 1994.

Rainwater, Percy Lee. *Mississippi: Storm Center of Secession, 1856–1861*. Baton Rouge: O. Claitor, 1938.

Reed, Alfred Zantzinger. *Training for the Public Profession of the Law: Historical Development and Principal Contemporary Problems of Legal Education in the United States with Some Account of Conditions in England and Canada*. New York: Merrymount, 1921.

Reid, John Phillip. *In a Defiant Stance: The Conditions of Law in Massachusetts Bay, the Irish Comparison, and the Coming of the American Revolution*. University Park: Pennsylvania State University Press, 1977.

———. *Law for the Elephant: Property and Social Behavior on the Overland Trail*. San Marino: Huntington Library, 1980.

Reidy, Joseph P. *From Slavery to Agrarian Capitalism in the Cotton Plantation South, Central Georgia, 1800–1880*. Chapel Hill: University of North Carolina Press, 1992.

Roark, James L. *Masters without Slaves: Southern Planters in the Civil War and Reconstruction*. New York: Norton, 1977.

Roediger, David. *The Wages of Whiteness: Race and the Making of the American Working Class.* New York: Verso, 1991.

Roper, John Herbert. *C. Vann Woodward, Southerner.* Athens: University of Georgia Press, 1987.

Rose, Willie Lee. *Slavery and Freedom.* Edited by William W. Freehling. New York: Oxford University Press, 1982.

Rosenberg, Norman L. *Protecting the Best Men: An Interpretive History of the Law of Libel.* Chapel Hill: University of North Carolina Press, 1986.

Rosengarten, Theodore. *Tombee: Portrait of a Cotton Planter.* New York: William Morrow, 1986.

Rutman, Darrett B., with Anita H. Rutman. *Small Worlds, Large Questions: Explorations in Early American Social History, 1600–1850.* Charlottesville: University Press of Virginia, 1994.

Ryan, Mary P. *Women in Public: Between Banners and Ballots, 1825–1880.* Baltimore: Johns Hopkins University Press, 1990.

Satcher, Buford. *Blacks in Mississippi Politics, 1865–1900.* Washington, D.C.: University Press of America, 1978.

Saville, Julie. *The Work of Reconstruction: From Slave to Wage Laborer in South Carolina, 1860–1870.* New York: Cambridge University Press, 1994.

Saxon, Alexander. *The Rise and Fall of the White Republic: Class Politics and Mass Culture in Nineteenth-century America.* New York: Verso, 1990.

Schwarz, Philip J. *Twice Condemned: Slaves and the Criminal Laws of Virginia, 1705–1865.* Baton Rouge: Louisiana State University Press, 1988.

Schweninger, Loren. *Black Property Holders in the South, 1790–1915.* Urbana: University of Illinois Press, 1990.

Scott, George Ryley. *The History of Corporal Punishment: A Survey of Flagellation in its Historical, Anthropological, and Sociological Aspects.* London: Torchstream, 1950.

Scott, James C. *Weapons of the Weak: Everyday Forms of Peasant Resistance.* New Haven: Yale University Press, 1985.

Sellers, Charles. *The Market Revolution: Jacksonian America, 1815–1846.* New York: Oxford University Press, 1991.

Senechal, Roberta. *The Sociogenesis of a Race Riot: Springfield, Illinois, in 1908.* Urbana: University of Illinois Press, 1990.

Shafer, Judith Kelleher. *Slavery, the Civil Law, and the Supreme Court of Louisiana.* Baton Rouge: Louisiana State University Press, 1994.

Shapiro, Barbara J. *"Beyond Reasonable Doubt" and "Probable Cause": Historical Perspectives on the Anglo-American Law of Evidence.* Berkeley: University of California Press, 1991.

Shapiro, Herbert. *White Violence and Black Response: From Reconstruction to Montgomery.* Amherst: University of Massachusetts Press, 1988.

Shields, Joseph D. *The Life and Times of Seargent Smith Prentiss.* Philadelphia: Lippincott, 1883.

Simpson, Brooks D. *Let Us Have Peace: Ulysses S. Grant and the Politics of War and Reconstruction, 1861–1868.* Chapel Hill: University of North Carolina Press, 1991.

Smith, J. Clay, Jr. *Emancipation: The Making of the Black Lawyer, 1844–1944.* Philadelphia: University of Pennsylvania Press, 1993.

Spain, August O. *The Political Theory of John C. Calhoun*. New York: Bookman, 1951.

Sparks, Randy J. *On Jordan's Stormy Banks: Evangelicalism in Mississippi, 1773–1876*. Athens: University of Georgia Press, 1994.

Stampp, Kenneth M. *The Era of Reconstruction, 1865–1877*. New York: Knopf, 1966.

Starobin, Robert S. *Industrial Slavery in the Old South*. New York: Oxford University Press, 1970.

Starr, June, and Jane F. Collier. *History and Power in the Study of Law: New Directions in Legal Anthropology*. Ithaca: Cornell University Press, 1989.

Steinberg, Allen. *The Transformation of Criminal Justice: Philadelphia, 1800–1880*. Chapel Hill: University of North Carolina Press, 1989.

Stowe, Steven M. *Intimacy and Power in the Old South: Ritual in the Lives of the Planters*. Baltimore: Johns Hopkins University Press, 1987.

Summers, Robert Samuel. *Instrumentalism and American Legal Theory*. Ithaca: Cornell University Press, 1982.

Sydnor, Charles Sackett. *Slavery in Mississippi*. New York: D. Appleton, 1933.

Tadman, Michael. *Speculators and Slaves: Masters, Traders, and Slaves in the Old South*. Madison: University of Wisconsin Press, 1989.

Taylor, Alrutheus Ambus. *The Negro in South Carolina during Reconstruction*. 1924. Reprint. New York: Russell and Russell, 1969.

Taylor, William Banks. *Brokered Justice: Race, Politics, and Mississippi Prisons, 1798–1992*. Columbus: Ohio State University Press, 1993.

Thomas, Keith. *Man and the Natural World: Changing Attitudes in England, 1500–1800*. London: Lane, 1983.

Thornton, J. Mills, III. *Politics and Power in a Slave Society: Alabama, 1800–1860*. Baton Rouge: Louisiana State University Press, 1978.

Tolnay, Stewart E., and E. M. Beck. *A Festival of Violence: An Analysis of Southern Lynchings, 1882–1930*. Urbana: University of Illinois Press, 1995.

Tomlins, Christopher. *Law, Labor, and Ideology in the Early American Republic*. New York: Cambridge University Press, 1993.

Trelease, Allen W. *White Terror: The Ku Klux Klan Conspiracy and Southern Reconstruction*. New York: Harper and Row, 1971.

Tucher, Andie. *Froth and Scum: Truth, Beauty, Goodness, and the Ax Murder in America's First Mass Medium*. Chapel Hill: University of North Carolina Press, 1994.

Tukey, John W. *Exploratory Data Analysis*. Reading: Addison-Wesley, 1977.

Tunnell, Ted. *Crucible of Reconstruction: War, Radicalism, and Race in Louisiana, 1862–1877*. Baton Rouge: Louisiana State University Press, 1984.

Turitz, Leo F., and Evelyn Turitz. *Jews in Early Mississippi*. Jackson: University Press of Mississippi, 1983.

Tushnet, Mark. *The American Law of Slavery, 1810–1860: Considerations of Humanity and Interest*. Princeton: Princeton University Press, 1981.

Vincent, Charles. *Black Legislators in Louisiana during Reconstruction*. Baton Rouge: Lousiana State University Press, 1976.

Wade, Richard C. *Slavery in the Cities: The South, 1820–1860*. New York: Oxford University Press, 1964.

Walker, Peter F. *Vicksburg: A People at War, 1860–1865*. Chapel Hill: University of North Carolina Press, 1960.

Walker, Samuel. *Popular Justice: A History of American Criminal Justice.* New York: Oxford University Press, 1980.

Warren, Robert Penn. *World Enough and Time.* New York: Random House, 1950.

Watson, Harry L. *Jacksonian Politics and Community Conflict: The Emergence of the Second American Party System in Cumberland County, North Carolina.* Baton Rouge: Louisiana State University Press, 1981.

Wayne, Michael. *The Reshaping of Plantation Society: The Natchez District, 1860–1880.* Baton Rouge: Louisiana State University Press, 1983.

Weaver, Herbert. *Mississippi Farmers, 1850–1860.* Nashville: Vanderbilt University Press, 1945.

Weaver, John C. *Constables and Courts: Order and Transgression in a Canadian City, 1816–1970.* Montreal: McGill-Queens University Press, 1995.

Wharton, Vernon Lane. *The Negro In Mississippi, 1865–1890.* Chapel Hill: University of North Carolina Press, 1947.

Wheeler, Jacob D. *A Practical Treatise on the Law of Slavery. Being a Compilation of All the Decisions Made on That Subject, in the Several Courts of the United States and State Courts.* 1837. Reprint. New York: Negro Universities Press, 1968.

White, Walter. *Rope and Faggot: A Biography of Judge Lynch.* 1929. Reprint. New York: Arno Press, 1969.

Whites, Lee Ann. *The Civil War as a Crisis in Gender: Augusta, Georgia, 1860–1890.* Athens: University of Georgia Press, 1995.

Whitfield, Stephen J. *A Death in the Delta: The Story of Emmett Till.* New York: Free Press, 1988.

Wigmore, John Henry. *A Panorama of the World's Legal Systems.* 3 vols. St. Paul: West, 1928.

Williams, Patricia J. *The Alchemy of Race and Rights.* Cambridge: Harvard University Press, 1991.

Williamson, Joel. *After Slavery: The Negro in South Carolina during Reconstruction, 1861–1877.* Chapel Hill: University of North Carolina Press, 1965.

———. *The Crucible of Race: Black-White Relations in the American South since Emancipation.* New York: Oxford University Press, 1984.

Wilson, Theodore Brantner. *The Black Codes of the South.* University: University of Alabama, 1965.

Wiltse, Charles M. *John C. Calhoun: Sectionalist, 1840–1850.* Indianapolis: Bobbs-Merrill, 1951.

Wood, Betty. *Women's Work and Men's Work: The Informal Slave Economies of Low-country Georgia.* Athens: University of Georgia Press, 1995.

Wood, Gordon. *The Radicalism of the American Revolution.* New York: Knopf, 1992.

Woodward, C. Vann. *Origins of the New South, 1877–1913.* Baton Rouge: Louisiana State University Press, 1951.

———. *Thinking Back: The Perils of Writing History.* Baton Rouge: Louisiana State University Press, 1986.

Wrigley, E. A., ed. *Nineteenth-century Society: Essays in the Use of Quantitative Methods for the Study of Social Data.* New York: Cambridge University Press, 1972.

Wright, George C. *Racial Violence in Kentucky, 1865–1940: Lynchings, Mob Rule, and "Legal Lynchings."* Baton Rouge: Louisiana State University Press, 1990.

Wunder, John R. *Inferior Courts, Superior Justice: A History of the Justices of the Peace on the Northwest Frontier.* Westport: Greenwood Press, 1979.

Wyatt-Brown, Bertram. *The House of Percy.* New York: Oxford University Press, 1994.

———. *Southern Honor: Ethics and Behavior in the Old South.* New York: Oxford University Press, 1982.

Younger, Richard D. *The People's Panel: The Grand Jury in the United States, 1634–1941.* Providence: Brown University Press, 1963.

Zainaldin, Jamil. *Law in Antebellum Society: Legal Change and Economic Expansion.* New York: Knopf, 1983.

Zangrando, Robert L. *The NAACP Crusade against Lynching, 1909–1950.* Philadelphia: Temple University Press, 1980.

ARTICLES AND CHAPTERS IN BOOKS

Abbott, Richard H. "The Republican Party Press in Reconstruction Georgia, 1867–1874." *Journal of Southern History* 61 (Nov. 1995): 725–60.

Abney, M. G. "Reconstruction in Pontotoc County." *Publications of the Mississippi Historical Society* 11 (1910): 229–69.

Baker, Paula C. "The Domestication of Politics: Women and American Political Society, 1780–1920." *American Historical Review* 89 (June 1984): 620–47.

Bardaglio, Peter W. "Rape and the Law in the Old South: 'Calculated to Excite Indignation in Every Heart.'" *Journal of Southern History* 60 (Nov. 1994): 749–72.

Bauer, Raymond, and Alice Bauer. "Day to Day Resistance to Slavery." *Journal of Negro History* 27 (Oct. 1942): 388–419.

Beasley, Jonathan. "Blacks—Slave and Free—Vicksburg, 1850–1860." *Journal of Mississippi History* 38 (Feb. 1976): 1–32.

Beattie, J. M. "Towards a Study of Crime in Eighteenth-century England: A Note on Indictments." In *The Triumph of Culture: Eighteenth-century Perspectives,* 299–314. Edited by Paul Fritz and David Williams. Toronto: A. M. Hakkert, 1972.

Bellesiles, Michael A. "The Origins of Gun Culture in the United States, 1760–1865." *Journal of American History* 83 (Sept. 1996): 425–55.

Benedict, Michael Les. "Laissez-Faire and Liberty: A Re-Evaluation of the Meaning and Origins of Laissez-Faire Constitutionalism." *Law and History Review* 3 (Fall 1985): 293–331.

———. "Preserving the Constitution: The Conservative Basis of Radical Reconstruction." *Journal of American History* 61 (June 1974): 65–90.

———. "Victorian Moralism and Civil Liberty in the Nineteenth-Century United States." In *The Constitution, Law, and American Life: Critical Aspects of the Nineteenth-Century Experience,* 91–122. Edited by Donald G. Nieman. Athens: University of Georgia Press, 1992.

Berlin, Ira. "Time, Space, and the Evolution of Afro-American Society in British Mainland North America." *American Historical Review* 85 (Feb. 1980): 15–43.

Berlin, Ira, and Herbert G. Gutman. "Natives and Immigrants, Free Men and Slaves: Urban Workingmen in the Antebellum South." *American Historical Review* 88 (Dec. 1983): 1175–200.

Berlin, Ira, Steven F. Miller, and Leslie S. Rowland. "Afro-American Families in the Transition from Slavery to Freedom." *Radical History Review* 42 (Fall 1988): 89–121.

Bigelow, Martha Mitchell. "Public Opinion and the Passage of the Mississippi Black Codes." *Negro History Bulletin* 33 (Jan. 1970): 11–16.

Billings, Warren M. "The Growth of Political Institutions in Virginia, 1634–1676." *William and Mary Quarterly* 31 (April 1974): 225–42.

Bode, Frederick A. "The Formation of Evangelical Communities in Middle Georgia: Twiggs County, 1820–1861." *Journal of Southern History* 60 (Nov. 1994): 711–48.

Bodenhamer, David J. "Criminal Justice and Democratic Theory in Antebellum America: The Grand Jury Debate in Indiana." *Journal of the Early Republic* 5 (Winter 1985): 481–502.

———. "The Democratic Impulse and Legal Change in the Age of Jackson: The Example of Criminal Juries in Antebellum Indiana." *Historian* 45 (Feb. 1983): 206–19.

Bonner, James C. "Profile of a Late Ante-Bellum Community." *American Historical Review* 49 (July 1944): 663–80.

Braden, W. H. "Reconstruction in Lee County." *Publications of the Mississippi Historical Society* 10 (1909): 135–46.

Brock, Euline W. "Thomas W. Cardozo: Fallible Black Reconstruction Leader." *Journal of Southern History* 47 (May 1981): 183–206.

Campbell, Randolph B. "Intermittent Slave Ownership: Texas as a Test Case." *Journal of Southern History* 51 (Feb. 1985): 15–23.

———. "Planters and Plain Folk: Harrison County, Texas, as a Test Case, 1850–1860." *Journal of Southern History* 40 (Aug. 1974): 369–92.

Cantor, Milton. "The Writ of Habeas Corpus: Early American Origins and Development." In *Freedom and Reform: Essays in Honor of Henry Steele Commager*, 55–77. Edited by Harold M. Hyman and Leonard W. Levy. New York: Harper and Row, 1967.

Cantrell, Gregg. "Racial Violence and Reconstruction Politics in Texas, 1867–1868." *Southwestern Historical Quarterly* 93 (Jan. 1990): 333–55.

Censer, Jane Turner. "Southwestern Migration among North Carolina Planter Families: 'That Disposition to Emigrate.'" *Journal of Southern History* 57 (Aug. 1991): 407–26.

Chapin, Joyce E. "Slavery and the Principle of Humanity: A Modern Idea in the Early Lower South." *Journal of Social History* 24 (Winter 1990): 299–311.

Cogan, Jacob Katz. "The Reynolds Affair and the Politics of Character." *Journal of the Early Republic* 16 (Fall 1996): 389–418.

Cohen, William. "Negro Involuntary Servitude in the South, 1885–1940: A Preliminary Analysis." *Journal of Southern History* 42 (Feb. 1976): 35–50.

Coleman, Edward Clarke, Jr. "Reconstruction in Attala County." *Publications of the Mississippi Historical Society* 10 (1909): 147–61.

Corwin, Edward S. "The Doctrine of Due Process of Law before the Civil War." *Harvard Law Review* 24 (March 1911): 366–85.

Currie, James T. "From Slavery to Freedom in Mississippi's Legal System." *Journal of Negro History* 65 (Spring 1980): 112–25.

de la Roche, Roberta Senechal. "Collective Violence as Social Control." *Sociological Forum* 11, no. 1 (1996): 97–128.

————. "The Sociogenesis of Lynching." In *Under Sentence of Death: Essays on Lynching in the South*, 48–76. Edited by W. Fitzhugh Brundage. Chapel Hill: University of North Carolina Press, 1997.

Donald, David. "The Scalawag in Mississippi Reconstruction." *Journal of Southern History* 10 (Nov. 1944): 447–60.

Drake, Winbourne Magruder. "The Mississippi Reconstruction Convention of 1865." *Journal of Mississippi History* 21 (Oct. 1959): 225–56.

Edwards, Laura F. "'The Marriage Covenant Is at the Foundation of All Our Rights': The Politics of Slave Marriages in North Carolina after Emancipation." *Law and History Review* 14 (Spring 1996): 81–124.

————. "Sexual Violence, Gender, Reconstruction, and the Extension of Patriarchy in Granville County, North Carolina." *North Carolina Historical Review* 68 (July 1991): 237–60.

Egerton, Douglas R. "Markets without a Market Revolution: Southern Planters and Capitalism." *Journal of the Early Republic* 16 (Summer 1996): 207–21.

Ellem, Warren A. "Who Were the Mississippi Scalawags?" *Journal of Southern History* 38 (May 1972): 217–40.

Ellison, Mary. "Resistance to Oppression: Black Women's Response to Slavery in the United States." *Slavery and Abolition* 4 (May 1983): 56–63.

Etcherson, Nicole. "Manliness and the Poltical Culture of the Old Northwest." *Journal of the Early Republic* 15 (Spring 1995): 59–77.

Eubank, Sever L. "The McCardle Case." *Journal of Mississippi History* 18 (April 1956): 111–27.

Fabel, Robin F. A. "An Eighteenth Colony: Dreams for Mississippi on the Eve of the Revolution." *Journal of Southern History* 59 (Nov. 1993): 647–72.

Fede, Andrew. "Legal Protection for Slave Buyers in the U.S. South: A Caveat Concerning *Caveat Emptor.*" *American Journal of Legal History* 31 (Oct. 1987): 322–58.

Fields, Barbara J. "Ideology and Race in American History." In *Region, Race, and Reconstruction: Essays in Honor of C. Vann Woodward*, 143–77. Edited by J. Morgan Kousser and James M. McPherson. New York: Oxford University Press, 1982.

Foner, Eric. "Black Reconstruction Leaders at the Grass Roots." In *Black Leaders of the Nineteenth Century*, 219–34. Edited by Leon Litwack and August Meier. Urbana: University of Illinois Press, 1988.

————. "Reconstruction and the Crisis of Free Labor." In Eric Foner, *Politics and Ideology in the Age of the Civil War*, 97–127. New York: Oxford University Press, 1980.

Finkelman, Paul. "Exploring Southern Legal History." *North Carolina Law Review* 64 (Nov. 1985): 77–116.

————. "Sorting Out *Prigg v. Pennsylvania.*" *Rutgers Law Review* 24 (Spring 1993): 605–64.

Fisher, William W. III. "Ideology and Imagery in the Law of Slavery." *Chicago-Kent Law Review* 68 (1993): 1051–83.

Flanigan, Daniel J. "Criminal Procedure in Slave Trials in the Antebellum South." *Journal of Southern History* 40 (Nov. 1974): 537–64.

Franklin, John Hope. "Mirror for Americans: A Century of Reconstruction History." *American Historical Review* 85 (Feb. 1980): 1–14.

————. "Slaves Virtually Free in Antebellum North Carolina." *Journal of Negro History* 28 (July 1943) 284–310.

Freeman, Joanne B. "Dueling as Politics: Reinterpreting the Burr-Hamilton Duel." *William and Mary Quarterly* 3d ser., 53 (April 1996): 289–318.

————. "Slander, Poison, Whispers, and Fame: Jefferson's 'Anas' and Political Gossip in the Early Republic." *Journal of the Early Republic* 15 (Spring 1995): 25–57.

Friedman, Lawrence. "Legal Culture and Social Development." *Law and Society Review* 4 (Aug. 1969): 29–44.

Gatrell, V. A. C., and T. B. Hadden. "Criminal Statistics and Their Interpretation." In *Nineteenth-Century Society: Essays in the Use of Quantitative Methods for the Study of Social Data*, 336–96. Edited by E. A. Wrigley. New York: Cambridge University Press, 1972.

Genovese, Eugene D. "Yeoman Farmers in a Slaveholders' Democracy." *Agricultural History* 49 (April 1975): 331–42.

Goldstein, Robert D. "*Blyew:* Variations on a Jurisdictional Theme." *Stanford Law Review* 41 (Feb. 1989): 469–566.

Gottfredson, Michael, and Travis Hirschi. "National Crime Control Policies." *Society* 32 (Jan.–Feb. 1995): 30–37.

Graham, Howard Jay. "Procedure to Substance: Extra-Judicial Rise of Due Process." *California Law Review* 40 (Winter 1952–53): 483–500.

Granade, Ray. "Violence: An Instrument of Policy in Reconstruction Alabama." *Alabama Historical Quarterly* 30 (Fall–Winter 1968): 181–202.

Greenberg, Kenneth S. "The Nose, the Lie, and the Duel in the Antebellum South." *American Historical Review* 95 (Feb. 1990): 57–74.

Gross, Ariela. "Pandora's Box: Slave Character on Trial in the Antebellum Deep South." *Yale Journal of Law and the Humanities* 7 (Summer 1995): 267–316.

Grossberg, Michael. "Legal History and Social Science: Friedman's *History of American Law* the Second Time Around." *Law and Social Inquiry* 13 (1988): 359–83.

————. "Social History Update: 'Fighting Faiths' and the Challenges of Legal History." *Journal of Social History* 25 (Fall 1991): 191–201.

Grossmann, Atina. "German Women Doctors from Berlin to New York: Maternity and Modernity in Weimar and in Exile." *Feminist Studies* 19 (Spring 1993): 65–86.

Guarneri, Carl J. "Reconstructing the Antebellum Communitarian Movement: Oneida and Fourierism." *Journal of the Early Republic* 16 (Fall 1996): 463–88.

Harris, J. William. "Etiquette, Lynching, and Racial Boundaries in Southern History: A Mississippi Example." *American Historical Review* 100 (April 1995): 387–410.

Harris, William C. "A Reconsideration of the Mississippi Scalawag." *Journal of Mississippi History* 32 (Feb. 1970): 2–42.

Hartog, Hendrik. "Lawyering, Husbands' Rights, and 'the Unwritten Law' in Nineteenth-Century America." *Journal of American History* 84 (June 1997): 67–96.

————. "Pigs and Positivism." *Wisconsin Law Review* (1985): 899–935.

Hay, Douglas. "Property, Authority, and the Criminal Law." In *Albion's Fatal Tree: Crime and Society in Eighteenth-century England*, 17–63. Edited by Douglas Hay et al. New York: Pantheon, 1975.

Heineman, Elizabeth. "The Hour of the Woman: Memories of Germany's 'Crisis Years' and West German National Identity." *American Historical Review* 101 (April 1996): 354–95.

Henderson, William C. "The Slave Court System in Spartanburg County." *Proceedings of the South Carolina Historical Association* (1976): 24–38.

Hermann, Janet Sharp. "Isiaih T. Montgomery's Balancing Act." In *Black Leaders of the Nineteenth Century,* 291–304. Edited by Leon Litwack and August Meier. Urbana: University of Illinois Press, 1988.

Hindus, Michael Stephen, and Douglas Lamar Jones. "Quantitative Method or *Quantum Meruit?* Tactics for Early American Legal History." *Historical Methods* 13 (Winter 1980): 63–74.

———. "Quantitative and Theoretical Approaches to the History of Crime and Law." *The Newberry Papers in Family and Community History* (1977): 26.

Hodes, Martha. "The Sexualization of Reconstruction Politics: White Women and Black Men in the South after the Civil War." *Journal of the History of Sexuality* 3 (Jan. 1993): 402–17.

Hoffer, Peter C. "Counting Crime in Premodern England and America: A Review Essay." *Historical Methods* 14 (Fall 1981): 187–93.

Hoffheimer, Michael H. "Mississippi Courts: 1790–1868." *Mississippi Law Journal* 65 (Fall 1995): 99–170.

Horwitz, Morton J. "The Rise of Legal Formalism." *American Journal of Legal History* 19 (Oct. 1975): 251–64.

Howe, Lowell J. "The Meaning of 'Due Process of Law' prior to the Adoption of the Fourteenth Amendment." *California Law Review* 18 (Sept. 1930): 583–610.

Ingalls, Robert. "Lynchings and Establishment Violence in Tampa, 1858–1935." *Journal of Southern History* 53 (Nov. 1987): 613–44.

Johnson, Michael P. "Planters and Patriarchy: Charleston, 1800–1860." *Journal of Southern History* 46 (Feb. 1980): 45–72.

———. "Smothered Slave Infants: Were Slave Mothers at Fault?" *Journal of Southern History* 47 (Nov. 1981): 493–520.

———. "Work Culture and the Slave Community: Slave Occupations in the Cotton Belt in 1860." *Labor History* 27 (Summer 1986): 325–55.

Johnston, Robert G. "Jury Subordination through Judicial Control." *Law and Contemporary Problems* 43 (Autumn 1980): 24–50.

Kerber, Linda K. "Separate Spheres, Female Worlds, Woman's Place: The Rhetoric of Women's History." *Journal of American History* 75 (June 1988): 9–39.

King, Andrew J. "The Law of Slander in Early Antebellum America." *American Journal of Legal History* 35 (Jan. 1991): 1–43.

Kitsuse, John I., and Aaron V. Cicourel. "A Note on the Uses of Official Statistics." *Social Problems* 11 (Fall 1963): 131–39.

Klein, Rachel N. "Ordering the Backcountry: The South Carolina Regulation." *William and Mary Quarterly* 38 (Oct. 1981): 661–80.

Kutler, Stanley I. "*Ex Parte McCardle:* Judicial Impotency? The Supreme Court and Reconstruction Reconsidered." *American Historical Review* 72 (April 1967): 835–51.

Lacey, Nannie. "Reconstruction in Leake County." *Publications of the Mississippi Historical Society* 11 (1910): 271–93.

Leftwich, George J. "Reconstruction in Monroe County." *Publications of the Mississippi Historical Society* 9 (1906): 53–84.

Lewis, Jan. "The Republican Wife: Virtue and Seduction in the Early Republic." *William and Mary Quarterly* 44 (Oct. 1987): 689–721.

Linden, Fabian. "Economic Democracy in the Slave South." *Journal of Negro History* 32 (April 1946): 140–89.

Lively, Robert A. "The American System." *Business History Review* 29 (March 1955): 81–96.

Magee, Hattie. "Reconstruction in Lawrence and Jefferson Davis Counties." *Publications of the Mississippi Historical Society* 11 (1910): 163–204.

McCain, Paul M. "Magistrates Courts in Early North Carolina." *North Carolina Historical Review* 48 (Jan. 1971): 32–40.

McCurry, Stephanie. "The Two Faces of Republicanism: Gender and Proslavery Politics in Antebellum South Carolina." *Journal of American History* 78 (March 1992): 1245–64.

McDonnell, Lawrence T. "Money Knows No Master: Market Relations and the American Slave Community." In *Developing Dixie: Modernization in a Traditional Society,* 31–44. Edited by Winfred B. Moore, Jr., Joseph F. Tripp, and Lyon G. Tyler, Jr. Westport: Greenwood Press, 1988.

McGerr, Michael. "Political Style and Women's Power, 1830–1930." *Journal of American History* 77 (Dec. 1990): 866–67.

McKibben, Davidson B. "Negro Slave Insurrections in Mississippi, 1800–1865." *Journal of Negro History* 34 (Jan. 1949): 73–90.

Mendelson, Wallace. "A Missing Link in the Evolution of Due Process." *Vanderbilt Law Review* 10 (Dec. 1956): 125–37.

Mering, John V. "Persistent Whiggery in the Confederate South: A Reconsideration." *South Atlantic Quarterly* 69 (Winter 1970): 124–43.

Merritt, Adrian. "The Nature and Function of Law: A Criticism of E. P. Thompson's 'Whigs and Hunters.'" *British Journal of Law and Society* 7 (Winter 1980): 194–214.

Monkkonen, Eric. "Systematic Criminal Justice History: Some Suggestions." *Journal of Interdisciplinary History* 9 (Winter 1979): 451–64.

Moore, John Hebron. "Local and State Governments of Antebellum Mississippi." *Journal of Mississippi History* 44 (May 1982): 104–34.

Morgan, Philip. "The Ownership of Property by Slaves in the Mid-Nineteenth-century Low Country." *Journal of Southern History* 49 (Aug. 1983): 399–420.

———. "Work and Culture: The Task System and the World of Lowcountry Blacks, 1700 to 1880." *William and Mary Quarterly* 3d ser., 39 (Oct. 1982): 563–99.

Morris, Christopher. "An Event in Community Organization: The Mississippi Slave Insurrection Scare of 1835." *Journal of Social History* 22 (Fall 1988): 93–111.

Morris, Thomas D. "Equality, Extraordinary Law, and Criminal Justice: The South Carolina Experience, 1865–1866." *South Carolina History Magazine* 83 (Jan. 1982): 15–33.

Myers, John B. "The Freedman and the Law in Post-Bellum Alabama, 1865–1867." *Alabama Review* 23 (Jan. 1970): 56–69.

Nash, A. E. Keir. "Fairness and Formalism in the Trials of Blacks in the State Supreme Courts of the Old South." *Virginia Law Review* 56 (Feb. 1970): 64–100.

———. "A More Equitable Past? Southern Supreme Courts and the Protection of the Antebellum Negro." *North Carolina Law Review* 48 (Fall 1970): 197–241.

———. "Negro Rights, Unionism, and Greatness on the South Carolina Court of Appeals: The Extraordinary Chief Justice John Belton O'Neall." *South Carolina Law Review* 21 (Spring 1969): 141–90.

———. "Reason of Slavery: Understanding the Judicial Role of the Peculiar Institution." *Vanderbilt Law Review* 32 (Jan. 1979): 7–218.

———. "The Texas Supreme Court and the Trial Rights of Blacks, 1845–1860." *Journal of American History* 58 (Dec. 1971): 622–42.

Nelson, William E. "The Impact of the Antislavery Movement upon Styles of Judicial Reasoning in Nineteenth-century America." *Harvard Law Review* 87 (Jan. 1974): 513–66.

Nichols, Irby C. "Reconstruction in Desoto County." *Publications of the Mississippi Historical Society* 11 (1910): 295–316.

Nieman, Donald. "Black Political Power and Criminal Justice: Washington County, Texas, 1868–1884." *Journal of Southern History* 55 (Aug. 1989): 391–420.

———. "The Freedmen's Bureau and the Mississippi Black Code." *Journal of Mississippi History* 40 (May 1978): 91–118.

———. "The Language of Liberation: African Americans and the Equalitarian Constitutionalism, 1830–1950." In *The Constitution, Law, and American Life: Critical Aspects of the Nineteenth-Century Experience*, 67–90. Edited by Donald G. Nieman. Athens: University of Georgia Press, 1992.

———. "Republicanism, the Confederate Constitution, and the American Constitutional Tradition." In *An Uncertain Tradition: Constitutionalism and the History of the South*, 201–24. Edited by Kermit Hall and James W. Ely, Jr. Athens: University of Georgia Press, 1989.

Oaks, Dallin H. "Habeas Corpus in the States." *University of Chicago Law Review* 32 (Winter 1965): 243–88.

Oakes, James. "A Failure of Vision: The Collapse of the Freedmen's Bureau Courts." *Civil War History* 25 (March 1979): 66–76.

———. "A Response." *Journal of Southern History* 51 (Feb. 1985): 23–28.

Oldfield, J. R. "A High and Honorable Calling: Black Lawyers in South Carolina, 1868–1915." *Journal of American Studies* 23 (Dec. 1989): 395–406.

O'Reilly, Kenneth. "The FBI and the Civil Rights Movement during the Kennedy Years: From the Freedom Rides to Albany." *Journal of Southern History* 54 (May 1988): 201–32.

Paludan, Phillip S. "The American Civil War Considered as a Crisis in Law and Order." *American Historical Review* 77 (Oct. 1972): 1013–34.

Patton, W. H. "History of the Prohibition Movement in Mississippi." *Publications of the Mississippi Historical Society* 10 (1909): 181–201.

Pederson, Jane M. "Gender, Justice, and a Wisconsin Lynching, 1889–1890." *Agricultural History* 67 (Spring 1993): 65–82.

Phillips, Ulrich Bonnell. "Racial Problems, Adjustments, and Disturbances." In *The South in the Building of the Nation*, vol. 4: *Political History of the Southern States*,

194–241. Edited by Franklin L. Riley. Richmond: Southern Historical Publication Society, 1909.

Powell, Lawrence. "Correcting for Fraud: A Quantitative Reassessment of the Mississippi Ratification Election of 1868." *Journal of Southern History* 55 (Nov. 1989): 633–58.

————. "The Politics of Livelihood: Carpetbaggers in the Deep South." In *Region, Race, and Reconstruction: Essays in Honor of C. Vann Woodward*, 315–47. Edited by J. Morgan Kousser and James M. McPherson. New York: Oxford Unversity Press, 1982.

Puckett, E. F. "Reconstruction in Monroe County." *Publications of the Mississippi Historical Society* 11 (1910): 103–61.

Rabinowitz, Howard. "The Conflict between Blacks and the Police in the Urban South, 1865–1900." *Historian* 39 (Nov. 1976): 72–76.

Rainwater, P. L., Jr., ed. "The Autobiography of Benjamin Grubb Humphreys, August 26, 1808–December 20, 1882." *Mississippi Valley Historical Review* 21 (Sept. 1934): 247.

"Reminiscences of Sergeant Wm. Sparks of the 72nd Illinois Volunteers." *Illinois Central Magazine* 3 (Sept. 1914): 17–21.

Richardson, Joe M. "Florida Black Codes." *Florida Historical Quarterly* 47 (Spring 1969): 365–79.

Richter, William L. "'The Revolver Rules the Day!': Colonel DeWitt C. Brown and the Freedmen's Bureau in Paris, Texas, 1867–1868." *Southwestern Historical Quarterly* 93 (Jan. 1990): 303–32.

Riegel, Stephen J. "The Persistent Career of Jim Crow: Lower Federal Courts and the 'Separate but Equal' Doctrine, 1865–1896." *American Journal of Legal History* 20 (Jan. 1984): 17.

Rorabaugh, W. J. "The Political Duel in the Early Republic: Burr v. Hamilton." *Journal of the Early Republic* 15 (Spring 1995): 1–23.

Russell, Thomas D. "South Carolina's Largest Slave Auctioneering Firm." *Chicago-Kent Law Review* 68, no. 3 (1993): 1241–82.

Schafer, Judith K. "'Details of a Most Revolting Character': Cruelty to Slaves as Seen in Appeals to the Supreme Court of Louisiana." *Chicago-Kent Law Review* 68, no. 3 (1993): 1283–311.

Shofner, Jerrell H. "Custom, Law, and History: The Enduring Influence of Florida's 'Black Code.'" *Florida Historical Quarterly* 55 (Jan. 1977): 277–98.

Shore, Lawrence. "Making Mississippi Safe for Slavery: The Insurrectionary Panic of 1835." In *Class, Conflict, and Consensus: Antebellum Southern Community Studies*, 96–127. Edited by Orville Vernon Burton and Robert C. McGrath. Westport: Greenwood Press, 1982

Simon, Bryant. "The Appeal of Cole Blease of South Carolina: Race, Class, and Sex in the New South." *Journal of Southern History* 62 (Feb. 1996): 57–86.

Smith, Albert C. "'Southern Violence' Reconsidered: Arson as Protest in Black-Belt Georgia, 1865–1910." *Journal of Southern History* 51 (Nov. 1985): 527–64.

Sommerville, Diane Miller. "The Rape Myth in the Old South Reconsidered." *Journal of Southern History* 61 (Aug. 1995): 481–518.

Steckel, Richard H. "A Dreadful Childhood: The Excess Mortality of American Slaves." *Social Science History* 10 (1986): 427–66.

Steiner, Mark E. "The Lawyer as Peacemaker: Law and Community in Abraham Lincoln's Slander Cases." *Journal of the Abraham Lincoln Association* 16 (Summer 1995): 1–22.

Surrency, Erwin C. "The First American Criminal Code: The Georgia Code of 1816." *Georgia Historical Quarterly* 63 (Winter 1979): 420–34.

Tomlins, Christopher L. "A Mirror Crack'd? The Rule of Law in American History." *William and Mary Law Review* 32 (Winter 1991): 353–97.

Tubbs, William B. "A Bibliography of Illinois Civil War Regimental Sources in the Illinois State Historical Library: Part I, Published and Printed Sources." *Illinois Historical Journal* 87 (Autumn 1994): 185–232.

Turner, Victor. "Social Dramas and Stories about Them." In *On Narrative*, 137–64. Edited by W. J. T. Mitchell. Chicago: University of Chicago Press, 1982.

Tyrrell, Ian R. "Drink and Temperance in the Antebellum South: An Overview and Interpretation." *Journal of Southern History* 48 (Nov. 1982): 485–510.

Varon, Elizabeth R. "Tippecanoe and the Ladies, Too: White Women and Party Politics in Antebellum Virginia." *Journal of American History* 82 (Sept. 1995): 494–521.

Wahl, Jenny B. "American Slavery and the Path of the Law." *Social Science History* 20 (Summer 1996): 281–316.

Waldrep, Christopher. "Black Access to Law in Reconstruction: The Case of Warren County, Mississippi." *Chicago-Kent Law Review* 70, no. 2 (1994): 583–624.

———. "Substituting Law for the Lash: Emancipation and Legal Formalism in a Mississippi County Court." *Journal of American History* 82 (March 1996): 1425–51.

Waller, Altina. "Community, Class, and Race in the Memphis Draft Riot of 1866." *Journal of Social History* 18 (Winter 1984): 233–46.

Watkins, Ruth. "Reconstruction in Newton County." *Publications of the Mississippi Historical Society* 11 (1910): 205–28.

Watson, Alan D. "North Carolina Slave Courts, 1715–1785." *North Carolina Historical Review* 60 (Jan. 1983): 24–36.

Watson, Harry L. "'The Common Rights of Mankind': Subsistence, Shad, and Commerce in the Early Republican South." *Journal of American History* 83 (June 1996): 13–43.

Wayne, Michael. "An Old South Morality Play: Reconsidering the Social Underpinnings of the Proslavery Ideology." *Journal of American History* 77 (Dec. 1990): 838–63.

Webb, Samuel L. "A Jacksonian Democrat in Postbellum Alabama: The Ideology and Influence of Journalist Robert McKee, 1869–1896." *Journal of Southern History* 62 (May 1996): 239–74.

Welke, Barbara Y. "When All the Women Were White, and All the Blacks Were Men: Gender, Class, Race, and the Road to *Plessy*, 1855–1914." *Law and History Review* 13 (Fall 1995): 261–316.

Wells, W. Calvin. "Reconstruction and Its Destruction in Hinds County." *Publications of the Mississippi Historical Society* 9 (1906): 85–108.

Westwood, Howard C. "Getting Justice for the Freedman." *Howard Law Journal* 16 (Spring 1971): 492–537.

Whittenburg, James P. "Planters, Merchants, and Lawyers: Social Change and the Origins of the North Carolina Regulation." *William and Mary Quarterly* 34 (April 1977): 215–38.

Wiecek, William M. "Slavery and Abolition before the United States Supreme Court, 1820–1860." *Journal of American History* 65 (June 1978): 34–59.

Williams, E. Russ. "Slave Patrol Ordinances of St. Tammany Parish, Louisiana, 1835–1838." *Louisiana History* 13 (Fall 1962): 399–412.

Witty, Fred M. "Reconstruction in Carroll and Montgomery Counties." *Publications of the Mississippi Historical Society* 10 (1909): 115–61.

Wright, Gavin. "'Economic Democracy' and the Concentration of Agricultural Wealth in the Cotton South, 1850–1860." *Agricultural History* 44 (Jan. 1970): 83–93.

Wunder, John. "American Law and Order Comes to Mississippi Territory: The Making of Sargent's Code, 1798–1800." *Journal of Mississippi History* 38 (May 1976): 131–56.

Wyatt-Brown, Bertram. "The Mask of Obedience: Male Slave Psychology in the Old South." *American Historical Review* 93 (Dec. 1988): 1228–52.

———. "Modernizing Southern Slavery: The Proslavery Argument Revisited." In *Region, Race, and Reconstruction: Essays in Honor of C. Vann Woodward,* 27–49. Edited by J. Morgan Kousser and James M. McPherson. New York: Oxford University Press.

Unpublished Manuscripts

Aquirre, Carlos. "Working the System: Black Slaves and the Courts in Lima, Peru, 1821–1854." Delivered at the conference on "The History of Black People in Diaspora," East Lansing, Mich., April 1995.

Bardaglio, Peter W. "Lawyers, Lynching, and Governance in the New South, 1880–1900." Delivered at the annual meeting of the Southern Historical Association, Louisville, Ky., Nov. 1994.

Bryant, Jonathan M. "'A County Where Plenty Should Abound': Race, Law, and Markets in Greene County, Georgia, 1850–1885." Ph.D. diss., University of Georgia, 1992.

Carlson, Douglas Wiley. "Temperance Reform in the Cotton Kingdom." Ph.D. diss., University of Illinois at Urbana-Champaign, 1982.

Davis, William Graham. "Attacking the 'Matchless Evil': Temperance and Prohibition in Mississippi, 1817–1908." Ph.D. diss., Mississippi State College, 1975.

Eubank, Sever Landon. "The Yerger Case: A Side Light of Reconstruction." M.A. thesis, Colorado College, 1950.

Finnegan, Terence. "'At the Hands of Parties Unknown': Lynching in Mississippi and South Carolina, 1881–1940." Ph.D. diss., University of Illinois at Urbana-Champaign, 1993.

Freeman, Joanne B. "Aristocratic Murder and Democratic Fury: Honor and Politics in Early National New England." Delivered at the annual meeting of the Society for Historians of the Early American Republic, Nashville, Tenn., July 20, 1996.

Harris, James Griffith. "The Background and Development of Early Missouri Trial Courts." Ph.D. diss., University of Missouri, 1949.

Kinsel, Amy L. "American Identity, National Reconciliation, and the Memory of the Civil War." Delivered at the annual meeting of the Organization of American Historians, Chicago, Ill., March 29, 1996.

Landi, Debbielee. "Best Evidence: A Social History of the County Court of Lafayette County, 1865–1870." M.A. thesis, University of Mississippi, 1992.

Modey, Yao Foli. "Black Justice under White Law: Criminal Prosecutions of Blacks in Antebellum North Carolina." M.A. thesis, Wake Forest University 1978.

Mounger, Dwyn M. "Lynching in Mississippi, 1830–1930." M.A. thesis, Mississippi State College, 1961.

Novak, William. "The Road to *Slaughterhouse:* The Regulation of Noxious Trades, 1830–1872." Delivered at the annual meeting of the American Society for Legal History, Memphis, 1993.

Index

Christopher Waldrep is associate professor of history at Eastern Illinois University, Charleston, and the author of *Night Riders: Defending Community in the Black Patch, 1890–1915,* as well as many articles in scholarly journals. He holds a Ph.D. from Ohio State University and an M.A. from Purdue University.

DATE DUE

DEMCO 38-296